AMERICAN IMMIGRATION

SECOND EDITION

An Encyclopedia of Political, Social, and Cultural Change

Volume 4

James Ciment and **John Radzilowski,** Editors

SHARPE REFERENCE

an imprint of M.E. Sharpe, Inc.

SHARPE REFERENCE

Sharpe Reference is an imprint of M.E. Sharpe, Inc.

M.E. Sharpe, Inc.
80 Business Park Drive
Armonk, NY 10504

© 2014 by M.E. Sharpe, Inc.

Cover photos (top to bottom): Dirck Halstead/Getty Images; Edwin Levick/Getty Images; AP Photo/Chris Carlson. *Maps:* Carto-graphics.

Library of Congress Cataloging-in-Publication Data

Encyclopedia of American immigration
American immigration: an encyclopedia of political, social, and cultural change / James Ciment and John Radzilowski, editors.—Second edition.
    4 volumes cm.
Originally published as: Encyclopedia of American immigration, 2001.
Includes bibliographical references and index.
ISBN 978-0-7656-8212-3 (hardcover)
1. United States—Emigration and immigration—Encyclopedias. 2. Immigrants—United States—Encyclopedias. I. Ciment, James. II. Radzilowski, John, 1965– III. Title.

JV6465.E53 2013 (2014)
304.8′73003–dc23   2013010015

Printed and bound in the United States

The paper used in this publication meets the minimum requirements of
American National Standard for Information Sciences—Permanence of
Paper for Printed Library Materials,
ANSI Z 39.48.1984.

CW (c) 10 9 8 7 6 5 4 3 2 1

Publisher: Myron E. Sharpe
Vice President and Director of New Product Development: Donna Sanzone
Executive Development Editor: Jeff Hacker
Project Manager: Laura Brengelman
Program Coordinator: Cathleen Prisco
Editorial Assistant: Meredith Day
Text Design and Cover Design: Jesse Sanchez
Typesetter: Nancy Connick

Contents

VOLUME 2

Part 3
Society, Culture, and Politics

Religion: Groups and Practice

VOLUME 3

Part 4
Nations of Origin and
U.S. Destinations

Nations of Origin and Immigration Groups

U.S. Destinations

Part 5
International Perspectives

VOLUME 4

Part 6
Documents

AMERICAN IMMIGRATION

SECOND EDITION

Documents

Documents

Revolutionary War Correspondence of George Washington (1775–1778)

In the following letters written by George Washington during the Revolutionary War, the commanding general of the Continental Army expresses his belief that native-born Americans should be given priority in recruitment, sentry duty, and other critical military situations. To do otherwise, he said, would undermine the morale of native-born troops. In addition, Washington suspected that foreign-born troops, who did not have family in North America, would have less allegiance to the patriot cause than native-born troops and would be more likely to desert the army.

General Order to the Army, July 7, 1775

The General has great Reason; and is highly displeased, with the Negligence and Inattention of those Officers, who have placed as Centries, at the outposts, Men with whose Characters they are not acquainted. He therefore orders, that for the future, no Man shall be appointed to those important Stations, who is not a Native of this Country, or has a Wife, or Family in it, to whom he is known to be attached. This order is to be consider'd as a standing one and the Officers are to pay obedience to it at their peril.

Letter to Colonel Alexander Spotswood, April 30, 1777

I want to form a company for my guard. In doing this I wish to be extremely cautious, because it is more than probable, that, in the course of the campaign, my baggage, papers, and other matters of great public import, may be committed to the sole care of these men. This being premised, in order to impress you with proper attention in the choice, I have to request, that you will immediately furnish me with four men of your regiments, . . . I think it [*fidelity*] most likely to be found in those, who have family connexions in the country. You will therefore send me none but natives, and men of some property, if you have them.

Letter to Colonel George Baylor, June 19, 1777

You should be extremely cautious in your enquiries into the character of those who are not natives who offer to enlist. Desertions among men of that class have been so frequent that unless you find 'em on examination to be of good & unsuspicious conduct, they should not be taken by any means. Otherwise, most probably, they will deceive you—add no strength to our arms, but much expence to the Public account and upon first opportunity will join the Enemy.

Letter to Henry Laurens, July 24, 1778

I will further add, that we have already a full proportion of foreign officers in our general councils; and, should their number be increased, it may happen upon many occasions, that their voices may be equal if not exceed the rest. I trust you think me so much a citizen of the world, as to believe I am not easily warped or led away by attachments merely local or American; yet I confess I am not entirely without 'em, nor does it appear to me that they are unwarrantable, if confined within proper limits. Fewer promotions in the foreign line would have been productive of more harmony, and made our warfare more agreeable to all parties. The frequency of them is the source of jealousy and of disunion.

Source: Worthington Chauncey Ford, ed. *The Writings of George Washington* (New York: G.P. Putnam's Sons, 1889).

Letters from an American Farmer, J. Hector St. John de Crèvecoeur (1782)

Michel Crèvecoeur, a Frenchman who had spent more than two decades in North America, returned to Europe in 1780 and, two years later, published his observations about life in the British colonies under the title Letters from an American Farmer. *Issued under the pen name J. Hector St. John de Crèvecoeur, the book was one of the earliest detailed accounts of the social scene in the colonies. Among Crèvecoeur's many observations were the ways in which America transformed immigrants into citizens. In the excerpt that follows, he highlights how America, in contrast to Europe, offered newcomers a home free of class distinctions, grinding poverty, lack of economic opportunity, and religious prejudice and strife.*

I wish I could be acquainted with the feelings and thoughts which must agitate the heart and present themselves to the mind of an enlightened Englishman when he first lands on this continent. He must greatly rejoice that he lived at a time to see this fair country discovered and settled; he must necessarily feel a share of national pride, when he views the chain of settlements which embellishes these extended shores. When he says to himself, this is the work of my countrymen, who, when convulsed by factions, afflicted by a variety of miseries and wants, restless and impatient, took refuge here. They brought along with them their national genius, to which they principally owe what liberty they enjoy, and what substance they possess. Here he sees the industry of his native country displayed in a new manner, and traces in their works the embryos of all the arts, sciences, and ingenuity which flourish in Europe. Here he beholds fair cities, substantial villages, extensive fields, an immense country filled with decent houses, good roads, orchards, meadows, and bridges, where an hundred years ago all was wild, woody, and uncultivated! What a train of pleasing ideas this fair spectacle must suggest; it is a prospect which must inspire a good citizen with the most heartfelt pleasure. The difficulty consists in the manner of viewing so extensive a scene. He is arrived on a new continent; a modern society offers itself to his contemplation, different from what he had hitherto seen. It is not composed, as in Europe, of great lords who possess everything, and of a herd of people who have nothing. Here are no aristocratical families, no courts, no kings, no bishops, no ecclesiastical dominion, no invisible power giving to a few a very visible one; no great manufacturers employing thousands, no great refinements of luxury. The rich and the poor are not so far removed from each other as they are in Europe. Some few towns excepted, we are all tillers of the earth, from Nova Scotia to West Florida. We are a people of cultivators, scattered over an immense territory, communicating with each other by means of good roads and navigable rivers, united by the silken bands of mild government, all respecting the laws, without dreading their power, because they are equitable. We are all animated with the spirit of an industry which is unfettered and unrestrained, because each person works for himself. . . . We have no princes, for whom we toil, starve, and bleed: we are the most perfect society now existing in the world. Here man is free as he ought to be; nor is this pleasing equality so transitory as many others are. Many ages will not see the shores of our great lakes replenished with inland nations, nor the unknown bounds of North America entirely peopled. Who can tell how far it extends? Who can tell the millions of men whom it will feed and contain? for no European foot has as yet travelled half the extent of this mighty continent!

The next wish of this traveller will be to know whence came all these people? They are a mixture of English, Scotch, Irish, French, Dutch, Germans, and Swedes. From this promiscuous breed, that race now called Americans have arisen. The eastern provinces must indeed be excepted, as being the unmixed descendants of Englishmen. I have heard many wish that they had been more intermixed also: for my part, I am no wisher, and think it much better as it has happened. They exhibit a most conspicuous figure in this great and variegated picture; they too enter for a great share in the pleasing perspective displayed in these thirteen provinces. . . .

In this great American asylum, the poor of Europe have by some means met together, and in consequence of various causes; to what purpose should they ask one another what countrymen they are? Alas, two thirds of them had no country. Can a wretch who wanders about, who works and starves, whose life is a continual scene of sore affliction or pinching penury; can that man call England or any other kingdom his country? A country that had no bread for him, whose fields procured him no harvest, who met with nothing but the frowns of the rich, the severity of the laws, with jails and punishments; who owned not a single foot of the extensive surface of this planet? No! urged by a variety of motives, here they came. Everything has tended to regenerate them; new laws, a new mode of living, a new social system; here they are become men; in Europe they were as so many useless plants, wanting vegetative mould, and refreshing showers; they withered, and were mowed down by want, hunger, and war; but now by the power of transplantation, like all other plants they have taken root and flourished! Formerly they were not numbered in any civil lists of their country, except in those of the poor; here they rank as citizens. By what invisible power has this surprising metamorphosis been performed? By that of the laws and that of their industry. The laws, the indulgent laws protect them as they arrive, stamping on them the symbol of adoption; they receive ample rewards for their labours; these accumulated rewards procure them lands; those lands confer on them the title of freeman, and to that title every benefit is affixed which men can possibly require. This is the great operation daily performed by our laws. . . .

What attachment can a poor European emigrant have for a country where he had nothing? The knowledge of the language, the love of a few kindred as poor as himself, were the only cords that tied him: his country is now that which gives him land, bread, protection, and consequence: *Ubi panis ibi patria,* is the motto of all emigrants. What then is the American, this new man? He is either an European, or the descendant of an European, hence that strange mixture of blood, which you will find in no other country. I could point out to you a family whose grandfather was an Englishman, whose wife was Dutch, whose son married a French woman, and whose present four sons have now four wives of different nations. *He* is an American, who leaving behind him all his ancient prejudices and manners, receives new ones from the new mode of life he has embraced, the new government he obeys, and the new rank he holds. He becomes an American by being received in the broad lap of our great *Alma Mater.* Here individuals of all nations are melted into a new race of men, whose labours and posterity will one day cause great changes in the world. Americans are the western pilgrims, who are carrying along with them that great mass of arts, sciences, vigour, and industry which began long since in the east; they will finish the great circle. The Americans were once scattered all over Europe; here they are incorporated into one of the finest systems of population which has ever appeared, and which will hereafter become distinct by the power of the different climates they inhabit. The American ought therefore to love this country much better than that wherein either he or his forefathers were born. Here the rewards of his industry follow with equal steps the progress of his labour; his labour is founded on the basis of nature, self-interest; can it want a stronger allurement? Wives and children, who before in vain demanded of him a morsel of bread, now, fat and frolicksome, gladly help their father to clear those fields whence exuberant crops are to arise to feed and to clothe them all; without any part being claimed, either by a despotic prince, a rich abbot, or a mighty lord. Here religion demands but little of him; a small voluntary salary to the minister, and gratitude to God; can he refuse these? The American is a new man, who acts upon new principles; he must therefore entertain new ideas, and form new opinions. From involuntary idleness, servile dependence, penury, and useless labour, he has passed to toils of a very different nature, rewarded by ample subsistence. This is an American. . . .

As I have endeavoured to shew you how Europeans become Americans; it may not be disagreeable to shew you likewise how the various Christian sects introduced, wear out, and how religious indifference becomes prevalent. When any considerable number of a particular sect happen to dwell contiguous to each other, they immediately erect a temple, and there worship the Divinity agreeably to their own peculiar ideas. Nobody disturbs them. If any new sect springs up in Europe, it may happen that many of its professors will come and settle in America. As they bring their zeal with them, they are at liberty to make proselytes if they can, and to build a meeting and to follow the dictates of their consciences; for neither the government nor any other power interferes. If they are peaceable subjects, and are industrious, what is it to their neighbours how and in what manner they think fit to address their prayers to the Supreme Being? But if the sectaries are not settled close together, if they are mixed with other denominations, their zeal will cool for want of fuel, and will be extinguished in a little time. Then the Americans become as to religion, what they are as to country, allied to all. In them the name of Englishman, Frenchman, and European is lost, and in like manner, the strict modes of Christianity as practised in Europe are lost also. This effect will extend itself still farther hereafter, and though this may appear to you as a strange idea, yet it is a very true one. I shall be able perhaps hereafter to explain myself better, in the meanwhile, let the following example serve as my first justification.

Let us suppose you and I to be travelling; we observe that in this house, to the right, lives a Catholic, who prays to God as he has been taught, and believes in transubstantiation; he works and raises wheat, he has a large family of children, all hale and robust; his belief, his prayers offend nobody. About one mile farther on the same road, his next neighbour may be a good honest plodding German Lutheran, who addresses himself to the same God, the God of all, agreeably to the modes he has been educated in, and believes in consubstantiation; by so doing he scandalizes nobody; he also works in his fields, embellishes the earth, clears swamps, etc. What has the world to do with his Lutheran principles? He persecutes nobody, and nobody persecutes him, he visits his neighbours, and his neighbours visit him. Next to him lives a seceder, the most enthusiastic of all sectaries; his zeal is hot and fiery, but separated as he is from others of the same complexion, he has no congregation of his own to resort to, where he might cabal and mingle religious pride with worldly obstinacy. He likewise raises good crops, his house is handsomely painted, his orchard is one of the fairest in the neighborhood. How does it concern the welfare of the country, or of the province at large, what this man's religious sentiments are, or whether he has any at all? He is a good farmer, he is a sober, peaceable, good citizen: William Penn himself would not wish for more. This is the visible character, the invisible one is only guessed at and is nobody's business. Next again lives a Low Dutchman, who implicitly believes the rules laid down by the synod of Dort. He conceives no other idea of a clergyman than that of an hired man; if he does his work well he will pay him the stipulated sum; if not he will dismiss him, and do without his sermons, and let his church be shut up for years. But notwithstanding this coarse idea, you will find his house and farm to be the neatest in all the country; and you will judge by his wagon and fat horses, that he thinks more of the affairs of this world than of those of the next. He is sober and laborious, therefore he is all he ought to be as to the affairs of this life, as for those of the next, he must trust to the great Creator. Each of these people instruct their children as well as they can, but these instructions are feeble compared to those which are given to the youth of the poorest class in Europe. Their children will therefore grow up less zealous and more indifferent in matters of religion than their parents. The foolish vanity or rather the fury of making proselytes, is unknown here; they have no time, the seasons call for all their attention, and thus in a few years, this mixed neighbourhood will exhibit a strange religious medley, that will be neither pure Catholicism nor pure Calvinism. A very perceptible indifference even in the first generation, will become apparent; and it may happen that the daughter of the Catholic will marry the son of the seceder, and settle by themselves at a distance from their parents. What religious education will they give their children? A very imperfect one. If there happens to be in the neighbourhood any place of worship, we will suppose a Quaker's meeting; rather than not shew their fine clothes, they will go to it, and some of them may perhaps attach themselves to that society. Others will remain in a perfect state of indifference; the children of these zealous parents will not be able to tell what their religious principles are, and their grandchildren still less. The neighbourhood of a place of worship generally leads them to it, and the action of going thither, is the strongest evidence they can give of their attachment to any sect. Thus all sects are mixed as well as all nations; thus religious indifference is imperceptibly disseminated from one end of the continent to the other; which is at present one of the strongest characteristics of the Americans. Where this will reach no one can tell, perhaps it may leave a vacuum fit to receive other systems. Persecution, religious pride, the love of contradiction, are the food of what the world commonly calls religion. These mo-

tives have ceased here: zeal in Europe is confined; here it evaporates in the great distance it has to travel; there it is a grain of powder inclosed, here it burns away in the open air, and consumes without effect. . .

Europe contains hardly any other distinctions but lords and tenants; this fair country alone is settled by freeholders, the possessors of the soil they cultivate, members of the government they obey, and the framers of their own laws, by means of their representatives. This is a thought which you have taught me to cherish; our distance from Europe, far from diminishing, rather adds to our usefulness and consequence as men and subjects. Had our forefathers remained there, they would only have crowded it, and perhaps prolonged those convulsions which had shook . . . it so long. . . . . Colonists are entitled to the consideration due to the most useful subjects; a hundred families barely existing in some parts of Scotland will here, in six years, cause an annual exportation of 10,000 bushels of wheat: 100 bushels being but a common quantity for an industrious family to sell, if they cultivate good land. It is here, then, that the idle may be employed, the useless become useful, and the poor become rich; but by riches I do not mean gold and silver, we have but little of those metals; I mean a better sort of wealth, cleared lands, cattle, good houses, good clothes, and an increase of people to enjoy them.

There is no wonder that this country has so many charms, and presents to Europeans so many temptations to remain in it. A traveller in Europe becomes a stranger as soon as he quits his own kingdom; but it is otherwise here. We know, properly speaking, no strangers; this is every person's country; the variety of our soils, situations, climates, governments, and produce, hath something which must please every body. No sooner does an European arrive, no matter of what condition, than his eyes are opened upon the fair prospect; he hears his language spoke, he retraces many of his own country manners, he perpetually hears the names of families and towns with which he is acquainted; he sees happiness and prosperity in all places disseminated; he meets with hospitality, kindness, and plenty every where; he beholds hardly any poor, he seldom hears of punishments and executions, and he wonders at the elegance of our towns, those miracles of industry and freedom. He cannot admire enough our rural districts, our convenient roads, good taverns, and our many accommodations; he involuntarily loves a country where every thing is so lovely. When in England, he was a mere Englishman; here he stands on a larger portion of the globe, not less than its fourth part, and may see the productions of the north, in iron and naval stores; the provisions of Ireland, the grain of Egypt, the indigo, the rice of China. He does not find, as in Europe, a crowded society, where every place is overstocked; he does not feel that perpetual collision of parties, that difficulty of beginning, that contention which oversets so many. There is room for every body, in America. Has he any particular talent, or industry? he exerts it in order to procure a livelihood, and it succeeds. Is he a merchant? the avenues of trade are infinite. Is he eminent in any respect? he will be employed and respected. Does he love a country life? pleasant farms present themselves; he may purchase what he wants, and thereby become an American farmer. Is he a laborer, sober and industrious? he need not go many miles, nor receive many informations before he will be hired, well fed at the table of his employer, and paid four or five times more than he can get in Europe. Does he want uncultivated lands? thousands of acres present themselves, which he may purchase cheap. Whatever be his talents or inclinations, if they are moderate, he may satisfy them. I do not mean that every one who comes will grow rich in a little time; no, but he may procure an easy, decent maintenance, by his industry. Instead of starving, he will be fed; instead of being idle, he will have employment; and these are riches enough for such men as come over here. The rich stay in Europe, it is only the middling and the poor that emigrate. Would you wish to travel in independent idleness, from north to south, you will find easy access, and the most cheerful reception at every house; society without ostentation, good cheer without pride, and every decent diversion which the country affords, with little expence. It is no wonder that the European who has lived here a few years is desirous to remain; Europe with all its pomp is not to be compared to this continent, for men of middle stations, or labourers.

An European, when he first arrives, seems limited in his intentions, as well as in his views; but he very suddenly alters his scale; two hundred miles formerly appeared a very great distance, it is now but a trifle; he no sooner breathes our air than he forms schemes, and embarks in designs he never would have thought of in his own country. There the plentitude of society confines many useful ideas, and often extinguishes the most laudable schemes which here ripen into maturity. Thus Europeans become Americans.

But how is this accomplished in that crowd of low, indigent people, who flock here every year from all parts of Europe? I will tell you; they no sooner arrive than they immediately feel the good effects of that plenty of provisions we possess; they fare on our best food, and are kindly entertained; their talents, character, and peculiar industry are immediately inquired into; they find countrymen every where disseminated, let them come from whatever part of Europe. Let me select one as an epitome of the rest. He is hired, he goes to work, and works moderately; instead of being employed by a haughty person, he finds himself with his equal, placed at the substantial table of the farmer, or else at an inferior one as good; his wages are high, his bed is not like that bed of sorrow on which he used to lie; if he behaves with propriety, and is faithful, he is caressed, and becomes, as it were, a member of the family. He begins to feel the effects of a sort of resurrection; hitherto he had not lived, but simply vegetated; he now feels himself a man, because he is treated as such; the laws of his own country had overlooked him in his insignificancy; the laws of this cover him with their mantle. Judge what an alteration there must arise in the mind and thoughts of this man; he begins to forget his former servitude and dependence, his heart involuntarily swells and glows; this first swell inspires him with those new thoughts which constitute an American. What love can he entertain for a country where his existence was a burthen to him; if he is a generous good man, the love of his new adoptive parent will sink deep into his heart. He looks around, and sees many a prosperous person, who but a few years before was as poor as himself. This encourages him much, he begins to form some little scheme, the first, alas, he ever formed in his life. If he is wise he thus spends two or three years, in which time he acquires knowledge, the use of tools, the modes of working the lands, felling trees, etc. This prepares the foundation of a good name, the most useful acquisition he can make. He is encouraged, he has gained friends; he is advised and directed, he feels bold, he purchases some land; he gives all the money he has brought over, as well as what he has earned, and trusts to the God of harvests for the discharge of the rest. His good name procures him credit. He is now possessed of the deed, conveying to him and his posterity the fee simple and absolute property of two hundred acres of land, situated on such a river. What an epoch in this man's life! He is become a freeholder, from perhaps a German boor—he is now an American, a Pennsylvanian, an English subject. He is naturalized, his name is enrolled with those of the other citizens of the province. Instead of being a vagrant, he has a place of residence; he is called the inhabitant of such a county, or of such a district, and for the first time in his life counts for something; for hitherto he has been a cypher. I only repeat what I have heard many say, and no wonder their hearts should glow, and be agitated with a multitude of feelings, not easy to describe. From nothing to start into being; from a servant to the rank of master; from being the slave of some despotic prince, to become a free man, invested with lands, to which every municipal blessing is annexed! What a change indeed! It is in consequence of that change that he becomes an American. . . . Ye poor Europeans, ye, who sweat, and work for the great—ye, who are obliged to give so many sheaves to the church, so many to your lords, so many to your government, and have hardly any left for yourselves—ye, who are held in less estimation than favourite hunters or useless lap-dogs—ye, who only breathe the air of nature, because it cannot be withheld from you; it is here that ye can conceive the possibility of those feelings I have been describing; it is here the laws of naturalization invite every one to partake of our great labours and felicity, to till unrented, untaxed lands! . . . It is not every emigrant who succeeds; no, it is only the sober, the honest, and industrious: happy those to whom this transition has served as a powerful spur to labour, to prosperity, and to the good establishment of children, born in the days of their poverty, and who had no other portion to expect but the rags of their parents, had it not been for their happy emigration. Others again have been led astray by this enchanting scene; . . . they have mouldered away their time in inactivity, misinformed husbandry, and ineffectual endeavours. How much wiser, in general, the honest Germans than almost all other Europeans; they hire themselves to some of their wealthy landsmen, and in that apprenticeship learn every thing that is neces-sary . . . and by dint of sobriety, rigid parsimony, and the most persevering industry, they commonly succeed. Their astonishment at their first arrival from Germany is very great—it is to them a dream; the contrast must be powerful indeed; they observe their countrymen flourish-ing in every place; they travel through whole counties where not a word of English is spoken; and in the names and the language of the people, they retrace Germany. They have been an useful acquisition to this continent, and to Pennsylvania in particular; to them it owes some share of its prosperity: to their mechanical knowledge and patience, it owes the finest mills in all America, the best teams of horses, and many other advantages. The recollection of their former poverty and slavery never quits them as long as they live.

The Scotch and the Irish might have lived in their own country perhaps as poor, but enjoying more civil advantages, the effects of their new situation do not strike them so forcibly, nor has it so lasting an effect. From whence the difference arises I know not, but out of twelve families of emigrants of each country, generally seven Scotch will succeed, nine German, and four Irish. The Scotch are frugal and laborious, but their wives cannot work so hard as German women, who, on the contrary, vie with their husbands, and often share with them the most severe toils of the field, which they understand better. They have therefore nothing to struggle against but the common casualties of nature. The Irish do not prosper so well; they love to drink and to quarrel; they are litigious, and soon take to the gun, which is the ruin of every thing; they seem beside to labour under a greater degree of ignorance in husbandry than the others; per-

haps it is that their industry had less scope, and was less exercised at home. . . .

There is no tracing observations of this kind, with-out making at the same time very great allowances, as there are every where to be found a great many excep-tions. The Irish themselves, from different parts of that kingdom, are very different. It is difficult to account for this surprising locality; one would think on so small an island an Irishman must be an Irishman; yet it is not so, they are different in their aptitude to, and in their love of labour.

The Scotch, on the contrary, are all industrious and saving; they want nothing more than a field to exert themselves in, and they are commonly sure of succeed-ing. The only difficulty they labour under is that tech-nical American knowledge which requires some time to obtain; it is not easy for those who seldom saw a tree, to conceive how it is to be felled, cut up, and split into rails and posts. . . .

Agreeable to the account which several Scotchmen have given me of the north of Britain, of the Orkneys, and the Hebride Islands, they seem, on many accounts, to be unfit for the habitation of men; they appear to be calculated only for great sheep pastures. Who then can blame the inhabitants of these countries for transport-ing themselves hither? This great continent must in time absorb the poorest part of Europe; and this will happen in proportion as it becomes better known, and as war, taxation, oppression, and misery increase there. The Hebrides appear to be fit only for the residence of malefactors, and it would be much better to send felons there than either to Virginia or Maryland. What a strange compliment has our mother country paid to two of the finest provinces in America! England has entertained in that respect very mistaken ideas; what was intended as a punishment is become the good fortune of several; many of those who have been transported as felons, are now rich, and strangers to the stings of those wants that urged them to violations of the law: they are become industrious, exemplary, and useful citizens. . . . This is no place of punishment; were I a poor hopeless, breadless Englishman, and not restrained by the power of shame, I should be very thankful for the passage. It is of very little importance how and in what manner an indigent man arrives; for if he is but sober, honest, and industrious, he has nothing more to ask of heaven. Let him go to work, he will have opportunities enough to earn a comfortable support, and even the means of procuring some land; which ought to be the utmost wish of every person who has health and hands to work. . . .

After a foreigner from any part of Europe is arrived, and become a citizen; let him devoutly listen to the voice of our great parent, which says to him, "Welcome to my shores, distressed European; bless the hour in which thou didst see my verdant fields, my fair navigable rivers, and my green mountains! If thou wilt work, I have bread for thee; if thou wilt be honest, sober, and industrious, I have greater rewards to confer on thee—ease and independence. I will give thee fields to feed and clothe thee; a comfortable fire-side to sit by, and tell thy children by what means thou hast prospered; and a decent bed to repose on. I shall endow thee beside with the immunities of a freeman. If thou wilt carefully educate thy children, teach them gratitude to God, and reverence to that government, that philanthropic government, which has collected here so many men and made them happy. . . . Go thou and work and till; thou shalt prosper, provided thou be just, grateful, and industrious."

Source: J. Hector St. John de Crèvecoeur. *Letters from an American Farmer* (London: Thomas Davies, 1782).

Article I, Sections 8 and 9, the U.S. Constitution (1787)

Article I, Section 8, of the Constitution of the United States grants Congress the power to regulate naturalization. In recent years, however, this power has been challenged by states enacting legislation that cut off social services to immigrants and allowed local and state authorities to enforce various aspects of immigration policy. Although federal courts have rejected most of such state legislation, the U.S. Supreme Court in 2012 upheld the provision of an Arizona statute, Senate Bill 1070, that allowed police to check the immigration status of individuals during routine law enforcement stops. (The high court struck down three other provisions of SB 1070.) Another article of the U.S. Constitution pertaining to a form of immigration, Article I, Section 9, permitted the slave trade to continue for twenty years after ratification of the Constitution. The authors conspicuously avoided using the word "slaves" in the text, reflecting the reservations many of them held about the slave trade and the entire institution of slavery.

Section 8. The Congress shall have the power. . . . To establish a uniform Rule of Naturalization . . . . .

Section 9. The Migration of Importation of such Persons as any of the States now existing shall think proper to admit, shall not be prohibited by the Congress prior to the Year one thousand eight hundred and eight but a tax or duty may be imposed on such Importation, not exceeding ten dollars for each person.

Source: U.S. Constitution.

An Act to Establish an Uniform Rule of Naturalization (1790)

Granted power by the Constitution to pass laws concerning naturalization and citizenship, the U.S. Congress passed the first legislation regulating the naturalization process on March 26, 1790; President George Washington promptly signed the bill into law. The legislation, excerpted below, introduced naturalization requirements based on race and years of residency in the United States.

Be it enacted by the Senate and House of Representatives of the United States of America in Congress assembled, That any alien, being a free white person, who shall have resided within the limits and under the jurisdiction of the United States for the term of two years, may be admitted to become a citizen thereof, on application to any common court of record, in any one of the states wherein he shall have resided for the term of one year at least, and making proof to the satisfaction of such court, that he is a person of good character, and taking the oath or affirmation prescribed by law, to support the constitution of the United States, which oath or affirmation such court shall administer; and the clerk of such court shall record such application, and the proceedings thereon; and thereupon such person shall be considered as a citizen of the United States. And the children of such persons so naturalized, dwelling within the United States, being under the age of twenty-one years at the time of such naturalization, shall also be considered as citizens of the United States. And the children of citizens of the United States, that may be born beyond sea, or out of the limits of the United States, shall be considered as natural born citizens; Provided, That the right of citizenship shall not descend to persons whose fathers have never been resident in the United States; Provided also, That no person heretofore proscribed by any state, shall be admitted a citizen as aforesaid, except by an act of the legislature in the state in which such person was proscribed.

Source: Statutes at Large of the United States of America, 1789–1845, vol. 1 (Boston: Little, Brown, 1845–1867).

Look Before You Leap, Anonymous (1796)

The following tract, issued anonymously during the presidency of George Washington, warns of the dangers facing indentured (or "indented") servants in the new United States. With the unwieldy title Look Before You Leap; or A Few Hints to Such Artizans, Mechanics, Labourers, Farmers, and Husbandmen, as Are Desirous of Emigrating to America, *the text includes two letters by eyewitnesses to the abuses visited upon indentured servants. Advisory documents such as this, along with rising prosperity in Europe and the declining cost of transatlantic transportation, reduced the influx of indentured servants to a trickle in the early nineteenth century.*

Preface

One species of abject misery consequent upon emigration has been hitherto unnoticed—but to the *labouring poor* it is tremendously awful, and pregnant with horrors of the most unprecedented nature. I mean the custom of *indenting,* or, to speak perhaps more precisely, of buying a voluntary exile and a bitter slavery. Those voracious harpies of whom in this preface we have had already too much occasion to make mention are in the habits of stimulating the *labouring poor* to cross the Atlantic upon an indenture—by which they bind themselves for a certain term, from two to seven years, as the indented servants of an austere captain or imperious landholder, whose only object is to derive a profit from their misfortune, and to aggrandize himself at the expense of industry in distress. These contracts have been common on the coasts of Ireland and Scotland for some time, but lately, even the metropolis is invested with them, and the panders of American opulence walk unblushingly to practice their delusions through the streets of London.

The situations of the unfortunate labourers who fall into their hands may be in some degree conceived, but cannot be easily described. They are sometimes employed on the coasts, but more generally sent into the interior, where every species of brutal insolence and overbearing tyranny is exercised upon their feelings. . . .

(The following letters were written by a master carpenter, who was so far distempered with the American mania, as to quit a very genteel situation and respectable connection in order to accumulate a rapid fortune at the Federal City of Washington.)

Norfolk, August 16, 1794

If you come to NORFOLK for that boasted encouragement our countrymen are taught to expect in England, you will be most *miserably disappointed.* I have seen upwards of three hundred poor persons, chiefly from Ireland, landed from one ship bemoaning with tears their own credulity, and lamenting most pathetically their departure from their native homes. These poor creatures are marched in small bodies by persons employed for that purpose to the different plantations where they are forced to indent themselves for *so many years* to the plant-

ers, who pay the captains what is called the *redemption money* for them. You will perhaps be surprised that such transactions are permitted in what is called the *land of liberty,* but I assure you this is thought nothing of here, and is actually the case. . . . There is one very unpleasant circumstance which attends us Englishmen here, which is, that most of the natives entertain the idea, *we quit our country for crimes,* and dare not return. I assure you I have been taunted with this already several times. . . .

George-town near Washington, January 21, 1795

Doubtless you have heard much of Kentucky. To this country, all the abandoned, the credulous, the unsettled, and the wretched in these states, are flocking in numbers. Most of the poor distressed objects I meet are indenting themselves to proprietors of land in Kentucky, in order to be conveyed there, carriage free; although the probability of such persons ever returning is scarcely possible. . . . The substance of what I have been able to collect is, that the poor creatures who have been induced to *indent themselves* are in situations the most pitiable; they are treated by their *masters* in a similar manner *to the felons formerly transported from England to Virginia.* Instead of being put in possession of portions of land, and quickly discharging their engagements, they sink deeper into debt, and this by the means of being obliged to purchase on credit at the most extravagant charges from their masters the stores and necessaries of which they stand in need. Thus situated they are never free from the landholder who is an absolute tyrant, while his miserable *indented servants are likely to remain slaves forever.* Great numbers die from the change of climate, want of proper sustenance, and the very unusual and laborious employ to which they are rigorously subjected by their vigilant overseers. Those situated upon the bordering territory are often scalped by the Indians, and their lives are in continual jeopardy. If my paper would contain all the information I have received respecting this enticing country, and also if I had time to write, I assure you it would form a striking contrast to a pamphlet, now laying beside me, and which I received when in London, from the *Kentucky agents in Threadneedle Street.*

Source: Anonymous. *Look Before You Leap* (London: W. Row, 1796).

Alien Act (1798)

In the late 1790s, tensions between Federalists and Democratic-Republicans in Congress reached a critical point. The two parties differed on a number of issues, including foreign policy, free speech, and immigration. On June 18, 1798, President John Adams, a Federalist, signed the Naturalization Act, which lengthened the period of residence required for citizenship from five to fourteen years. One week later, he signed the Alien Act, which gave the president broad authority to remove foreigners from the country. The Alien Act remained in force for two years and angered many Democratic-Republicans, who saw it both as an infringement of civil liberties and as a threat to their own electoral chances. Then, as now, most immigrants tended to vote for the party that would eventually be known as the Democratic Party.

Section 1. Be it enacted by the Senate and the House of Representatives of the United States of America in Congress assembled, That it shall be lawful for the President of the United States at any time during the continuance of this act, to order all such aliens as he shall judge dangerous to the peace and safety of the United States, or shall have reasonable grounds to suspect are concerned in any treasonable or secret machinations against the government thereof, to depart out of the territory of the United States within such time as shall be expressed in such order, which order shall be served to the alien by delivering a copy thereof, or leaving the same at his usual abode, and returned to the office of the Secretary of State, by the marshal or other person to whom the same shall be directed. And in case any alien, so ordered to depart, shall be found at large within the United States after the time limited in such order for his departure, and not having obtained a license from the President to reside therein, or having obtained such license shall not have conformed thereto, every such alien shall, on conviction thereof, be imprisoned for a term not exceeding three years, and shall never after be admitted to become a citizen of the United States. Provided always, and be it further enacted, that if any alien so ordered to depart shall prove to the satisfaction of the President, by evidence to be taken before such person or persons as the President shall direct, who are for that purpose hereby authorized to administer oaths, that no injury or danger to the United States will arise from suffering such alien to reside therein, the President may grant a license to such alien to remain within the United States for such time as he shall judge proper, and at such place as he may designate. And the President may also require of such alien to enter into a bond to the United States, in such penal sum as he may direct, with one or more sufficient sureties to the satisfaction of the person authorized by the President to take the same, conditioned for the good behavior of such alien during his residence in the United States, and not violating his license, which license the President may revoke, whenever he shall think proper.

Sect. 2. And be it further enacted, That it shall be lawful for the President of the United States, whenever he may deem it necessary for the public safety, to order to be removed out of the territory thereof, any alien who may or shall be in prison in pursuance of this act; and to cause to be arrested and sent out of the United States such of those aliens as shall have been ordered to depart therefrom and shall not have obtained a license as aforesaid, in all cases where, in the opinion of the President, public safety requires a speedy removal. And if any alien so removed or sent out of the United States by the President shall voluntarily return thereto, such alien on conviction thereof, shall be imprisoned so long as, in the opinion of the President, the public safety may require. . . .

Sect. 4. And be it further enacted, That the circuit and district courts of the United States, shall respectively have cognizance of all crimes and offenses against this act. And all marshals and other officers of the United States are required to execute all precepts and orders of the President of the United States issued in pursuance or by virtue of this act.

Sect. 5. And be it further enacted, That it shall be lawful for any alien who may be ordered to be removed from the United States, by virtue of this act, to take with him such part of his goods, chattels, or other property, as he may find convenient; and all property left in the United States by any alien, who may be removed, as aforesaid, shall be, and remain subject to his order and disposal, in the same manner as if this act had not been passed.

Sect. 6. And be it further enacted, That this act shall continue and be in force for . . . two years.

Source: Statutes at Large of the United States of America, 1789–1845, vol. 1 (Boston: Little, Brown, 1845–1867).

History of the English Settlement in Edwards County, Illinois, George Flower (1817–1818)

George Flower and Morris Birkbeck, socially progressive pioneers from England in the early nineteenth century, sought to establish a settlement in the rural backwoods of Illinois that would be based on communitarian principles and agricultural innovation. In the following account, Flower describes the process by which a group of newcomers came to settle the prairie in what is now southeastern Illinois. In contrast to the classic image of immigrants as rugged individualists pioneering the wilderness, Flower's description emphasizes community and cooperation as the essence of successful frontier settlement. In reality, such experiments attracted only a small portion of the waves of immigrants coming to the United States during the early republic and antebellum eras.

During the winter [1817–1818] I was preparing and assisting others to prepare for a final emigration in the spring. . . . I was constantly applied to in person and by letter for information and advice on the subject of emigration, by persons in every rank, but chiefly from those in moderate circumstances.

In describing western America, and the mode of living there, I found some difficulty in giving a truthful picture to the Englishman who had never been out of England. In speaking of a field, the only field he had ever seen was a plot of ground, from five to fifty acres in extent, surrounded by a ditch, a bank, and a live hawthorn fence; it has two or more well-made gates, that swing freely on their hinges, and clasp firmly when shut. The word field brings this picture to his eye. . .

The publication in England of our travels, my return, and personal communication with a host of individuals, had given a wide-spread knowledge of what we had done and what we intended to do. Our call had received a response from the farmers of England, the miners of Cornwall, the drovers of Wales, the mechanics of Scotland, the West India planter, the inhabitants of the Channel Isles, and the "gentleman of no particular business" of the Emerald Isle. All were moving or preparing to move to join us in another hemisphere. The cockneys of London had decided on the reversal of their city habits, to breathe the fresh air of the prairies. Parties were moving, or preparing to move, in all directions. At one time, the movement appeared as if it would be national. Representatives from each locality, and descendants from every class that I have mentioned, are now living in the English Settlement of Edwards County, Illinois. The preparatory movements were completed. The first act of our drama here properly closes, and the history of the actual emigration, with the accidents and incidents of the journeyings by sea and land, now begins. . .

Early in March, 1818, the ship "Achilles" sailed from Bristol with the first party of emigrants destined for our settlement in Illinois. . . . Forty-four men and one married woman sailed in this ship. The men were chiefly farm laborers and mechanics from Surrey. . . . Another party, of about equal number, composed of London mechanics, and tradesmen from various parts of England, formed another party that sailed in the same ship. . . . [This] party landed safely at Philadelphia early in June. They made their way,

some in wagons; some on horseback, over the mountains to Pittsburgh, then descending the Ohio in flat-boats to Shawneetown, in August, proceeded without delay on foot, in wagons and on horseback, to Mr. Birkbeck's cabin on the Boltenhouse Prairie. . . .

The next ship with emigrants for the prairies, which sailed from Liverpool in the following month of April, was chartered by myself for the party that came with me. My own immediate family and friends occupied the cabin; my domestic servants, and other emigrants going out to join us, filled the steerage; and my live-stock of cows, hogs, and sheep, of the choicest breeds of England, took up all the spare room on deck. . . . We arrived without accident at New York, after a passage of fifty days, and but one week after the Bristol ship, that sailed a month before us. To remove all these people and their luggage, and the animals that I had brought, to our Settlement, nearly a thousand miles inland, was no small undertaking, at a time when there was neither turnpike nor railroad, and steam-boats few, and in the infancy of their management. Patience, toil, time, and money were all required and all were freely bestowed.

On reaching land, the ship's party was broken up, and smaller parties were formed of people of similar habits and tastes, clubbing together for mutual assistance on the way. Those of small means, proceeded on without loss of time. Those of more means, lingered a little in the cities, and with their new friends, before taking their departure for what was then the Far West. . . .

In this manner, the various individuals and parties made the best way they could. Some of them were joined by individuals and families of English, that were lingering on the sea-board, without any specific reference to our Settlement; but seeing the emigration, and having read the publications, joined and went on. I think every accession from the East was English. . . .

The various objects we had in view, for which I was sent to England, were all accomplished with singular success. My voyage across the Atlantic was of unusual speed. By a singular coincidence, my father had sold, a few days before my arrival in England, his dwelling and lands in Marden for £23,000, thus giving to himself, my mother, brothers, and sisters, an opportunity of returning with me in the spring, which they willingly embraced, to take up their abode in the prairies. . . .

On entering the prairie, my large horses were covered with the tall prairie-grass, and laboriously dragged the heavy-laden vehicle. The cabin built for me was well sheltered by wood from the north and east, with an arm of the prairie lying south in a gently descending slope for a quarter of a mile; it was as pretty a situation as could be desired. The cabin could not boast of many comforts. With a clap-board roof, held on by weight-poles, and a rough puncheon floor, it had neither door nor window. Two door-ways were cut out, and the rough logs were scutched down inside. All the chips and ends of logs left by the backwoods builders lay strewed upon the floor. We were now face to face with the privations and difficulties of a first settlement in the wilderness. But greater than all other inconveniences was the want of water. There was no water nearer than the cabin in which the French family lived, a quarter of a mile off. . . .

For a moment let us glance at the situation of these settlers, a thousand miles inland, at the heels of the retreating Indians. A forest from the Atlantic shore behind them, but thinly settled with small villages, far apart from each other. To the west, one vast uninhabited wilderness of prairie, interspersed with timber, extending two thousand miles to the Pacific Ocean. Excepting St. Louis, on the Mississippi, then a small place, and Kaskaskia, yet smaller, there were no inhabitants west of us. About the same time, one or two small American settlements were forming a few miles east of the Mississippi, as we were planting ourselves a few miles west of the Wabash. . . .

There were no roads on land, no steam-boats on the waters. The road, so-called, leading to Vandalia (then composed of about a dozen log-houses), was made by one man on horseback following in the track of another, every rider making the way a little easier to find, until you came to some slush, or swampy place, where all trace was lost, and you got through as others had done, by guessing at the direction, often riding at hazard for miles until you stumbled on the track again. And of these blind traces there were but three or four in the southern half of the State. No roads were worked, no watercourses bridged. Before getting to Vandalia, there was a low piece of timbered bottom-land, wet and swampy, and often covered with water, through which every traveler had to make his way as he best could, often at the risk of his life. Such was the state of the country. No man could feel sure that he was within the limits of the State, but from knowing that he was west of the Wabash and east of the Mississippi. We had some difficulties, peculiar to ourselves, as a foreign people. The Americans, by pushing onward and onward for almost two generations, had a training in handling the axe and opening farms, and, from experience, bestowing their labor in the most appropriate manner, which we, from our inexperience, often did not. Fresh from an old country, teeming with the conveniences of civilized life, at once in a wilderness with all our inexperiences, our losses were large from misplaced labor. Many were discouraged, and some returned, but the mass of the settlers stayed, and, by gradual experience, corrected their first errors, thus overcoming difficulties which had well-nigh overcome them. The future success of the Settlement was obtained by individual toil and

industry. Of the first inconveniences and sufferings, my family had its full share. . . .

Emigrants kept coming in, some on foot, some on horseback, and some in wagons. Some sought employment, and took up with such labor as they could find. Others struck out and made small beginnings for themselves. Some, with feelings of petulance, went farther and fared worse; others dropped back into the towns and settlements in Indiana. At first, I had as much as I could do to build a few cabins for the workmen I then employed, and in erecting a large farmyard a hundred feet square, enclosed by log-buildings, two stories high; also in building for my father's family a house of considerable size, and appointed with somewhat more of comforts than is generally found in new settlements. I had as yet done nothing in erecting buildings for the public in general, as there had been no time. . . .

The first double-cabin built, was designated for a tavern, and a single one for its stable. Another and second double and single cabin were occupied as dwelling and shop by a blacksmith. I had brought bellows, anvils, tools, and appliances for three or four blacksmith-shops, from the City of Birmingham, England. There were three brothers that came with us, all excellent mechanics, and one of them, a blacksmith, was immediately installed, and went to work. There stood Albion, no longer a myth, but a reality, a fixed fact. A log-tavern and a blacksmith-shop. Two germs of civilization were now planted—one of the useful arts, the other a necessary institution of present civilization. Any man could now get his horse shod and get drunk in Albion, privileges which were soon enjoyed, the latter especially. . . .

From time to time little parties came in year after year, chiefly small tradesmen and farm-laborers. The latter, a most valuable class, came from all parts of England. The farmers brought with them their various experiences and tools, necessary to work the different soils. In this way a greater variety of workmen and tools are to be found in the English Settlement than perhaps in any one neighborhood in England.

Three brothers, Joseph, Thomas, and Kelsey Crackles, able-bodied farm-laborers, from Lincolnshire, came with a full experience in the cultivation of flat, wet land; and brought with them the light fly-tool for digging ditches and drains, by which a practised hand can do double the work that can be done by a heavy steel spade. They lived with me three years before going on farms of their own. Their experience has shown us that the flat, wet prairies, generally shunned, are the most valuable wheat lands we possess. . . .

It is a noticeable fact that emigrants bound for the English Settlement in Illinois, landed at every port from the St. Lawrence to the Gulf of Mexico. This arises from the fact that the laborers and small farmers of England are very imperfectly acquainted with the geography of America. Indeed, among all classes in England there is a very inadequate idea of the extent of the United States. . . . As various as their ports of debarkation, were the routes they took, and the modes of conveyance they adopted.

Some came in wagons and light carriages, overland; some on horseback; some in arks; some in skiffs; and some by steam-boat, by New Orleans. One Welshman landed at Charleston, S.C. "How did you get here?" I asked. "Oh," he innocently replied, "I just bought me a horse, sir, and inquired the way." It seems our Settlement was then known at the plantations in Carolina and in the mountains of Tennessee. The great variety found among our people, coming as they did from almost every county in the kingdom, in complexion, stature, and dialect, was in the early days of our Settlement very remarkable. . . .

It will be seen that our position is not on any of the great highways of travel. We caught none of the floating population as they passed. Most of those who came set out expressly to come to us. . . .

After [a temporary] check to emigration . . . the tide began to flow again. Individuals and families were frequently arriving, and occasionally a party of thirty and forty. A fresh cause induced this tide of emigration. It arose from the private correspondence of the first poor men who came. Having done well themselves, and by a few years of hard labor acquired more wealth than they ever expected to obtain—they wrote home to friend or relative an account of their success. These letters handed round in the remote villages of England, in which many of them lived, reached individuals in a class to whom information in book form was wholly inaccessible. Each letter had its scores of readers, and, passing from hand to hand, traversed its scores of miles. The writer, known at home as a poor man, earning perhaps a scanty subsistence by his daily labor, telling of the wages he received, his bountiful living, of his own farm and the number of his live-stock, produced a greater impression in the limited circle of its readers than a printed publication had the power of doing. His fellow-laborer who heard these accounts, and feeling that he was no better off than when his fellow-laborer left him for America, now exerted every nerve to come and do likewise. . . . In this way we have given to Illinois a valuable population, men that are a great acquisition to the Country. It was observed that these emigrants who came in the second emigration, from five to ten years after the first settlement, complained more of the hardships of the country than those who came first. These would complain of a leaky roof, or a broken fence, and all such inconveniences. The first-comers had no cabins or fences to complain of; with them it was conquer or die. And thus emigrants came dropping in from year to year. . . .

But it was the class of farm-laborers and small farmers, of whom I have before spoken, that furnished the bone and sinew of the Settlement. Well instructed in all agricultural labor, as plowmen, seedsmen, and drainers of land, habituated to follow these occupations with continuous industry, the result was certain success. Their course was a uniform progress and advance. Many of them without money, and some in debt for their passage, they at first hired out at the then usual price of fifty cents a day without board, and seventy-five cents for haytime and harvest. In two or three years they became tenants, or bought a piece of unimproved Congress-land at a dollar and a quarter an acre, and gradually made their own farms. Several of them, now the wealthiest farmers of the county, earned their first money on my farm at Park House. It is chiefly the labor of these men, extending over twenty, thirty, and even forty years, that has given to the Settlement the many fine farms to be seen around Albion. . . .

The first years of our settlement, from 1818 to 1825, were spent by our settlers in putting up small houses (chiefly of logs), and shelter of the same sort for the work-horses and other domestic animals used in breaking up and fencing in the prairie for the first fields. In about three years [after 1818], a surplus of corn, pork, and beef was obtained, but no market. Before they could derive any benefit from the sale of their surplus produce, the farmers themselves had to quit their farms and open the channels of commerce, and convey their produce along until they found a market. At first there were no produce-buyers, and the first attempts at mercantile adventures were almost failures. In the rising towns, a few buyers began to appear, but with too small a capital to pay money, even at the low price produce then was. They generally bought on credit, to pay on their return from New Orleans. In this way, the farmers were at disadvantage; if the markets were good, the merchant made a handsome profit. If bad, they often had not enough to pay the farmer. Then the farmers began to build their own flat-boats, load them with the produce of their own growth, and navigate them by their own hands. They traded down the Mississippi to New Orleans, and often on the coast beyond. Thus were the channels of trade opened, and in this way was the chief trade of the country carried on for many years.

Afterward, partly from capital made in the place and foreign capital coming in, trade was established in a more regular way. The farmer is no longer called from his farm, but sells at home to the storekeepers and merchants, now found in all the small but growing towns from ten to fifteen miles distant from each other, all over the country. They have now sufficient capital to pay for the produce on its delivery. In this way the trade established has continued, excepting in its increasing magnitude.

When considered, the enlarged sphere of action and change of destiny of these farm-laborers of England, now substantial farmers and merchants in our land is truly wonderful. Once poor laborers, their experience comprised within their parish bounds, or the limits of the farm on which they toiled for a bare subsistence; now farmers themselves in another hemisphere, boat-builders, annually taking adventurous trading-voyages of over a thousand miles, and many of them becoming tradesmen and merchants on a large scale, and commanding an amount of wealth they once never dreamed of possessing. And well they deserve their success. They have earned it by perseverance and hard labor, flinching at nothing. . . .

A valuable experience was gained in the gradual taking up of land. Of course, the most inviting situations were first secured. The last land, left as refuse, was flat, wet prairie, that had not much thickness of hazle mould, so much sought after by the farmer. The surface wet, but aridly dry in summer, with a subsoil of whitish clay. The Americans said they could not get a living off such land. The English laborers, by a little judicious ditching, which made part of their fencing, found it to be the best soil for small grain and meadow in the country. . . .

Another favorable circumstance was the happy adaptation of the country to the settlers. Had our European settlers been placed in a heavy-timbered country, they would have desponded, despaired, and died. The cost of denuding a heavy-wooded district of its timber and preparing it for cultivation, is not less than twelve dollars an acre. What a source of national wealth this item is to a state like Illinois, with its thirty-six million acres of prairie land. Every individual, thus fortunately placed, is saved a generation of hard and unprofitable labor. This circumstance is not sufficiently appreciated by a pioneer settler.

One element of success may be traced to a happy proportion among the settlers of men of money, men of intelligence, and men of toil. A settlement all of needy laborers would have suffered much, and would probably have dispersed . . . as many others have done. It was the men of property that sustained the weight of the Settlement for the first five years, not only by its first supply of food and the building of its first houses, but in hiring the laborers as they came from the old country. This gave to the poor, but hard-working man, some knowledge of the ways of the country, while he was laying up a little store of money for his independent beginning. The sterling qualities found in the great bulk of the English laborers and little farmers, is another element of success. Their general sobriety, persevering industry, and habitual hard work, carried them through periods of long discouragements to final success. The first founders gave what they had of

ability and money to the very last. All these circumstances working together have given that solid prosperity, which is characteristic of the English Settlement in Illinois.

Source: George Flower. *History of the English Settlement in Edwards County, Illinois, Founded in 1817 and 1818 by Morris Birkbeck and George Flower* (Chicago: Fergus Printing, 1882).

Plea for Change of Venue by James Brown, Petitioner in Case to Retrieve Runaway Indentured Servants (1819)

In the federal court filing reproduced below, petitioner James Brown of Nashville, Tennessee, contends that his case against the persons who helped his indentured servants run away—and who then prevented Brown from reclaiming them—could not be heard fairly in Ohio, where the alleged crime took place. The indentured servants in question were "redemptioners" from Germany, whose passage to America the petitioner had paid for in exchange for a period of service. Brown's basic argument is that he had reached an agreement with the servants regarding the work they would be expected to perform in exchange for their passage, and that their flight was therefore both unjustified and an unjust imposition on him.

To the honorable Congress of the United States: The memorial of James Brown, a citizen of the State of Tennessee, and the town of Nashville:

Your memorialist humbly represents to your honorable body that he purchased in the city of Philadelphia, about the last of October, 1818, a number of German redemptioners; advanced a considerable sum of money in their behalf; and took their indentures for three years and five months, commencing when they should arrive at the place of their destination. Your memorialist, before indenturing of said servants, described to them the climate, and explained to them the kind of business which they would be required to follow. Your memorialist further represents to your honorable body that he informed said servants, and also suggested to some gentlemen in Philadelphia, that, if he did purchase said slaves, it was not with the prospect of great emolument to himself, but that he thought their residence in the State of Tennessee or Alabama would greatly ameliorate their condition, and, at the same time, their particular avocations would be of incalculable advantage in that section of country. With these laudable objects in view, your memorialist made the purchase, selecting vine-dressers and mechanics for the purpose above stated to your honorable body, and said servants urged with much solicitude your memorialist to make said advances for them; and your memorialist, in conformity with the agreement between himself and said servants, and at a very great expense, conveyed the said servants on their way to the place for which they had indented themselves as far as Marietta, in the State of Ohio, when, by the interposition, persuasion, and aid of Caleb Emmerson . . . with many others whose names are unknown to your memorialist, the said indented servants were induced to make their escape from out of the possession of your memorialist, and were conveyed away and secreted by the said persons, or some of them, before mentioned. Your memorialist applied to the proper authorities for the purpose of reclaiming said servants, but all his efforts were defeated by the violent, oppressive, and illegal conduct of said persons, your memorialist being by the said persons unjustly arrested and imprisoned, together with the officer who had in his possession a precept authorizing the apprehension and arrest of said servants, the details of which transaction will more fully appear by the accompanying documents, to which your honorable body is particularly referred. Your memorialist would have sought redress by an appeal to the laws of his country at the time that this extraordinary proceeding took place, but was advised by counsel that there was no probability, under the present state of public feeling, that restitution would be made for the injury which your memorialist had sustained both in person and property; and your memorialist was further advised by several respectable citizens that, if he went into the country again for the purpose of arresting his servants, his life would be jeopardized. Application was made through his excellency Joseph McMinn, Governor of the State of Tennessee, on behalf of your memorialist, to the Governor of the State of Ohio; and he, in reply to the Governor of the State of Tennessee, in substance acknowledges the wrong and injury which your memorialist has sustained in that State, and regrets, in language equally just and proper, that such individuals should be permitted to disturb the public tranquility, and concludes by stating that he has been informed that justice had been rendered your memorialist: which is not the fact; for the six [servants] which he arrested by authority from the honorable Judge Bird were forcibly taken from him by the citizens of Cincinnati. . . . And your memorialist represents to your honorable body that he has lost his servants entirely, and that he has no other redress than by suits at law; and your memorialist begs leave to state, furthermore, that such is the extent of the influence of the individuals, and such their activity in exerting that influence, and that such is the temper and feeling of the people generally, that your memorialist believes he would be unable in the State of

Ohio to have justice done in the trial of his suits; and your memorialist is advised that there is no law which authorizes a change of venue from one State to another. Your memorialist therefore prays your honorable body to pass some general law authorizing such change of venue upon the case made out before the judge of the federal courts, or a special law to permit it in this particular case, so that your memorialist can have a trial in Virginia or Kentucky, or some adjacent State.

And your memorialist, as in duty bound, will ever pray, &c.

[Signed] James Brown

Source: Change of Venue, December 28, 1818, *American State Papers: Miscellaneous* 2:550–51.

Manifest of Immigrants Act (1819)

Calling on ship owners and masters to supply information to the federal government regarding the passengers on board and their intentions upon arrival in the United States, the Manifest of Immigrants Act, passed on March 2, 1819, was the first piece of federal legislation calling for the gathering of immigration statistics. A century later, such statistics would be used to establish quotas regulating the influx of immigrants by national origin.

Be it enacted by the Senate and the House of Representatives of the United States of America in Congress assembled . . .

Sec. 4. And be it further enacted, That the captain or master of any ship or vessel arriving in the United States or any of the territories thereof, from any foreign place whatever, at the same time that he delivers a manifest of all cargo, and, if there be no cargo, then at the time of making a report or entry of the ship or vessel, pursuant to the existing laws of the United States, shall also deliver and report, to the collector of the district in which such ship or vessel shall arrive, a list or manifest of all passengers taken on board of the said ship or vessel at any foreign port or place; in which list or manifest it shall be the duty of the said master to designate, particularly, the age, sex, and occupation, of the said passengers, respectively, the country to which they severally belong, and that of which it is their intention to become inhabitants; and shall further set forth whether any, and what number, have died on the voyage; which report and manifest shall be sworn to by the said master, in the same manner as is directed by the existing laws of the United States, in relation to the manifest of the cargo, and that the refusal or neglect of the master aforesaid, to comply with the provisions of this section, shall incur the same penalties, disabilities, and forfeitures, as are at present provided for a refusal or neglect to report and deliver a manifest of the cargo aforesaid.

Source: Statutes at Large of the United States of America, 1789–1845, vol. 3 (Boston: Little, Brown, 1845–1867).

Selections from Letters Written During a Tour through the United States, in the Autumn of 1819, Emanuel Howitt (1819)

In his Selections from Letters Written During a Tour through the United States, in the Autumn of 1819, *Emanuel Howitt describes to fellow Englishmen the harsh economic conditions facing immigrants to America. He also criticizes the contemptuous attitude toward immigrants he perceives among native-born Americans, as well as the latter's propensity for taking financial advantage of innocent newcomers. Howitt's basic message is that anyone who comes to America with capital or valuable skills will do well, but that anyone less fortunate would be better advised to stay in England. The effect of such warnings on immigration numbers is not known, though the Panic of 1819, to which Howitt alludes, did reduce the flow.*

The tide of emigration, like that of the ocean, must ebb as well as flow, and this is the ebbing period; but, if such be the distress of England, and so gloomy its prospects, that emigration is (to anyone) an object of desire, I would certainly advise them to remove hither rather than to a new colony. The pioneers of civilization, those who advance first into an untrodden desert, and begin the work of culture and population, ought to be schooled to the office by a suitable education; they must be inured from childhood to a rude and desultory life, to every inconvenience of poverty and irregularity of climate, to struggle against difficulties which would daunt, and amidst sufferings which would destroy all besides. The towns-man, the mechanic, and even the farmer, accustomed to regularity of life, must, in such a situation, become a wretched object, and, most probably, the victim of his change of habits. But here, at least, they may find some degree of civil security, and may fix themselves on a track which has felt the first efforts of civilization, and is still in the verge of society: but it must be *the distressed* alone, who can hope to find alleviation here. There may be some who may improve their situations. Farmers, of considerable

capital, who, by purchasing a track that will supply their families with food, and reserve a portion of that capital, to procure clothes and other necessaries, may live comfortably, and look forward to an increasing value of their estates. Mechanics, whose superior skill or good fortune, may meet with profitable employ; but the state of trade and glut of emigration, both preclude the possibility of the majority securing to themselves situations which will counterbalance the difficulties and hardships they will certainly find: amongst these, the impositions of the older inhabitants are not the least. The old American (or Yankee) looks with the most sovereign contempt upon the emigrant: he considers him a wretch, driven out of a wretched country, and seeking a subsistence in his glorious land. His pride is swelled, and his scorn of the poor emigrant doubled, not merely by this consideration, but by the prevailing notion that but few come here who have not violated the laws of their native realm. If a word is said of one returning, "Oh (says the Yankee), he'll none return: the stolen horse will keep him here."

With their insatiate thirst of gain, and these contemptuous notions of emigrants, they seem to consider them fair objects of plunder; and are prepared, in every transaction, to profit by their ignorance of the value of their goods, the custom and laws of the country, and the character of the people. Whoever comes here, should come with his eyes and ears open, and with the confirmed notion, that he is going to deal with sharpers. If he is not careful in purchasing necessaries for his inland journey, he will pay ten-fold for them; and when he is there, without equal caution, he will be liable to purchase land of a squatter: that is, a man who has taken possession of it, cultivated it without any title, and is subject to be ejected every day by the legal owner. With this, the evils of the banking system are to be taken into the account. I have stated, in a former letter, the causes which tend to bind a purchaser to the soil, and make him a pauper and a slave upon it; add to this, the extremes of heat and cold, the tormenting and disgusting swarms of vermin.

Source: E. Howitt. Selections from Letters Written During a Tour through the United States, in the Autumn of 1819 (Nottingham, UK: J. Dunn, 1819).

Imminent Dangers, Samuel Morse (1835)

Best known for his invention of the telegraph and the code that bears his name, Samuel Morse was also active in nativist politics in the mid-nineteenth century. In 1835, a year before he ran for mayor of New York City, Morse wrote an anti-immigration book titled Imminent Dangers to the Free Institutions of the United States through Foreign Immigration, and the Present State of the Naturalization Laws. *As the following excerpt makes clear, Morse was an ardent opponent of free immigration, especially involving Catholics and the Irish. While Morse's claim that foreign governments were using immigrants as a way to bring down American democracy was extreme even for his era, his argument that Catholic immigrants represented a threat to the American way of life was not out of the mainstream. During the great wave of Catholic Irish immigration in the late 1840s and early 1850s, many native-born Americans would join the Know-Nothing Party, whose primary goals included keeping out the Irish.*

Few, out of the great cities, are aware what sophistry has of late been spread among the more ignorant class of foreigners, to induce them to clan together, and to assert what they are pleased to call their rights. The ridiculous claim to superior privileges over native citizens, which I have noticed, is a specimen. . . . Already has the influence of bad councils led the deluded emigrant, particularly the Irish emigrant, to adopt such a course as to alienate from him the American people. Emigrants have been induced to prefer such arrogant claims, they have nurtured their foreign feelings and their foreign nationality to such a degree, and manifested such a determination to create and strengthen a separate and a foreign interest, that the American people can endure it no longer, and a direct hostile interest is now in array against them. This is an effect natural from such a cause; it is one long predicted in the hope of averting the evil. If evil is the consequence, the writer at least washes his hands of the guilt. The name and character of foreigner has, by this conduct of emigrants and their advocates, become odious, and the public voice is becoming louder and louder, and it will increase to unanimity, or at least so far as real American feeling pervades the hearts of Americans, until its language will be intelligible and audible even to those deaf ears, who now affect neither to hear, nor to heed it. . . . It is that anomalous, nondescript . . . thing, neither foreigner nor native, yet a moiety of each, now one, now the other, both or neither, as circumstances suit, against whom I war; a naturalized *foreigner,* not a naturalized citizen; a man who from Ireland, or France, or Germany, or other foreign lands, renounces his native country and adopts America, professes to become an American, and still, being received and sworn to be a citizen, talks (for example) of Ireland as "his home," as "his beloved country," resents anything said against the Irish as said against him, glories in being Irish, forms and cherishes an Irish interest, brings hither Irish local feuds, and forgets, in short, all his new obligations as an American, and retains both a name and a feeling and a practice in regard to his adopted country at war with propriety, with decency, with gratitude, and with true patriotism. I hold no parley with such contradictions as Irish fellow-citizens, French fellow-citizens, or German fellow-citizens. With as much consistency might we say *foreign natives,* or *hostile friends.* But the present is no time either for compliment or nice discrimination. When the country is invaded by an army, it is not the moment to indulge in pity towards the deluded soldiers of the various hostile corps, who act as they are commanded by their superior officers. It is then no time to make distinctions among the officers, lest we injure those who are voluntarily fighting against us, or who may be friends in the enemy's camp. The first thing is to bring the whole army to unconditional surrender, and when they have laid down their arms in a body, and acknowledged our sovereignty, then good fellowship, and courtesy, and pity will have leisure to indulge in discriminating friends from foes, and in showing to each their respective and appropriate sympathies.

We have now to resist the *momentous* evil that threatens us from *Foreign Conspiracy.* The Conspirators are in the *foreign importations.* Innocent and guilty are brought over together. We must of necessity suspect them all. That we are most seriously endangered, admits not of the slightest doubt; we are experiencing the natural reaction of European upon American principles, and it is infatuation, it is madness not to see it, not to guard against it. A subtle attack is making upon us by foreign powers. The proofs are as strong as the nature of the case allows. They have been adduced again and again, and they have not only been uncontradicted, but silently acquiesced in, and have acquired fresh confirmation by every day's observation. The arbitrary governments of Europe—those governments who keep the people in the most abject obedience at the point of the bayonet, with Austria at their head, have combined to attack us in every vulnerable point that the nation exposes to their assault. They are compelled by self-preservation to attempt our destruction—they must destroy democracy. It is with them a case of life and death, they must succeed or perish. If they do not overthrow American liberty, American liberty will overthrow their despotism. . . . Will you despise the cry of danger? Well, be it so. Believe the foreign Jesuit rather than your own countrymen. Open wide your doors. Yes, throw down your walls. Invite, nay allure, your enemies. Enlarge your almshouses and your prisons; be not sparing of your money; complain not of the outrages in your streets, nor the burden of your taxes. You will be repaid in praises of your toleration and liberty. What though European despots have compelled you to the necessity of employing your lives in toiling and providing for their outcast poor, and have caused you to be vexed, and your habit outraged by the expatriated turbulence of their cities, instead of allowing you to rejoice in the prosperity, and happiness, and peaceful neighbourhood of your own well-provided, well-instructed children. . . .

What were the circumstances of the country when laws so favourable to the foreigner were passed to induce him to emigrate and settle in this country? The answer is obvious. Our early history explains it. In our national infancy we needed the strength of *numbers*. Powerful nations, to whom we were accessible by fleets, and consequently also by armies, threatened us. Our land had been the theatre of contests between French, and English, and Spanish armies, for more than a century. Our numbers were so few and so scattered, that as a people we could not unite to repel aggression. The war of Independence, too, had wasted us. We wanted *numerical strength;* we felt our weakness in numbers. *Safety,* then, national *safety,* was the motive which urged us to use every effort to increase our population, and to induce a foreign emigration. Then foreigners seemed all-important, and the policy of alluring them hither, too palpable to be opposed successfully even by the remonstrances of Jefferson. We could be benefited by the emigrants, and we in return could bestow on them a gift beyond price, by simply making them citizens. Manifest as this advantage seemed in the increase of our numerical strength, Mr. Jefferson looked beyond the advantage of the moment, and saw the distant evil. . . . Now, if under the most favourable circumstances for the country, when it could most be benefited, when numbers were most urgently needed, Mr. Jefferson could discover the evil afar off, and protest against encouraging foreign immigration, how much more is the measure to be deprecated, when circumstances have so entirely changed, that instead of *adding strength* to the country, immigration *adds weakness,* weakness physical and moral! And what overwhelming force does Mr. Jefferson's reasoning acquire, by the vast change of circumstances which has taken place both in Europe and in this country, in our earlier and in our later condition. *Then* we were few, feeble, and scattered. *Now* we are numerous, strong, and concentrated. *Then* our accessions by immigration were real accessions of strength from the ranks of the learned and the good, from the enlightened mechanic and artisan, and intelligent husbandman. *Now* immigration is the accession of weakness, from the ignorant and the vicious, or the priest-ridden slaves of Ireland and Germany, or the outcast tenants of the poorhouses and prisons of Europe. And again: *Then* our beautiful system of government had not been unfolded to the world to the terror of tyrants; the rising brightness of American Democracy was not yet so far above the horizon as to wake their slumbering anxieties, or more than to gleam faintly, in hope, upon their enslaved subjects. *Then* emigration was natural, it was an attraction of affinities, it was an attraction of liberty to liberty. Emigrants were the proscribed for conscience's sake, and for opinion's sake, the real lovers of liberty, Europe's loss, and our gain. . . . Now emigrants are selected for a service to their tyrants, and by their tyrants; not for their affinity to liberty, but for their mental servitude, and their docility in obeying the orders of their priests. They are transported in thousands, nay, in *hundreds of thousands,* to our shores, to our loss and Europe's gain. Again, I say, let . . . the law of the land be so changed, that no foreigner who comes into the country after the law is passed shall ever be entitled to the right of suffrage. This is just ground; it is practicable ground; it is defensible ground; and it is safe and prudent ground; and I cannot better close than in the words of Mr. Jefferson: "The time to guard against corruption and tyranny is before they shall have gotten hold on us; it is better to keep the wolf out of the fold, than to trust to drawing his teeth and talons after he has entered."

. . . What reason can be assigned, why they who profess to have become Americans, should organize themselves into Foreign National Societies all over the country; and under their foreign appellation, hold correspondence with each other to promote their foreign interest? Can any good reason be given why such *foreign associations* should be allowed to exist in this country? The Irish have been thus organized for many years. The objects of *one* of these Irish societies will serve to illustrate the objects generally of all these associations in the midst of us. "The Boston Hibernian Lyceum," says the *Catholic Diary* of March 14, 1835, "organized about *two years ago,* is composed of Irish young men, for the diffusion among each other["]—of what?—"of mutual sympathy and mutual co-operation, in whatever may aid to qualify them to meet and discharge their responsibilities as the representatives of their native, as well as citizens of their adopted, country, as Irishmen and Americans." Here we have an avowal directly of an organization to promote a foreign interest in this country! . . .

It is notorious that the excitement respecting the Roman Catholic emigrant has existed scarcely a year. The exposure of foreign designs through the Roman Catholic religion, and the discussions arising out of it, all the riotous conduct of Catholics and others, and among other things the public notices of these very *organizations,* have all occurred within the last year. But the organizations of the Catholics, and particularly of the Irish, are of many years standing. The Society at Boston above quoted, and one of the most recent, was formed long before any excitement on the subject "two years ago," says the *Catholic Diary.* It was discovering these organizations, already formed on the part of foreigners, that excited the jealousy and distrust on the part of the American people.

Source: Samuel F.B. Morse. *Imminent Dangers to the Free Institutions of the United States through Foreign Immigration, and the Present State of the Naturalization Laws.* Originally published in the *Journal of Commerce*, 1835.

Stimulating Emigration from Ireland, Court Deposition by Michael Gaugan (1837)

With the great wave of Irish immigrants fleeing the potato famine—and the nativist hostility it would spark in the United States—still a decade in the future, this New York court deposition, taken from an Irish immigrant in 1837, reflects the fact that some Americans were eager to see more immigration from Ireland. Specifically, businessmen and early industrialists seeking cheap labor offered promises of high wages that in many cases never materialized. The tactic of luring immigrants from Europe to fill American factories would become much more widespread after the Civil War.

State of New York. City and County of New York. Michael Gaugan, at present in the city of New York, being duly sworn, doth depose and say, that he is a native of Ireland, and last resided in the city of Dublin in Ireland, previous to his coming to this country with his family, consisting of himself, wife, son, and daughter. That up to the time of his coming to this country, he was employed as assistant engineer on the grand canal Ballanhasloe, to Dublin, which situation he had held for the last thirteen years, at a salary of one pound one shilling sterling per week, besides a house and an acre of ground or more; in which situation he lived respectably and comfortably with his family; and should have continued to do so had he not been induced by the false representations held out to his countrymen generally, in an evil hour, to quit his employment, his home and his friends, to come to this country, under an expectation that with his acquirements in civil engineering, he should soon become a wealthy man.

And this deponent further says, that there were hand bills, placarded on every corner, tree, and pump and public place in the city of Dublin, and for forty or fifty miles in the surrounding country, stating, in substance, that the people were fools not to leave the country, where there was nothing but poverty staring them in the face. That laborers were so much wanted in America, that even women were employed to work at men's work—that work was plenty in America, and wages high, to wit, 9 or 10 shillings a day, British money, and his diet. And deponent further says that William Wiley of Dublin, the agent of Rawson and McMurray of New York, told this deponent that he, deponent, could get ten pounds British money

per month, and his diet as wages; that every one was on a perfect equality in America; that the common laboring man received high wages, and sat at the same table and ate with his master, and gave deponent such a glowing picture of the wealth of America, and that with ease, an independent fortune could be made; that he (deponent) determined to relinquish his situation on the grand canal and bring his family to America, expecting, and so stated to his employer, that he might expect to see him return again in three years a rich man.

And this deponent further states, that there is one or more agent in every principal town in Ireland, who receives a commission for collecting and forwarding emigrants to Liverpool, where they take ship for America.

And this deponent further says, that he arrived in this city in the ship "Troy," Captain Allen, on the 16th day of June last past, with 204 passengers, that a majority of them were men in good employment at home, and lived comfortably and contented, until these passenger agents appeared in the country, a great part of whom have already returned home to Ireland, disappointed and disgusted at the gross impositions that had been practised upon them. That deponent is now without means for the support of himself and his family, and has no employment, and has already suffered great deprivation since he arrived in this country; and is now soliciting means to enable him to return with his family home to Ireland.

[Signed] Mich'l Gaugan

Source: *Niles' Weekly Register,* vol. 52 (August 26, 1837).

Four Years of Irish History, 1845–1849, Charles Gavan Duffy (1883)

In his book on the Irish potato famine of the late 1840s, Irish nationalist Charles Gavan Duffy summarizes the report of an English Quaker who toured the country in 1847. As the report describes, conditions in Ireland in the midst of famine were nothing short of catastrophic for the general population. Beyond the widespread starvation, Duffy observes the breakdown of institutions of civil society and the lack of help offered by the British government. He further condemns the British for not inspecting the emigrant ships, whose terrible conditions made more deaths inevitable.

The state of the country grew worse from day to day. It is difficult now to realise the condition of the western population in the autumn of 1847; but a witness of unexceptionable impartiality has painted it in permanent colours. A young Englishman representing the Society of Friends, who in that tragic time did work worthy of the Good Samaritan, reported what he saw in Mayo and Galway in language which for plain vigour rivals the narratives of [novelist Daniel] Defoe. This is what he saw in Westport:

The town of Westport was in itself a strange and fearful sight, like what we read of in beleaguered cities; its streets crowded with gaunt wanderers, sauntering to and fro with hopeless air and hunger-struck look—a mob of starved, almost naked, women around the poor-house clamouring for soup tickets—our inn, the head-quarters of the road engineer and pay clerks, beset by a crowd of beggars for work.

As he approached Galway, the rural population were found to be in a more miserable condition:

Some of the women and children that we saw on the road were abject cases of poverty and almost naked. The few rags they had on were with the greatest difficulty held together, and in a few weeks, as they are utterly unable to provide themselves with fresh clothes unless they be given them, they must become absolutely naked.

And in another district:

As we went along, our wonder was not that the people died, but that they lived; and I have no doubt whatever that in any other country the mortality would have been far greater; that many lives have been prolonged, perhaps saved, by the long apprenticeship to want in which the Irish peasant has been trained, and by that lovely, touching charity which prompts him to share his scanty meal with his starving neighbour.

The fishermen of the Cladagh, who were induced to send the Whig Attorney-General to Parliament a few months before, had to pledge the implements of their calling for a little daily bread:

Even the very nets and tackling of these poor fishermen, I heard, were pawned, and, unless they be assisted to redeem them, they will be unable to take advantage of the herring shoals, even when they approach their coast. . . . In order to ascertain the truth of this statement, I went into two or three of the largest pawnshops, the owners of which fully confirmed it and said they had in pledge at least a thousand pounds' worth of such property and saw no likelihood of its being redeemed.

In a rural district which he revisited after an interval he paints a scene which can scarcely be matched in the annals of a mediaeval plague:

One poor woman whose cabin I had visited said, "There will be nothing for us but to lie down and die." I tried to give her hope of English aid, but, alas! her prophecy has been too true. Out of a population of 240 I found thirteen already dead from want. The survivors were like walking skeletons—the men gaunt and haggard, stamped with the livid mark of hunger—the children crying with pain—the women in some of the cabins too weak to stand. When there before I had seen cows at almost every cabin, and there were besides many sheep and pigs owned in the village. But now all the sheep were gone—all the cows—all the poultry killed—only one pig left—the very dogs which had barked at me before had disappeared; no potatoes—no oats.

Speaking of Clifden, he says:

To get to their work many of the men have to walk five, even seven, Irish miles; the sergeant of a police station by the road-side told us that the custom of these men was to take a little meal gruel before starting in the morning, taking but one meal one day and treating themselves with two the next. He mentioned cases in which they had worked till they fell over their tools. Four-and-sixpence per week thus earned, the sole resource of a family of six, with Indian meal, their cheapest food, at 2/10 to 4/-per stone! What is this but slow death—a mere enabling the patient to endure for a little longer time the disease of hunger?

The young man pointed the moral which these horrible spectacles suggested with laudable courage:

I would not now discuss the causes of this condition, nor attempt to apportion blame to its authors; but of this one fact there can be no question: that the result of our social system is that vast numbers of our fellow-countrymen—of the peasantry of one of the richest nations the world ever knew—have not leave to live. . . .

The weekly returns of the dead were like the bulletin of a fierce campaign. As the end of the year approached, villages and rural districts, which had been prosperous and populous a year before, were desolate. In some places the loss amounted to half the resident population. Even the paupers shut up in poor-houses did not escape. More than one in six perished of the unaccustomed food. The people did not everywhere consent to die patiently. In Armagh and Down groups of men went from house to house in the rural districts and insisted on being fed. In Tipperary and Waterford corn-stores and bakers' shops were sacked. In Donegal the people seized upon a flour-mill and pillaged it. In Limerick 5,000 men assembled on Tory Hill, and declared that they would not starve. A local clergyman restrained them by the promise of speedy relief. "If the Government did not act promptly, he himself would show them where food could be had." In a few cases crops were carried away from farms. The offences which spring from suffering and fear were heard of in many districts, but they were encountered with instant resistance. There were 30,000 men in red jackets, carefully fed, clothed, and lodged, ready to maintain the law. Four prisoners were convicted at the Galway assizes of stealing a filly, which they killed and ate to preserve their own lives. In Enniskillen two boys under twelve years of age were convicted of stealing one pint of Indian meal cooked into "stirabout," and Chief Justice Blackburn vindicated the outraged law by transporting them for seven years. Other children committed larcenies that they might be sent to gaol, where there was still daily bread to be had. In Mayo the people were eating carrion wherever it could be procured, and the coroner could not keep pace with the inquests; for the law sometimes spent more to ascertain the cause of a pauper's death than would have sufficed to preserve his life.

The social disorganisation was a spectacle as afflicting as the waste of life; it was the waste of whatever makes life worth possessing. All the institutions which civilise and elevate the people were disappearing one after another. The churches were half empty; the temperance reading-rooms were shut up; the mechanics' institute no longer got support; only the gaols and the poor-houses were crowded. A new generation, born in disease and reared in destitution, pithless and imbecile, threatened to drag down the nation to hopeless slavery. Trade was paralysed; no one bought anything which was not indispensable at the hour. The loss of the farmers in potatoes was estimated at more than twenty millions sterling, and with the potatoes the pigs which fed on them disappeared. The seed procured at a high price in spring again failed; time, money, and labour were lost, and another year of famine was certain. All who depended on the farmer had sunk with him; shopkeepers were beggared, tradesmen were starving, the priests living on voluntary offerings were sometimes in fearful distress when the people had no longer anything to offer. . . .

When the increased mortality was pressed on the attention of the Government, Lord John Russell replied that the owners of property in Ireland ought to support the poor born on their estates. It was a perfectly just proposition if the ratepayers were empowered to determine the object and method of the expenditure; but prohibiting reproductive work, and forcing them to turn strong men into paupers, and keep them sweltering in workhouses instead of labouring to reclaim the waste lands—this was not justice. . . .

The people fled before the famine to England, America, and the British colonies. They carried with them the seed of disease and death. In England a bishop and more than twenty priests died of typhus, caught in attendance on the sick and dying. The English people clamoured against such an infliction, which it cannot be denied would be altogether intolerable if these fugitives were not made exiles and paupers by English law. They were ordered home again, that they might be supported on the resources of their own country; for though we had no country for the purpose of self-government and self-protection, we were acknowledged to have a country when the necessity of bearing burdens arose.

More than a hundred thousand souls fled to the United States and Canada. The United States maintained sanitary regulations on shipboard which were effectual to a certain extent. But the emigration to Canada was left to the individual greed of ship-owners, and the emigrant ships rivalled the cabins of Mayo or the fever sheds of Skibbereen. Crowded and filthy, carrying double the legal number of passengers, who were ill-fed and imperfectly clothed, and having no doctor on board, the holds, says an eye-witness, were like the Black Hole of Calcutta, and deaths occurred in myriads. The survivors, on their arrival in the new country, continued to die and to scatter death around them. At Montreal, during nine weeks, eight hundred emigrants perished, and over nine hundred residents died of diseases caught from emigrants. During six months the deaths of the new arrivals exceeded three thousand. No preparations were made by the British Government for the reception, or the employment, of these helpless multitudes. The *Times* pronounced the neglect to be an eternal disgrace to the British name. Ships carrying German emigrants and English emigrants arrived in Canada at the same time in a perfectly healthy state. The Chief Secretary for Ireland was able to inform the House of Commons that of a hundred thousand Irishmen who fled to Canada in a year 6,100 perished on the voyage, 4,100 on their arrival, 5,200 in the hospitals, and 1,900 in the towns to which they repaired. The Emigrant Society of Montreal paints the result during the whole period of the famine, in language not easily to be forgotten.

Source: Sir Charles Gavan Duffy. *Four Years of Irish History, 1845–1849* (London: Cassell, Petter, Galpin, 1883).

Treaty of Guadalupe Hidalgo (1848)

To mark the official end of the Mexican-American War (1846–1848), in which the United States seized the northern third of Mexican sovereign territory, diplomatic representatives of the two countries signed the Treaty of Guadalupe Hidalgo on February 2, 1848. Article 8 of the treaty, reprinted below, granted full U.S. citizenship to any of the thousands of Mexicans living in those territories, including the modern-day U.S. states of California, Arizona, Nevada, and Utah, and parts of New Mexico, Colorado, and Wyoming.

Mexicans now established in territories previously belonging to Mexico, and which remain for the future within the limits of the United States as defined by the present treaty, shall be free to continue where they now reside, or to remove at any time to the Mexican republic, retaining the property which they possess in the said territories, or disposing thereof, and removing the proceeds wherever they please, without their being subjected on this account, to any contribution, tax, or charge whatever.

Those who shall prefer to remain in the said territories, may either retain the title and rights of Mexican citizens, or acquire those of citizens of the United States. But they shall be under the obligation to make their election within one year from the date of the exchange of ratifications of this treaty, and those who shall remain in the said territories after the expiration of that year, without having declared their intention to retain the character of Mexicans, shall be considered to have elected to become citizens of the United States.

Source: William Malloy, ed. *Conventions, International Acts, Protocols, and Agreements Between the United States of America and Other Powers, 1776–1909,* vol. 1 (Holmes Beach, FL: Gaunt, 1996).

The United States of North America, with Particular Consideration Paid to German Emigration There, Gottfried Menzel (1853)

Originally published in German in Berlin, Gottfried Menzel's The United States of North America, with Particular Consideration Paid to German Emigration There *attempted to offer a balanced picture to German immigrants considering a move to the United States. Before embarking, he advised, prospective émigrés should investigate the true conditions of life in America for impoverished newcomers. Economic hard times, followed by the abortive revolutions of 1848, sent tens of thousands of German-speaking émigrés to the United States in the mid-nineteenth century.*

The motive common to all men for changing their homes is the hope of improving their condition. If something is annoying or oppressive to a man in one place and he cannot remove the untoward conditions, he is then inclined to betake himself to the place where he thinks he can remain undisturbed by such vexations. In Germany as elsewhere, there are two things particularly which are disagreeable and burdensome to many of the inhabitants and from which they escape by emigrating to America.

In Germany as in most of the European states many people are dissatisfied with the state organization and institutions. They feel themselves hampered by the government, complain of lack of freedom, of too much government, and the like, and direct their gaze to the free states of the great North American Republic, as the land of desired freedom. . . .

Germans who voluntarily exchanged their homes in Germany for new homes in North America to obtain greater freedom, especially those who have emigrated since the year 1848, always say in their accounts from America that they are entirely satisfied with American freedom, and sincerely pity all those who are not yet sharers in it. But through the newspapers of the day other opinions are heard. There are many things with which they are really dissatisfied. Some existing institutions they wish to remove and to replace with others, but they have not yet been able to change anything in these republican constitutions and democratic institutions. The Americans do not approve of these efforts at reformation and say, "These Germans wish to dictate everything, but do not wish to be dictated to themselves."

Much greater is the number of those who leave their fatherland on account of the poverty of its material resources and in order to better their condition in America. For many people industrial conditions in Germany are such that you cannot blame them for emigrating when they learn that in North America there are far greater productive natural resources and that work has a greater value than in Germany.

He who in Germany has to suffer from want and misery, or must expect these in the near future, finds that hope of better fortune overcomes his attachment to the *Vaterland.* He easily separates himself from his old home and wanders to a distant land believing that he will find life more favorable there.

That it is easier to make a living in America cannot be denied; but it is a matter of regret that those who could better their condition in this way frequently lack the means. Many people who take this risk find only their misfortune or ruin. The numbers of those who return to Germany from America prove that many are not successful there. When an emigrant ship is prepared to sail from the harbor of New York for Hamburg or Bremen, there are usually twenty or more people leaving the land of their disappointed hopes for the old home country after one or two years' bitter experiences. They have left, out of their fortunes, scarcely the necessary money for the return passage. Still others would follow them if they had the means for the trip or if they were not ashamed to return.

Therefore everyone who is thinking of emigrating to America should take care to determine whether or not he is fit for America. He should carefully weigh what he leaves here against what he may find there, lest he should be guilty of too great haste or light-mindedness and make a mistake that he may regret only too soon and bitterly. . . . The emigrant must rely upon others and believe what they tell him about that country, either to give up his decision or to fulfil it. But most of them are guilty of credulity which may be regarded as the chief cause of the numerous emigrations.

A great many books about emigration to America have been written, and every year new ones appear. *Rathgeber, Führer, Wegweiser* for emigrants are the customary titles of these books. A book written against emigration, or one advising emigration only for the few, would have little charm and would find few purchasers. But as soon as a book appears which describes the land to which the emigrant would go as a land of paradise, then it is sold and read diligently, and thousands are moved in this way to become emigrants. Many a book on emigration very truly describes what is good and what is agreeable in America, but passes over in silence the disadvantages or disagreeable features of American life. Through this one-sided presentation of American conditions many are lured to emigrate. It is obvious that the countless speculators who every year gain many millions of emigrants will make a great effort to bring to the attention of the people many books through which the desire for emigration is awakened and increased. They are themselves completely indifferent to the fate of the emigrants, and if emigration turns out to be for their ruin they do not care. Again, many who read books on emigration see only what they like; and they overlook the disagreeable, which is moreover only painted in faint colors, and do not give it mature consideration. Thus they themselves help to make the work of deception easy and complete.

But the descriptions and the letters of the emigrants to their relatives and friends and acquaintances—are they not then true and reliable? This I deny. First, because no one who has emigrated will confess that he was disappointed, that he had not found there that on which he had counted with certainty and which he had so joyfully anticipated. He is very right in thinking that few in the old home will have sympathetic pity for him, and many only malicious joy and bitter ridicule. Even sympathy for misfortune brought on one's self is not agreeable. One does not wish to confess to those who advised against emigration that they were right in their forebodings and warnings, and that they had seen more clearly and correctly than he had.

Secondly, the immigrants wish, for many reasons, to have many of their relatives and countrymen follow them and settle near them. On the one hand, because of the neighborly society and support, the need of which

many of them have bitterly experienced. On the other hand, one desires everywhere new arrivals of immigrants because they will buy land, and stock, and so on from those already settled, by which ready money, of which there is always need, comes into this part of the country and the value of the land and its produce increases. The following of relatives, especially if they are well off, is much desired by their predecessors whether circumstances are favorable or unfavorable.

Therefore, it is easy to understand that there are no complaints in the letters of the immigrants in spite of the causes of complaint that many a writer may have. Before my trip to America I received many letters from people living there, who described their condition as quite satisfactory, but when I had personally investigated their condition and when I expressed my surprise at their letters which had gone so far from reality, I received the answer, "Others ought to try their life too. In Germany there are more than enough people, while here there are too few."

What does North America offer that is good?

This great country offers its inhabitants noteworthy advantages which may be summarized as follows:

1. Although the citizens of the United States are not, as is popularly supposed, free from taxes, yet the taxes on land and cattle which the farmer has to pay are not high, and artisans pay no taxes on their business.

2. The citizens are, during a certain age, under obligation to serve in the militia, but except in the case of war this is rarely asked of them except perhaps for suppression of a riot. For regular military service volunteers are always available, since they are well paid. The quartering of soldiers in time of peace is not allowed.

3. Complete freedom in the trades and professions, hunting and fishing is allowed to everyone. . .

4. There is no difference in rank. The terms "upper class" and "lower class" have no significance. The public official has no advantage not shared by the farmer, the merchant, or the teamster.

5. North America, as a country with fertile land still partly unoccupied, a country thinly populated with flourishing trade and general freedom of trade, offers far greater and more abundant means of livelihood than Germany.

6. Labor there has a high, and cost of living a lower, value; therefore on the whole the people are far less oppressed

by want and need and the tormenting anxiety for one's daily bread.

Against the advantages just enumerated . . . the following disadvantages will not please those who are eager to emigrate.

The long and distant sea-voyage appears to many of them as the great hardship of emigration, and they think if only this were accomplished all would be well. Although this is accompanied by danger and much inconvenience, it is soon over. Seasickness is indeed painful for many, but it is not dangerous, and need not be feared since it is good for their health after the sea journey. Far more hazardous and more serious in their consequences are the following:

1. [The danger, after landing in America, of losing one's property through the deception and thievery of the runners.]

2. The unhealthy climate. . . .

3. The German in America is a complete stranger. Everything is strange, the country, the climate, laws, and customs. One ought to realize what it means to be an alien in a far distant land. More than this, the German in America is despised as alien, and he must often hear the nickname "Dutchman," at least until he learns to speak English fluently. It is horrible what the German immigrants must endure from the Americans, Irish, and English. I was more than once a witness to the way German immigrants were forced by the American captain or pilot with terrible brutality, kicking, etc., to carry wood from the shore to the boat, although they had paid their full fare and had not been engaged for those duties. Only in the places where the Germans are in the majority does the newly arrived immigrant find, after all the hardships of the journey, an endurable existence. The Americans are accustomed to alter their behavior to him only after he has become Americanized. The rabble who also emigrated from Germany in former times have brought the German name into discredit.

4. The educational institutions are, in America, defective and expensive or they are completely lacking. Therefore parents can give their children the necessary education only through great sacrifices or, in case they are poor, the children must be allowed to run wild. . . .

5. The majority of the Germans emigrating to America wish to seek their fortunes in agriculture. But the purchase of land has its dangers and difficulties. The price of the land is, in proportion to its productivity, not so low as is generally believed. To establish a farm on new and uncultivated land is for the newcomer an almost impossible task. The life of a North American farmer is not at all enviable as many think. Where labor is so dear and where agricultural products are so cheap, there no one can exist except the man who is able and willing to do all his own work and does not need to employ outside labor. . . .

I have been approached since my return from North America by a large number of persons for information concerning conditions there and for advice concerning their projected plan of emigration. Either because of their personal qualifications or circumstances, hardly one-fourth of these people could be advised with confidence to undertake this important step. I found most of them unsuitable for emigration for the following more or less serious reasons:

1. *A weak constitution or shattered health.*—The emigrant to America needs a strong and healthy body.

2. *Advanced age.*—The man who is already over forty years of age, unless he has some sons who can help him with their labor, cannot count upon success and prosperity in America.

3. *Childlessness with somewhat advanced age.*—What will a married couple do when their capacity to labor disappears with the years? They could not earn enough when young to support them in later years. If they have a substantial property to bring over from Germany, then emigration would be a very unwise step for them, since for the man without employment living is much higher in America than in Europe, especially if one needs servants or cannot do without the comforts and luxuries of life.

4. *Lack of experience in the field of labor on the part of those who expect to establish their fortunes there through hard labor.*—The duties of the agriculturists, as well as the occupations of the artisan, involve heavy labor. Many harbor the delusion that they are already accustomed to the labor required there, or that they will easily learn it if they have worked a little here in this country. But he who has not from his youth up been performing continuously the most severe labor, so much the more will he lack, in America, where work is harder, the necessary strength and ability. He will certainly not be a competent and contented workingman. In America . . . labor is much more severe and much more work is required for the higher wages he receives than is usual in Germany. Those who spent their youth in schools, offices, or in other sedentary work, play in America a very sad and pitiable role.

5. *A slow easy-going habit of living a life of ease and comfort.*—One may find in the great cities of North America all the comforts and conveniences which European cities offer, but in America they are only for the few—for the rich—and to this class German emigrants do not usually belong. Not many persons in America can command even the comforts of the ordinary citizen of Europe. Many people seek compensation in whiskey for their many privations and hardships and this is the way to certain ruin.

6. *Destitution.*—If the passage for a single emigrant costs only 50 thaler, at least as much again must be counted for the land journey here and in America. Unfortunately this amount is beyond the reach of those who would have the best chance of improving their condition in America. The artisan, even though he cannot carry on his business there independently but must work in great workshops and factories must often make yet a further land journey in order to find the most suitable place, and he needs, especially if he has a family, a not inconsiderable amount of money. Seldom is a place found in the vicinity of the port of arrival where places are not already filled with laborers. If the means of traveling are not available, he falls into difficulties and distress, is obliged to sell the effects he brought with him for a trifling sum, or considers himself fortunate if he finds a job anywhere at the lowest wage—a wage that will barely keep him and his family from hunger. Those who wish to move on to the land should not come to America without capital unless they are young, strong, and eager to work. It is necessary to earn the means to independence through service or through daily labor which is, to be sure, not easy, but is surer than to purchase immediately an independent position with money brought from Germany.

Source: Gottfried Menzel. *The United States of North America, with Particular Consideration Paid to German Emigration There* (Berlin: G. Reimer, 1853).

Emigration, Emigrants, and Know-Nothings, Anonymous (1854)

With vast numbers of newcomers entering the country from Ireland, Germany, and other parts of Europe, anti-immigrant sentiment in the United States reached new heights in the 1850s. The anonymous author of the book excerpted here described himself as an Englishman who had lived in the United States for thirteen years and had been a naturalized citizen for seven of them. The arguments he makes against unfettered immigration are common in the annals of American history—that immigrants contribute to crime and that they compete with the native-born for jobs, lowering wages for everyone in the process. The writer thus fits into a classic pattern in the nation's history—previous immigrants who want to close the gates behind them.

And what have I learned in the course of my travels and observations concerning the unlimited and unguarded admittance of foreigners into the country? What conclusion have I come to? That it is a glaring and grievous evil; an evil to the United States, and an evil to many of the emigrants themselves. Why? Because anybody, or everybody, may come without let or hindrance. The rogues and vagabonds from London, Paris, Amsterdam, Vienna, Naples, Hamburg, Berlin, Rome, Genoa, Leghorn, Geneva, &c., may come and do come. The outpouring of alms and work houses, and prisons and penitentiaries, may come and do come. Monarchies, oligarchies, and aristocracies may and do reduce the millions of the people to poverty and beggary, and compel the most valueless to seek for a shelter and a home in the United States of America, and they do so. And what are the consequences? The consequences are that about 400,000 souls, from Europe, chiefly Germans, Irish, and Dutch are annually arriving in this country and making it their permanent abode. That a vast number of these emigrants come without money, occupation, friends, or business; many, very many, have not the means of buying land, getting to it, stocking it, and waiting for first crops, and many others would not settle upon land if they could. That, go where you will in the United States, you find nearly all the dens of iniquity, taverns, grog-shops, beer houses, gambling places, and houses of ill fame and worse deeds, are kept by foreigners. That, at the various ports, the alms-houses and hospitals are, in the main, occupied by foreigners; and that numerous objects of poverty and destitution are to be seen crawling along the streets in every direction. That not a few become criminals, filling our prisons and putting the country to great expense.

This is a fearful catalogue of consequences, but they are by no means all. This unlimited and unrestricted admission of foreign emigrants is a serious injury to the native laboring population, socially, morally, religiously, and politically; socially, by overstocking the labor market and thus keeping wages down; morally and religiously, by unavoidable contact and intercourse; and politically, by consequence of want of employment and low wages, making them needy and dependent, whereby they become the easy prey or willing tools of designing and unprincipled politicians. And in this way the native population is deteriorated and made poor, needy, and subservient: and these realities produce want of self-respect, hopelessness, laxity in morals, recklessness, delinquencies, and crimes.

But there is another consequence which is deserving

of notice, and it is this: Our manufacturers, ironmakers, machinists, miners, agriculturists, railway, canal, and other contractors, private families, hotelkeepers, and many others, have got into the way of expecting and seeking for cheap labor, through the supply of operatives, workmen, laborers, house-help, and various kinds of workers, kept up by the indiscriminate and unrestrained admission of emigrants. Indeed it is no secret that emigrants, or rather foreign workers, have become an article of importation; professedly for the purpose of providing for the deficiency of supply in the labor market, but in reality with the intention of obtaining efficient workers at lower wages.

I remember well in the early part of 1846, when our manufacturers and ironmakers, far and near, were struggling hard for the retention of the high protective tariff then in existence, and the profits on cotton spinning and manufacturing ranged from thirty to one hundred per cent, that hundreds of operatives were imported from England for the purpose of obtaining practised hands and to keep wages from rising. And I remember also that some years ago when there was an attempt to reduce the wages of ironmakers and machinists at Pittsburgh and elsewhere, and the men resisted, that importation was resorted to with considerable success; and that those importations, and others both before and since, were obtained in a great measure by partial, fallacious, and incorrect representations.

This last mentioned consequence has had, and probably will continue to have, a very unfair and deplorable effect upon the native laboring population; for it needs no proof to sustain the assertion, that but for these specific and large importations of cotton and woolen manufacturing operatives, machinists and ironworkers, the wages of the then located population must have risen, and the natives been made better off. It is worthy of mention and attention in this connexion, that master coal miners, master ironmakers, master machinists, master cotton and woollen manufacturers, &c., are to a man advocates for a very high tariff upon coal, iron, steel, machines, tools, and cotton and woollen goods; and for the unlimited admission of workers without a sixpence of duty; by which means the consumers of all those articles are made to pay exorbitant prices for their benefit (the benefit of the masters), while they can and do avail themselves of the free importation of labor in order to keep wages from rising or for the purpose of lowering them. This is certainly the protective system, but it is protecting the masters and not the workers; the strong against the weak; the high livers and little workers, against the low livers and hard workers. If any protective system is wanted, I am an advocate for a protective system which shall prevent pauper labor from coming into the country, and admitting all

merchandise free, which by making it abundant and cheap would add to the comfort of the masses. . . .

Then what ought to be done? I will say what I am convinced ought to be done, and what would be for the honor and welfare of the country at large; and that is, restrict by law the admission and importation of emigrants to within prudent limits. None should be permitted to land at any of our ports and remain in the country unless he, she, or they could show satisfactorily to the proper authorities (made and provided for that purpose) that they were engaged in trade, had a living occupation to go to, or were fully prepared to comply with the regulations which require them immediately to settle upon and cultivate permanently the public lands appropriated to that purpose.

We would have these public lands given in limited quantities, say from fifty and not exceeding one hundred acres, to emigrant settlers, according to the number of persons in a family and their power of improving and cultivating it. Plain and full instructions in pamphlet form should be prepared and given to every settler, whereby they would learn how to get to the lands at the least cost and in the most direct way, requiring them to go in companies and to own and occupy adjoining allotments, and recommending them to adopt a simple, reciprocal associative manner of labor and living. Nay, rather than we should continue emigration upon its present basis, through which we should go on producing paupers, delinquents, and criminals, and causing numbers of new comers to take up low and vile occupations, and for the much to be desired and wise purpose of raising up "A bold peasantry, their country's pride," we would even consent to defray the expense of conveying them to their new homes out of the national exchequer.

Such an alteration of the system, or rather such an introduction of a system, would soon become generally known throughout Europe, and would deter and prevent the vicious, the destitute, and the very ignorant from coming among us, and would in consequence stop the rapid increase of pauperism, degradation, and crime at our ports. On the other hand, it would encourage such foreigners as had laid up a little money, and were likely to prove industrious and respectable citizens, to come over and help us to become truly great, by intelligent industry, honesty, and frugality.

Among other regulations, under the new system, all owners and captains of vessels should be formally notified of the fact, and that they would be held liable to take all emigrants back, free from charge, and to maintain them whilst in port, whom they had brought out contrary to the emigration law.

But I expect this scheme or proposition will be objected to by many, who will say, "such restrictions would be inconsistent with our liberties and the spirit of true republicanism, would prevent hundreds and thousands of monarchially oppressed subjects from participating in the benefits to be derived from our free institutions and more equitable governments, and that without the present free and unlimited admission of emigrants we should be prevented from executing great public works as heretofore."

To these objections, I reply, that the unrestricted exercise of any liberty or privilege which is productive of so much evil as this is, ought to be restrained; not only for the sake of our national respectability and the well-being of our native population, but for the sake also of those unfortunate persons who having already filled our ports, cities, and towns, with the poor and the helpless, are, some of them, in worse positions than when at home and living under European governments. Moreover, it is evidently injudicious and impolitic for us to place it in the power of kings and aristocracies and their suborganizations, to send hither hundreds of thousands of their ignorant, superstitious, and least valuable subjects for us to educate, reform, and maintain. And as it respects the prosecution of great public works, I say, that a great number are got up without necessity, as matters of speculation, and go into forgetfulness, never having been intended for the public use, and never brought to maturity; I say that we have no occasion to do the work of five centuries in one, and whatever is done hastily and recklessly is sure to be done ill; and therefore we had better do less and do it well. But railroad, canal, and other companies might, upon showing that they could not obtain laborers and operatives, be permitted to import workers and become chargeable with their maintenance and traveling expenses on their arrival.

Source: Anonymous. *Emigration, Emigrants, and Know-Nothings* (Philadelphia: By the Author, 1854).

Irish Response to Nativism, Editorial, New York *Citizen* (1854)

In this extract from an 1854 editorial published in the Citizen, *a New York City newspaper for Irish Americans, the editors discourage readers from supporting all "No-Nothing" candidates. The Know-Nothing Party—officially the American Party—was a rabid anti-immigrant, anti-Catholic political organization that gained wide support among native-born voters in the early 1850s.*

Since the establishment of the *Citizen,* we have uniformly urged upon Irish citizens that they should not act together

as Irishmen—should not isolate themselves from other American parties, should not place themselves in the hands of Irish priests, still less of Irish grog-sellers, to be disposed of as a political capital. We have made bold to propound the doctrine, that every Irish voter ought to vote upon his individual judgment about measures and men—not because the "Irish vote" goes this way or the other; that there ought, in short, to be no Irish vote at all; but that Irishmen in America should be so entirely absorbed into the American system as to be indifferently Democrats or Whigs, Hards, Softs, Silver-greys—anything except Garrisonian abolitionists.

But there is an element coming in, that alters the whole case. Here come a set of ignorant malignants, taking it upon them to represent the great nation, to maintain its honor and to guard its religion (the vagabonds!) and they say to their Irish fellow-citizens, "No, you shall never become wholly American—you are to be isolated for ever—you are unfit to enjoy the liberties, or to exercise the franchises of Americans—your religion is not to our taste—your brogue is unmusical to our ears."

Can there be any doubt as to how any Irish, or any German citizen, ought to treat these creatures? In this one case, at any rate, foreign-born men *are* isolated, though not by their own act. Whatever may be their political predilections, and however various on other points, here, at least, they must be one. No Irish voter, no German citizen, can, without abject disgrace, support—we do not say a No-Nothing candidate, but any candidate who courts or relies upon, or does not repudiate and spit upon, No-Nothing support.

Whosoever shall act otherwise at the approaching elections fawns upon the foot that spurns him, kisses the hand that would wrest the franchise from his children, and confesses that he and his are content to be helots and Pariahs in the free land of their adoption, as their strong tyrants made them Pariahs and helots in the land of their birth!

Source: Citizen (New York City), vol. 1 (October 28, 1854).

U.S. Senate Report on the Demand for Immigrant Labor (1864)

With thousands of men fighting in the Civil War, the United States experienced a severe labor shortage in the early 1860s. In 1864, a U.S. congressional committee investigated the situation and issued a report on agricultural conditions and the need for immigrant labor. The report, excerpted below, points out that new wage laborers would be needed both to run the factories of the North and to rebuild the South in the years after the war.

The special wants for labor in this country at the present time are very great. The war has depleted our workshops, and materially lessened our supply of labor in every department of industry and mechanism. In their noble response to the call of their country, our workmen in every branch of the useful arts have left vacancies which must be filled, or the material interest of the country must suffer. The immense amount of native labor occupied by the war calls for a large increase of foreign immigration to make up the deficiency at home. The demand for labor never was greater than at present, and the fields of usefulness were never so varied and promising.

The south, having torn down the fabric of its labor system by its own hands, will, when the war shall have ceased, present a wide field for voluntary white labor, and it must look to immigration for its supply.

The following may be mentioned as the special inducements to immigration:

1st. High price of labor and low price of food, compared with other countries.

2d. Our land policy, giving to every immigrant, after he shall have declared his intentions to become a citizen, a home and a farm, substantially as a free gift, charging him less for 160 acres in fee-simple than is paid as the annual rent of a single acre in England.

3d. The political rights conferred upon persons of foreign birth.

4th. Our system of free schools, melting in a common crucible all differences of religion, language, and race, and giving to the child of the day laborer and the son of the millionaire equal opportunities to excel in the pursuit and acquirement of knowledge. This is an advantage and a blessing which the poor man enjoys in no other country.

Source: U.S. Senate Committee on Agriculture. *Report on the Enactment of Suitable Laws for the Encouragement and Protection of Foreign Immigrants Arriving Within Jurisdiction of the United States.* 38th Cong., 1st sess., February 18, 1864, Committee Print 15.

Report of the Minnesota Board of Immigration (1871)

Like many other Western states with a lot of land but small populations after the Civil War, Minnesota actively encouraged the settlement of immigrants, especially from Britain, Ireland, *and Scandinavia. As summarized in this report, the government of Minnesota expended significant amounts of money and energy to promote immigration, including the hiring of agents and the writing and translating of pamphlets. As the document also makes clear, Minnesota faced significant competition from other states in the recruitment of European settlers.*

Organization of the Board.—The act of March 3d, 1871, created a Board of five persons, two of whom were designated in said act by name; the Governor, Secretary of State and Treasurer of State constituting the other members *ex-officio.* It was made the duty of the said Board generally, "to adopt measures, which will insure the establishment of a thorough system of inducing immigration to the State."

Certain plans of carrying out this act were recommended, which we will give in detail:

Correspondence in newspapers.—One plan was to "engage suitable correspondents, publish or cause to be published, articles treating on and describing in a true light the developed and undeveloped resources of the State of Minnesota," etc. As far as desirable and effective this plan was adopted in our operations both in America and in Europe. Our agent in Germany, whose time expired in March last, caused to be inserted in a number of German papers ably written articles on our State. Our Commissioner of Immigration in New York has among his many successful enterprises for promoting immigration, also caused to be inserted advertisements calling the attention of the public to Minnesota and to the State Pamphlet and other publications on the subject, in some 600 newspapers in the New England and Middle States. Hans Mattson, formerly Secretary of State, and the clerk of the State Board have for the same purpose issued a series of letters in the different Scandinavian newspapers in America, and as many hundred copies of these papers every week go to regular subscribers in Europe, said articles have also reached their destination abroad. The board found the promulgation of said semi-official articles the more useful, as the surrounding States through the Scandinavian press made strong efforts to turn the flood of Scandinavian immigration from Minnesota.

Emigration direct from England and Scotland has not been overlooked. Not only have there been many calls from there for information answered by letters and pamphlets, but the regular immigration pamphlet, by direction of the Board, has been republished in monthly installments in the columns of the *Free West,* an emigration paper of ability and extensive circulation published in London. By this means it has reached many thousands of additional readers. The immigration has been greater from the British Isles and less from Germany during the last two years (for obvious reasons) than during any one of several years.

Distribution of pamphlets.—The main work required may be divided into two branches: (1) Furnishing the necessary information as to the inducements and advantages offered by the State to all classes of desirable immigrants. (2) Aiding, protecting, and advising the immigrant on his way to our State.

The first part has been and is pursued to great effect by sending the State pamphlet to the very heart of the most remote emigrant districts in Northern Europe, in the English, German, Norwegian, and Swedish languages, and by addressing them, not by boxes sent to agents, but in every case to individuals, who contemplate leaving their fatherland. The most of them make up their minds as to their final destination before they leave. Letters and counsels from their friends and relations in America, will govern their movements, and as the State pamphlet is nothing but a condensed series of answered questions upon immigration, the people, as indicated by their thousands of applications, deem this or similar pamphlets the best medium for enlightening their transatlantic friends.

To this end an extra edition of 15,000 copies of the pamphlet prepared in 1870 by the commissioners of statistics was re-printed in English in the winter of 1871.

An edition of 5,000 copies translated into German, with some abbreviations and alterations, has been printed. Also 5,700 copies in Norwegian, and 3,500 copies in Swedish; the two latter distributed in the countries of Norway, Sweden, Denmark, and among the Scandinavians in the United States. An edition of 5,000 copies in English, especially for the Irish immigration, was also printed.

The editions printed in foreign languages contained, besides most of the information of the English pamphlet, many facts of value, especially to immigrants from Europe, which were not deemed necessary to those sent to citizens of the United States.

The throng of applications, for pamphlets, and of questions touching our State to be answered by letters, may be understood from the fact, that the immigration bureau received during the season from 50 to 100 letters per day, each of them containing more applications. Early in the season the Norwegian pamphlets—originally 5,000—were exhausted; so several thousand English pamphlets had to be sent Scandinavians in America, until a new issue could be procured for filling waiting applications to Norway and Denmark.

Thus altogether over 34,000 pamphlets have been printed, and mostly distributed in various tongues, and even this amount proved to be insufficient for the Scandinavian demand.

Mode of distribution.—The plan adopted in the distribution of the pamphlets was, as above stated, calculated to place them in the hands of the very persons seeking information in regard to Minnesota. In brief advertisements the Board stated that anyone wishing the pamphlet could have the same sent him free of postage by forwarding his address to the Secretary of State. This plan has worked still more admirably than in 1870, as the requisitions, partly direct from Europe and partly through friends in the United States, have amounted this season to several thousands. The high rates of postage on copies sent to foreign countries have greatly increased that item of our expenditures, but this may possibly be saved to a great extent in the future, if it should be found advisable to let the applicants themselves pay the postage to foreign countries.

Maps.—In all 23,800 copies of the pamphlet have been furnished with maps (English maps, 14,000; German, 4,000; Norwegian, 3,500; Swedish, 2,300). As most of the applications ask for pamphlets with maps, and as other States have adopted the plan of circulating their immigration documents with maps, the Board deemed it necessary to continue to provide the same. The maps last season were furnished at a considerable lower price than the preceding year.

Agents and their work.—The Board was also empowered to appoint agents for the purpose of aiding, protecting, and advising the immigrant on his way to our State, etc.

Local agents can do a great deal of good work in keeping runners from taking hold of new comers, in seeing the immigrants without unnecessary delay forwarded to their destination, and not the least in aiding the unfortunate and preventing imposition. On account of a deficiency from the foregoing year, which had to be covered by last year's appropriation, the Board did not feel at liberty to sustain more than one agency. The Board deemed it proper to establish as a rule, that its operations had to be limited and regulated in accordance with the fund appropriated. Consequently, it had to abstain from creating local agencies in Milwaukee, Chicago, and Quebec. The demand for these agencies had diminished from the fact, that the railroads during last season had procured experienced agents and guides, who performed their duties to the satisfaction of all parties, without expense to our State, and partly because the greater number of immigrants had taken notice of our timely warning in 1870: not to use the uncertain water routes, when railroad transportation was obtainable at reasonable prices.

The Milwaukee and St. Paul road deserves our thanks for having treated the immigrants liberally; the St. Paul and Pacific, and the Superior and Mississippi roads have erected more immigrant houses along their lines, thereby enabling immigrants to find shelter until they find their friends, or decide where to settle. The St. Paul and Pacific's agent, Mr. Christiansen, last season, as before, bestowed upon immigrants arriving at St. Paul all the kindness and care they are in need of in their often helpless condition after a journey of thousands of miles.

Statistics of immigration.—The whole number of immigrants for 1870 to our State is estimated at 30,000, namely: 22,000 direct from Europe, and the rest from the United States and Canada. Out of said 22,000, nearly 10,000 came from the Scandinavian countries.

As the Board during last summer had no agencies or reporters in the principal landing-places, it is of course impossible to give any accurate account concerning the actual number of foreign immigrants but from close observation of figures given in newspapers during the entire season, and judging from other sources of information, the immigration has certainly been as large this year as last. Attracted to lands available under the homestead laws, the majority of immigrants located on the surveyed and unsurveyed lands, especially in the Red River region and in the frontier counties farther South. The hardwood timber land belonging to the Lake Superior, and Mississippi R.R. Co. has also, to some extent, been settled. Northern Europe parts yearly with from 0.39 to 0.86 per cent of their population, nearly all of which emigrate to America. Of immigration last season from Northern Europe, Wisconsin received 3,000 Scandinavians; Minnesota 10,000. . . .

The increasing correspondence and other pressing work connected with the duties of the Board—almost enough to make it a department of its own—necessitated the employ of a clerk acting under the direction of the Board.

His business has mainly been: (1) Receiving and filing some 9,000 letters and mailing pamphlets to at least 20,000 different applicants. Of this number about 3,500 are sent to Norway, 1,500 to London, and 300 to Denmark. About 4,000 copies were forwarded to Germany. (2) Answering letters in different languages upon immigration. (3) Assisting immigrants in cases of lost baggage and money. (4) Writing articles and answering attacks made on our State. (5) Translating the State pamphlet into the Norwegian language. . . .

Of the value of an extensive immigration to the State, the Board has not had any good reason to change their views as expressed in their last annual report. Not only does our immigration add hundreds of thousands of dollars in property of all descriptions to the common wealth of the community, but it furnishes, from year to year, by far the greater numbers of those who supply the demand for hired laborers, as well as to replenish and multiply the artisans, mechanics, and skilled laborers, upon whom we depend to build up and extend our manufacturing, mining, and mechanical interests. Yet exceeding by far any of these interests is that resulting from bringing the cheap European labor in contact with our wild land. The national wealth has been by no other means so rapidly developed and accumulated as by bringing the cheap, and *there,* nearly valueless labor of the old world into direct contact with our equally cheap lands, which, *without that labor,* are of as little value to us, as is the surplus labor of the old world to it, without our lands.

From Northern Europe a man, only capable of earning a bare subsistence there, can be transported to, and set down upon, a homestead in Minnesota for from $50 to $75. He locates on land, which, in its raw condition is not worth over $1.25 per acre, and at the end of five years he has subsisted his family and by his labor has advanced his quarter-section of land to an average value of $1,000, an advance of 300 per cent on the capital with which the settler commenced. Persons residing in the older portions of the State and not on any of the thoroughfares leading to those sections, into which immigrants are flocking by the thousands, often fall into the error, that the State is receiving no immigration—that nothing is realized in exchange for the appropriation made for the promotion of immigration—in short, that the fund is *squandered.* Such objectors can easily be undeceived by taking a journey along our western frontier or sojourning for a time, from the first of May till the close of the season, on some one of the numerous routes of travel leading to those counties, into which the annual tide is flowing.

Source: Report of the Board of Immigration to the Legislature of Minnesota (St. Paul, MN: D. Ramaley, 1871).

Economic Value of an Immigrant, Special Report of the U.S. Congress (1871)

In this investigative report issued by the U.S. Congress in 1871, researchers examined the degree to which immigrants added to or detracted from the American economy. The question—still a controversial one today—was answered in the affirmative, at least in this case. According to the report, "the sum of $800 seems to be the full average capital value of each {wage-earning} immigrant" over the course of his or her lifetime. The calculation was based on how much they earned and how much they consumed, minus the value of goods consumed by non-wage-earning members of immigrants' families.

In making an intelligent estimate of the addition to the material wealth of the country by immigration, several distinct conditions should be regarded. The character of the immigrants as industrious and law-abiding citizens, their nationalities, education, and previous condition, as well as their occupation and ages, are elements to be considered when determining their value.

As regards nationality, more than one-half of those who have thus far arrived in the United States are British, and come from the United Kingdom, or from the British possessions of North America. These speak our language, and a large part are acquainted with our laws and institutions, and are soon assimilated with, and absorbed into, our body-politic.

The German element comes next, and embraces nearly two-thirds of the remainder, being at once an industrious and an intelligent people, a large proportion settling in rural districts and developing the agricultural resources of the West and South, while the remainder, consisting largely of artisans and skilled workmen, find profitable employment in the cities and manufacturing towns.

The influx of Scandinavians, who have already made extensive settlements in the Northwestern States, constitutes a distinctive feature of the movement, and though but a few years since it received its first impetus, is already large and rapidly increasing. Industrious, economical, and temperate, their advent should be especially welcomed. . . .

The Latin nations contribute very little to our population, and the Slavic still less, while today, as from time immemorial, the different branches of the great Teutonic trunk are swarming forth from the most populous regions, to aid in the progress of civilization.

While a brief review of the ethnic derivation of the millions who have transferred their allegiance from the Old World to the New, exhibits a favorable result, other elements of their value to this country require consideration. The wide contrasts between skilled and unskilled labor, between industry and laziness, between economical habits and unthrift, indicates a marked variation in the capital value of the immigrant to the country. The unskilled laborers, who at once engage in subduing the forests, or cultivating the prairies, are of far more value to the country than those who remain in the large cities.

Deducting the women and children, who pursue no occupation, about 46 per cent of the whole immigration have been trained to various pursuits. Nearly half of these are skilled laborers and workmen who have acquired their trades under the rigorous system which prevails in the Old World, and come here to give us the benefit of their training and skill without repayment of the cost of such education. Nor are the farm laborers and servants destitute of the necessary training to fit them for their several duties, while those classed as common or unskilled laborers are well qualified to perform the labor required, especially in the construction of works of internal improvement. Nearly 10 per cent consist of merchants and traders, who doubtless bring with them considerable capital as well as mercantile experience, while the smaller number of professional men and artists, embracing architects, engineers, inventors, men of thorough training and a high order of talent, contribute to our widely extended community not only material, but artistic, aesthetic, intellectual, and moral wealth. . . .

Recurring to the money value of an immigrant, it may be stated that the sum of $1,000 has usually been regarded as the average worth of each permanent addition to our population, an amount somewhat too large, but yet an approximation to the true value. Mr. Kapp, one of the commissioners of emigration of the State of New York, who has given much consideration to the subject now under review, assumes the average value to be $1,125. . . .

But the question, what is the average money value of an immigrant, is yet unanswered. To resolve it, other elements than those already mentioned must receive consideration. The immigrant must be regarded both as a producer and as a consumer. In treating the whole number of immigrants as producers, the non-producers must first be excluded. These consist of the very aged and the very young, and of those who are unable to labor, whether from sickness, physical inability, or mental condition, whether in or out of charitable or reformatory institutions, and of the criminal or vicious class, whether in or out of prison. In this category may also be included those whose occupations or pursuits tend to demoralize or injure society. The social statistics of the foreign-born population being imperfect, it will perhaps be possible to estimate the productiveness of the whole by taking the earnings of unskilled laborers; offsetting the increased productiveness and earnings of the skilled workmen against the unproductiveness of the classes above mentioned.

The wages of laborers and unskilled workmen throughout the country average very nearly $400 per year. Assuming that the families of these men consist of four persons, we have $100 as the amount which each individual produces, and to which also he is restricted in consumption. The estimated yearly expenditures of the family of a laborer, consisting of two adults and two small children (if any are larger it is probable that they earn something in addition), is as follows: For tea, coffee, sugar, and other foreign goods, which pay a duty of about 60 per cent to the Government, $60; flour, meat, and butter, about $150; rent, $50; fuel and light, $30; vegetables, $30; milk, eggs, &c., $20; leaving $60 for clothing, housekeeping goods, &c. As most of these expenditures are for articles of domestic product which pay a succession of profits not only to the retailer, wholesale dealer, and producer, but to the transporter, the sum of these net profits constitutes the aggregate amount which this family contributes to the wealth of the country. A careful computation gives $160, which sum is the measure alike of their production and consumption. As producers and consumers, then, each is worth to the country $40 per annum, which capitalized at five per cent, gives $800 as the average value of an immigrant.

As a large number, especially those from Northern Europe, engage at once in the cultivation of the soil on their own account, it is desirable to ascertain the increment to the wealth of the country consequent upon their industry. This appears in the form of productive fields reclaimed from the wilderness, buildings and fences erected, agricultural implements and stock accumulated, &c. In the absence of correct data, the sum of $160 by a family of four persons, or $40 each, is considered an approximate estimate of the yearly addition to the realized wealth of the country by such improvements. The figures of the census recently taken will doubtless show that an immense aggregate increase in the national wealth is due to this source alone. Being the result of voluntary industry and self-imposed economy, it is an increase which remains in the hands of the immigrants themselves, who thus contribute to the state that highest form of wealth, a sturdy, moral, intelligent, and independent yeomanry, the very balance-wheel of national machinery. Data will soon exist by which the average production will be tested. It is believed that the statistics of the census of 1870, when compiled, will exhibit the average value of real and personal estate in the Union at about $800 per capita, and the annual increase about 5 per cent, or $40. Now, while the property owned by the foreign-born population does not average $800, yet in productiveness, it is believed, they contribute their full share.

It should not be forgotten, however, that these immigrants bring with them some money, estimated at $100 by Mr. Kapp, and at $80 by Mr. Wells, but inasmuch as a careful investigation was made at Castle Garden, New York, which resulted in establishing $68 as the average sum brought by alien passengers, that amount is assumed as the correct one. As the greater part, if not the whole of this sum, is required to take the immigrant to his destination, and to support him until he becomes a producer, the amount of money which he brings with him is omitted in the foregoing estimate of his capital value. If his annual value to the country be capitalized at 6 per cent instead of 5, and the largest estimate of money brought with him ($100) included, it would aggregate less than $800, the amount already estimated as his capital value.

From the foregoing considerations, therefore, the sum of $800 seems to be the full average capital value of each immigrant. At this rate those who landed upon our shores during the year just closed, added upwards of $85,000,000 to our national wealth, while during the last half-century the increment from this source exceeds $6,243,880,800. It is impossible to make an intelligent estimate of the value to the country of those foreign-born citizens who brought their educated minds, their cultivated tastes, their skill in the arts, and their inventive genius. In almost every walk of life their influence has been felt. Alike in the fearful ordeal of war and in the pursuits of peace, in our legislative halls, and in the various learned professions, the adopted sons of America have attained eminence. Among the many who rendered timely aid to our country during the late war, it may seem invidious to mention a single name, except for the purpose of illustration. In the year 1839 there arrived at the port of New York, in the steamship "British Queen," which sailed from the port of London, a Swedish immigrant, better known as Captain John Ericsson. What was his value to the country, as estimated on the 9th day of March, 1862? Was it eight hundred, eight hundred thousand, or eight millions of dollars?

Source: House Committee, *Special Report on Immigration; Accompanying Information for Immigrants.* March 15, 1871. 42nd Cong., 1st sess., Doc. 1.

Page Act (1875)

During the gold rush of the late 1840s and 1850s and the construction of the transcontinental railroad in the 1860s, tens of thousands of Chinese arrived on the West Coast of the United States. White residents, many immigrants themselves, greeted the Chinese with hostility, and the state of California enacted a number of statutes that expressly limited the rights and privileges of Asian newcomers. In 1875, Congress passed the first national law aimed at limiting Chinese immigration. Named after its sponsor, Representative Horace F. Page (R-CA), the Page Act had two aims: to prevent Chinese immigrants from coming to America under contract or obligation without their free and voluntary consent (that is, to end "coolie labor") and to bar the entry of Asian prostitutes. The law ultimately made it difficult for any Asian—and especially Chinese women—to enter the country, thereby hindering Chinese immigrants from establishing families in the United States.

Be it enacted . . . , That in determining whether the immigration of any subject of China, Japan, or any Oriental country, to the United States, is free and voluntary . . .

it shall be the duty of the consul-general or consul of the United States residing at the port from which it is proposed to convey such subjects, in any vessel enrolled or licensed in the United States, or any port within the same, before delivering to the masters of any such vessels the permit or certificate provided for in such section, to ascertain whether such immigrant has entered into a contract or agreement for a term of service within the United States, for lewd and immoral purposes; and if there be such contract or agreement, the said consul-general or consul shall not deliver the required permit or certificate.

Sec. 2. That if any citizen of the United States, or other person amenable to the laws of the United States, shall take, or cause to be taken or transported, to or from the United States any subject of China, Japan, or any Oriental country, without their free and voluntary consent, for the purpose of holding them to a term of service, such citizen or other person shall be liable to be indicted therefor, and, on conviction of such offense, shall be punished by a fine not to exceed two thousand dollars and be imprisoned not exceeding one year; and all contracts and agreements for a term of service of such persons in the United States, whether made in advance or in pursuance of such illegal importation, and whether such importation shall have been in American or other vessels, are hereby declared void.

Sec. 3. That the importation into the United States of women for the purposes of prostitution is hereby forbidden; and all contracts and agreements in relation thereto, made in advance or in pursuance of such illegal importation and purposes are hereby declared void; and whoever shall knowingly and willfully import, or cause any importation of, women to the United States for purposes of prostitution, or shall knowingly and willfully hold, or attempt to hold, any woman to such purposes, in pursuance of such illegal importation and contract or agreement, shall be deemed guilty of a felony, and on conviction thereof, shall be imprisoned not exceeding five years and pay a fine not exceeding five thousand dollars. . . .

Source: Act of March 3, 1975, ch. 141, 18 Stat. 477.

Angell Treaty (1881)

The Burlingame Treaty between the United States and China in 1868 opened the way to increased trade between the two countries and gave Chinese nationals the right to immigrate to America. Eleven years later, Congress passed legislation that restricted Chinese immigration, but President Rutherford B. Hayes vetoed the measure because of its conflict with the Burlingame Treaty. In the aftermath, Hayes appointed a commission headed by University of Michigan President James B. Angell to go to China and negotiate a new treaty that would give the United States authority to restrict Chinese immigration. The Angell Treaty, as it came to be called, was negotiated in 1880 and ratified in 1881.

Whenever in the opinion of the Government of the United States, the coming of Chinese laborers to the United States, or their residence therein, affects or threatens to affect the interests of that country, or to endanger the good order of the said country or any locality within the territory thereof, the Government of China agrees that the Government of the United States may regulate, limit, or suspend such coming or residence, but may not absolutely prohibit it. The limitation or suspension shall be reasonable, and apply only to Chinese who may go to the United States as laborers, other classes not being included in the limitations. Legislation taken in regard to Chinese laborers will be of such a character only as is necessary to enforce the regulation, limitation, or suspension of immigration, and immigrants shall not be subject to personal maltreatment or abuse.

Article II

Chinese subjects, whether proceeding to the United States as teachers, students, merchants, or from curiosity, together with their body and household servants, and Chinese laborers who are now in the United States shall be allowed to go and come of their own free will and accord, and shall be accorded all the rights, privileges, immunities, and exemptions which are accorded to citizens and subjects of the most favored nation.

Article III

If Chinese laborers, or Chinese of any other class, now either permanently or temporarily residing in the territory of the United States, meet with ill treatment at the hands of any other persons, the Government of the United States will exert all its powers to devise measures for their protection and to secure to them the same rights, privileges, immunities, and exemptions as may be enjoyed by the citizens or subjects of the most favored nation, and to which they are entitled by treaty.

Source: Act of May 5, 1881, ch. 126, 22 Stat. 826.

Report on German Emigration, Interview with a Government Official of Würtemburg (1881)

The document that follows summarizes an 1881 interview with a "prominent official" of the government of Würtemburg, a component jurisdiction of the German Empire. As the official makes clear, major causes of European emigration in the late nineteenth century included the plight of farmers and workers. The interviewer, probably connected with the local U.S. consulate, expresses concern that "criminals" and "paupers" were being urged to emigrate. The official assures him that this is not the case. Instead, he maintains, overpopulation and a dearth of jobs were driving hard-working people to America.

Consular Report on Immigrants from Germany

Views of a prominent official.—I have recently been favored with an opportunity for a quite extended and, at the same time, informal conversation on this subject with a prominent official of the Würtemberg government. Allusion having been made to the recent remarkable increase in the number of those departing hence for America, the official replied that the question had indeed of late been occupying public attention, on account not so much of the actual loss in numbers occasioned thereby as the excellent quality of the material that is at present leaving this kingdom for the United States. . . .

Question.—Of what class of people is the present emigration principally composed?

Reply.—Chiefly of tillers of the soil, hardy and robust men whose loss from the rural districts will be much more felt than would be the drawing off of a corresponding number of the population from the cities, which are comparatively overcrowded, and where the unemployed and criminal classes are generally found. As for the actual loss in population it is really no great subject for regret, for our rate of increase is very rapid. The kingdom is quite thickly peopled, its productive capacities are taxed to the utmost for the support of its inhabitants, and a moderate emigration may therefore be considered rather a relief than otherwise. But those who are emigrating are the tillers in the fields and vineyards, men who are necessarily the largest contributors to our agricultural welfare, and who have generally some mechanical skill as well. They compose the element we can least afford to lose.

Question.—Is there any reason for supposing that paupers and criminals are sent from here to the United States as emigrants?

Reply.—None whatever; that is, in the case of persons known to be such. It is of course impossible for the emigrant agents to make thorough inquiry into the antecedents of every one of the many hundreds presenting themselves to be registered as intending to emigrate. But there is no organized movement either on the part of local, county, or town authorities, or of any philanthropic association, to send such persons to the United States. A general belief and understanding exists here that even if sent thither they would not be permitted to land.

Question.—Are there any means by which the authorities here can, if they so desire, arrest this tide of emigration?

Reply.—Practically none. Even the restrictions existing at the German ports of embarkation, Hamburg and Bremen, are rendered fruitless by the fact that any German, wishing to emigrate to America, can easily avoid them by passing over into Belgium or Holland, and taking steamer at Antwerp or Rotterdam. On the French frontier the passport regulations are enforced with a somewhat greater show of vigor, so that but few emigrants from Germany leave by way of Havre, or other ports of France. Most of those leaving covertly go by way of one or the other of the two non-German ports previously mentioned.

Question.—To what, in your opinion, may this sudden increase, or rather revival, of emigration to the United States be attributed?

Reply.—Every season disastrous to agricultural interests gives an impetus to emigration. The grape and grain crops have been poor for three or four years now, causing much distress and want among the lower classes and in the rural populations. These latter, hearing from their friends in America of the, to them, fabulous rates of wages (two or three dollars a day) paid there, and of the good crops and general prosperity, naturally turn thither with longing eyes, and come to look with discontent upon their lot here, where they see no chance of bettering themselves. Do what they will, few if any of them lay aside any money here. The great evil in our rural districts is the tavern, where workingmen pass their evenings drinking beer instead of remaining at home with their wives and families. When their working hours are over they repair to the tavern; when Sunday comes they pass the entire day there. The result is they save nothing, and are no better off at the end of the year than they were at the beginning.

Question.—Is there no remedy for this prevalence of beer shops?

Reply.—Not so long as licenses to keep them are so easily obtained. Were only one or two allowed in each village, the evil would be to a great extent done away with, whereas now almost every other house is a beer saloon, and a laboring man finds it almost impossible, in passing along the street, to resist the temptation of dropping in at one or another of them before he reaches his home.

Question.—Are the peasantry here kept well informed of the condition of affairs in America by those who have previously emigrated thither?
Reply.—Perfectly. Every letter brings glowing accounts of high wages, good crops, and general welfare, and virtually says, "Come over and join us." It is easy to understand how ready a poor man with no prospects before him here is to listen to such an invitation.

Source: "Emigration from the Kingdom of Würtemburg, Report by Consul Catlin, of Stuttgart, on Its Cause, Character, and Extent, and the Laws by Which It is Governed," in *United States Consular Reports,* vol. 2, no. 6 (April 1881).

Chinese Exclusion Act (1882)

After ratification of the Angell Treaty with China in 1881, the U.S. Congress began drafting legislation to restrict Chinese immigration. The first version of the Chinese Exclusion Act, passed in March 1882, would have excluded all Chinese laborers from entering the United States for twenty years. President Chester Arthur vetoed the bill, claiming that the twenty-year provision was excessive and a violation of the Angell Treaty. Congress reduced the length of exclusion to ten years and passed the measure overwhelmingly: 201–37 in the House of Representatives and 32–15 in the Senate. On May 6, 1882, President Arthur signed the bill into law. The Chinese Exclusion Act, which barred virtually all Chinese from U.S. shores, was the first federal law ever passed that banned a group of immigrants solely on the basis of race or nationality. The law also denied the more than 100,000 Chinese immigrants already in the United States the right to become citizens. Renewed in 1892 and 1902, and made permanent in 1904, the Chinese Exclusion Act remained in effect for a total of sixty-one years. It was repealed in 1943 when China became an ally of the United States in World War II.

Whereas, in the opinion of the Government of the United States the coming of Chinese laborers to this country endangers the good order of certain localities within the territory thereof: Therefore, *Be it enacted by the Senate and the House of Representatives of the United States of America in Congress assembled,* That from and after the expiration of ninety days next after the passage of this act, and until the expiration of ten years next after the passage of this act, the coming of Chinese laborers to the United States

be, and the same is hereby, suspended; and during such suspension it shall not be lawful for any Chinese laborer to come, or having so come after the expiration of said ninety days, to remain within the United States.

Sec. 2. That the master of any vessel who shall knowingly bring within the United States on such vessel, and land or permit to be landed, any Chinese laborer, from any foreign port or place, shall be deemed guilty of a misdemeanor, and on conviction thereof shall be punished by a fine of not more than five hundred dollars for each and every such Chinese laborer so brought, and may also be imprisoned for a term not exceeding one year. . . .

Sec. 4. That for the purpose of properly identifying Chinese laborers who were in the United States . . . or shall come into the same before the expiration of ninety days next after the passage of this act, and in order to furnish them with the proper evidence of their right to go from and to come to the United States of their own free will and accord, as provided by the treaty of the United States and China . . . the collector of customs of the district from which any such Chinese laborer shall depart from the United States shall, in person or by deputy, go on board each vessel having on board any such Chinese laborer and cleared or about to sail from his district for a foreign port, and on such vessel make a list of all such Chinese laborers, which shall be entered in registry-books to be kept for that purpose, in which shall be stated the name, age, occupation, last place of residence, physical marks or peculiarities, and all facts necessary for the identification of each of such Chinese laborers, which books shall be kept in the custom-house; and every such Chinese laborer so departing from the United States shall be entitled to, and shall receive free of any charge or cost upon application thereof, from the collector or his deputy, at the time such a list is taken, a certificate, signed by the collector or his deputy and attested by his seal of office, in such form as the Secretary of the Treasury shall prescribe, which certificate shall contain a statement of the name, age, occupation, last place of residence, personal description, and facts of identification of the Chinese laborer to whom the certificate is issued, corresponding with the said list and registry in all particulars. . . . The certificate herein provided for shall entitle the Chinese laborer to whom the same is issued to return to and re-enter the United States upon producing and delivering the same to the collector of customs of the district at which the Chinese laborer shall re-enter; and upon delivery of such certificate by such Chinese laborer to the collector of customs at the time of re-entry in the United States, said collector shall cause the same to be filed in the custom-house and duly canceled. . . .

Sec. 6. That in order to the faithful execution of articles one and two of the treaty in this act before mentioned, every Chinese person other than a laborer who may be entitled by said treaty to come within the United States, and who shall be about to come to the United States, shall be identified as so entitled by the Chinese government in each case, such identity to be evidenced by a certificate issued under the authority of said government, which certificate shall be in the English language . . . stating such right to come, and which certificate shall state the name, title, or official rank, if any, the age, height, and all physical peculiarities, former and present occupation or profession, and place of residence in China of the person to whom the certificate is issued. . . . Such certificate shall be prima-facie evidence of the fact set forth therein. . . .

Sec. 7. That any person who shall knowingly and falsely alter or substitute any name for the name written in such certificate or forge any such certificate, or knowingly utter any forged or fraudulent certificate, or falsely personate any person named in any such certificate, shall be deemed guilty of a misdemeanor; and upon conviction thereof shall be fined in sum not exceeding one thousand dollars, and imprisoned in a penitentiary for a term of not more than five years.

Sec. 8. That the master of any vessel arriving in the United States from any foreign port or place shall, at the same time he delivers a manifest of the cargo, . . . deliver and report to the collector of customs of the district in which such vessel shall have arrived a separate list of all Chinese passengers on board the vessel at that time. Such list shall show the names of such passengers . . . and such list shall be sworn to by the master in the manner required by law in relation to the manifest of the cargo. Any willful refusal or neglect of any such master to comply with the provisions of this section shall incur the same penalties and forfeiture as are provided for a refusal or neglect to report and deliver a manifest of cargo.

Sec. 9. That before any Chinese passengers are landed from any such vessel, the collector, or his deputy, shall proceed to examine such passengers, comparing the certificates with the list and with the passengers; and no passenger shall be allowed to land in the United States from such vessel in violation of law.

Sec. 10. That every vessel whose master shall knowingly violate any of the provisions of this act shall be deemed forfeited to the United States, and shall be liable to seizure and condemnation in any district of the United States into which such vessel may enter or in which she may be found.

Sec. 11. That any person who shall knowingly bring into or cause to be brought into the United States by land, or who shall knowingly aid and abet the same, or aid and abet the landing in the United States from any vessel of any Chinese person not lawfully entitled to enter the United States, shall be deemed guilty of a misdemeanor, and shall, on conviction thereof, be fined in a sum not exceeding one thousand dollars, and imprisoned for a term not exceeding one year.

Sec. 12. That no Chinese person shall be permitted to enter the United States by land without producing the certificate in this act required of Chinese persons seeking to land from a vessel. And any Chinese person found unlawfully within the United States shall be caused to be removed therefrom to the country from whence he came . . . after being brought before some justice, judge, or commissioner of a court of the United States and found to be one not lawfully entitled to be or remain in the United States.

Sec. 13. That this act shall not apply to diplomatic and other officers of the Chinese Government traveling upon the business of that government . . . and shall exempt them and their body and household servants from the provisions of this act as to other Chinese persons.

Sec. 14. That hereafter no State court or court of the United States shall admit Chinese to citizenship; and all laws in conflict with this act are hereby repealed.

Sec. 15. That the words "Chinese laborers," wherever used in this act, shall be construed to mean both skilled and unskilled laborers and Chinese employed in mining.

Source: Act of May 6, 1882, ch. 126, 22 Stat. 58.

Alien Contract Labor Law (Foran Act) (1885)

Contract labor involves the importation of foreign workers—usually in groups—by a business or contracting firm. The contractor pays the workers' passage, and the workers are required to pay back the costs with their labor. In the decades after the Civil War, American workers and unions fought to outlaw contract labor, which threatened both their bargaining power and their wages, as employers could always argue in labor negotiations that they might hire contract laborers to replace dissatisfied employees. In 1885, Congress passed the Alien Contract Labor Law, also known as the Foran Act (after its sponsor, Representative Martin A. Foran, D-OH), which prohibited the practice of contract labor.

Be it enacted by the Senate and House of Representative of the United States of America in Congress assembled, That from and after the passage of this act it shall be unlawful for any person, company, partnership, or corporation, in any manner whatsoever, to prepay the transportation, or in any way assist or encourage the importation or migration of any alien or aliens, any foreigner or foreigners, into the United States, its Territories, or the District of Columbia, under contract or agreement, parol [*sic*] from or special, express or implied, made previous to the importation or migration of such alien or aliens, foreigner or foreigners, to perform labor or service of any kind in the United States, its Territories, or the District of Columbia.

Sec. 2. That all contracts or agreements, express or implied, parol, or special, which may hereafter be made by and between any person, company, partnership, or corporation, and any foreigner or foreigners, alien or aliens, to perform labor or service or having reference to the performance of labor or service by any person in the United States, its Territories, or the District of Columbia previous to the migration or importation of the person or persons whose labor or service is contracted for into the United States, shall be utterly void and of no effect.

Sec. 3. That for every violation of any of the provisions of section one of this act the person, partnership, company, or corporation violating the same, by knowingly assisting, encouraging or soliciting the migration or importation of any alien or aliens, foreigner or foreigners, into the United States . . . shall forfeit and pay for every such offense the sum of one thousand dollars. . . .

Sec. 4. That the master of any vessel who knowingly brings within the United States on any such vessel and land, or permit to be landed, from any foreign port or place, any alien laborer, mechanic, or artisan, who, previous to embarkation on such vessel, had entered into contract or agreement, parol or special, express or implied, to perform labor or service in the United States, shall be deemed guilty of a misdemeanor, and on the conviction thereof, shall be punished by a fine of not more than five hundred dollars for each and every such alien laborer, mechanic, or artisan so brought as aforesaid, and may also be imprisoned for a term not exceeding six months.

Sec. 5. That nothing in this act shall be so construed as to prevent any citizen or subject of any foreign country temporarily residing in the United States, either in private or official capacity, from engaging, under contract or otherwise, persons not residents or citizens of the United States to act as private secretaries, servants, or domestics for such foreigner temporarily residing in the United States as aforesaid; nor shall this act be construed so as to prevent any person, or persons, partnership, or corporation from engaging, under contract or agreement, skilled workmen in foreign countries to perform labor in the United States in or upon any new industry not at present established in the United States; Provided, That the skilled labor for that purpose cannot be otherwise obtained; nor shall the provisions of this act apply to professional actors, artists, lecturers, or singers, nor to persons employed strictly as the personal or domestic servants, nor to ministers of any recognized religious denomination, nor persons belonging to any recognized profession, nor professors for colleges and seminaries; Provided, That nothing in this act shall be construed as prohibiting any individual from assisting any member of his family to migrate from any foreign country to the United States for the purpose of settlement here. . . .

Source: Act of February 26, 1885, ch. 164, 23 Stat. 332.

Scott Act (1888)

The Scott Act, passed by Congress on September 13, 1888, added new restrictions to the Chinese Exclusion Act of 1882. Previously, Chinese workers already in the United States could come and go to China as they pleased. Under the Scott Act, named after its sponsor, Representative William Scott (D-PA), Chinese immigrants were required to get certificates to do so in advance; the certificates were not easy to come by.

Be it enacted by the Senate and the House of Representatives of the United States of America in Congress assembled, That from and after the date of the exchange of ratifications of the pending treaty between the United States of America and His Imperial Majesty the Emperor of China, signed on the twelfth day of March, anno Domini eighteen hundred and eighty-eight, it shall be unlawful for any Chinese person, whether a subject of China or any other power, to enter the United States except as hereinafter provided.

Sec. 2. That Chinese officials, teachers, students, merchants, or travelers for pleasure or curiosity, shall be permitted to enter the United States, but in order to entitle themselves to do so, they shall first obtain the permission of the Chinese Government, or other Government of which they may at the time be citizens or subjects. Such permission and also their personal identity shall in such case be evidenced by a certificate to be made out by the diplomatic representative of the United States in that country, or of the consular representative of the United States at the port or place from which the person therein named comes. The certificate shall contain a full description of such person, of his age, height, and general physical features, and shall state his former and present occupation or profession and place of residence, and shall be made out in duplicate. One copy shall be delivered open to the person named and described, and the other copy shall be sealed up and delivered by the diplomatic or consular officer as aforesaid to the captain of the vessel on which the person named in the certificate sets sail for the United States, together with the sealed certificate, which shall be addressed to the collector of customs at the port where such person is to land. . . . And any captain who lands or attempts to land a Chinese person in the United States, without having in his possession a sealed certificate, as required in this section, shall be liable to the penalties prescribed in section nine of this act.

Sec. 3. That the provisions of this act shall apply to all persons of the Chinese race, whether subjects of China or other foreign power, excepting Chinese diplomatic or consular officers and their attendants; and the words "Chinese laborers," whenever used in this act, shall be construed to mean both skilled and unskilled laborers and Chinese employed in mining.

Sec. 4. That the master of any vessel arriving in the United States from any foreign port or place with any Chinese passengers on board shall, when he delivers his manifest of cargo, and if there be no cargo, when he makes legal entry of this vessel, and before landing or permitting to land any Chinese person (unless a diplomatic or consular officer, or attendant of such officer) deliver to the collector of customs of the district in which the vessel shall have arrived the sealed certificates and letters as aforesaid, and a separate list of all Chinese persons taken on board of his vessel at any foreign port or place, and of all such persons on board at the time of the arrival as aforesaid. Such list shall show the names of such persons and other particulars as shown by their open certificates, or other evidences required by this act, and such list shall be sworn to by the master in the manner required by law in relation to the manifest of the cargo.

The master of any vessel as aforesaid shall not permit any Chinese diplomatic or consular officer or attendant of such officer to land without having first been informed by the collector of customs of the official character of such officer or attendant. Any refusal or willful neglect of the master of any vessel to comply with the provisions of this section shall incur the same penalties and forfeitures as are provided for a refusal or neglect to report and deliver a manifest of the cargo.

Sec. 5. That from and hereafter the passage of this act, no Chinese laborer in the United States shall be permit-ted, after having left, to return thereto, except under the conditions stated in the following sections.

Sec. 6. That no Chinese laborer within the purview of the preceding section shall be permitted to return to the United States unless he has a lawful wife, child, or parent in the United States, or property therein of the value of one thousand dollars, or debts of like amount due him and pending settlement. The marriage to such wife must have taken place at least one year prior to the application of the laborer for a permit to return to the United States, and must have been followed by the continuous cohabitation of the parties as man and wife.

If the right to return be claimed on the ground of property or of debts, it must appear that the property is bona fide and not colorably acquired for the purpose of evading this act, or that the debts are unascertained and unsettled, and not promissory notes or other similar acknowledgments of ascertained liability.

Sec. 7. That a Chinese person claiming the right to be permitted to leave the United States and return thereto on any of the grounds stated in the foregoing section, shall apply to the collector of customs of the district from which he wishes to depart at least one month prior to the time of his departure, and shall make an oath before the said collector a full statement descriptive of his family, or property, or debts, as the case may be, and shall furnish to the said collector such proofs of the facts entitling him to return as shall be required by the rules and regulations prescribed from time to time by the Secretary of the Treasury, and for any false swearing in relation thereto he shall incur the penalties of perjury. He shall also permit the collector to take a full description of his person, which description the collector shall retain and mark with a number. And if the collector, after hearing the proofs and investigating all the circumstances of the case, shall decide to issue a certificate of return, he shall at such time and place as he may designate, sign and give to the person applying a certificate containing the number of the description last aforesaid, which shall be the sole evidence given to such person of his right to return. If the last named certificate be transferred, it shall become void, and the person to whom it was given shall forfeit his right to return to the United States. The right of return under said certificate shall be limited to one year; but it may be extended for an additional period, not to exceed a year, in cases where, by reason of sickness or other cause of disability beyond his control, the holder thereof shall be rendered unable sooner to return, which facts shall be fully reported to and investigated by the consular representative of the United States at the port or place from which such laborer departs for the United

States, and certified by such representatives of the United States to the satisfaction of the collector of customs at the port where such Chinese person shall seek to land in the United States, such certificate to be delivered by said representative to the master of the vessel on which he departs for the United States. And no Chinese laborer shall be permitted to re-enter the United States without producing to the proper officer of the customs of the port of such entry the return certificate herein required. A Chinese laborer possessing a certificate under this section shall be admitted to the United States only at the port from which he departed therefrom. . . .

Sec. 13. That any Chinese person, or persons of Chinese descent, found unlawfully in the United States, or its Territories, may be arrested upon a warrant issued upon a complaint, under oath, filed by any party on behalf of the United States, by any justice, judge, or commissioner of any United States court, returnable before any justice, judge, or commissioner of a United States court, or before any United States court, and when convicted, upon a hearing, and found and adjudged to be one not lawfully entitled to be or remain in the United States, such person shall be removed from the United States to the country from whence he came. . . . And in all such cases the person who brought or aided in bringing such person into the United States shall be liable to the Government of the United States for all necessary expenses incurred in such investigation and removal; and all peace officers of the several States and Territories of the United States are hereby invested with the same authority in reference to carrying out the provisions of this act, as a marshal or deputy marshal of the United States, and shall be entitled to like compensation, to be audited and paid by the same officers.

Sec. 14. That the preceding sections shall not apply to Chinese diplomatic or consular officers or their attendants, who shall be admitted to the United States under special instructions of the Treasury Department, without production of other evidence than that of personal identity.

Source: Act of September 13, 1888, ch. 1015, 25 Stat. 476.

Act Banning Naturalization of Anarchists (1903)

Although the Red Scare of the post–World War I era was still nearly two decades away, fear of anarchists rose in the United States in the late nineteenth and early twentieth centuries, especially following the assassination of President William McKinley in 1901 by self-proclaimed anarchist Leon Czolgosz. Anarchists believed in both individual freedom and an end to all governments, and some advocated violence to achieve their ends. On March 3, 1903, Congress passed legislation banning the naturalization and citizenship of alleged anarchists.

Sec. 39. That no person who believes in or who is opposed to all organized government, or who is a member of or affiliated with any organization entertaining and teaching such disbelief in or opposition to all organized government, or who advocates or teaches the duty, necessity, or propriety of the unlawful assaulting or killing of any officers, either of specific individuals or of officers generally, of the Government of the United States or of any other government, because of his or their official character, or who has violated the provisions of this Act, shall be naturalized or be made a citizen of the United States. All courts and tribunals and all judges and officers thereof having jurisdiction of naturalization proceedings or duties to perform in regard thereto shall, on the final application for naturalization, make careful inquiry into such matters, and before issuing the final order or certificate of naturalization cause to be entered of record the affidavit of the applicant and of his witnesses so far as applicable, reciting and affirming the truth of every material requisite for naturalization. All final orders and certificates of naturalization hereafter made shall show on their face specifically that said affidavits were duly made and recorded, and all orders and certificates that fail to show such facts shall be null and void.

That any person who purposely procures naturalization in violation of the provisions of this section shall be fined not more than five thousand dollars, or shall be imprisoned not less than one nor more than ten years, or both, and the court in which such conviction is had shall thereupon adjudge and declare the order or decree and all certificates admitting such person to citizenship null and void. Jurisdiction is hereby conferred on the courts having jurisdiction of the trial of such offense to make such adjudication.

That any person who knowingly aids, advises, or encourages any such person to apply for or to secure naturalization or to file the preliminary papers declaring an intent to become a citizen of the United States, or who in any naturalization proceeding knowingly procures or gives false testimony as to any material fact, or who knowingly makes an affidavit false as to any material fact required to be proved in such proceeding, shall be fined not more than five thousand dollars, or imprisoned not less than one nor more than ten years, or both.

Source: Act of March 3, 1903, ch. 1012, 32 Stat. 1222.

Gentlemen's Agreement (1907)

Although not as numerous as the Chinese in the middle years of the nineteenth century, Japanese immigrants to the West Coast of the United States in the latter part of the century sparked anti-Asian hostility as well. But, unlike Chinese immigrants, who came from a country with little geopolitical weight, the Japanese hailed from a rising world power, requiring the U.S. government to seek out their involvement in any immigration restriction measures. In March 1907, President Theodore Roosevelt negotiated the so-called Gentlemen's Agreement calling for the Japanese government to impose voluntary restrictions on the emigration of its citizens (and those of Korea, then in the process of being absorbed as a Japanese colony) to the United States.

Whereas, by the act entitled "An Act to regulate the immigration of aliens into the United States," approved February 20, 1907, whenever the President is satisfied that passports issued by any foreign Government to its citizens to go to any country other than the United States or to the Canal Zone, are being used for the purpose of enabling the holders to come to the continental territory of the United States from such country or from such insular possession or from the Canal Zone;

AND WHEREAS, upon sufficient evidence produced before me by the Department of Commerce and Labor, I am satisfied that passports issued by the Government of Japan to citizens of that country or Korea and who are laborers, skilled or unskilled, to go to Mexico, to Canada and to Hawaii, are being used for the purpose of enabling the holders thereof to come to the continental territory of the United States to the detriment of labor conditions therein;

I hereby order that such citizens of Japan or Korea, to wit: Japanese and Korean laborers, skilled and unskilled, who have received passports to go to Mexico, Canada, or Hawaii, and come therefrom, be refused permission to enter the continental territory of the United States.

It is further ordered that the Secretary of Commerce and Labor be, and he hereby is, directed to take, through the Bureau of Immigration and Naturalization, such measures and to make and enforce such rules and regulations as may be necessary to carry this order into effect.

Source: Executive Order 589, March 14, 1907.

White-Slave Traffic Act (Mann Act) (1910)

In 1910, Congress passed the so-called White-Slave Traffic Act of 1910, also called the Mann Act, after its sponsor, Representative James R. Mann (R-IL). Much of the act focused on the interstate transport of women for "immoral purpos{es}." It also contained a clause outlawing the importation of women for the purpose of prostitution, though there is little evidence this was a major problem. Many historians believe that this aspect of the law offered a politically expedient way for Congress to appear that it was doing something about the overwhelming number of immigrants pouring into the country in the early twentieth century—a flow that was beginning to arouse opposition among native-born Americans.

Sec. 1. That the term "interstate commerce" as used in this Act, shall include transportation from any State or Territory or the District of Columbia to any other State or Territory or the District of Columbia, and the term "foreign commerce," as used in this Act, shall include transportation from any State or Territory or the District of Columbia to any foreign country and from any foreign country to any State or Territory or the District of Columbia.

Sec. 2. That any person who shall knowingly transport or cause to be transported, or aid or assist in obtaining transportation for, or in transporting, in interstate or foreign commerce, or in any Territory or in the District of Columbia, any woman or girl for the purpose of prostitution or debauchery, or for any other immoral purpose, or with the intent and purpose to induce, entice, or compel such woman or girl to become a prostitute or to give herself up to debauchery, or to engage in any other immoral practice; or who shall knowingly procure or obtain, or cause to be procured or obtained, or aid or assist in procuring or obtaining, any ticket or tickets, or any form of transportation or evidence of the right thereto, to be used by any woman or girl in interstate or foreign commerce, or in any Territory or the District of Columbia, in going to any place for the purpose of prostitution or debauchery, or for any other immoral purpose, or with the intent or purpose on the part of such person to induce, entice, or compel her to give herself up to the practice of prostitution, or to give herself up to debauchery, or any other immoral purpose, whereby such woman or girl shall be transported in interstate or foreign commerce, or in any Territory or the District of Columbia, shall be deemed guilty of a felony, and upon conviction thereof shall be punished by a fine not exceeding five thousand dollars, or by imprisonment of not more than five years, or by both such fine and imprisonment, in the discretion of the court. . . .

Sec. 3. That any person who shall knowingly persuade, induce, entice, or coerce, or cause to be persuaded, induced, enticed, or coerced, or aid or assist in persuading, inducing, enticing, or coercing any woman or girl to go from one place to another in interstate or foreign commerce . . . for the purpose of prostitution or debauchery, or for any other immoral purpose . . . shall be deemed guilty of a felony and on conviction thereof, shall be punished by a fine of not more than five thousand dollars, or by imprisonment for a term not exceeding five years, or by both such fine and imprisonment. . . .

Sec. 6. That for the purpose of regulating and preventing the transportation in foreign commerce of alien women and girls for the purpose of prostitution and debauchery, and in pursuance of and for the purpose of carrying out the terms of the agreement or project of arrangement for the suppression of the white-slavery traffic . . . the Commissioner of Immigration and Naturalization is hereby designated as the authority of the United States to receive and centralize information concerning the procuration of alien women and girls with a view to their debauchery, and to exercise supervision over such alien women and girls. . . .

Every person who shall keep, maintain, control, support, or harbor in any house or place for the purpose of prostitution, or for any other immoral purpose, any alien woman or girl within three years after she shall have entered the United States from any country . . . shall be deemed guilty of a felony, and on conviction thereof shall be punished by a fine of not more than ten thousand dollars, or by imprisonment for a term of not exceeding ten years, or by both such fine and imprisonment, in the discretion of the court.

Source: Act of June 25, 1910, ch. 395, 36 Stat. 825.

Immigration Act (1917)

Popularly referred to as the Literacy Act, the Immigration Act of 1917 was the first American piece of restrictive legislation aimed at all immigrants, including those from Europe. While the law called for the exclusion of persons with physical or mental disease—as well as those with allegedly dangerous political convictions—it also included a clause that banned immigrants over the age of sixteen who were illiterate in English or their native tongue. Finally, the law prohibited immigration for anyone from the "Asiatic Barred Zone," an artificially defined area covering most of the Asian continent and Pacific Islands.

Sec. 1. That the word "alien" wherever used in this Act shall include any person not a native-born or naturalized citizen of the United States; but this definition shall not be held to include Indians of the United States not taxed or citizens of the islands under the jurisdiction of the United States. That the term "United States" as used in the title as well as in the various sections of this Act shall be construed to mean the United States, and any waters, territory, or other place subject to the jurisdiction thereof, except the Isthmian Canal Zone. . . .

Sec. 2. That there shall be levied, collected, and paid a tax of $8 for every alien, including alien seamen regularly admitted as provided in this Act, entering the United States. . . .

Sec. 3. That the following classes of aliens shall be excluded from admission into the United States: All idiots, imbeciles, feeble-minded persons, epileptics, insane persons . . . persons with chronic alcoholism; paupers; professional beggars; vagrants; persons afflicted with tuberculosis in any form or a loathsome or dangerous contagious disease; persons not comprehended within any of the foregoing excluded classes who are found to be and are certified by the examining surgeon as being mentally or physically defective, such physical defect being of a nature which may affect the ability of such alien to earn a living; persons who have been convicted . . . of a felony or other crime or misdemeanor involving moral turpitude; polygamists, or persons who practice polygamy or believe in and advocate the practice of polygamy; anarchists, or persons who advocate the overthrow by force or violence of the Government of the United States, or of all forms of law . . . or who advocate the assassination of public officials, or who advocate and teach the unlawful destruction of property . . . ; prostitutes, or persons coming to the United States for the purpose of prostitution or immoral purposes . . . ; persons hereinafter called contract laborers . . . ; persons likely to become public charges . . . ; persons whose ticket or passage is paid for with the money of another; persons whose ticket or passage is paid for by any corporation, association, society, municipality, or foreign government, either directly or indirectly; stowaways . . . ; all children under sixteen years of age unaccompanied by or not coming to one or both of their parents . . . unless otherwise provided for by existing treaties, persons who are natives of islands not possessed by the United States adjacent to the continent of Asia, situate [*sic*] south of the twentieth parallel latitude north, west of the one hundred and sixtieth meridian of longitude east from Greenwich, and north of the tenth parallel of latitude south, or who are natives of any country, province, or dependency situate on the Continent of Asia west of the one hundred and tenth meridian of longitude east from Greenwich and east of the fiftieth meridian of longitude east from Greenwich and south of the fiftieth parallel of latitude north, except that portion of said territory situate between the fiftieth and sixty-fourth and thirty-eighth parallels of latitude north, and no alien now in any way excluded from, or prevented from entering the United States shall be admitted to the United States. . . .

That after three months from the passage of this Act in addition to the aliens who are by law now excluded from admission into the United States, the following persons shall also be excluded:

All aliens over sixteen years of age, physically capable of reading, who cannot read the English language, or some other language or dialect, including Hebrew or Yiddish: Provided, That any admissible alien, or any alien heretofore or hereafter legally admitted, or any citizen of the United States, may bring in or send for his father or grandfather over fifty-five years of age, his wife, his mother, his grandmother, or his unmarried or widowed daughter, if otherwise admissible, whether such relative can read or not; and such relative shall be permitted to enter. That for the purpose of ascertaining whether aliens can read the immigrant inspectors shall be furnished with slips of uniform size, prepared under the direction of the Attorney General, each containing not less than thirty nor more than forty words in ordinary use, printed in plainly legible type in some one of the various languages or dialects of immigrants. Each alien may designate the particular language or dialect in which he desires the examination to be made, and shall be required to read the words printed on the slip in such language or dialect. . . .

Provided, That nothing in this Act shall exclude, if otherwise admissible, persons convicted, or who admit to the commission, or who teach or advocate the commission, of an offense purely political. . . .

Provided further, That skilled labor, if otherwise admissible, may be imported if labor of the kind unemployed can not be found in this country, and the question of the necessity of importing such skilled labor in any particular instance may be determined by the Attorney General upon the application of any person interested, such application to be made before such importation, and such determination by the Attorney General to be reached after a full hearing and an investigation into the facts of the case. . . .

It shall also be unlawful for any person to bring to any port of the United States any alien who is excluded by the provisions of section 3 of this Act because unable to read, or who is excluded by the terms of section 3 of this Act as a native of that portion of the Continent of Asia and the islands adjacent thereto described in said section. . . .

Sec. 27. That for the preservation of the peace and in order that arrests may be made for crimes under the laws of the States and Territories of the United States where the various immigration stations are located, the officers in charge of such stations, as occasion may require, shall admit therein the proper State and municipal officers charged with the enforcement of such laws, and for the purpose of this section the jurisdiction of such officers and of the local courts shall extend over such stations. . . .

Sec. 29. That the President of the United States is authorized, in the name of the Government of the United States, to call, in his discretion, an international conference, to assemble at such point as may be agreed upon, or to send special commissioners to any foreign country, for the purpose of regulating by international agreement, subject to the advice and consent of the Senate of the United States, the immigration of aliens to the United States; of providing for the mental, moral, and physical examination of such aliens by American consuls or other officers of the United States Government at the ports of embarkation, or elsewhere; of securing the assistance of foreign Governments in their own territories to prevent the evasion of the laws of the United States governing immigration to the United States; of entering into such international agreements as may be proper to prevent the immigration of aliens who, under the laws of the United States, are or may be excluded from entering the United States, and of regulating any matters pertaining to such immigration. . . .

Source: Act of February 5, 1917, ch. 29, 39 Stat. 874.

Jones-Shafroth Act (1917)

Following the Spanish-American War in 1898, the United States annexed Puerto Rico as a colony. Nineteen years later, Congress acted to extend a limited form of citizenship to the people of Puerto Rico. According to many historians, however, the Jones-Shafroth Act (named for its congressional sponsors, Representative William Atkinson Jones, D-VA, and Senator John Shafroth, D-CO) was passed in order to draft Puerto Ricans into the armed forces as U.S. entry into World War I loomed. Ultimately, after World War II, the law allowed millions of Puerto Ricans to immigrate without restriction to the continental United States.

Sec. 5. That all citizens of Puerto Rico, as defined by section seven of the Act of April twelfth, nineteen hundred, "temporarily to provide revenues and a civil government for Puerto Rico, and for other purposes," and all natives of Puerto Rico, who were temporarily absent from that island on April eleventh, eighteen hundred and ninety-nine, and have since returned and are permanently residing in that island, and are not citizens of any foreign country, are hereby declared, and shall be deemed and held to be, citizens of the United States: *Provided,* That any person hereinbefore described may retain his present political status by making a declaration, under oath, of his decision to do so within six months of the taking effect of this Act before a district court in which he resides, the declaration to be in form as follows:

"I, _____, being duly sworn, hereby declare my intention not to become a citizen of the United States as provided in the Act of Congress conferring United States citizenship upon citizens of Puerto Rico and certain natives permanently residing in said island." . . .

After making such declaration and submitting such proofs, such persons shall be admitted to take the oath of allegiance before the court, and thereupon shall be considered a citizen of the United States.

Source: Act of March 2, 1917, ch. 145, 39 Stat. 951.

The Immigrant and the Community, Grace Abbott (1917)

In her 1917 book The Immigrant and the Community, *Progressive Era reformer Grace Abbott outlined the many difficulties facing American immigrants before, during, and after their arrival. In Chapter 1, reproduced below, Abbott describes conditions aboard the ships carrying immigrants across the Atlantic Ocean, what happens to the newcomers once they arrive, and how they are treated during transport around the country. While she notes some improvement in the treatment of immigrants, she says there is much yet to be done. Among other things, Abbott calls for federal legislation that would protect immigrants against fraud and abuse by individuals and firms involved in their transport.*

Chapter 1: The Journey of the Immigrant

The stories of hardship, danger, and exploitation that the immigrants suffered on their journey to the United States during the early part of the nineteenth century do not make pleasant reading. When the sailing vessel was still the usual means of crossing the Atlantic, travelers were required to furnish their own food and bedding for a journey that usually lasted a month or six weeks, and sometimes days or even weeks longer. Complaints of fearful overcrowding without regard for sex or age, of gross immorality, and of cruelty on the part of officers and crew were made in newspapers as well as before congressional investigating committees.

The death-rate during the crossing was appalling. According to Friedrich Kapp, chairman of the New York Board of Emigration Commissioners, a death-rate of 10 per cent was not uncommon, while sometimes as many as one third of the entire number died. Often, for example, the Irish famine victims, whose power of resistance had already been shattered, escaped from their stricken country only to die at sea.

Conditions of passenger traffic across the ocean were, however, greatly improved as a result of the statutes regulating steerage conditions passed by the United States in 1819, 1846, 1847, 1855, and 1860, and similar legislation adopted at about the same time by England, Holland, and the German cities. The shortening of the journey by the use of steam and the competition of rival companies also resulted in more comforts for the immigrant.

But the journey is still very far from being what decency demands. In ships which still have what is known as the "old-type steerage" as many as three hundred persons often sleep and live during the crossing in the large dormitories which have rows and rows of doubledeck berths. These berths are six feet long, two feet wide, and are two and one-half feet apart. Into thirty cubic feet of space, therefore, the immigrant must pack himself, his hand luggage, his towels and other toilet necessities, and the eating utensils which the ship furnishes him.

The misery of these conditions is greatly aggravated on bad days when the immigrants cannot use the small open deck allotted to them, when the hatches are closed, and the three hundred steerage passengers spend day and night in their berths, sometimes compelled to sleep in their clothes because the bedding furnished them is insufficient.

A number of excellent reports on steerage condition have been made in recent years which are based on experiences of men and women who traveled as immigrants both to and from Europe. As is to be expected, all the investigators who have made the trip and know these conditions at first hand have agreed that this old-style steerage should be abolished. The law should require more deck space, more and better food, and better sleeping quarters. Now, when immigration is in a sense at a standstill, would seem to be a time to set a new standard, so that with the new immigration, which will probably come after the war, safe, sanitary, and reasonably comfortable quarters can be assured for all those who come. The steerage with its huge and promiscuous dormitories should become a thing of the past, and the four- or six-passenger cabins that are now found in the third-class accommodations of some of the boats should be substituted. There is also general agreement that the treatment of the immigrants by the crew, complaint of which is frequently made by the immigrant women, would be much improved if a government inspector traveled with every boat, or if it were known that he might be on any boat disguised as an immigrant.

In the early nineteenth century, the trials of the immigrant did not end with the fearful journey across the Atlantic, for wherever they landed they were met by a small army of exploiters. Runners who spoke their language piloted them to boarding houses where they were held until their little money was exhausted, or employment agents and bogus railroad representatives robbed and misdirected them. Before the regulation of immigration was taken over by the United States, a number of the States had taken steps to prevent these abuses. New York especially had developed machinery that had for its object the guarding of the newly arrived immigrant from fraud and exploitation, not only at the port of New York but in cities in the interior of the State. The statute enacted by New York in 1848 and improved in 1849 established a strict control of immigrant boarding houses, runners, and passenger and baggage agents, and provided for the appointment of officials who were to give advice to the immigrants and put them on their guard against fraud and imposition. A further act of 1855 required transportation companies to furnish the mayors of different cities with a statement of the rates and charges for conveying immigrants; and one of 1868 gave the Commissioner of Immigration supervision over the sale of passenger tickets to immigrants. In their efforts to protect the immigrants the state authorities in New York cooperated with private agencies, especially the German and Irish societies formed to assist the immigrants of those nationalities who were coming in such large numbers at that time.

The decisions of the United States Supreme Court holding the state head tax on immigrants unconstitutional ended state regulation and compelled the United States Government to take over this work. Since then public attention has in the main been so fastened on the 2 or 3 per cent. of the immigrants who are excluded as undesirable that little thought has been given to the 97 or 98 per cent. of them who are admitted, although self-interest alone should long ago have suggested that special precautions be taken by the United States for the protection of the morals and the health of the immigrant who is permitted to remain.

Much improvement in the methods of inspection, detention, and release of immigrants at the various ports of arrival has been made in recent years. Because of the more efficient organization of the service, immigrants are now treated with humane consideration by government officials; runners from cheap hotels, expressmen, employment agents, and all those who might profit by their ignorance and dependence are generally denied access to them. The moral exploitation of the girl is guarded against by an examination of the persons to whom she is released.

But in contrast to these improvements made at the ports, there is, for the girl destined to Chicago and other interior points, no corresponding protective machinery. She is carefully guarded by the federal authorities until she is placed on the train, but the Government then considers that its responsibility is at an end. It is not considered a matter of national concern whether she is sent to her destination by the most direct or by a long, circuitous route. She may be approached by any one while traveling and persuaded to leave the train. Through her own mistake or intention or the carelessness of railroad officials, she may be put off before she reaches her destination.

Immigrants are no longer sold bogus railroad tickets at the ports as they were before the railroads had official representatives at Castle Garden, but they still do not always get a square deal from the railroads. The steamship companies hold the key to the present situation because relatives and friends who send prepaid tickets from the United States as well as those who purchase their transportation abroad are usually persuaded to buy through tickets to the final destination. This means that most of the immigrants land with an order which shows that they have paid a steamship company for a railroad ticket to their destination. The steamship companies have, therefore, the power of saying whether all those who come on their boats with these orders shall travel over one railroad or whether this patronage shall be more generally distributed. By a "friendly" agreement between the steamship companies and practically all the railroads of the country, a railroad office, maintained under the joint control of the railroads at Ellis Island, is recognized by the steamship companies and each railroad is given its share of the patronage. This agreement is based, however, upon the business ideal of fairness to the competing railroads and not upon consideration of the comfort of the immigrants. In order that all the roads may enjoy their share of the traffic, immigrants are sometimes sent by the most indirect routes to their destinations. For example, those who are coming to Chicago are often sent from New York by boat on the Old Dominion Line to Norfolk, Virginia, and from there on by the Chesapeake and Ohio and connecting lines to Chicago.

In the year ending June 30, 1916, immigrants were sent by nine different routes from New York to Chicago, but nearly three times as many were sent around by Norfolk, Virginia, as by any other single route. Instances less flagrant but which result in much discomfort and sometimes real suffering also occur.

Immigrants constantly arrive in Chicago on their way to the Pacific coast who could make the journey without a single change but are given tickets at Ellis Island which call for several changes en route.

A Norwegian girl arrived in May of 1916 on the *Kristiania fjord* and was going to a town in Iowa. No change should have been necessary after she left Chicago, but she was put on a train that left the city in the afternoon and then put off at a railroad junction in Illinois at nine o'clock at night to wait for another train. She sat up all night in the railroad station and then spent the next day waiting for her train, alone and frightened because she was unable to speak a word of English and did not know how to make herself safe and comfortable. The railroad agent made no effort to protect her from three men who he saw were annoying her. To add to the anxiety that any girl would feel under these circumstances, she was robbed of the little money she had carefully saved because she did not want to reach her relatives quite empty-handed.

Passengers on the immigrant trains frequently expect to arrive in a much shorter time than the indirect route requires, and they do not provide themselves with the additional food which the roundabout journey makes necessary. No arrangement is made for them to purchase food en route, so they sometimes arrive hungry and exhausted. One tired Bohemian mother who came to the office of the Immigrants' Protective League with her four little children had had the difficult task of keeping them quiet when they had had no food for the last thirty-six hours of their trip.

Some improvement has been made recently in the routing of the immigrants, but Mr. Frederic C. Howe, the present Commissioner of Immigration at Ellis Island, who is very much interested in eradicating this and all other abuses, thinks that the evils of the present system cannot be cured until the Immigration Bureau is authorized by Congress to take entire charge of this matter.

This neglect on the part of the United States to take any measure to protect the immigrant after he has been admitted to the United States was especially inexcusable. The Government's experience with the ocean-going steamers gave every reason for anticipating that, in the absence of regulation and inspection, overcrowding, insanitary conditions, and inadequate provisions for the women and girls were sure to be found on the boats which carried immigrants from New York to Fall River, [Massachusetts,] or on the immigrant trains which took so many scores of thousands west each year during the periods of heavy immigration which preceded the war.

The Massachusetts Commission on Immigration, an investigating commission appointed in 1913, received complaints about conditions on the Fall River boats on which, in accordance with an agreement with the transatlantic steamship companies, all the immigrants were then sent from New York to Boston or from Boston to New York.

Investigators for the Commission who were sent to make the trip as immigrants reported shocking conditions: "beds filthy, ventilation incredibly inadequate, and the overcrowding serious." Worse than this, the immigrant men were the butt of coarse and cruel jokes and pranks, and the Polish girls were compelled to defend themselves against the advances of the crew who freely entered the women's dormitory and tried to drag the girls into the crew's quarters.

The steamship company was directly responsible for these conditions, but the United States Government was equally to blame for taking no precautions to insure decency on these boats inasmuch as its experience in regulating ocean travel since 1819 had shown the necessity of official regulation and supervision.

In the hope of securing immediate improvement, the Massachusetts Commission submitted the result of its investigation to the officers of the steamship company, and steps were at once taken by the company to improve conditions. By the time its report was submitted to the legislature, the Commission was therefore able to report that the boats were being rebuilt so as to provide outside ventilation for both men's and women's quarters, more sanitary washrooms, and complete separation of the crew's quarters from the quarters of the immigrant women. Furthermore, an immigrant steward and a stewardess were placed in charge of the immigrant service. All this promised much greater safety and comfort for the immigrant. But the Commission called attention to the fact that if conditions were to be kept decent, legislation regulating these boats and continuous inspection were necessary. The temptation to overcrowd dangerously and in consequence to lower the moral safeguards is great. A permanent commission on immigration was not created in Massachusetts, however, and the United States Government, although it holds that the way in which immigrants travel before they are admitted is a matter of national concern, still takes the position that after they are admitted it is quite indifferent as to what they suffer from carelessness, neglect, or exploitation.

The railroad journey also needs supervision. At present, it is practically impossible to trace the girls who leave New York but who never reach their friends in Chicago. Sometimes it is possible to reach some conclusion as to what became of them, but these conclusions only point to the necessity for safeguarding the journey. For example, two Polish girls, seventeen and twenty-two years of age, whose experience before they started for America had been bounded by the limits of a small farm in Galicia, were coming to their cousins who lived back of the Stockyards in Chicago. Their names and addresses had been sent to the Immigrants' Protective League on one of the lists of unaccompanied girls received regularly from the ports of entry. When one of the visitors of the League called at the house, she found the cousin and the entire household much alarmed because the girls had not arrived. Through inquiries of others who came on the same boat, it was learned that the girls had become acquainted on the way over with a man from Rochester and that he was "looking out for them." The only official information which could be secured was a description of the railroad tickets that the girls held when they left Ellis Island. Investigation by the railroad showed that on that date one ticket had been sold to Rochester and two Chicago tickets had been used only as far as Rochester. The girls had completely disappeared, and there was no official responsibility for their failure to arrive in Chicago.

Sometimes the girls, to whom nothing really serious happens, are for a time in an extremely dangerous position. For example, one seventeen-year-old girl was put off the train at South Chicago by mistake and wandered about for several hours at night. Finally a man offered to take her to her friends. He proved worthy of the confidence she had in his kindly intent, and she was conducted safely to the Northwest Side, many miles from where she had been left. Another girl, nineteen years old, who came in by way of Quebec, became separated from her sister and friends at Detroit. She was taken to a police station for the night and in the morning continued her journey. She arrived in South Chicago without money or the address of her relatives. She was therefore taken to the South Chicago Police Station and after spending a night there was taken to the Women's Annex of the Harrison Street Police Station. The police regarded it as impossible to find the girl's friends, so the matron of the Annex found her work in a downtown hotel. A visitor of the League returning from South Chicago reported great excitement in one neighborhood over the fact that an immigrant girl had been lost at Detroit. This report was connected with the story of the police matron, and a visit to the hotel proved the identity of the girl. Except for this she would have been alone in Chicago, ignorant of our language and the dangers of the city, with no one to turn to in case of sickness or unemployment.

Several girls have told of being approached on the trains and invited by strange men to get off at "some big city and see the town," but they wisely concluded to continue their journey without these gay excursions into the unknown.

More immigrants have been arriving at great distributing centers like Chicago, Pittsburgh, or Cleveland than came to the port of New York during the days when the State of New York was adopting its comprehensive program for the protection of the immigrants. During the early part of the nineteenth century it is said, that "the hapless strangers, ignorant of the customs and laws of the country, often unable to speak the language that would procure police assistance, more liable by reason of their 'outlandish' dress and manners to meet ridicule than sympathy from the masses of native citizens, were browbeaten and fleeced without mercy." This reads like a description of the situation in which those who have been coming in the twentieth century have found themselves on getting off an immigrant train in Chicago.

Any woman can understand the nervous apprehension which the immigrant girl must feel as she comes into one of Chicago's bewildering railroad stations, but very few realize how well grounded her fears are. Eager friends and relatives find it almost impossible to meet the immigrants because immigrant trains are sidetracked for all other kinds of traffic, so that it is extremely difficult to determine just when they will reach Chicago. Merely talking with the girls about their experiences is not so convincing as seeing the actual situation which they meet on leaving a train in Chicago.

On one occasion, for example, the train was due at seven thirty in the morning, but finally arrived shortly after four o'clock in the afternoon. It had been reported as coming at various hours so that three trips were made to the station, although each time inquiry had been made by telephone and assurance given that the train was reported due at once. Several hundred immigrants got off the train when it finally came. Many of them were very young, and one felt their disappointment as they peered eagerly and anxiously for the father or sister or friend they expected to see. Those who were going north or west of Chicago came out the main gate already ticketed by a representative of the transfer company and were taken as American travelers are to another depot without any confusion. But those who were to remain in Chicago were directed into a small immigrant waiting-room which opened on a narrow side street. Here they were hastily sorted into groups and then pushed out the door into the midst of ten or twelve express-men, who were crowding and pushing and quarreling over the division of spoils. In a short time the struggle was over and they had all been loaded into the waiting wagons. By this time it was almost dark and they drove away.

This unsupervised, irresponsible method of disposing of these people explains the plight of the Irish girl who had started on a wagon with a group of other immigrants for the South Side. After going some distance, the expressman discovered she had a North Side address; so, charging her four dollars, he put her off the wagon and left her without any suggestion as to what she should do. It explains, too, the disposition that was made of a Polish girl of seventeen who was taken at three o'clock in the morning to the place where her sister was supposed to live. The address proved to be incorrect, however, and the woman who lived there angrily refused to let her stay until morning. The girl had no money and wept disconsolately when the expressman told her in a language she did not understand that "nobody could find her sister if nobody knew her address and that he wasn't going to take her back to the depot for nothing." The saloon-keeper next door finally offered her a refuge, and she lived with his family behind the saloon three days before her sister, who was making daily trips to the depot, was found.

Not long before this, a girl had been brought to the office of the Immigrants' Protective League who had arrived in Chicago on Sunday afternoon and because her friends could not be found had been taken to the Annex of the Harrison Street Police Station, where, like many immigrant girls, she had received her first initiation into Chicago life. She had the name and address of the girl friend who lived in Chicago and had promised to get her work, written in the front of her prayer-book, and she could not understand that it was incorrect. She tearfully insisted on accompanying the Polish visitor of the Immigrants' Protective League on the search for her friend and grew more and more discouraged as one clue after another was tried and failed. Finally the girl said that her friend worked in a bed-spring factory. Starting out anew on this clue, she was found in the third bed-spring factory they visited. Then the friend explained that one number had been left off the address which the girl had so carefully written in her prayer-book.

Since the summer of 1908, the Immigrants' Protective League has received from the various ports of entry the names and addresses of the unaccompanied women and girls who are coming to Chicago. The plan has been to have these women and girls visited by a representative of the League who was able to speak their language and was prepared to help them in making a beginning of their life in Chicago. Since 1908, 20,304 girls have been thus visited by the League—not all those whose names were received, because the resources of the League were not such as to enable us to do this during the seasons when immigration was heaviest. It was through these visits that we learned that some girls did not reach their relatives and friends, and that an extension of the care and supervision which is given girls at the ports of entry should be extended to the interior. For example, in one year of normal immigration when 3338 girls were visited, 434 of the addresses sent us were obviously incorrect and no visit was attempted. We found some trace of 364 others, but after several visits the attempt to locate them

was abandoned, although we had not followed up every possible clue. But 504 could not be located, although every possible effort was made to find them. In thirty-four instances, we found the persons whose names and addresses the girls had given at the port, but they were not expecting the girls and knew nothing of what had become of them. Typical cases of failure to find the girls whose names were received from the ports will illustrate the reasons for anxiety. A Lithuanian girl of eighteen, for example, gave the address of a local steamship agency, and subsequently we learned that she had been called for by a notoriously disreputable man and taken to a rooming house. We traced her to two other addresses but were not able to find her. In another case, investigation of an address which a twenty-year-old Polish girl gave revealed the fact that three years previously a telegram had been received from the port announcing the arrival of a girl who was unknown to any one at the address given. No girl had come. The next year this had happened again. This particular year neither the telegram nor the girl had arrived, and although the name and address was correct no explanation of the use of the name could be given. The evidence which we have had year after year has convinced us that many of these girls whom we were unable to locate undoubtedly reached their relatives and friends; many others, although they did not succeed in doing this, have, by the merest chance, found people who were kind to them and helped them in securing work and in making their connections in Chicago; but from much evidence we are sure that a considerable number cannot be accounted for in these ways.

Whether in cases like those last cited the giving of the incorrect name and address was intentional on the part of the girl, the result of some mistake, or serious deception, federal protection and supervision is the only way of reducing the resulting danger to the community and to the girls. In the administration of the immigration law the girls are required to give the name and address of some one to whom they are coming as a condition of admission. But experience has shown how little protection there is either for the community or for the girl in this requirement.

In 1910 the Immigrants' Protective League was given by the Chicago and Western Indiana Railroad the use of a building across from its depot, and all the immigrants who arrived at that station were sent across to the League's waiting-room. As this was the terminal used by the Erie, the Wabash, and the Grand Trunk railroads, more than three times as many immigrants arrived at this as at any other station in the city. The plan worked out by the League was that its officers, speaking the languages of the immigrants, should arrange to send them to their friends. If possible, relatives were to be reached by telephone; if this could not be done, they were to be sent sometimes with a cab or expressman, sometimes in charge of a messenger boy, or, when they were able to speak English or had some knowledge of how to get about in a city, they were to be directed or taken to a street car; and finally all those who were peculiarly helpless or who had doubtful or suspicious addresses were to be sent out accompanied by one of the officers of the League. This plan was followed for four years. Cards printed in their native languages were given the immigrants as they left the League's waiting-room, telling them what they were to do in case of an overcharge or neglect on the part of the driver or messenger. The name and address of each immigrant, the number of the expressman or cab driver, the name of the relative or officer or messenger boy to whom each was entrusted, as well as any charges made, were carefully recorded.

As was anticipated, the expressmen and cabmen opposed this supervision as an invasion of the right to exploit the immigrant which they thought the city had guaranteed them when they paid their license of one dollar and a half. With their official-looking badges and caps and their stock of foreign phrases, the drivers and runner would secure the attention of the immigrants and then by a combination of force and persuasion would load them on their wagons and drive off with them. During the first six months of the League's work at this station, although a vigorous fight was kept up with the drivers by night as well as by day, we were able to get hold of only 1903 immigrants, the next year 5204 reached our waiting room and their delivery was arranged for in the orderly manner planned. In 1912 the number increased to 15,537. By 1913 we had convinced the exploiters that we were really in earnest and that prosecutions would be pushed and licenses suspended, and during that year 41,322 immigrants were cared for in the League's waiting room and their delivery arranged for by officers of the League.

Although complaints of abuses were very much less frequent in 1913 than in former years, it was still necessary for us to report thirty-three drivers of express wagon and cabs to the Inspector of Vehicles, who promptly imposed the penalties prescribed by the city ordinance for overcharges and similar offenses.

A very large number of the immigrant trains were found to arrive between midnight and six o'clock in the morning. Some of the immigrants had addresses to which they could not be taken at night, and others having dangerous or doubtful addresses could not be sent out until an investigation had been made in the morning. So the Immigrants' Protective League found it necessary to keep many of the immigrants over night, and some bedrooms were therefore provided on the second floor of its building. In one year ninety-five arrived who had lost their addresses, and it was necessary for us to spend much time in the search for their relatives or friends.

In undertaking this work, the Immigrants' Protective League had two objects: first, to give to the very large numbers arriving at this depot the assistance they so badly needed; and second, and more important, to demonstrate that official supervision was both necessary and practical. The limitations upon the work of a private organization were evident from the beginning. We lacked the authority necessary to make the protection as effective as it should be made; the space we had was quite inadequate to prevent serious overcrowding of the waiting-room; and it was impossible to secure, through private subscription, funds adequate for doing work which so clearly belonged to the Federal Government. Moreover, the organization did not feel justified in appealing to interested citizens to donate the money for this work when the head tax which the Government levied upon the immigrant was much more than enough to pay for really adequate protection and assistance during the first period of adjustment. The need of the Federal Government's undertaking this work was therefore constantly urged; and in 1913 a law was passed by Congress that authorized the Secretary of Labor to establish immigrant stations at points in the interior, and an appropriation was made for the maintenance of such a station in Chicago. This law also authorized the Secretary to detail immigrant inspectors to travel on immigrant trains.

With some difficulty, a location was found for the station in 1913, and the receiving-room, dormitories, bathrooms, and laundry were furnished and ready for use in January, 1914. The following summer, certain additional officers were assigned to the Chicago Station to undertake this work, but these were later withdrawn.

The delay in the operation of the Station was declared in the Annual Report of the Secretary of Labor for 1911 to be due to the fact that the immigrants were required to pay a local transfer agency for transportation from the railway stations to the Immigrant Station. This difficulty was removed during the summer of 1914 through the agreement by all the railroads carrying Chicago-bound immigrants to transfer them from the terminal station to the Immigrant Station without extra charge. But this agreement has not been utilized by the Federal Government except when the immigrant on his arrival at Ellis Island asks to be transferred to the Federal Station in Chicago.

The large receiving-room, after being locked for year, is now being used for the much-needed labor exchange work that the Department of Labor has recently undertaken. But the dormitories, bathrooms, laundry rooms, etc., have never been used. The Government has been paying rent for this unused space for more than two years. This illustration of the way in which an administrative department of the Government can refuse to carry out the laws passed by Congress should be interesting to students of political science.

That the duty of protecting and caring for the immigrant on his journey belongs to the federal rather than the local government is obvious. The former controls the admission of immigrants and is informed as to the number arriving. Protection and supervision of release is given the immigrants who arrive at the ports of entry, and it is logical, therefore, to ask an extension of this care to the interior. The protection needed by immigrants arriving in Chicago is also needed in Pittsburgh, Cleveland, St. Louis, and other important centers of arrival and distribution. Official inspectors, both men and women, should travel on immigrant trains to insure considerate treatment on the part of the railroads and to protect the immigrant from the organized exploitation which develops when there is no official supervision.

The first federal statute that provided for regulation of immigration (1882), as well as the statutes of 1903 and 1907, authorized the Commissioner-General of Immigration "to establish such regulations, not inconsistent with law, as he shall deem best calculated for protecting the United States and the immigrant *from fraud and loss*," and gave him authority to enter into contracts for the support and relief of such immigrants as may fall into distress or need public aid. These provisions were not made without a quite definite understanding of the need for the protection which was here authorized. It may be assumed that the provision in the federal statutes recognizing the duty of the Government to guard the immigrant from fraud and loss was suggested by the similar functions of the New York officials. In view of this, it would seem that a moral duty rests on the Federal Government to give proper consideration to the protective aspect of immigrant control.

National and even international attention has been drawn to the prosecution of so-called "white slavers." Important as this work is, it should not be the only form of control attempted. For in prosecutions we must, of necessity, wait until the girl has been ruined, and no fine or penitentiary sentence inflicted upon the man or woman responsible for her downfall can undo for her or for society the damage that has been wrought. Some constructive, preventive measures should be undertaken as well. First among these, perhaps, should be the guarantee to every immigrant girl of a safe arrival at her destination.

In his annual report for 1915, the Commissioner-General of Immigration calls attention to the fact that "since the law providing for the collection of a head tax from arriving immigrants has been in force, up to the end of this fiscal year (1915) there has been collected over $9,000,000 in excess of the expenditures for the immigration service." The Immigration Bill which has just been passed over the President's veto increases this head tax for adults from four to eight dollars. And so it is probable that in the future larger sums will be collected. The obligation of regarding the money collected in this way as a trust fund to be used in behalf of the immigrant cannot be too strongly insisted upon.

The first evidence of the "new nationalism" should be in the nation's affording the kind of protection which shall give to the immigrant such ideas of America as we should like him to have when he begins his life among us. Only too frequently, under present conditions, the idealistic picture of America which he brings with him is destroyed immediately on his arrival, and instead he begins with a knowledge of some of the ugliest and meanest aspects of our life.

Source: Grace Abbott. *The Immigrant and the Community* (New York: Century, 1917).

Quota Act (1921)

As its name suggests, the Quota Act of 1921 was the first U.S. federal legislation designed to restrict immigration by means of a national quota system. Under that system, the allowable number of immigrants from a given country would be set at 3 percent of the total number of persons from that country living in the United States in 1910. This method of calculation still allowed for a heavy influx of immigrants from Eastern and Southern European countries—people whom nativists considered inferior, dangerous, and incapable of assimilating to the American way of life. Three years later, Congress would pass the much more restrictive Quota Act of 1924.

Be it enacted by the Senate and the House of Representatives . . . ,

Sec. 2. (a) That the number of aliens of any nationality who may be admitted under the immigration laws to the United States in any fiscal year shall be limited to 3 per centum of the number of foreign-born persons of such nationality resident in the United States as determined by the United States census of 1910. This provision shall not apply to the following, and they shall not be counted in reckoning any of the percentage limits provided in this Act: (1) Government officials, their families, attendants, servants, and employees; (2) aliens in continuous transit through the United States; (3) aliens lawfully admitted to the United States who later go in transit . . . to another foreign contiguous territory; (4) aliens visiting the United States as tourists or temporarily for business or pleasure; (5) aliens from countries immigration from which is regulated in accordance with treaties or agreements relating solely to immigration; (6) aliens from the so-called Asiatic barred zone . . . (7) aliens who have resided continuously for at least five years immediately preceding the time of their application for admission . . . in the Dominion of Canada, Newfoundland, the Republic of Cuba, the Republic of Mexico, countries of Central and South America, or adjacent islands; or (8) aliens under the age of eighteen who are children of citizens of the United States.

(b) For the purposes of this Act nationality shall be determined by country of birth, treating as separate countries the colonies or dependencies for which separate enumeration was made in the United States census of 1910;

(c) That the Secretary of State, the Secretary of Commerce, and the Attorney General, jointly, shall, as soon as feasible after enactment of this Act, prepare a statement showing the number of persons of the various nationalities resident in the United States as determined by the census of 1910, which statement shall be the population basis for the purposes of this Act. . . .

(d) When the maximum number of aliens from any nationality who may be admitted in any fiscal year under this Act shall have been admitted all other aliens of such nationality, except as otherwise provided for by this Act . . . shall be excluded. . . .

Provided further, That in the enforcement of this Act preference shall be given so far as possible to the wives, parents, brothers, sisters, children under eighteen years of age, and fiancees, (1) of citizens of the United States, (2) of aliens now in the United States who have applied for citizenship in the manner provided by law, or (3) of persons eligible to United States citizenship who served in the military or naval forces of the United States at any time between April 6, 1917 and November 11, 1918 . . . and have been separated from such forces under honorable conditions.

Sec. 3. That the Commissioner of Immigration and Naturalization, with the approval of the Attorney General, shall as soon as feasible after the enactment of this Act, and from time to time hereafter, prescribe rules and regulations necessary to carry the provisions of this Act into effect. He shall, as soon as feasible . . . publish a statement showing the number of aliens of the various nationalities who may be admitted to the United States. . . . Thereafter he shall publish monthly statements during the time this Act remains in force showing the number of aliens of each nationality already admitted under provisions of this Act . . . and the number who may be admitted . . . during the then current fiscal year . . . but when 75 per centum of the maximum number of any nationality . . . shall have been admitted such statements shall be issued weekly thereafter. . . . The Attorney General shall also submit such statements to the Secretary of State, who shall transmit the information contained therein to the proper diplomatic and consular officials of the United States, which officials shall make the same available to persons intending to emigrate to the United States and to others who may apply.

Sec. 5. That this Act shall take effect and be enforced 15 days after its enactment . . . and shall continue in force until June 30, 1924 [originally "1922" but extended for two more years], and the number of aliens of any nationality who may be admitted during the remaining period of the current fiscal year, from the date when this Act becomes effective until June 30, shall be limited in proportion to the number admissible during the fiscal year 1922.

Sec. 6. That it shall be unlawful for any person, including any transportation company other than railway lines entering the United States from foreign contiguous territory, or the owner, master, agent, or consignee of any vessel, to bring to the United States either from a foreign country or any insular possession of the United States any alien not admissible under the terms of this Act or regulations made thereunder.

Source: Act of May 19, 1921, ch. 8, 42 Stat. 5.

United States v. Bhagat Singh Thind (1923)

On February 19, 1923, the U.S. Supreme Court ruled against the petition of Bhagat Singh Thind, an immigrant from Punjab in northern India, requesting U.S. citizenship as a "free, White person" (a requirement established by the Naturalization Act of 1790). Thind argued that he was eligible for naturalization as a member of the Caucasian race (as many people from northern India are), but the Court ruled against him on grounds that the term "White person" should be interpreted in commonsense terms rather than strictly anthropological terms.

Mr. Justice [George] Sutherland delivered the opinion of the court:

The cause is here upon a certificate from the circuit

court of appeals, requesting instruction of this court in respect to the following questions: 1. Is a high caste Hindu of full Indian blood, born in Amritsar, Punjab, India, a white person within the meaning of #2169, Revised Statutes (Comp. Stat. #4358, 6 Fed. Stat. Anno. 2d ed. P. 944)?

2. Does the Act of February 5, 1917 . . . disqualify from naturalization as citizens those Hindus now barred by that act, who had lawfully entered the United States prior to passage of said act?

. . . No question was made in respect to the individual qualifications of the appellee. The sole question is whether he falls within the class designated by Congress as eligible. Section #2169, Revised Statutes, provides that the provision of the Naturalization Act "shall apply to aliens being free white persons and to aliens of African nativity and to persons of African descent."

If the applicant is a white person within the meaning of this section he is entitled to naturalization; otherwise not. . . .

In the endeavor to ascertain the meaning of the statute we must not fail to keep in mind that it does not apply the word "Caucasian," but the words "white persons," and these are words of common speech, and not of scientific origin. The word "Caucasian" not only was not employed in the law, but was probably wholly unfamiliar to the original framers of the statute in 1790. When we employ it, we do so as an aid to the ascertainment of the legislative intent, and not as an invariable substitute for the statutory words. . . . But in this country, during the last half century especially, the word by common usage has acquired a popular meaning, not clearly defined, to be sure, but sufficiently so to enable us to say that its popular, as distinguished from its scientific application, is of appreciably narrower scope. It is in the popular sense of the word, therefore, that we employ it as an aid to the construction of the statute, for it would be obviously illogical to convert words from common speech, used in a statute, into words of scientific terminology, when neither the latter nor the science for whose purposes they were coined was within the contemplation of the framers of the statute or of the people for whom it was framed. . . .

The words of familiar speech, which were used by the original framers of the law, were intended to include only the type of man whom they knew as white. The immigration of that day was almost exclusively from the British Isles and northwestern Europe, whence they and their forebears had come. When they extended the privilege of American citizenship to "any alien being a free white person," it was these immigrants—bone of their bone, flesh of their flesh—and their kind whom they must have had affirmatively in mind. The succeeding years brought immigration from eastern, southern, and middle Europe, among them the Slavs and the dark-eyed, swarthy people

of Alpine and Mediterranean stock, and these were received as unquestionably akin to those already here, and readily amalgamated with them. It was the descendants of these and other immigrants of like origin, who constituted the white population of the country when . . . the naturalization test [was reenacted]. . . .

What we now hold is that the words "free white persons" are words of common speech, to be interpreted in accordance with the understanding of the common man, synonymous with the word "Caucasian" only as that word is popularly understood. As so understood and used, whatever may be the speculations of the ethnologist, it does not include the body of people to whom the appellee belongs. It is a matter of familiar observation and knowledge that the physical group characteristics of the Hindus render them readily distinguishable from the various groups of persons in this country commonly recognized as white. . . . It is very far from our thought to suggest the slightest question of racial superiority or inferiority. What we suggest is merely racial difference, and it is of such character and extent that the great body of our people instinctively recognize it and reject the thought of assimilation.

It is not without significance in this connection that Congress, by the Act of February 5, 1917, . . . has now excluded from admission to this country all natives of Asia within designated limits of latitude and longitude, including the whole of India. This not only constitutes conclusive evidence of the congressional attitude of opposition to Asiatic immigration generally, but is persuasive of a similar attitude toward Asiatic naturalization as well, since it is not likely that Congress would be willing to accept as citizens a class of persons whom it rejects as immigrants.

It follows that a negative answer must be given to that first question, which disposes of the case and renders an answer to the second question unnecessary, and it will be so certified. Answer to question No. 1, No.

Source: United States v. Bhagat Singh Thind, 261 U.S. 204 (1923).

Quota Act (1924)

Three years after passing the first Quota Act in 1921, Congress moved to restrict U.S. immigration even further through the Quota Act of 1924. The 1921 law had set a limit on annual immigration from a given country at 3 percent of the total number of persons of that nationality living in the United States in 1910; the 1924 legislation lowered the percentage to 2 percent and established 1890 as the base year. Because much of the burgeoning immigration from Eastern and Southern Europe had occurred after 1890, the quotas for countries in those regions were thereby lowered to a significant degree. Opponents of open immigration had long argued that people from Eastern and Southern Europe were culturally inferior to those from Northern and Western Europe and that they were less capable of being assimilated into American life.

Sec. 2. (a) A consular officer upon the application of any immigrant . . . may . . . issue to such an immigrant an immigration visa which shall consist of one copy of the application provided for in section 7, visaed by such consular officer. Such visa shall specify (1) the nationality of the immigrant; (2) whether he is a quota immigrant (as defined in section 5) or a non-quota immigrant (as defined in section 4); (3) the date on which the validity of the immigration visa shall expire; and (4) such additional information necessary to the proper enforcement of the immigration laws and the naturalization laws as may be by regulation prescribed.

Sec. 6. (a) Immigration visas to quota immigrants shall be issued in each fiscal year as follows:

(1) Fifty per centum of the quotas of each nationality for such year shall be made available . . . to the following classes of immigrants, without priority of preference as between such classes: (A) Quota immigrants who are the fathers or mothers of citizens of the United States . . . or who are the husbands of citizens of the United States by marriages occurring on or after May 31, 1928, of citizens who are citizens of the United States who are twenty-one years of age or over; and (B) in the case of any nationality the quota of which is three hundred or more, quota immigrants who are skilled in agriculture, and the wives, and the dependent children under the age of eighteen years, of such immigrants skilled in agriculture, if accompanying or following to join them.

(2) The remainder of the quota of each nationality for such year . . . shall be made available in such year for the issuance of immigration visas to quota immigrants of such nationality who are the unmarried children under twenty-one years of age, or the wives, of alien residents of the United States who were lawfully admitted to the United States for permanent residence. . . .

Sec. 10. (a) Any alien about to depart temporarily from the United States may make application to the Commissioner of Immigration and Naturalization for a permit to reenter the United States stating the length of his intended absence, and the reasons therefor. . . .

Sec. 11. (a) The annual quota of any nationality shall be 2 per centum of the number of foreign-born individuals of such nationality resident in continental United States as determined by the United States census of 1890, but the minimum quota of any nationality shall be 100. . . .

Sec. 12. (a) For the purpose of this Act nationality shall be determined by country of birth, treating as separate countries the colonies, dependencies, or self-governing dominions for which separate enumeration was made in the United States census of 1890 and which was not included in the enumeration for the country to which such colony or dependency belonged. . . .

Sec. 13. (a) No immigrant shall be admitted . . . unless he (1) has an unexpired immigration visa . . . ; (2) is of the nationality specified in the visa; (3) is a nonquota immigrant if specified in the visa as such; (4) is a preference-quota immigrant if specified . . . as such; and (5) is otherwise admissible under the immigration laws. . . .

(c) No alien ineligible to citizenship shall be admitted to the United States unless such alien (1) is admissible as a non-quota immigrant under the provisions of subdivisions (b), (d) or (e) of section 4, or (2) is the wife, or the unmarried child under 18 years of age, of an immigrant admissible . . . , and is accompanying or following to join him, or (3) is not an immigrant as defined in section 3. . . .

(e) No quota immigrant shall be admitted under subdivision (d) if the entire number of immigrant visas which may be issued to quota immigrants of the same nationality for the fiscal year has already been issued. . . .

Sec. 18. If a quota immigrant of any nationality having an immigration visa is excluded from admission to the United States under the immigration laws and deported, or does not apply for admission to the United States before the expiration of the validity of the immigration visa, or if any alien of any nationality having an immigration visa issued to him as a quota immigrant is found not to be a quota immigrant, no additional immigration visa shall be issued in lieu thereof to any other immigrant.

Sec. 19. No alien seaman excluded from admission . . . shall be permitted to land . . . except temporarily for medical treatment, or pursuant to such regulations as the Attorney General may prescribe for the ultimate departure, removal, or deportation of such alien from the United States.

Sec. 23. Whenever any alien attempts to enter the United States the burden of proof shall be upon the alien to establish that he is not subject to exclusion under any of the provisions of the immigration laws.

Source: Act of May 26, 1924, ch. 190, 43 Stat. 153.

Indian Citizenship Act (1924)

Although Native Americans were the first people to live in what would later become the sovereign United States, those living on reservations were the very last to become full citizens. They received that status by an act of Congress on June 2, 1924.

Be it enacted by the Senate and House of Representatives of the United States of America in Congress assembled, That all non-citizen Indians born within the territorial limits of the United States be and they are hereby, declared to be citizens of the United States: *Provided,* That the granting of such citizenship shall not in any manner impair or otherwise affect the right of any Indian to tribal or other property. (43 Stat. 253; 8 U.S.C. 3.)

Source: Immigration and Nationality Laws and Regulations as of March 1, 1944 (Washington, DC: U.S. Government Printing Office, 1944).

Executive Order 9066, President Franklin D. Roosevelt (1942)

Following the Japanese attack on the U.S. naval base at Pearl Harbor, Hawaii, on December 7, 1941, and the U.S. declaration of war against the empire of Japan the following day, fears of an even larger attack on the U.S. mainland swept the West Coast. Rumors circulated that Japanese agents on American soil were helping prepare for an invasion. Although no proof of such a conspiracy ever surfaced, Japanese Americans came under suspicion by the federal government no less than by fellow citizens. On February 19, 1942, President Franklin D. Roosevelt issued Executive Order 9066, calling for the internment of all Japanese Americans (citizens or not) residing in the Western United States. By August 1942, more than 120,000 Japanese Americans had been rounded up and relocated to ten internment, or concentration, camps in the West and elsewhere; most were held until the conclusion of hostilities in 1945.

NOW, THEREFORE, by virtue of the authority vested in me as President of the United States, and Commander in Chief of the Army and Navy, I hereby authorize and direct the Secretary of War, and the Military commanders whom he may from time to time designate, whenever he or any designated Commander deems such action necessary or desirable, to prescribe military areas in such places and of such extent as he or the appropriate Military Commander may determine, from which any and all persons may be excluded, and with respect to which, the right of any person to enter, remain in, or leave shall be subject to whatever restrictions the Secretary of War or the appropriate Military Commander may impose in his discretion. The Secretary of War is hereby authorized to provide for residents of any such area who are excluded therefrom, such transportation, food, shelter, and other accommodations as may be necessary, in the judgment of the Secretary of War, of the said Military Commander, and until other arrangements are made, to accomplish the purpose of this order. The designation of military areas in any region or locality shall supersede designations of prohibited or restricted areas by the Attorney General under the proclamations of December 7 and 8, 1941, and shall supersede the responsibility and authority of the Attorney General under the said Proclamation in respect of such prohibited and restricted areas.

I hereby further authorize and direct the Secretary of War and the said Military Commanders to take such other steps as he or the appropriate Military Commander may deem advisable to enforce compliance with the restrictions applicable to each Military area hereinabove authorized to be designated, including the use of Federal troops and other Federal Agencies, with authority to accept assistance of state and local agencies.

I hereby further authorize and direct all Executive commanders in carrying out this Executive Order, including the furnishing of medical aid, hospitalization, food, clothing, transportation, use of land, shelter, and other supplies, equipment, utilities, facilities, and services.

This order shall not be construed as modifying or limiting in any way the authority granted under Executive Order 8972, dated December 12, 1941, nor shall it be construed as limiting or modifying the duty and responsibility of the Federal Bureau of Investigation, with respect to the investigation of alleged acts of sabotage or the duty and responsibility of the Attorney General and the Department of Justice under the Proclamations of December 7, and 8, 1941, prescribing regulations for the conduct and control of alien enemies, except as such duty and responsibility is superseded by the designation of military areas hereunder.

Source: Federal Register, vol. 7, no. 38 (February 1942).

Hirabayashi v. United States (1943)

In February 1942, President Franklin D. Roosevelt issued Executive Order 9066, calling for the internment of all Japanese Americans on the West Coast because of the threat they posed to national security amid war against Japan. One month later, on March 21, Congress passed legislation to enable the executive order and mobilize deportations. Almost immediately, Japanese Americans began to challenge the constitutionality of both the executive order and the congressional legislation. Among the first to do so was Gordon Hirabayashi, a U.S. citizen and student at the University of Washington at Seattle. Rather than report for relocation, Hirabayashi turned himself in to police for refusing to comply with the order. For his act of civil disobedience, Hirabayashi was arrested and sentenced to six months in prison. He appealed the case, which ultimately went before the U.S. Supreme Court. In Hirabayashi v. United States, *the high court ruled unanimously that Executive Order 9066 was constitutional on grounds of national security and military necessity and that Hirabayashi's conviction would stand.*

Mr. Chief Justice [Harlan] Stone delivered the opinion of the Court:

Appellant, an American citizen of Japanese ancestry, was convicted in the district court of violating the Act of Congress of March 21, 1942 . . . which makes it a misdemeanor knowingly to disregard restrictions made applicable by a military commander to persons in a military area prescribed by him as such, all as authorized by an Executive Order of the President.

The questions for our decision are whether the particular restriction violated, namely that all persons of Japanese ancestry residing in such an area be within their place of residence daily between the hours of 8:00 p.m. and 6:00 a.m., was adopted by the military command in the exercise of an unconstitutional delegation by Congress of its legislative power, and whether the restriction unconstitutionally discriminated between citizens of Japanese ancestry and those of other ancestries in violation of the Fifth Amendment.

The evidence showed that appellant had failed to report to the Civil Control Station on May 11 or May 12, 1942, as directed, to register for evacuation from the military area. He admitted failure to do so, and stated it had at all times been his belief that he would be waiving his rights as an American citizen by so [registering]. . . .

. . . [O]n March 22, 1942, General DeWitt issued Public Proclamation No. 3, 7 Federal Register 2543. After referring to the previous designation of military areas . . . it recited that "the present situation within these Military Areas and Zones requires as a matter of military necessity the establishment of certain regulations pertaining to all enemy aliens and all persons of Japanese ancestry within said Military Areas and Zones." . . . It accordingly declared and established that from and after March 27, 1942, "all alien Japanese . . . and all persons of Japanese ancestry residing or being within the geographic limits of Military Zone 1 . . . shall be within their place of residence between the hours of 8:00 p.m. and 6:00

a.m., which period is hereinafter referred to as the hours of curfew." . . .

The Chairman of the Senate Military Affairs Committee explained on the floor of the Senate that the purpose of the proposed legislation was to provide a means of enforcement of curfew orders and other military orders made pursuant to Executive Order 9066. . . . He also stated to the Senate that "reasons for suspected widespread fifth-column activity among Japanese" were to be found in the system of dual citizenship which Japan deemed applicable to American-born Japanese, and in the propaganda disseminated by Japanese consuls, Buddhist priests and other leaders among American-born children of Japanese. Such was stated to be the explanation of the contemplated evacuation from the Pacific Coast area of persons of Japanese ancestry, citizens as well as aliens.

The conclusion is inescapable that Congress, by the Act of March 21, 1942, ratified and confirmed Executive Order 9066. . . . The question then is not one of congressional power to delegate to the President the promulgation of the Executive Order, but whether, acting in cooperation, Congress and the Executive have constitutional authority to impose the curfew restrictions here complained of. . . .

. . . In the critical days of March, 1942, the danger to our war production by sabotage and espionage in this area [from Washington State to California] seems obvious. . . . The military commander's appraisal of facts in the light of the authorized standard, and the inferences which he drew from those facts, involved the exercise of his informed judgment. But as we have seen, those facts, and the inferences drawn from them, support the judgment of the military commander, that the danger of espionage and sabotage to our military resources was imminent, and that the curfew order was an appropriate measure to meet it. . . .

The Constitution as a continuously operating charter of government does not demand the impossible or the impractical. The essentials of the legislative function are preserved when Congress authorizes a statutory command to be operative, upon ascertainment of a basic conclusion of fact by a designated representative of the government. . . . The present statute, which authorized curfew orders made pursuant to Executive Order No. 9066 for the protection of war resources from espionage and sabotage, satisfies those requirements. Under the Executive Order the basic facts, determined by the military commander in light of knowledge then available, were whether that danger existed and whether a curfew order was an appropriate means of minimizing the danger. Since his findings to that effect were, as we have said, not without adequate support, the legislative function was performed and the sanction of the statute attached to violations of the curfew order. It is unnecessary to consider whether or to what extent such findings would support orders differing from the curfew order.

The conviction under the second count is without constitutional infirmity. Hence we have no occasion to review the conviction on the first count, since, as already stated, the sentences on the two counts are to run concurrently and conviction on the second is to sustain the sentence. For this reason also it is unnecessary to consider the Government's argument that compliance with the order to report at the Civilian Station did not necessarily entail confinement in a relocation center. Affirmed.

Source: 320 U.S. 81.

Repeal of Chinese Exclusion Acts (1943)

Beginning in 1882, Congress passed a series of laws that barred virtually all Chinese immigration into the United States. During World War II, however, China became a critical ally of the United States in the struggle against the Japanese Empire. As part of that alliance—and as a reflection of diminishing anti-Chinese prejudice in the United States—Congress repealed the Chinese Exclusion Acts in December 1943. Even in doing so, however, it established an annual national quota of just 105 per year. More Chinese would be allowed into the United States under various refugee laws following the communist takeover of mainland China in 1949, but large-scale Chinese immigration would have to await passage of the Immigration and Nationality Act of 1965, which ended the national quota system.

Be it enacted by the Senate and House of Representatives of the United States of America in Congress assembled, That the following Acts or parts of Acts relating to the exclusion or deportation of persons of the Chinese race are hereby repealed: [The Act then lists every Act or part of an Act passed since 1882.] *Provided,* That all charges for the maintenance or return of Chinese persons applying for admission to the United States shall hereafter be paid or reimbursed to the United States by the person, company, partnership, or corporation bringing such Chinese to a port of the United States as applicants for admission. . . .

Sec. 2. With the exception of Chinese wives of American citizens and those Chinese aliens coming under subsections (b), (d), (e) and (f) of section 4, Immigration Act of 1924 . . . all Chinese persons entering the United States annually as immigrants shall be allocated to the quota for the Chinese computed under the provisions of section 11 of the said Act. A preference up to 75 per centum of the quota shall be given to Chinese born and resident in China.

Source: Act of December 17, 1943, ch. 344, 57 Stat. 600.

Directive on European Refugees, President Harry S. Truman (1945)

Before and during World War II, the U.S. government generally refused to accept the large number of refugees—many of them Jewish—fleeing the horrors of Nazi genocide and expansionism. The end of the war left untold numbers of displaced persons scattered across Europe. To provide them refuge—and to assuage any guilt associated with the failure to take in more Nazi victims during the war—the United States moved to welcome more of the dispossessed. On December 22, 1945, President Harry S. Truman issued a directive on this subject.

The war has brought in its wake an appalling dislocation of populations in Europe. Many humanitarian organizations, including the United Nations Relief and Rehabilitation Administration are doing their utmost to solve the multitude of problems arising in connection with this dislocation of hundreds of thousands of persons. Every effort is being made to return the displaced persons and refugees in the various countries of Europe to their former homes. The great difficulty is that so many of these persons have no homes to which they may return. The immensity of the problem of displaced persons and refugees is almost beyond comprehension.

A number of countries in Europe, including Switzerland, Sweden, France, and England, are working toward its solution. The United States shares the responsibility to relieve the suffering. To the extent that our present immigration laws permit, everything possible should be done at once to facilitate the entrance of some of these displaced persons and refugees into the United States.

In this way we may do something to relieve human misery, and set an example to the other countries of the world which are able to receive some of these war sufferers. I feel that it is essential that we do this ourselves to show our good faith in requesting other nations to open their doors for this purpose.

Most of these persons are natives of Central and Eastern Europe and the Balkans. The immediate quotas for all those countries for one year total approximately 39,000, two-thirds of which are allotted to Germany. Under the law, in any single month the number of visas issued cannot exceed ten percent of the annual quota. This means that from now on only about 3,900 visas can be issued each month to persons who are natives of these countries.

Very few persons from Europe have migrated to the United States during the war years. In fiscal year 1942 only ten percent of the immigration quotas was used; in 1943, five percent; in 1944, six percent; and in 1945, seven percent. As of November 30, 1945, the end of the fifth month of the current fiscal year, only about ten percent of the quotas for the European countries has been used. These unused quotas however do not accumulate through the years, and I do not intend to ask the Congress to change this rule. . . .

I consider that common decency and fundamental comradeship of all human beings require us to do what lies within our power to see that our established immigration quotas are used in order to reduce human suffering. I am taking the necessary steps to see that this is done as quickly as possible. . . .

I am informed that there are various measures now pending before the Congress which would either prohibit or severely reduce further immigration. I hope that such legislation will not be passed. This period of unspeakable human distress is not the time for us to close or to narrow our gates. I wish to emphasize, however, that any effort to bring relief to these displaced persons and refugees must and will be strictly within the limits of the present quotas as imposed by law.

Upon the basis of a careful survey by the Department of State and the Immigration and Naturalization Service, it has been determined that if these persons were now applying for admission to the United States most of them would be admissible under the immigration laws. In the circumstances, it would be inhumane and wasteful to require these people to go all the way back to Europe merely for the purpose of applying there for immigration visas and returning to the United States. Many of them have close relatives, including sons and daughters, who are citizens of the United States and who have served and are serving honorably in the armed forces of our country. I am therefore directing the Secretary of State and the Attorney General to adjust the immigration status of the members of this group who may wish to remain here, in strict accordance with existing laws and regulations. . . .

The attached directive has been issued by me to the responsible government agencies to carry out this policy. I wish to emphasize, above all, that nothing in the directive will deprive a single American soldier or his wife or children of a berth on a vessel homeward bound, or delay their return. This is the opportunity for America to set an example for the rest of the world in cooperation towards alleviating human misery.

Source: Public Papers of the Presidents: Harry S. Truman (December 22, 1945).

Agricultural Act of 1949

To ensure a steady and adequate supply of agricultural workers, the United States moved to allow Mexican workers into the country in 1949, extending the Bracero Program begun in 1942 to address World War II labor shortages. Under the program, Mexican guest workers were allowed to enter the United States on a temporary basis for contract labor. While the 1949 legislation included measures designed to prevent abuse of workers, critics complained that such abuses continued anyway. The program was discontinued in 1964, by which time some 4.6 million guest workers had taken part.

Be it enacted by the Senate and House of Representatives of the United States of America in Congress assembled, That this Act may be cited as the "Agricultural Act of 1949."

Sec. 501. For the purpose of assisting in such production of agricultural commodities and products as the Secretary of Agriculture deems necessary, by supplying agricultural workers from the Republic of Mexico . . . the Secretary of Labor is authorized—

(1) to recruit workers . . .

(2) to establish and operate reception centers at or near places of actual entry of such workers into the continental United States for the purpose of receiving and housing such workers for their employment in, or departure from, the continental United States;

(3) to provide transportation for such workers . . .

(4) to provide workers with such subsistence . . . at reception centers;

(5) to assist such workers and employers in negotiating contracts for agricultural employment . . .

(6) to guarantee the performance by employers of provisions of such contracts. . . .

Sec. 502. No workers shall be made available under this title to any employer unless such employer enters into an agreement with the United States—

(1) to indemnify the United States against loss . . .

(2) to reimburse the United States for essential expenses . . .

(3) to pay to the United States, in any case in which a worker is not returned [costs]. . . .

Sec. 505. Workers recruited under this title who are not citizens of the United States shall be admitted to the United States subject to the immigration laws. . . .

Sec. 506.(c) Workers recruited under the provisions of this title shall not be subject to the head tax levied under section 2 of the Immigration Act of 1917. . . .

Source: Act of October 31, 1949, ch. 792, 63 Stat. 1051.

Immigration and Nationality Act (McCarran-Walter Act) (1952)

As the Cold War and anticommunist sentiment intensified in the late 1940s and early 1950s, Congress moved to alter immigration and naturalization laws to meet changing national security interests. The Immigration and Nationality Act of 1952, also known as the McCarran-Walter Act (after its congressional sponsors, Senator Patrick McCarran, D-NY, and Representative Francis Walter, D-PA), was largely a reiteration of the 1917 and 1924 literacy and quota acts, with some increase in immigration from Asia. But in a key provision prompted by the Cold War, Congress also sought to block the naturalization of any person deemed a threat to national security; that section of the legislation is excerpted below. The Immigration and Nationality Act of 1952 passed over President Harry S. Truman's veto.

Chapter 2—Nationality Through Naturalization

Sec. 311. The right of a person to become a naturalized citizen of the United States shall not be denied or abridged because of race or sex or because such a person is married. Notwithstanding section 405(b), this section shall apply to any person whose petition for naturalization shall hereafter be filed, or shall have been pending on the effective date of this Act.

Sec. 312. No person except as otherwise provided in this title shall hereafter be naturalized as a citizen of the United States upon his own petition who cannot demonstrate—

(1) an understanding of the English language, including the ability to read, write, and speak words in ordinary usage in the English language. . . .

(2) a knowledge and understanding of the fundamentals of the history, and of the principles and form of government, of the United States.

Sec. 313. (a) Notwithstanding the provisions of section 405(b), no person shall be naturalized as a citizen of the United States—[the act lists subsections (1) through (6) which prohibit the naturalization of anarchists, communists, totalitarians, and those who believe or publish such, etc.]. . . .

Sec. 316. (a) No person, except as otherwise provided for in this title, shall be naturalized unless such petitioner, (1) immediately preceding the date of filing his petition for naturalization has resided continuously, after being lawfully admitted for permanent residence, within the United States for at least five years and during the five years . . . has been physically present therein for periods totaling at least half of that time, and who has resided within the State in which petition is filed for at least six months, (2) has resided continuously within the United States from the date of the petition up to the time of admission to citizenship, and (3) during all the periods referred to in this subsection has been and still is a person of good moral character, attached to the principles of the Constitution of the United States, and well disposed to the good order and happiness of the United States. [The subsection then specifies when and how absences are accepted as exceptions to the "continuous" residing provision.] . . .

Sec. 337. (a) A person who has petitioned for naturalization shall, in order to be and before being admitted to citizenship, take in open court an oath (1) to support the Constitution of the United States; (2) to renounce and abjure absolutely and entirely all allegiance and fidelity to any foreign prince, potentate, state, or sovereignty of whom or which the petitioner was before a subject or citizen; (3) to support and defend the Constitution and laws of the United States against all enemies, foreign and domestic; (4) to bear true faith and allegiance [to] the same; and (5) (A) to bear arms on behalf of the United States when required by law, or (B) to perform noncombatant service in the Armed Forces of the United States when required by law, or (C) to perform work of national importance under civilian direction when required by law. . . .

Sec. 349. (a) From and after the effective date of this Act a person who is a national of the United States whether by birth or naturalization, shall lose his nationality by—

(1) obtaining naturalization in a foreign state upon his own application, upon an application filed in his behalf by a parent, guardian, or duly authorized agent, or through the naturalization of a parent having legal custody of such person. . . .

(2) taking an oath or making an affirmation or other formal declaration of allegiance to a foreign state or a political subdivision thereof . . .

(3) entering, or serving in, the armed forces of a foreign state . . . unless [prior to doing so] authorized by the Secretary of State and the Secretary of Defense . . .

(4) accepting, serving in, or performing the duties of any office, post, or employment under the government of a foreign state or a political subdivision thereof . . .

(5) voting in a political election in a foreign state . . .

(6) making a formal renunciation of nationality before a diplomatic or consular officer of the United States in a foreign state, in such form as may be prescribed by the Secretary of State . . .

(7) making in the United States a formal written renunciation of nationality in such form as may be prescribed by . . . the Attorney General . . .

(8) deserting the military, air, or naval forces of the United States in a time of war, if and when he is convicted thereof by court martial and as the result of such conviction is dismissed or dishonorably discharged from the service . . .

(9) committing any act of treason against, or attempting to overthrow, or bearing arms against, the United States . . .

(10) departing from or remaining outside of the jurisdiction of the United States in time of war . . . for the purpose of evading or avoiding . . . service in the military. . . .

Source: Act of June 27, 1952, ch. 477, 66 Stat. 163.

Whom We Shall Welcome, Report of the President's Commission on Immigration and Naturalization (1953)

In January 1953, the President's Commission on Immigration and Naturalization published its report on U.S. immigration and immigration policy, including proposals for change. Formally titled Whom We Shall Welcome, *the report called for abolishing the national quota system and opening America's gates to more immigrants. In the sections reproduced here, the*

writers of the report outline the impact of U.S. immigration law on national security and the worldwide struggle against communism. Their recommendations include entry for more refugees from communism but vigilance against "subversives." The commission's recommendation to end quotas would have to await the more liberal political climate of the 1960s, finally becoming law with the Immigration and Nationality Act of 1965.

Chapter 3. Immigration and our Foreign Policy

Escapees from Iron Curtain Countries

The escapee situation is even more critical at the present time. There are 20,000–25,000 persons, housed in camps in Germany, Austria, Italy, Trieste, Greece, and Turkey, who have escaped from behind the Iron Curtain since January 1, 1948. These escapees are non-Germans. They are, in general, the people from behind the Iron Curtain who have most recently arrived, risking life and limb, leaving behind everything but the clothes on their backs, in order to live in freedom. Some of them have come because of the enticements held out to them by the Voice of America or by other Western propaganda for democracy.

Now that the Communists have tightened up the border watch, the flow has dropped to about 500 a month. How many try and fail, paying for the attempt with their lives, is anyone's guess, but at one point the mortality rate was estimated to be over 80 percent.

Unfortunately, escapees are not likely to find the welcome and freedom they thought would await them. They arrive in countries already surfeited with refugees. They cannot, for the most part, continue on to the United States, because of restrictions in our immigration law. And so most of them are put in camps, without work, with none of the comforts and few of the privileges or rights of free men.

The United States has a special responsibility toward these people, and a special interest in them. At least some of them have come because our propaganda lured them. If sacrifice earns the right to liberty, they have earned it. We cannot turn them away and expect those still behind the Iron Curtain to believe us ever again.

Furthermore, they are, generally speaking, convinced opponents of Communist tyranny. They have experienced it, and they want no more of it. They can be helpful to us. And yet, we have done very little for them and nothing to welcome them to our shores.

Out of the current Mutual Security appropriation, a fund of $4,300,000 has been set aside to help the resettlement of escapees. The announcement caused hopes to rise among those escapees in camps in Europe. It brought a short-lived increase in the rate of escape through the Iron

Curtain. Its results have been negligible because the fund is too small and because the United States and the other free nations have formulated no adequate programs for their care and resettlement.

The Commission believes that effective measures should be taken and adequate appropriations made to provide reasonable reception, care, and migration opportunities for escapees from Communism.

The escapee problem is not a partisan political issue. It is generally agreed that something should be done immediately. President Truman said in his special Message to the Congress on March 24, 1952:

> . . . specific aid and assistance should be provided for the people who are fleeing at the risk of their lives from southern and eastern Europe. These people are Balts, Poles, Czechs, Slovaks, Hungarians, Bulgarians, Rumanians, Albanians, Ukrainians, and Russians.
>
> These people face a desperate situation. Not only do they arrive destitute, with only what they can carry on their backs, but they find themselves in totally strange lands among strange peoples speaking strange languages. The local authorities do not have adequate resources to care for them properly. These people need better care when they first arrive, and they need assistance if they are to move on and resettle elsewhere.
>
> The miserable conditions in which these fugitives from communism find themselves, and their present inability to emigrate to new homes and start new lives, lead inevitably to despair. Their disillusionment is being effectively exploited by Communist propaganda. These men and women are friends of freedom. They include able and courageous fighters against communism. They ask only for an opportunity to play a useful role in the fight for freedom. It is the responsibility of the free world to afford them this opportunity.

He recommended a program authorizing 21,000 escapees to migrate to the United States over a 3-year period, plus supplemental reception, care, payment of cost of ocean transportation, and a program of education for leadership for those who choose to remain in Europe.

President-Elect Eisenhower said in a speech on October 17, 1952:

> A contest for world leadership—in fact, for survival—exists between the Communist idea and the American ideal. That contest is being waged in the minds and hearts of human beings. We say—and we sincerely believe—that we are on the side of freedom; that we are on the side of humanity. We say—and we know—that the Communists are on the side of slavery, the side of inhumanity.
>
> Yet to the Czech, the Pole, the Hungarian who takes his life in his hands and crosses the frontier tonight—or to the Italian who goes to some American consulate—this ideal that beckoned him can be a mirage because of the McCarran Act.

Secretary of State Acheson said, in his statement to the Commission:

> Another special problem of equal importance is that of the escapees from Communist countries. These people arrive in the border countries destitute. They have lost their homes, their property, and often their families. They have a deep hatred for communism—they know from experience what it means. They have a deep love of freedom, having been so long without it. If they are left to shift for themselves in lands already burdened with surplus population they will not be able to find work, and will be disillusioned about the meaning of Western Democracy. As their disillusion grows, and word of it spreads, it will be difficult for us to convince the captive populations behind the Iron Curtain that the free world is interested in their fate. With our aid other countries are trying to make possible a new life for these escapees. But these efforts do not by themselves meet the need. To welcome escapees to the United States on a scale impossible under the present quota restrictions, would be a vital step in making our policy toward the satellite peoples effective.

Prof. Philip E. Mosley, president of the East European fund set up by the Ford Foundation, and member of the Russian Institute of Columbia University, testified:

> I feel that we will strengthen our own country and the free world . . . if we will open a door, or rather if we will reopen a door to the people who under intolerable pressure are escaping every day and every week from the Iron Curtain countries.

American foreign policy toward the countries behind the Iron Curtain, particularly the satellites, is to emphasize that their people would be better off on our side. **But in connection with escapees, a most vital aspect of the "cold war," American immigration law lies directly athwart our foreign policy....**

Chapter 15. Security Protections

Since the earliest days of the Republic, Congress has expressed concern over the activities of subversive aliens in our midst. The Alien Act of 1798 authorized the President to order the departure of any alien whom he deemed dangerous to the United States. The Alien Enemy Act of 1798, passed 2 weeks later, permitted the apprehension, restraint, and removal of alien enemies, if deemed necessary for the public safety. The first law was so unpopular and violated such fundamental American principles that it was allowed to expire after 2 years. The second, limited in application to time of war or threatened invasion, is still in effect.

It was not, however, until 1903 that the law barred

the entry of aliens who were regarded as inimical to the safety and security of the country. By a 1903 statute, anarchists and those who believed in or advocated the forcible overthrow of the Government of the United States, or of all forms of Government, or the assassination of public officials, were denied admission to the United States. These provisions were continued and strengthened in 1907 and 1917. The Anarchist Act of 1918, as amended in 1920, enlarged the description of aliens classed as subversive. It barred from the United States aliens who write, publish or cause to be written or published, or circulate, distribute or display, or possess for such purposes, any written or printed matter advising, advocating, or teaching opposition to organized forms of Government, or the overthrow by force or violence of Government, or the killing of officers generally, or unlawful damage to or destruction of property, or sabotage.

The Supreme Court, in 1939, had occasion to interpret the laws which authorize the exclusion of aliens deemed subversive, and the deportation of those in the United States who were members of or affiliated with subversive organizations. The Supreme Court's decision required a finding by the Government of present membership or affiliation, in order to support the exclusion or deportation of an alien.

However, the Congress reversed this situation in the Alien Registration Act of 1940, which made such membership at any time a ground for exclusion and deportation. Other enactments between 1940 and 1950 generally strengthened and, to some extent, enlarged the description of classes to be excluded or deported from the United States as subversives; and authorized the denial of visas to, and the exclusion of, aliens seeking to enter the United States for the purpose of engaging in activities which would endanger public safety.

In the years immediately following the close of hostilities of World War II, a growing awareness developed of the inadequacies of existing law to cope with Communism's drive for world domination. To meet this increasing threat, Congress enacted the Internal Security Act of 1950. This Act greatly enlarged the proscribed classes of subversive aliens. For the first time the Communist Party was mentioned by name. The terms "communism," "Communist organization," "Communist front organization," "totalitarianism," "advocates," and "doctrine" were defined by statute. Moreover, the Act makes membership, association or affiliation with an organization required to register as a subversive organization under the Subversive Activities Control Act of 1950, a ground for exclusion and deportation.

In addition the discretion of the Attorney General to admit subversive aliens, under preexisting legislation, was completely eliminated with respect to aliens returning to the United States to resume a permanent residence after a temporary absence abroad. Subversive aliens seeking temporary admission could do so only under a severely curtailed discretion of the Attorney General, and, where exercised, the Attorney General was required to make a detailed report to Congress. Many provisions of the Internal Security Act of 1950 were attacked at the time as being unnecessarily harsh, improper, and not in the best interests of the country.

The provisions of the Internal Security Act of 1950 have been carried forward into the Immigration and Nationality Act of 1952, without substantial change. The only significant difference in the treatment of subversive aliens under the 1952 Act is that the definition of "totalitarian party" is limited to an organization which advocates the establishment of a totalitarian dictatorship or totalitarianism in the United States. This would bar admission of members of the Communist Party, but some have expressed concern that it would not bar from the United States members of the Nazi, Fascist, or Falange parties.

Security Screening Process

The various administrative agencies have endeavored to establish effective processes to screen out and bar subversive people. The State Department has devised an elaborate screening process in an attempt to ascertain whether applicants for visas come within the statutory designations of subversives. The law requires each applicant for a visa to prepare a lengthy, documented application. In addition, the consular officers usually require the alien to submit a questionnaire designed, when completed, to provide a basis for a background check of the alien from a security point of view.

After an examination of the papers submitted by the alien, sources of information available in the local Foreign Service posts of the United States and so-called "look-out" notices from the Department of State and the Department of Justice are checked. American officers at the Foreign Service post, such as the military, naval, air, or economic attachés, are consulted to ascertain whether their respective spheres of operation have uncovered any information which might have a bearing on the alien's admissibility. Checks with other sources of information available abroad are utilized wherever practicable.

The alien is invited to appear at the consular establishment to be examined under oath concerning his background and other factors bearing upon his eligibility for admission to the United States. If any derogatory information is uncovered, further action on the alien's application is suspended pending additional examination or pending reference of the application to the Department of State. Should the derogatory information indicate that the alien falls within one of the proscribed subversive classes, the interrogation is usually conducted more thoroughly in order firmly to establish the facts relating to the alien's admissibility. The alien may or may not be given an opportunity to rebut the derogatory information on file.

The consular officer may, of course, refuse to issue a visa at any stage of the investigation, but if he entertains any doubt as to the alien's admissibility from a security standpoint, he is required by regulation to refer the case to the Department of State for an advisory opinion. For former voluntary members of proscribed organizations, no visa may be issued without an advisory opinion. If an advisory opinion from the Department of State is unfavorable, no visa may be issued. However, even if the Department of State renders a favorable advisory opinion, the consular officer may still refuse a visa as he sees fit. Wherever possible the Department of State conducts an independent and supplemental security check, utilizing various intelligence facilities of our Government.

Special provisions of law which relate to accredited officials of foreign governments, or representatives of foreign governments to international organizations, generally make impossible the application of normal screening processes to them. On the other hand, classes of aliens who, because of their profession, occupation, or previous status, present special problems, are subjected to even closer scrutiny and additional checks.

Possession of a visa does not entitle an alien to enter the United States; a visa is, in effect, a permit to apply for admission. An alien with a visa, who applies for admission to the United States, is required to satisfy the Attorney General that he is eligible under the immigration laws for admission. The Immigration and Naturalization Service has authority to make a completely independent security check upon an alien presenting a visa. Immigration officials at this point have the benefit of advice and information from various intelligence sources in the United States and elsewhere.

Once an alien is in the United States, he may be deported for subversive activities. The investigations preceding the arrest in deportation and the consequent hearing may have been made by one or more of the several intelligence agencies of the United States Government or may have been conducted by the Immigration and Naturalization Service.

Thus, at each stage of the immigration process, the issuance of a visa, the admission at ports of entry, or deportation, the facilities for the detection or apprehension of the subversive alien represent the combined efforts of many intelligence and investigating agencies in addition to the agencies administering the immigration law.

The Commission made efforts to learn whether security agencies, and those responsible for the administration of the immigration laws had any specific recommendations to make in order to strengthen the security provisions of such and related laws. At the time these efforts were made, the act of 1952 had not become effective. However, the Commission is able to report that as of the time of its inquiry, the security measures in the laws and regulations were believed to be adequate. The sole exception was the suggestion that the Commission recommend provisions to enable immigration authorities to exclude applicants for visas who are active members of, or believe in the principles advocated by, Nazi, Fascist, and other such totalitarian organizations.

Generally speaking, the immigration laws deal with three groups of subversives: (1) spies and saboteurs; (2) present members and affiliates of subversive organizations; and (3) former members or affiliates of subversive organizations.

Spies and Saboteurs

The act of 1952 makes ineligible to receive a visa and requires the exclusion of:

> Aliens who the consular officer or the Attorney General knows or has reason to believe seek to enter the United States solely, principally, or incidentally to engage in activities which would be prejudicial to the public interest, or endanger the welfare, safety, or security of the United States; . . .
>
> Aliens with respect to whom the consular officer or the Attorney General knows or has reasonable ground to believe probably would, after entry, (A) engage in activities which would be prohibited by the laws of the United States relating to espionage, sabotage, public disorder, or in other activity subversive to the national security, (B) engage in any activity a purpose of which is the opposition to, or the control or overthrow of, the Government of the United States, by force, violence, or other unconstitutional means, or (C) Join, affiliate with, or participate in the activities of any organization which is registered or required to be registered under section 7 of the Subversive Activities Control Act of 1950 . . .

Such aliens, even if they are permanent residents returning after a temporary absence abroad, are specifically denied the benefits of the exercise of discretion. Provisions relating to the parole of aliens into the United States, or to the waiver of documents for nonimmigrant aliens, are not intended by Congress to include these subversive aliens, save for the possible purpose of prosecution for crime. Such aliens may be deported at any time, without regard to when they entered the United States.

Legislation which establishes an absolute bar against admission to the United States of those whose purpose in entering is to engage in activities which violate our laws relating to espionage, sabotage, public disorder or national security must remain on our statute books and be strictly enforced.

These statutory provisions give authority to deal with spies and saboteurs. However, the act of 1952 gives a consular officer the absolute and unreviewable power to bar aliens whom he "knows or has reason to believe seek to enter the United States solely, principally, or incidentally to engage in activities which would be prejudicial to the public interest," or with respect to whom, the consular officer "knows or has reasonable ground to believe probably would, after entry" engage in subversive activities. . . . The difficulties are here aggravated because the statutory language is so undefined. It is susceptible of as many different interpretations as there are men applying it. Such absolute and unreviewable discretion is not necessary for the protection of the security of the United States.

The statute should without doubt leave ample room for the exercise of discretion for the protection of the national security, but it should contain definite standards to guide administrative action, so as to guard against abuse. The vague language of the act of 1952 does not meet this need, and it should be revised so as to specify that it applies to aliens who seek to enter, or who are believed to be seeking to enter for the purpose of violating the criminal laws of the United States relating to espionage, sabotage, and public order; or violating the laws relating to the protection of the conduct of military and foreign affairs; and relating to the protection of other activities and functions of the government and other public agencies, national, state and local, upon which the national security depends.

The administrative review elsewhere recommended for visa denial, exclusion, and deportation actions should be applicable here. . . .

Present Members and Affiliates of Subversive Organizations

The law forbids entry to aliens who are anarchists or who are members or affiliates of the Communist Party or other totalitarian organizations, or who advocate or teach opposition to or violent overthrow of all organized government, or who write, publish, display, or circulate or who possess for circulation any written or printed matter which teaches or advocates world communism, opposition to or forceful overthrow of government, the killing of officers of government, the destruction of property or sabotage. Subversive aliens barred from admission to the United States are not limited to those who are members of the proscribed organizations, but also includes those who are affiliated with such groups.

With respect to all classes of subversive aliens, except anarchists, the law authorizes the issuance of a visa to such an alien if he establishes to the satisfaction of a consular officer, and the consular officer finds, that the membership or affiliation of the alien in a subversive organization is involuntary or occurred when the alien was under 16 years of age. It is necessary, in addition, however, that at the time the alien applies for admission to the United States the Attorney General must independently be satisfied and also find that the alien to whom a visa was so issued was involuntarily a member of or affiliated with any of the enumerated subversive classes.

The law authorizes the deportation of any alien who at the time of entry was within any of the classes excluded by law. It also provides for the deportation of any member of each of the categories of subversive aliens who is, or at any time after entry has become, a member of any of the proscribed classes of subversive aliens. Discretionary relief in connection with deportation is denied to aliens who are present members of subversive groups.

There can be no doubt that present members or affiliates of subversive organizations should be excluded from the United States. The issue is what is to be regarded as "member," "affiliate," or a "subversive organization." In these respects, the Commission believes that our present laws are not adequate. In part, the difficulty is that the act of 1952 is lengthy, complex, repetitive, and obscure.

As to membership, the Commission believes that the provision of the present law exempting "involuntary" members is desirable and sound. The purpose of the immigration law should be to bar only those aliens who, by their membership or affiliation with subversive groups, have identified themselves with the aims and principles of those groups. These exemptions should be interpreted broadly, so that the statutory injunction will encompass only those who were subversives at heart and will not reach those who were merely nominal members, or as a result of compulsion or mistake. Such involuntary membership or affiliation merits the exception which the statute gives it.

"Affiliation" is not fully defined in the 1952 Act, and the statute merely states:

> The giving, loaning, or promising of support or of money or any other thing of value for any purpose to any organization shall be presumed to constitute affiliation therewith; but nothing in this paragraph shall be construed as an exclusive definition of affiliation.

This definition is an improvement over the similar one contained in the Internal Security Act of 1950 which made the giving, loaning, or promising of support or of money a conclusive presumption of affiliation. Nevertheless, even this improved definition should be read in the light of the congressional expression of need for legislation controlling subversive activities, contained in the Internal Security Act of 1950:

> In carrying on the activities referred to in paragraph 6 [establishment of Communist totalitarian dictatorship as part of the world Communist movement], such Communist organizations in various countries are organized on a secret, conspiratorial basis and operate to a substantial extent through organizations, commonly known as "Communist fronts," which in most instances are created and maintained, or used, in such manner as to conceal the facts as to their true character and purposes and their membership. One result of this method of operation is that such affiliated organizations are able to obtain financial and other support from persons who would not extend such support if they knew the true purposes of and the actual nature of the control and influence exerted upon such "Communist fronts."

The security of the United States must be protected against aliens guilty of true "affiliation" with subversive organizations. However, the statutory definition of "affiliation" condemns those who give support to front organizations "for any purpose," and thus may reach the innocent as well as the guilty.

The definition of "affiliation" should make it clear that the law bars those aliens who by their support or contribution or other form of affiliation knowingly and willingly seek to further the subversive aims and principles of the organizations. This proposal is in keeping with the present law's provision authorizing the admission to the United States and the naturalization of aliens who became affiliated with a communist organization without knowledge of its character.

In one respect, the act of 1952 leaves a security loophole, and so does not go far enough to protect the national security. Although the statute attempts to encompass every activity and belief that might be deemed subversive, it fails to ban members or affiliates of foreign totalitarian organizations, other than Communist. It bars admission to

> aliens who are members of or affiliated with . . . (IV) the Communist or any other totalitarian party of any State of the United States, of any foreign state, or of any political or geographical subdivision of any foreign state . . .

Comprehensive, though it sounds, this subsection may not bar Nazis, Fascists, or other totalitarian groups who are not Communists. This clause was carried forward verbatim from the Internal Security Act of 1950. But, whereas the Internal Security Act defines the terms "totalitarian dictatorship" and "totalitarianism" as

> . . . systems of government not representative in fact, characterized by (A) the existence of a single political party, organized on a dictatorial basis, with as close an identity between such party and its policies and the governmental policies of the country in which it exists, that the party and the government constitute an indistinguishable unit, and (B) the forcible suppression of opposition to such party, . . .

the act of 1952 adds to the above definition the following:

> The term "totalitarian party" means an organization which advocates the establishment in the United States of a totalitarian dictatorship or totalitarianism . . .

Both the Senate and House Committee reports are silent on the significance of the definition limiting a totalitarian party to one which advocates the establishment of totalitarianism "in the United States." It would appear, however, that the new definition is intended to exclude from the ban of the immigration laws totalitarian parties such as the Nazis, Fascists, and Falangists who are believed not to advocate the establishment of a totalitarian dictatorship in the United States.

No less than communism, other forms of totalitarianism degrade the dignity of man and deprive him of those rights which our Declaration of Independence holds to be unalienable. It is contended that the law should make a distinction between present membership in the Communist Party and present membership in other totalitarian parties, on the ground that communism is the only present menace.

While such a distinction appears plausible in the light of the imminence of the Communist peril, the resurgence of neo-Nazism and neo-Fascism in Germany and Italy underlines the danger of treating such totalitarian movements too lightly. Nazi and Fascists and other advocates of totalitarianism may not be developing plans today to overthrow the Government of the United States or any other democratic government by force and violence. There was a period, however, when they did attempt to dominate the world. The cost of stopping that effort was the heaviest ever paid in the history of the world. The millions of graves of those who died that democracy might survive, or who perished as victims of mass murder; the hundreds of thousands who were maimed; the millions who were stripped of their possessions and forced to undergo undescribable suffering, privation and misery; the destruction of the economic resources of once prosperous and happy peoples—these results of the evil ambitions, the cruelties of Nazism and Fascism should keep the United States alert forevermore to the danger from that source. The Communists and the Nazis pooled their ideologies and their plans for world conquest to begin World War II. The subsequent disintegration of that unholy partnership was fortunate for the democracies, but we shall be inviting disaster if we receive the disciples of one form of totalitarianism while arming for defense against the other.

The Commission deems the present adherents of all forms of totalitarianism to be hostile to our way of life and believes they should be banned from the United States.

A problem that has troubled the Commission has been the undesirable alien who is a product of our own society. Elsewhere, the Commission has urged that such aliens not be deported. Where such an alien is a present subversive, a special issue arises. Apart from the fact that such an alien is a product of our society, the difficulty, as pointed out to the Commission by the Immigration and Naturalization Service, is that deportation orders for subversives often prove futile. Mr. Justice Jackson succinctly stated the problem in his dissenting opinion in *United States v. Spector,* 343 U.S. 169 at pages 179–180.

> A deportation policy can be successful only to the extent that some other state is willing to receive those we expel. But, except selected individuals who can do us more harm abroad than here, what Communist power will cooperate with our deportation policy by receiving our expelled Communist aliens? And what non-Communist power feels such confidence in its own domestic security that it can risk taking in persons this stable and powerful Republic finds dangerous to its security? World conditions seem to frustrate the policy of deportation of subversives. Once they gain admission here, they are our problem and one that cannot be shipped off to some other part of the world.

A law which cannot be enforced brings the entire administration of justice into disrepute.

The Commission requested the Immigration and Naturalization Service for advice and recommendations to meet the problem of aliens who are under orders of deportation, but cannot be deported because no country will accept them. The answer was that the Internal Security Act of 1950 had provided, and the act of 1952 had continued, certain limited sanctions to aid in effectuating an order of deportation against persons in the subversive, criminal and other undesirable groups, and that no other methods of dealing with this matter had been devised.

Under such circumstances, therefore, the Commis-

sion believes that this country should accept as its own responsibility all those aliens who are the product of our own society.

The Commission recommends that

(1) **present members of subversive or totalitarian organizations, or persons who, by their present affiliation with such organizations, manifest their belief in or sympathy with the aims and principles of such organizations, should be denied visas and should be excluded from admission to the United States. Present membership or affiliation should create a presumption of such belief or sympathy, subject to countervailing evidence to prove that such membership or affiliation was involuntary.**

(2) **The definition of "totalitarian party," "totalitarian dictatorship," and "totalitarianism" should be clarified so that it embraces all aliens in sympathy with the governmental theories and policies of totalitarianism as that word is defined in the Internal Security Act of 1950.**

(3) **"Affiliation" as used in the immigration laws should be defined so that it embraces only those aliens who, by their action and conduct, have demonstrated an association with totalitarian groups because of sympathy for or agreement with the subversive aims and principles of such groups.**

(4) **Alien members or affiliates of subversive organizations who were lawfully admitted to the United States for permanent residence prior to reaching the age of 16 years, or who were lawfully admitted for permanent residence and have resided in the United States continuously for at least 20 years, should not be subject to deportation, but should be dealt with in the same manner as subversive citizens.**

Former Membership or Affiliation with Subversive Organizations

At one time, as witness the Alien Registration Act of 1940, present and former members of subversive organizations were treated alike. However, in the act of 1952, Congress recognized that former membership in or affiliation with subversive groups or organizations should not be an absolute bar to admission or stay in this country. It made two exceptions. The first is where such membership or affiliation was involuntary or occurred when the alien was under 16 years of age. The second is where membership or affiliation has been terminated for 5 years and for that period the alien has been "actively opposed" to such subversive ideologies, and where the admission of the alien "would be in the public interest." Each case in this last category must be reported to the Congress.

The deportation of former members or affiliates of subversive classes is, as in the case of present members, provided for by the law. However, unlike present members, former members or affiliates of subversive groups are eligible, under severely limited conditions, to receive discretionary relief by way of suspension of deportation.

The problem of past membership or affiliation is obviously a difficult one. If there is merely a severance of formal bonds of association without a corresponding repudiation of sympathetic belief in the aims and principles of the subversive group, such aliens continue to be threats to our security.

A former member who has made a genuine break with subversive ideology offers no threat to our security. Indeed experience has shown that such converts may represent very stable adherents to the principles of democracy because they are less likely again to succumb to the false blandishments of totalitarianism. **The removal of the absolute bar against former—and now reformed—subversive aliens strengthens our own internal and external security and advances our foreign policy.**

However, the act of 1952 contains other important defects. For example, the requirement of 5 year active opposition to a formerly held totalitarian ideology may defeat important objectives of our intelligence and foreign policy agencies. Escapees who come out from behind the Iron Curtain, or defectors from communism elsewhere, may be of vital and immediate importance to our security and defense as well as to our foreign policy. And yet they must wait 5 years, although there may be conclusive proof of complete reformation in a shorter period of time. Indeed, retention of an inflexible 5-year bar against former subversives might seriously impair the Commission's proposals to grant priority to refugees from communism (Chapter 9).

The requirement of "active" opposition to former doctrines misses the point. Most people who have genuinely renounced subversive ideas do not become active pamphleteers, speakers or professional antitotalitarians; the genuineness of their opposition to totalitarianism cannot be measured by the loudness of their disclaimers.

There is an inconsistency in our laws relating to former membership or affiliation in subversive organizations. The act of 1952 carries forward the previous law's failure to coordinate the naturalization and deportation directives aimed at former members of subversive organizations. The naturalization law permits the admission to citizenship of former subversives whose membership in the proscribed organization ended more than 10 years earlier. But the deportation statute apparently permits the expulsion of such former subversives at any time, even after 10 years has expired since the membership or association with the subversive group terminated. It would seem reasonable to

suppose that if a former member of a subversive group is eligible for naturalization after 10 years he should by the same token be able to avoid deportation.

There are also the grossly inconsistent provisions to the effect that a former member of a subversive organization, who actively opposed that subversive organization for a period of 5 years, may now be admitted into the United States although he was never here before, while a long-time resident alien who 30 years ago resigned from membership in a subversive organization, left it, and has since actively opposed it, must be deported.

The Commission believes that the provisions of the act of 1952 to the effect that membership in or affiliation with subversive organizations should not necessarily be a bar to entry into the United States are sound; and the Commission recommends that these same provisions be extended to cover deportation procedures, so that former membership in or affiliation with subversive organizations genuinely repudiated over a period of at least 5 years, should not be a ground for deportation.

The Commission recommends that the requirement of active opposition should be amended by deleting the word "active," thus making its benefits available to all opponents of totalitarianism. The Commission recommends that the requirement of 5 years opposition should be subject to waiver in appropriate cases, after thorough screening and approval by the appropriate security agencies of the United States. This would make possible the admission of bona fide escapees and defectors.

The Commission recommends that the immigration law apply the same conditions to former members and affiliates of all totalitarian parties, whether they were Communist, Nazi, Fascist, or other such parties.

It should be noted, too, that the law requires a finding by both the consular officer and the Attorney General that the admission of the alien would be in the public interest. Without criteria under which "in the public interest" may be measured, the phrase seems too vague for effective administration. It is quite conceivable that administrative officers might seldom, if ever, find that the admission of a former Communist, Nazi, or Fascist would affirmatively be in the public interest. **The Commission recommends that the law should require a finding that the admission of a former subversive would not be contrary to the public interest.**

Exclusion Without Hearing

Security considerations sometimes create special problems in connection with otherwise normal immigration procedures. At least for the past 60 years, an alien has been entitled to a hearing before he can be excluded at a port of entry. However, when the ground for his exclusion involves confidential information, the disclosure of which would be detrimental to the best interests of the United States, there is a conflict between two important values. On the one side is the security of the United States; on the other is the fundamental concept of American law that a person is entitled to a fair hearing before the Government takes action affecting him.

From at least 1893 until 1941, no alien—not even a subversive—could be excluded without a hearing. In 1941 such provision was made. The Passport Act of 1918 authorized the President in time of war or national emergency to impose additional restrictions and prohibitions on entry into and departure from the United States upon a finding that the interests of the United States so required. The President issued a proclamation on November 14, 1941, reciting the existence of a national emergency and declaring that "no alien should be permitted to enter the United States if it appears to the satisfaction of the Secretary of State that such entry would be prejudicial to the interests of the United States," as provided in regulations issued by the Secretary of State with the concurrence of the Attorney General. These regulations authorized the Attorney General to deny hearings when a person is excludable "on the basis of information of a confidential nature, the disclosure of which would be prejudicial to the public interest."

From the evidence before the Commission, including testimony before congressional committees and various United States Government briefs in the Supreme Court, this measure was intended to have only limited application. It seems that this procedure was designed to provide a legal sanction for denying access to the United States during war or national emergency only in those special cases where disclosure of the information or the source of the information, on the basis of which the exclusion is ordered for security reasons, would be contrary to the national interest.

During the war years, this new procedure was sparingly used. The Immigration and Naturalization Service reports that only a negligible number of aliens were excluded without a hearing. However, with the end of hostilities immigration to the United States was resumed on a larger scale. In addition, the nation became increasingly aware of the threat to its security by world communism. These two circumstances resulted in an enlarged application of the hitherto limited measure of denying entry without a hearing, because of confidential information. Aliens who had been or were associated with Communist activities and those suspected of such affiliation were excluded without hearing in substantial

numbers at seaports and to a much larger extent at land ports of entry. From December 1948, to July 1, 1952, approximately 2,000 aliens, other than seamen, were temporarily excluded without a hearing, and in about 500 cases the exclusion without hearing was made permanent. The constitutionality of exclusions of aliens without hearing was upheld by the Supreme Court.

The Internal Security Act of 1950 provided the first express statutory authority for excluding an alien without a hearing in security cases. Unlike the Passport Act, however, the Internal Security Act of 1950 does not limit the exercise of the power to exclude without hearing to time of war or national emergency. These provisions of the Internal Security Act of 1950 are carried forward into the act of 1952.

The consideration of exclusions without hearing cannot be isolated from the larger problems created by the efforts of the United States to safeguard its security during the current era of international tensions. At many levels in our national life, we have been confronted with the dilemma of attempting to resolve apparent conflicts between our national safety and traditional concepts of freedom. The attempt to discover a precise line of demarcation is a quest that has led us in many directions and has not yet resulted in any satisfactory solution.

The Commission believes that the present situation in connection with exclusions without hearing is unsatisfactory. The protection of the right to a fair hearing is essential to a democracy. Any legal process which affects people's rights without giving them a chance to be heard is ordinarily regarded as being repugnant to the American sense of fair play. It denies a person the opportunity to defend himself against what may be false accusations. It encourages slanders by people whose stories may be generated by malice, misinformation, or the desire for self-advancement. However, in time of crisis there may be need for extreme measures to protect the national security, and even perhaps for some relaxation of our traditional safeguards for individual rights.

Under present world circumstances, it may be necessary for the United States Government to have authority to bar, without a hearing, aliens whose admission would directly menace the national safety. However, such a power should not be exercised except in the extreme and unusual case where the national security or the lives, welfare, or continued usefulness of our intelligence agents and informants are immediately affected by the fact that the very holding of a hearing will cause disclosure of highly secret information.

The officials who have exercised the extraordinary power to exclude aliens from the United States without hearing have been motivated, the Commission believes, by a sincere desire to protect the nation. However, there is some public belief that this unusual power has been or may be used to excess and without adequate safeguards. And there is some evidence, including testimony of a responsible immigration official before a congressional committee, to substantiate this belief. The law should provide measures to avoid abuse of this extraordinary power and to limit its exercise to those few and rare cases in which the security of the United States is actually involved.

The Commission recommends that determination as to whether an alien should be excluded without a hearing, on the basis of confidential information, should be made by the proposed Board of Immigration and Visa Appeals. . . .

Each alien affected should, unless the proposed Board of Immigration and Visa Appeals decides to the contrary, receive notice of the nature of the charges against him, and such other information as the Board may determine, after consultation with intelligence agencies, will not prejudice the public interest. Any such alien should have the opportunity, before any such determination is made, to testify and to present in person or by counsel any information or evidence or argument he may desire to submit on his own behalf. These procedural safeguards should be incorporated into the statute or in regulations issued thereunder.

A determination to exclude without a hearing should be supported by strong and convincing evidence, not mere rumor or unsustained suspicion. It should be reached only after every effort is made to investigate the charges and evaluate the confidential information. It should never be used because evidence is not easily obtainable.

In this way, the Commission believes that the security of the United States would be protected and a procedure established to preserve the American concept of fair dealing.

Source: President's Commission on Immigration and Naturalization. *Whom Shall We Welcome* (Washington, DC: U.S. Government Printing Office, 1953).

Immigration and Nationality Act (1965)

The Immigration and Nationality Act of 1952 (also known as the McCarran-Walter Act) lifted the ban on immigration from Asia and the Pacific Islands, but kept in place most of the quota system established in the 1920s. Spurred by a booming economy, the civil rights movement, and rising liberal senti-

ment in the 1950s and 1960s, the American public took a more welcoming position on immigration. In 1965, Congress passed and President Lyndon B. Johnson signed sweeping new legislation, the Immigration and Nationality Act (technically a set of amendments to the 1952 law), which effectively ended the old quota system. In its place was a system based on broad hemispheric quotas and a new emphasis on family reunion as basis for granting legal status to immigrants.

Be it enacted by the Senate and House of Representatives of the United States of America in Congress assembled, That section 201 of the Immigration and Nationality Act [of 1952] . . . be amended to read as follows:

"Sec. 201. (a) Exclusive of special immigrants defined in section 101 (a) (27), and of the immediate relatives of United States citizens specified in subsection (b) of this section, the number of aliens who may be issued immigrant visas or who may otherwise acquire the status of an alien lawfully admitted to the United States for permanent residence, or who may, pursuant to section 203 (a) (7) enter conditionally, (i) shall not in any of the first three quarters of any fiscal year exceed a total of 45,000 and (ii) shall not in any fiscal year exceed a total of 170,000.

"(b) The "immediate relatives" referred to in subsection (a) of this section will mean the children, spouses, and parents of a citizen of the United States: *Provided,* That in the case of parents, such citizen must be at least twenty-one years of age. . . .

"(d) Quota numbers not issued or otherwise used during the previous fiscal year, as determined in accordance with subsection (c) hereof, shall be transferred to an immigration pool. Allocation of numbers from the pool and from national quotas shall not together exceed in any fiscal year the numerical limitations in subsection (a) of this section. The immigration pool shall be made available to immigrants otherwise admissible under the provisions of this Act who are unable to obtain prompt issuance of a preference visa due to oversubscription of their quotas, or subquotas as determined by the Secretary of State. . . .

"(e) The immigration pool and the quota areas shall terminate June 30, 1968. Thereafter immigrants admitted under the provisions of this Act who are subject to the numerical limitations of subsection (a) of this Act will be admitted in accordance with the percentage limitations and in the order of priority specified in section 203."

Sec. 2. Section 202 of the Immigration and Nationality Act [of 1952] . . . is amended to read as follows:

"(a) No person shall receive any preference or priority or be discriminated against in the issuance of an immigrant visa because of his race, sex, nationality, place of birth, or place of residence, except as specifically provided in section 101 (a) (27), section 201 (b), and section 203: *Provided,* That the total number of immigrant visas and the number of conditional entries made available to natives of any single foreign state . . . shall not exceed 20,000 in any fiscal year. . . .

"(b) Each independent country, self-governing dominion, mandated territory, and territory under the international trusteeship of the United Nations, other than the United States and its outlying possessions, shall be treated as a separate foreign state for the purposes of the numerical limitation set forth in the proviso to subsection (a) of this section when approved by the Secretary of State. All other inhabited lands shall be attributed to a foreign state specified by the Secretary of State. For the purposes of this Act the foreign state to which an immigrant is chargeable shall be determined by birth within such foreign state. . . ."

Sec. 3. Sec. 203 of the Immigration and Nationality Act [of 1952] . . . is amended as follows:
"Sec. 203. (a) Aliens who are subject to the numerical limitations . . . shall be allotted visas or their conditional entry authorized, as the case may be, as follows:

"(1) Visas shall be first made available, in a number not to exceed 20 per centum of the number specified in section 201 (a) (ii), to qualified immigrants who are the unmarried sons or daughters of citizens of the United States.

"(2) Visas shall next be made available, in a number not to exceed 20 per centum of the number specified in section 201 (a) (ii), plus visas not required to be classes specified in paragraph (1), to qualified immigrants who are spouses, unmarried sons or unmarried daughters of an alien admitted for permanent residence.

"(3) Visas shall next be made available, in a number not to exceed 10 per centum . . . to qualified immigrants who are members of the professions, or who because of their exceptional ability in the sciences or arts will substantially benefit prospectively the national economy, cultural interests, or welfare of the United States.

"(4) Visas shall next be made available, in a number not to exceed 10 per centum . . . to qualified immigrants who are the married sons or married daughters of citizens of the United States.

"(5) Visas shall next be made available, in a number not to exceed 24 per centum . . . to qualified immigrants who are the brothers or sisters of citizens of the United States.

"(6) Visas shall next be made available, in a number not to exceed 10 per centum of the number specified . . . to qualified immigrants who are capable of performing specified skilled or unskilled labor, not of a temporary or seasonal nature, for which a shortage of employable and willing persons exists in the United States.

"(7) Conditional entries shall next be made available by the Attorney General, pursuant to such regulations as he may prescribe and in a number not to exceed 6 per centum . . . to aliens who satisfy an Immigration and Naturalization Service officer at an examination in any non-Communist or non-Communist-dominated country, (A) that (i) because of persecution or fear of persecution on account of race, religion, or political opinion they have fled (I) from any Communist or Communist-dominated country or area, or (II) from any country within the general area of the Middle East, and (ii) are unable or unwilling to return to such country or area on account of race, religion, or political opinion, and (iii) are not nationals of the countries or areas in which their application for conditional entry is made; or (B) that they are persons uprooted by catastrophic natural calamity as defined by the President who are unable to return to their usual place of abode. For the purposes of the foregoing the term 'general area of the Middle East' means the area between and including (1) Libya on the west, (2) Turkey on the north, (3) Pakistan on the east, and (4) Saudi Arabia and Ethiopia on the south. . . .

"(8) Visas authorized in any fiscal year, less those required for issuance to the classes specified in paragraphs (1) through (6) and less the conditional entries and visas made available pursuant to paragraph (7), shall be made available to other qualified immigrants strictly in the chronological order in which they qualify. Waiting lists of applicants shall be maintained in accordance with regulations prescribed by the Secretary of State. No immigrant visa shall be issued to a nonpreference immigrant under this paragraph, or to an immigrant with a preference under paragraph (3) or (6) of this subsection, until the consular officer is in receipt of a determination made by the Secretary of Labor in pursuant to the provisions of section 212 (a) (14).

"(9) A spouse or child as defined in section 101 (b) (1) (A), (B), (C), (D), or (E) shall, if not otherwise entitled to an immigrant status and the immediate issuance of a visa, or to conditional entry under paragraph (1) through

(8), be entitled to the same status, and the same order of consideration provided in subsection (b), if accompanying, or following . . . his spouse or parent. . . .

"(d) Every immigrant shall be presumed to be a nonpreference immigrant until he establishes to the satisfaction of the consular officer and the immigration officer that he is entitled to a preference status. . . ."

Sec. 8. Section 101 of the Immigration and Nationality Act [of 1952] . . . is amended as follows:
(a) Paragraph (27) of subsection (a) is amended to read as follows:

"(27) The term 'special immigrant' means—

"(A) an immigrant who was born in any independent foreign country of the Western Hemisphere or in the Canal Zone and the spouse and children of any such immigrant, if accompanying, or following to join him . . .

"(B) an immigrant, lawfully admitted for permanent residence, who is returning from a temporary visit abroad;

"(C) an immigrant who was a citizen of the United States and may, under section 324 (a) or 327 of title III, apply for reacquisition of citizenship;

"(D) (i) an immigrant who continuously for at least two years immediately preceding the time of his application for admission . . . has been, and who seeks to enter the United States solely for the purpose of carrying on the vocation of minister of a religious denomination, and whose services are needed by such religious denomination having a bona fide organization in the United States; and (ii) the spouse or the child of any such immigrant, if accompanying or following to join him; or

"(E) an immigrant who is an employee, or an honorably retired former employee, of the United States Government abroad, and who has performed faithful service for a total of fifteen years or more, and his accompanying spouse and children. . . ."

Sec. 10. Section 212 (a) of the Immigration and Nationality Act [of 1952] . . . is amended as follows:
(a) Paragraph (14) is amended to read as follows: "Aliens seeking to enter the United States, for the purpose of performing skilled or unskilled labor, unless the Secretary of Labor has determined and certified to the Secretary of State and to the Attorney General that (A) there are not sufficient workers in the United States who are able, willing, qualified, and available at the time of the ap-

plication for a visa and admission to the United States and at the place to which the alien is destined to perform such skilled or unskilled labor, and (B) the employment of such aliens will not adversely affect the wages and working conditions of the workers in the United States similarly employed. . . ."

Sec. 11 (a) Section 221 (a) is amended by deleting the words "the particular nonquota category in which the immigrant is classified, if a nonquota immigrant," and substituting in lieu thereof the words "the preference, nonpreference, immediate relative, or special immigration classification to which the alien is charged. . . ."

Sec. 20. This Act shall become effective on the first day of the first month after the expiration of thirty days following the date of its enactment except as provided herein.

Source: Act of October 3, 1965, 79 Stat. 911.

Lau v. Nichols **(1974)**

In a landmark 1974 decision, the U.S. Supreme Court for the first time ruled that the failure of a public school to offer special instruction to non-English-speaking students—in this case, Chinese-speaking students—violates the Civil Rights Act of 1964. The Court's unanimous decision in Lau v. Nichols *guaranteed linguistically appropriate instruction to immigrant students, subsequently interpreted to mean bilingual instruction. Associate Justice William O. Douglas wrote the majority opinion, excerpted below, overturning a lower court ruling and affirming equal educational opportunity based on ethnicity.*

Certiorari to the United States Court of Appeals for the Ninth Circuit

The failure of the San Francisco school system to provide English language instruction to the approximately 1,800 students of Chinese ancestry who do not speak English, or to provide them with other adequate instructional procedures, denies them a meaningful opportunity to participate in the public educational program and thus violates 601 of the Civil Rights Act of 1964, which bans discrimination based "on the ground of race, color, or national origin," in "any program or activity receiving Federal financial assistance," and the implementing regulations of the Department of Health, Education, and Welfare.

Mr. Justice Douglas delivered the [unanimous] opinion of the Court:

The San Francisco, California, school system was integrated in 1971 as a result of a federal court decree, 339 F. Supp. 1315. See *Lee v. Johnson,* 404 U.S. 1215. The District Court found that there are 2,856 students of Chinese ancestry in the school system who do not speak English. Of those who have that language deficiency, about 1,000 are given supplemental courses in the English language. About 1,800, however, do not receive that instruction.

This class suit brought by non-English-speaking Chinese students against officials responsible for the operation of the San Francisco Unified School District seeks relief against the unequal educational opportunities, which are alleged to violate, inter alia, the Fourteenth Amendment. No specific remedy is urged upon us. [414 U.S. 563, 565] Teaching English to the students of Chinese ancestry who do not speak the language is one choice. Giving instructions to this group in Chinese is another. There may be others. Petitioners ask only that the Board of Education be directed to apply its expertise to the problem and rectify the situation.

The District Court denied relief. The Court of Appeals affirmed, holding that there was no violation of the Equal Protection Clause of the Fourteenth Amendment or of 601 of the Civil Rights Act of 1964, 78 Stat. 252, 42 U.S.C. 2000d, which excludes from participation in federal financial assistance, recipients of aid which discriminate against racial groups, 483 F.2d 791. One judge dissented. A hearing en banc was denied, two judges dissenting. Id., at 805. We granted the petition for certiorari because of the public importance of the question presented, 412 U.S. 938.

The Court of Appeals reasoned that "[e]very student brings to the starting line of his educational career different advantages and disadvantages caused in part by social, economic and cultural background, created and continued completely apart from any contribution by the school system," 483 F.2d, at 797. Yet in our view the case may not be so easily decided. This is a public school system of California and 71 of the California Education Code states that "English shall be the basic language of instruction in all schools." That section permits a school district to determine "when and under what circumstances instruction may be given bilingually." That section also states as "the policy of the state" to insure "the mastery of English by all pupils in the schools." And bilingual instruction is authorized "to the extent that it does not interfere with the systematic, sequential, and regular instruction of all pupils in the English language." [414 U.S. 563, 566]

Moreover, 8573 of the Education Code provides that no pupil shall receive a diploma of graduation from grade 12 who has not met the standards of proficiency in "English," as well as other prescribed subjects. Moreover, by 12101 of the Education Code (Supp. 1973) children between the ages of six and 16 years are (with exceptions not material here) "subject to compulsory full-time education."

Under these state-imposed standards there is no equality of treatment merely by providing students with the same facilities, textbooks, teachers, and curriculum; for students who do not understand English are effectively foreclosed from any meaningful education. Basic English skills are at the very core of what these public schools teach. Imposition of a requirement that, before a child can effectively participate in the educational program, he must already have acquired those basic skills is to make a mockery of public education. We know that those who do not understand English are certain to find their classroom experiences wholly incomprehensible and in no way meaningful. We do not reach the Equal Protection Clause argument which has been advanced but rely solely on 601 of the Civil Rights Act of 1964, 42 U.S.C. 2000d, to reverse the Court of Appeals.

That section bans discrimination based "on the ground of race, color, or national origin," in "any program or activity receiving Federal financial assistance." The school district involved in this litigation receives large amounts of federal financial assistance. The Department of Health, Education, and Welfare (HEW), which has authority to promulgate regulations prohibiting discrimination in federally assisted school systems, 42 U.S.C. 2000d-1, in 1968 issued one guideline that "[s]chool systems are responsible for assuring that students of a particular race, color, or national origin are not denied the [414 U.S. 563, 567] opportunity to obtain the education generally obtained by other students in the system." 33 Fed. Reg. 4956. In 1970 HEW made the guidelines more specific, requiring school districts that were federally funded "to rectify the language deficiency in order to open" the instruction to students who had "linguistic deficiencies," 35 Fed. Reg. 11595.

By 602 of the Act HEW is authorized to issue rules, regulations, and orders to make sure that recipients of federal aid under its jurisdiction conduct any federally financed projects consistently with 601. HEW's regulations, 45 CFR 80.3 (b) (1), specify that the recipients may not

(ii) Provide any service, financial aid, or other benefit to an individual which is different, or is provided in a different manner, from that provided to others under the program;. . . .

(iv) Restrict an individual in any way in the enjoyment of any advantage or privilege enjoyed by others receiving any service, financial aid, or other benefit under the program.

Discrimination among students on account of race or national origin that is prohibited includes "discrimination . . . in the availability or use of any academic . . . or [414 U.S. 563, 568] other facilities of the grantee or other recipient." Id., 80.5 (b). Discrimination is barred which has that effect even though no purposeful design is present: a recipient "may not . . . utilize criteria or methods of administration which have the effect of subjecting individuals to discrimination" or have "the effect of defeating or substantially impairing accomplishment of the objectives of the program as respect individuals of a particular race, color, or national origin." Id., 80.3 (b) (2).

It seems obvious that the Chinese-speaking minority receive fewer benefits than the English-speaking majority from respondents' school system which denies them a meaningful opportunity to participate in the educational program—all earmarks of the discrimination banned by the regulations. In 1970 HEW issued clarifying guidelines, 35 Fed. Reg. 11595, which include the following:

> Where inability to speak and understand the English language excludes national origin-minority group children from effective participation in the educational program offered by a school district, the district must take affirmative steps to rectify the language deficiency in order to open its instructional program to these students.

> Any ability grouping or tracking system employed by the school system to deal with the special language skill needs of national origin-minority group children must be designed to meet such language skill needs as soon as possible and must not operate as an educational deadend or permanent track.

Respondent school district contractually agreed to "comply with title VI of the Civil Rights Act of 1964 . . . and all requirements imposed by or pursuant to the [414 U.S. 563, 569] Regulation" of HEW (45 CFR pt. 80) which are "issued pursuant to that title . . ." and also immediately to "take any measures necessary to effectuate this agreement." The Federal Government has power to fix the terms on which its money allotments to the States shall be disbursed. *Oklahoma v. CSC,* 330 U.S. 127, 142–143. Whatever may be the limits of that power, *Steward Machine Co. v. Davis,* 301 U.S. 548, 590 et seq., they have not been reached here. Senator Humphrey, during the floor debates on the Civil Rights Act of 1964, said:

> "Simple justice requires that public funds, to which all taxpayers of all races contribute, not be spent in any fashion which encourages, entrenches, subsidizes, or results in racial discrimination."

We accordingly reverse the judgment of the Court of Appeals and remand the case for the fashioning of appropriate relief.

Source: Lau v. Nichols, 414 U.S. 563 (1974).

California Agricultural Labor Relations Act (1975)

After years of strikes, boycotts, and labor strife in the farmlands of California, the state legislature passed and Governor Jerry Brown, Jr., signed into law the California Agricultural Labor Relations Act, the first law in the nation's history protecting the rights of farmworkers to bargain collectively, free of punitive measures by employers. Enacted in June 1975, the law essentially followed the National Labor Relations Act of the 1930s and represented a major victory for the United Farm Workers union, its president, César Chávez, and the largely immigrant Mexican workforce the union represented.

The people of the State of California do enact as follows:

SEC. 1. In enacting this legislation the people of the State of California seek to ensure peace in the agricultural fields by guaranteeing justice for all agricultural workers and stability in labor relations.

This enactment is intended to bring certainty and a sense of fair play to a presently unstable and potentially volatile condition in the state. The Legislature recognizes that no law in itself resolves social injustice and economic dislocations.

However, in the belief the people affected desire a resolution to this dispute and will make a sincere effort to work through the procedures established in this legislation, it is the hope of the Legislature that farm laborers, farmers, and all the people of California will be served by the provisions of this act.

SEC. 1.5. It is the intent of the Legislature that collective-bargaining agreements between agricultural employers and labor organizations representing the employees of such employers entered into prior to the effective date of this legislation and continuing beyond such date are not to be automatically canceled, terminated, or voided on that effective date; rather, such a collective-bargaining agreement otherwise lawfully entered into and enforceable under the laws of this state shall be void upon the Agricultural Labor Relations Board certification of that election after the filing of an election petition by such employees pursuant to Section 1156.3 of the Labor Code.

SEC. 2. Part 3.5 (commencing with Section 1140) is added to Division 2 of the Labor Code, to read:

Part 3.5. Agricultural Labor Relations

Chapter 1. General Provisions and Definitions
1140. This part shall be known and may be referred to as the Alatorre-Zenovich-Dunlap-Berman Agricultural Labor Relations Act of 1975.

1140.2. It is hereby stated to be the policy of the State of California to encourage and protect the right of agricultural employees to full freedom of association, self-organization, and designation of representatives of their own choosing, to negotiate the terms and conditions of their employment, and to be free from the interference, restraint, or coercion of employers of labor, or their agents, in the designation of such representatives or in self-organization or in other concerted activities for the purpose of collective bargaining or other mutual aid or protection. For this purpose this part is adopted to provide for collective-bargaining rights for agricultural employees. . . .

1140.4. As used in this part:
(a) The term "agriculture" includes farming in all its branches, and, among other things, includes the cultivation and tillage of the soil, dairying, the production, cultivation, growing, and harvesting of any agricultural or horticultural commodities (including commodities defined as agricultural commodities in Section 1141j(g) of Title 12 of the United States Code), the raising of livestock, bees, fur-bearing animals, or poultry, and any practices (including any forestry or lumbering operations) performed by a farmer or on a farm as an incident to or in conjunction with such farming operations, including preparation for market and delivery to storage or to market or to carriers for transportation to market.

(b) The term "agricultural employee" or "employee" shall mean one engaged in agriculture, as such term is defined in subdivision (a). However, nothing in this subdivision shall be construed to include any person other than those employees excluded from the coverage of the National Labor Relations Act, as amended, as agricultural employees, pursuant to Section 2(3) of the Labor Management Relations Act (Section 152(3), Title 29, United States Code), and Section 3(f) of the Fair Labor Standards Act (Section 203(f), Title 29, United States Code).

Further, nothing in this part shall apply, or be construed to apply, to any employee who performs work to be done at the site of the construction, alteration, painting, or repair of a building, structure, or other work (as these terms have been construed under Section 8(e) of the Labor Management Relations Act, 29 USC Section 158(e)) or logging or timber-clearing operations in initial preparation of land for farming, or who does land leveling or only land surveying for any of the above.

As used in this subdivision, "land leveling" shall include only major land moving operations changing the contour of the land, but shall not include annual or seasonal tillage or preparation of land for cultivation.

(c) The term "agricultural employer" shall be liberally construed to include any person acting directly or indirectly in the interest of an employer in relation to an agricultural employee, any individual grower, corporate grower, cooperative grower, harvesting association, hiring association, land management group, any association of persons or cooperatives engaged in agriculture, and shall include any person who owns or leases or manages land used for agricultural purposes, but shall exclude any person supplying agricultural workers to an employer, any farm labor contractor as defined by Section 1682, and any person functioning in the capacity of a labor contractor. The employer engaging such labor contractor or person shall be deemed the employer for all purposes under this part.

(d) The term "person" shall mean one or more individuals, corporations, partnerships, associations, legal representatives, trustees in bankruptcy, receivers, or any other legal entity, employer, or labor organization having an interest in the outcome of a proceeding under this part.

(e) The term "representatives" includes any individual or labor organization.

(f) The term "labor organization" means any organization of any kind, or any agency or employee representation committee or plan, in which employees participate and which exists, in whole or in part, for the purpose of dealing with employers concerning grievances, labor disputes, wages, rates of pay, hours of employment, or conditions of work for agricultural employees.

(g) The term "unfair labor practice" means any unfair labor practice specified in Chapter 4 (commencing with Section 1153) of this part.

(h) The term "labor dispute" includes any controversy concerning terms, tenure, or conditions of employment, or concerning the association or representation of persons in negotiating, fixing, maintaining, changing, or seeking to arrange terms or conditions of employment, regardless of whether the disputants stand in the proximate relation of employer and employee.

(i) The term "board" means Agricultural Labor Relations Board.

(j) The term "supervisor" means any individual having the authority, in the interest of the employer, to hire, transfer, suspend, lay off, recall, promote, discharge, assign, reward, or discipline other employees, or the responsibility to direct them, or to adjust their grievances, or effectively to recommend such action, if, in connection with the foregoing, the exercise of such authority is not of a merely routine or clerical nature, but requires the use of independent judgment.

Chapter 2. Agricultural Labor Relations Board
Article 1. Agricultural Labor Relations Board: Organization

1141. (a) There is hereby created in state government the Agricultural Labor Relations Board, which shall consist of five members.

(b) The members of the board shall be appointed by the Governor with the advice and consent of the Senate. The term of office of the members shall be five years, and the terms shall be staggered at one-year intervals. Upon the initial appointment, one member shall be appointed for a term ending January 1, 1977, one member shall be appointed for a term ending January 1, 1978, one member shall be appointed for a term ending January 1, 1979, one member shall be appointed for a term ending January 1, 1980, and one member shall be appointed for a term ending January 1, 1981. Any individual appointed to fill a vacancy of any member shall be appointed only for the unexpired term of the member to whose term he is succeeding. The Governor shall designate one member to serve as chairperson of the board. Any member of the board may be removed by the Governor, upon notice and hearing, for neglect of duty or malfeasance in office, but for no other cause.

Chapter 3. Rights of Agricultural Employees
1152. Employees shall have the right to self-organization, to form, join, or assist labor organizations, to bargain collectively through representatives of their own choosing, and to engage in other concerted activities for the purpose of collective bargaining or other mutual aid or protection, and shall also have the right to refrain from any or all of such activities except to the extent that such right may be affected by an agreement requiring membership in a labor organization as a condition of continued employment as authorized in subdivision (c) of Section 1153.

Chapter 4. Unfair Labor Practices and Regulation of Secondary Boycotts
1153. It shall be an unfair labor practice for an agricultural employer to do any of the following:
(a) To interfere with, restrain, or coerce agricultural employees in the exercise of the rights guaranteed in Section 1152.

(b) To dominate or interfere with the formation or administration of any labor organization or contribute financial or other support to it. However, subject to such rules and regulations as may be made and published by the board pursuant to Section 1144, an agricultural employer shall not be prohibited from permitting agricultural employees to confer with him during working hours without loss of time or pay.

(c) By discrimination in regard to the hiring or tenure of employment, or any term or condition of employment, to encourage or discourage membership in any labor organization.

Nothing in this part, or in any other statute of this state, shall preclude an agricultural employer from making an agreement with a labor organization (not established, maintained, or assisted by any action defined in this section as an unfair labor practice) to require as a condition of employment, membership therein on or after the fifth day following the beginning of such employment, or the effective date of such agreement whichever is later, if such labor organization is the representative of the agricultural employees as provided in Section 1156 in the appropriate collective-bargaining unit covered by such agreement. No employee who has been required to pay dues to a labor organization by virtue of his employment as an agricultural worker during any calendar month, shall be required to pay dues to another labor organization by virtue of similar employment during such month. For purposes of this chapter, membership shall mean the satisfaction of all reasonable terms and conditions uniformly applicable to other members in good standing; provided, that such membership shall not be denied or terminated except in compliance with a constitution or bylaws which afford full and fair rights to speech, assembly, and equal voting and membership privileges for all members, and which contain adequate procedures to assure due process to members and applicants for membership.

(d) To discharge or otherwise discriminate against an agricultural employee because he has filed charges or given testimony under this part.

(e) To refuse to bargain collectively in good faith with

labor organizations certified pursuant to the provisions of Chapter 5 (commencing with Section 1156) of this part.

(f) To recognize, bargain with, or sign a collective-bargaining agreement with any labor organization not certified pursuant to the provisions of this part.

1154. It shall be an unfair labor practice for a labor organization or its agents to do any of the following:
(a) To restrain or coerce:

(1) Agricultural employees in the exercise of the rights guaranteed in Section 1152. This paragraph shall not impair the right of a labor organization to prescribe its own rules with respect to the acquisition or retention of membership therein.

(2) An agricultural employer in the selection of his representatives for the purposes of collective bargaining or the adjustment of grievances.

(b) To cause or attempt to cause an agricultural employer to discriminate against an employee in violation of subdivision (c) of Section 1153 or to discriminate against an employee with respect to whom membership in such organization has been denied or terminated for reasons other than failure to satisfy the membership requirements specified in subdivision (c) of Section 1153.

(c) To refuse to bargain collectively in good faith with an agricultural employer, provided it is the representative of his employees subject to the provisions of Chapter 5 (commencing with Section 1156) of this part.

(d) To do either of the following: (i) To engage in, or to induce or encourage any individual employed by any person to engage in, a strike or a refusal in the course of his employment to use, manufacture, process, transport, or otherwise handle or work on any goods, articles, materials, or commodities, or to perform any services; or (ii) to threaten, coerce, or restrain any person; where in either case (i) or (ii) an object thereof is any of the following:

(1) Forcing or requiring any employer or self-employed person to join any labor or employer organization or to enter into any agreement which is prohibited by Section 1154.5.

(2) Forcing or requiring any person to cease using, selling, transporting, or otherwise dealing in the products of any other producer, processor, or manufacturer, or to cease doing business with any other person, or forcing or

requiring any other employer to recognize or bargain with a labor organization as the representative of his employees unless such labor organization has been certified as the representative of such employees. Nothing contained in this paragraph shall be construed to make unlawful where not otherwise unlawful, any primary strike or primary picketing.

(3) Forcing or requiring any employer to recognize or bargain with a particular labor organization as the representative of his agricultural employees if another labor organization has been certified as the representative of such employees under the provisions of Chapter 5 (commencing with Section 1156) of this part.

(4) Forcing or requiring any employer to assign particular work to employees in a particular labor organization or in a particular trade, craft, or class unless such employer is failing to conform to an order or certification of the board determining the bargaining representative for employees performing such work.

Nothing contained in this subdivision (d) shall be construed to prohibit publicity including picketing for the purpose of truthfully advising the public, including consumers, that a product or products or ingredients thereof are produced by an agricultural employer with whom the labor organization has a primary dispute and are distributed by another employer, as long as such publicity does not have an effect of inducing any individual employed by any person other than the primary employer in the course of his employment to refuse to pick up, deliver, or transport any goods, or not to perform any services at the establishment of the employer engaged in such distribution, and as long as such publicity does not have the effect of requesting the public to cease patronizing such other employer.

However, publicity which includes picketing and has the effect of requesting the public to cease patronizing such other employer shall be permitted only if the labor organization is currently certified as the representative of the primary employer's employees.

Further, publicity other than picketing, but including peaceful distribution of literature which has the effect of requesting the public to cease patronizing such other employer, shall be permitted only if the labor organization has not lost an election for the primary employer's employees within the preceding 12-month period, and no other labor organization is currently certified as the representative of the primary employer's employees.

Nothing contained in this subdivision (d) shall be construed to prohibit publicity, including picketing, which may not be prohibited under the United States Constitution or the California Constitution.

Nor shall anything in this subdivision (d) be construed to apply or be applicable to any labor organization in its representation of workers who are not agricultural employees. Any such labor organization shall continue to be governed in its intrastate activities for nonagricultural workers by Section 923 and applicable judicial precedents.

(e) To require of employees covered by an agreement authorized under subdivision (c) of Section 1153 the payment, as a condition precedent to becoming a member of such organization, of a fee in an amount which the board finds excessive or discriminatory under all circumstances. In making such a finding, the board shall consider, among other relevant factors, the practices and customs of labor organizations in the agriculture industry and the wages currently paid to the employees affected.

(f) To cause or attempt to cause an agricultural employer to pay or deliver, or agree to pay or deliver, any money or other thing of value, in the nature of an exaction, for services which are not performed or not to be performed.

(g) To picket or cause to be picketed, or threaten to picket or cause to be picketed, any employer where an object thereof is either forcing or requiring an employer to recognize or bargain with a labor organization as the representative of his employees, or forcing or requiring the employees of an employer to accept or select such labor organization as their collective bargaining representative, unless such labor organization is currently certified as the representative of such employees, in any of the following cases:

(1) Where the employer has lawfully recognized in accordance with this part any other labor organization and a question concerning representation may not appropriately be raised under Section 1156.3.

(2) Where within the preceding 12 months a valid election under Chapter 5 (commencing with Section 1156) of this part has been conducted.

Nothing in this subdivision shall be construed to prohibit any picketing or other publicity for the purpose of truthfully advising the public (including consumers) that an employer does not employ members of, or have a contract with, a labor organization, unless an effect of such picketing is to induce an individual employed by any other person in the course of his employment, not to pick up, deliver, or transport any goods or not to perform any services.

Nothing in this subdivision (g) shall be construed to permit any act which would otherwise be an unfair labor practice under this section.

(h) To picket or cause to be picketed, or threaten to picket or cause to be picketed, any employer where an object thereof is either forcing or requiring an employer to recognize or bargain with the labor organization as a representative of his employees unless such labor organization is currently certified as the collective-bargaining representative of such employees.

(i) Nothing contained in this section shall be construed to make unlawful a refusal by any person to enter upon the premises of any agricultural employer, other than his own employer, if the employees of such employer are engaged in a strike ratified or approved by a representative of such employees whom such employer is required to recognize under this part. . . .

Chapter 5. Labor Representatives and Elections

1156. Representatives designated or selected by a secret ballot for the purposes of collective bargaining by the majority of the agricultural employees in the bargaining unit shall be the exclusive representatives of all the agricultural employees in such unit for the purpose of collective bargaining with respect to rates of pay, wages, hours of employment, or other conditions of employment. Any individual agricultural employee or a group of agricultural employees shall have the right at any time to present grievances to their agricultural employer and to have such grievances adjusted, without the intervention of the bargaining representative, as long as the adjustment is not inconsistent with the terms of a collective-bargaining contract or agreement then in effect, if the bargaining representative has been given opportunity to be present at such adjustment.

1156.2. The bargaining unit shall be all the agricultural employees of an employer. If the agricultural employees of the employer are employed in two or more contiguous geographical areas, the board shall determine the appropriate unit or units of agricultural employees in which a secret ballot election shall be conducted.

1156.3. (a) A petition which is either signed by, or accompanied by authorization cards signed by, a majority of the currently employed employees in the bargaining unit may be filed in accordance with such rules and regulations as may be prescribed by the board, by an agricultural employee or group of agricultural employees, or any individual or labor organization acting in their behalf alleging all the following:

(1) That the number of agricultural employees currently employed by the employer named in the petition, as determined from his payroll immediately preceding the filing of the petition, is not less than 50 percent of his peak agricultural employment for the current calendar year.

(2) That no valid election pursuant to this section has been conducted among the agricultural employees of the employer named in the petition within the 12 months immediately preceding the filing thereof.

(3) That no labor organization is currently certified as the exclusive collective-bargaining representative of the agricultural employees of the employer named in the petition.

(4) That the petition is not barred by an existing collective-bargaining agreement.

(b) Upon receipt of such a signed petition, the board shall immediately investigate such petition, and, if it has reasonable cause to believe that a bona fide question of representation exists, it shall direct a representation election by secret ballot to he held, upon due notice to all interested parties and within a maximum of seven days of the filing of the petition. If at the time the election petition is filed a majority of the employees in a bargaining unit are engaged in a strike, the board shall, with all due diligence, attempt to hold a secret ballot election within 48 hours of the filing of such petition. The holding of elections under strike circumstances shall take precedence over the holding of other secret ballot elections.

(c) The board shall make available at any election under this chapter ballots printed in English and Spanish. The board may also make available at such election ballots printed in any other language as may be requested by an agricultural labor organization, or agricultural employee eligible to vote under this part. Every election ballot, except ballots in runoff elections where the choice is between labor organizations, shall provide the employee with the opportunity to vote against representation by a labor organization by providing an appropriate space designated "No Labor Organizations."

(d) Any other labor organization shall be qualified to appear on the ballot if it presents authorization cards signed by at least 90 percent of the employees in the bargaining unit at least 24 hours prior to the election.

(e) (1) Within five days after an election, any person may file with the board a signed petition asserting that allegations made in the petition filed pursuant to subdivision

(a) were incorrect, that the board improperly determined the geographical scope of the bargaining unit, or objecting to the conduct of the election or conduct affecting the results of the election.

(2) Upon receipt of a petition under this subdivision, the board, upon due notice, shall conduct a hearing to determine whether the election shall be certified. Such hearing may be conducted by an officer or employee of a regional office of the board. He shall make no recommendations with respect thereto. If the board finds, on the record of such hearing, that any of the assertions made in the petition filed pursuant to this subdivision are correct, or that the election was not conducted properly, or misconduct affecting the results of the election occurred, the board may refuse to certify the election. Unless the board determines that there are sufficient grounds to refuse to do so, it shall certify the election. . .

(g) If no petition is filed pursuant to subdivision (e) within five days of the election the board shall certify the election.

(h) The board shall decertify a labor organization if the United States Equal Employment Opportunity Commission has found, pursuant to Section 2000(e) (5) of Title 42 of the United States Code, that the labor organization engaged in discrimination on the basis of race, color, national origin, religion, sex or any other arbitrary or invidious classification in violation of Subchapter VI of Chapter 21 of Title 42 of the United States Code during the period of such labor organization's present certification.

Harvest-Time Strikes
1156.4. Recognizing that agriculture is a seasonal occupation for a majority of agricultural employees, and wishing to provide the fullest scope for employees' enjoyment of the rights included in this part, the board shall not consider a representation petition or a petition to decertify as timely filed unless the employer's payroll reflects 50 percent of the peak agricultural employment for such employer for the current calendar year for the payroll period immediately preceding the filing of the petition.

In this connection, the peak agricultural employment for the prior season shall alone not be a basis for such determination, but rather the board shall estimate peak employment on the basis of acreage and crop statistics which shall be applied uniformly throughout the State of California and upon all other relevant data.

1156.5. The board shall not direct an election in any bargaining unit where a valid election has been held in the immediately preceding 12-month period.

1156.6. The board shall not direct an election in any bargaining unit which is represented by a labor organization that has been certified within the immediately preceding 12-month period or whose certification has been extended pursuant to subdivision (b) of Section 1155.2.

1156.7. (a). No collective-bargaining agreement executed prior to the effective date of this chapter shall bar a petition for an election.

(b) A collective-bargaining agreement executed by an employer and a labor organization certified as the exclusive bargaining representative of his employees pursuant to this chapter shall be a bar to a petition for an election among such employees for the term of the agreement, but in any event such bar shall not exceed three years, provided that both the following conditions are met:

(1) The agreement is in writing and executed by all parties thereto.

(2) It incorporates the substantive terms and conditions of employment of such employees.

(c) Upon the filing with the board by an employee or group of employees of a petition signed by 30 percent or more of the agricultural employees in a bargaining unit represented by a certified labor organization which is a party to a valid collective-bargaining agreement, requesting that such labor organization be decertified, the board shall conduct an election by secret ballot pursuant to the applicable provisions of this chapter, and shall certify the results to such labor organizations and employer.

However, such a petition shall not be deemed timely unless it is filed during the year preceding the expiration of a collective-bargaining agreement which would otherwise bar the holding of an election, and when the number of agricultural employees is not less than 50 percent of the employer's peak agricultural employment for the current calendar year.

(d) Upon the filing with the board of a signed petition by an agricultural employee or group of agricultural employees, or any individual or labor organization acting in their behalf, accompanied by authorization cards signed by a majority of the employees in an appropriate bargaining unit, and alleging all the conditions of paragraphs (1), (2), and (3), the board shall immediately investigate such petition and, if it has reasonable cause to believe that a bona fide question of representation exists, it shall direct an election by secret ballot pursuant to the applicable provisions of this chapter:

(1) That the number of agricultural employees currently employed by the employer named in the petition, as determined from his payroll immediately preceding the filing of the petition, is not less than 50 percent of his peak agricultural employment for the current calendar year.

(2) That no valid election pursuant to this section has been conducted among the agricultural employees of the employer named in the petition within the 12 months immediately preceding the filing thereof.

(3) That a labor organization, certified for an appropriate unit, has a collective-bargaining agreement with the employer which would otherwise bar the holding of an election and that this agreement will expire within the next 12 months.

1157. All agricultural employees of the employer whose names appear on the payroll applicable to the payroll period immediately preceding the filing of the petition of such an election shall be eligible to vote. An economic striker shall be eligible to vote under such regulations as the board shall find are consistent with the purposes and provisions of this part in any election, provided that the striker who has been permanently replaced shall not be eligible to vote in any election conducted more than 12 months after the commencement of the strike.

In the case of elections conducted within 18 months of the effective date of this part which involve labor disputes which commenced prior to such effective date, the board shall have the jurisdiction to adopt fair, equitable, and appropriate eligibility rules, which shall effectuate the policies of this part, with respect to the eligibility of economic strikers who were paid for work performed or for paid vacation during the payroll period immediately preceding the expiration of a collective-bargaining agreement or the commencement of a strike; provided, however, that in no event shall the board afford eligibility to any such striker who has not performed any services for the employer during the 36-month period immediately preceding the effective date of this part.

1157.2. In any election where none of the choices on the ballot receives a majority, a runoff shall be conducted, the ballot providing for a selection between the two choices receiving the largest and second largest number of valid votes cast in the election.

1157.3. Employers shall maintain accurate and current payroll lists containing the names and addresses of all their employees, and shall make such lists available to the board upon request.

1158. Whenever an order of the board made pursuant to Section 1160.3 is based in whole or in part upon the facts certified following an investigation pursuant to Sections 1156.3 to 1157.2 inclusive, and there is a petition for review of such order, such certification and the record of such investigation shall be included in the transcript of the entire record required to be filed under Section 1160.8 and thereupon the decree of the court enforcing, modifying, or setting aside in whole or in part the order of the board shall be made and entered upon the pleadings, testimony, and proceedings set forth in such transcript.

1159. In order to assure the full freedom of association, self-organization, and designation of representatives of the employees own choosing, only labor organizations certified pursuant to this part shall be parties to a legally valid collective-bargaining agreement.

Chapter 6. Prevention of Unfair Labor Practices and Judicial Review and Enforcement

1160. The board is empowered, as provided in this chapter, to prevent any person from engaging in any unfair labor practice, as set forth in Chapter 4 (commencing with Section 1153) of this part.

1160.2. Whenever it is charged that any person has engaged in or is engaging in any such unfair labor practice, the board, or any agent or agency designated by the board for such purposes, shall have power to issue and cause to be served upon such person a complaint stating the charges in that respect, and containing a notice of hearing before the board or a member thereof, or before a designated agency or agencies, at a place therein fixed, not less than five days after the serving of such complaint. No complaint shall issue based upon any unfair labor practice occurring more than six months prior to the filing of the charge with the board and the service of a copy thereof upon the person against whom such charge is made, unless the person aggrieved thereby was prevented from filing such charge by reason of service in the armed forces, in which event the six-month period shall be computed from the day of his discharge. Any such complaint may be amended by the member, agent, or agency conducting the hearing, or the board in its discretion, at any time prior to the issuance of an order based thereon. The person so complained against shall have the right to file an answer to the original or amended complaint and to appear in person or otherwise and give testimony at the place and time fixed in the complaint. In the discretion of the member, agent, or agency conducting the hearing or the board, any other person may be allowed to intervene in the proceeding and to present testimony. Any such proceeding shall, so far as practicable, be conducted in accordance with the Evidence Code. All proceedings shall be appropriately reported.

1160.3. The testimony taken by such member, agent, or agency, or the board in such hearing shall be reduced to writing and filed with the board. Thereafter, in its discretion, the board, upon notice, may take further testimony or hear argument. If, upon the preponderance of the testimony taken, the board shall be of the opinion that any person named in the complaint has engaged in or is engaging in any such unfair labor practice, the board shall state its findings of fact and shall issue and cause to be served on such person an order requiring such person to cease and desist from such unfair labor practice, to take affirmative action, including reinstatement of employees with or without backpay, and making employees whole, when the board deems such relief appropriate, for the loss of pay resulting from the employer's refusal to bargain, and to provide such other relief as will effectuate the policies of this part. Where an order directs reinstatement of an employee, backpay may be required of the employer or labor organization, as the case may be, responsible for the discrimination suffered by him. Such order may further require such person to make reports from time to time showing the extent to which it has complied with the order. If, upon the preponderance of the testimony taken, the board shall be of the opinion that the person named in the complaint has not engaged in or is not engaging in any unfair labor practice, the board shall state its findings of fact and shall issue an order dismissing the complaint. No order of the board shall require the reinstatement of any individual as an employee who has been suspended or discharged, or the payment to him of any backpay, if such individual was suspended or discharged for cause. In case the evidence is presented before a member of the board, or before an administrative law officer thereof, such member, or such administrative law officer, as the case may be, shall issue and cause to be served on the parties to the proceedings a proposed report, together with a recommended order, which shall be filed with the board, and, if no exceptions are filed within 20 days after service thereof upon such parties, or within such further period as the board may authorize, such recommended order shall become the order of the board and become effective as therein prescribed.

Until the record in a case shall have been filed in a court, as provided in this chapter, the board may, at any time upon reasonable notice and in such manner as it shall deem proper, modify or set aside, in whole or in part, any finding or order made or issued by it.

1160.4. The board shall have power, upon issuance of a complaint as provided in Section 1160.2 charging that any person has engaged in or is engaging in an unfair labor practice, to petition the superior court in any county wherein the unfair labor practice in question is alleged to have occurred, or wherein such person resides or transacts business, for appropriate temporary relief or restraining order. Upon the filing of any such petition, the board shall cause notice thereof to be served upon such person, and thereupon the court shall have jurisdiction to grant to the board such temporary relief or restraining order as the court deems just and proper.

1160.5. Whenever it is charged that any person has engaged in an unfair labor practice within the meaning of paragraph (4) of subdivision (d) of Section 1154, the board is empowered and directed to hear and determine the dispute out of which such unfair labor practice shall have arisen, unless within 10 days after notice that such charge has been filed, the parties to such dispute submit to the board satisfactory evidence that they have adjusted, or agreed upon methods for the voluntary adjustment of the dispute. Upon compliance by the parties to the dispute with the decision of the board or upon such voluntary adjustment of the dispute, such charge shall be dismissed.

1160.6. Whenever it is charged that any person has engaged in an unfair labor practice within the meaning of paragraph (1), (2), or (3) of subdivision (d), or of subdivision (g), of Section 1154, or of Section 1155, the preliminary investigation of such charge shall be made forthwith and given priority over all other cases except cases of like character in the office where it is filed or to which it is referred. If, after such investigation, the officer or regional attorney to whom the matter may be referred has reasonable cause to believe such charge is true and that a complaint should issue, he shall, on behalf of the board, petition the superior court in the county in which the unfair labor practice in question has occurred, is alleged to have occurred, or where the person alleged to have committed the unfair labor practice resides or transacts business, for appropriate injunctive relief pending the final adjudication of the board with respect to the matter. The officer or regional attorney shall make all reasonable efforts to advise the party against whom the restraining order is sought of his intention to seek such order at least 24 hours prior to doing so. In the event the officer or regional attorney has been unable to advise such party of his intent at least 24 hours in advance, he shall submit a declaration to the court under penalty of perjury setting forth in detail the efforts he has made. Upon the filing of any such petition, the superior court shall have jurisdiction to grant such injunctive relief or temporary restraining

order as it deems just and proper. Upon the filing of any such petition, the board shall cause notice thereof to be served upon any person involved in the charge and such person, including the charging party, shall be given an opportunity to appear by counsel and present any relevant testimony. For the purposes of this section, the superior court shall be deemed to have jurisdiction of a labor organization either in the county in which such organization maintains its principal office, or in any county in which its duly authorized officers or agents are engaged in promoting or protecting the interests of employee members. The service of legal process upon such officer or agent shall constitute service upon the labor organization and make such organization a party to the suit. In situations where such relief is appropriate, the procedures specified herein shall apply to charges with respect to paragraph (4) of subdivision (d) of Section 1154.

1160.7. Whenever it is charged that any person has engaged in an unfair labor practice within the meaning of subdivision (c) of Section 1153 or subdivision (b) of Section 1154, such charge shall be given priority over all other cases except cases of like character in the office where it is filed or to which it is referred and cases given priority under Section 1160.6.

1160.8. Any person aggrieved by the final order of the board granting or denying in whole or in part the relief sought may obtain a review of such order in the court of appeal having jurisdiction over the county wherein the unfair labor practice in question was alleged to have been engaged in, or wherein such person resides or transacts business, by filing in such court a written petition requesting that the order of the board be modified or set aside. Such petition shall be filed with the court within 30 days from the date of the issuance of the board's order. Upon the filing of such petition, the court shall cause notice to be served upon the board and thereupon shall have jurisdiction of the proceeding. The board shall file in the court the record of the proceeding, certified by the board within 10 days after the clerk's notice unless such time is extended by the court for good cause shown. The court shall have jurisdiction to grant to the board such temporary relief or restraining order it deems just and proper and in like manner to make and enter a decree enforcing, modifying and enforcing as so modified, or setting aside in whole or in part, the order of the board. The findings of the board with respect to questions of fact if supported by substantial evidence on the record considered as a whole shall in like manner be conclusive.

An order directing an election shall not be stayed

pending review, but such order may be reviewed as provided in Section 1158.

If the time for review of the board order has lapsed, and the person has not voluntarily complied with the board's order, the board may apply to the superior court in any county in which the unfair labor practice occurred or wherein such person resides or transacts business for enforcement of its order. If after the hearing, the court determines that the order was issued pursuant to procedures established by the board and that the person refuses to comply with the order, the court shall enforce such order by writ of injunction or other proper process. The court shall not review the merits of the order.

1160.9. The procedures set forth in this chapter shall be the exclusive method of redressing unfair labor practices.

Source: Congressional Quarterly. *Historic Documents of 1975* (Washington, DC: Congressional Quarterly, 1976).

Refugee Act of 1980

During much of the Cold War, U.S. immigration policy was geared to providing refuge to individuals fleeing communist countries, especially Cuba. In response to the Southeast Asian refugee crisis of the mid- to late 1970s, however, Congress passed the Refugee Act of 1980, which expanded the universe of people defined as refugees. Under the new law, the meaning of "refugee" was changed to that followed by the United Nations: any person with a "well-founded fear of persecution" due to race, religion, politics, or nationality.

Be it enacted by the Senate and House of Representatives of the United States of America in Congress assembled, That this Act may be cited as the "Refugee Act of 1980."

Sec. 101. (a) The Congress declares that it is the historic policy of the United States to respond to the urgent needs of persons subject to persecution in their homelands, including, where appropriate, humanitarian assistance for their care and maintenance in asylum areas, efforts to promote opportunities for resettlement or voluntary repatriation, aid for necessary transportation and processing, admission to this country of refugees for special humanitarian concern to the United States, and transitional assistance to refugees in the United States. The Congress further declares that it is the policy of the United States to encourage all nations to provide assistance and resettlement opportunities to refugees to the fullest extent possible.

(b) The objectives of this Act are to provide permanent and systematic procedures for the admission to this country of refugees of special humanitarian concern to the United States, and to provide comprehensive and uniform provisions for the effective resettlement and absorption of those refugees who are admitted. . . .

(42) The term "refugee" means (A) any person who is outside any country of such person's nationality or, in the case of a person having no nationality, is outside any country in which such person last habitually resided, and who is unable or unwilling to return to, and is unable or unwilling to avail himself or herself of the protection of, that country because of persecution or a well-founded fear of persecution on account of race, religion, nationality, membership in a particular social group, or political opinion, or (B) in such special circumstances as the President after appropriate consultation . . . may specify. . . . The term "refugee" does not include any person who ordered, incited, assisted, or otherwise participated in the persecution of any person on account of race, religion, nationality, membership in a particular social group, or political opinion. . . .

Sec. 207. (a) (1) Except as provided in subsection (b), the number of refugees who may be admitted under this section in fiscal year 1980, 1981, or 1982, may not exceed fifty thousand unless the President determines, before the beginning of the fiscal year and after appropriate consultation . . . , that admission of a specific number of refugees in excess of such number is justified by humanitarian concerns or is otherwise in the national interest.

(2) Except as provided in subsection (b), the number of refugees who may be admitted under this section in any fiscal year after fiscal year 1982 shall be such number as the President determines, before the beginning of the fiscal year and after appropriate consultation, is justified by humanitarian concerns or is otherwise in the national interest.

(3) Admissions under this subsection shall be allocated among refugees of special humanitarian concern to the United States in accordance with a determination made by the President after appropriate consultation.

(b) If the President determines, after appropriate consultation, that (1) an unforeseen emergency refugee situation exists, (2) the admission of certain refugees in response to the emergency refugee situation is justified by grave humanitarian concern or is otherwise in the national interest, and (3) the admission to the United States of these refugees cannot be accomplished under subsection (a), the

President may fix a number of refugees to be admitted to the United States during the succeeding period (not to exceed twelve months) in response to the emergency refugee situation and such admissions shall be allocated among refugees of special humanitarian concern to the United States in accordance with a determination made by the President after the appropriate consultation provided under this subsection. . . .

(4) The refugee status of any alien (and of the spouse or child of the alien) may be terminated by the Attorney General pursuant to such regulations as the Attorney General may prescribe if the Attorney General determines that alien was not in fact a refugee within the meaning of subsection 101 (a) (42) at the time of the alien's admission. . . .

(d)(1) Before the start of each fiscal year the President shall report to the Committees of the Judiciary of the House of Representatives and of the Senate regarding the foreseeable number of refugees who will be in need of resettlement during the fiscal year and the anticipated allocation of refugee admissions during the fiscal year. . . .

(3)(B) After the President initiates appropriate consultation prior to making a determination, under subsection (b), that the number of refugee admissions should be increased because of an unforeseen emergency refugee situation, to the extent that time and the nature of the emergency refugee situation permit, a hearing to review the proposal to increase refugee admissions shall be held unless public disclosure of the details of the proposal would jeopardize the lives or safety of individuals. . . .

Sec. 208. (a) The Attorney General shall establish a procedure for an alien physically present in the United States or at a land border or port of entry, irrespective of such alien's status, to apply for asylum, and the alien may be granted asylum at the discretion of the Attorney General if the Attorney General determines that such alien is a refugee within the meaning of section 101(a)(42)(a). . . .

Sec. 209. (b) Not more than five thousand of the refugee admissions authorized under section 207(a) in any fiscal year may be made available by the Attorney General, in the Attorney General's discretion and under such regulations as the Attorney General may prescribe, to adjust to the status of an alien lawfully permitted for permanent residence the status of any alien granted asylum who—

(1) applies for such adjustment;

(2) has been physically present in the U.S. for at least one year after being granted asylum,

(3) continues to be a refugee in the meaning of section 101(a)(42)(a) or a spouse or child of such refugee,

(4) is not firmly resettled in any foreign country, and

(5) is admissible (except as otherwise provided for under subsection (c) as an immigrant under this Act at the time of examination for adjustment of such alien. . . .

Sec. 203 . . . (a) Exclusive of special immigrants in section 101(a)(27), immediate relatives specified in subsection (b) of this section, and aliens who are admitted or granted asylum under section 207 or 208, the number of aliens born in any foreign country or dependent area who may be issued immigrant visas or who may otherwise acquire the status of an alien lawfully admitted to the United States for permanent residence, shall not in any of the first three quarters of any fiscal year exceed a total of seventy-two thousand and shall not in any fiscal year exceed two hundred and seventy thousand. . . .

(h)(1) The Attorney General shall not deport or return any alien (other than an alien described in section 241(a)(19)[)] to a country if the Attorney General determines that such alien's life or freedom would be threatened in such country on account of race, religion, nationality, membership in a particular social group, or political opinion. . . .

Sec. 204. (2) The Attorney General shall establish the asylum procedure referred to in section 208(a) of the Immigration and Nationality Act (as added by section 201(b) of this title) not later than June 1, 1980. . . .

Sec. 301. (a) The President shall appoint, by and with the advice and consent of the Senate, a United States Coordinator for Refugee Affairs (hereinafter referred to as the "Coordinator"). The Coordinator shall have the rank of Ambassador-at-Large.

Source: Public Law 96-212.

White House Statements on *Marielito* Refugees from Cuba (1980)

Between April and September 1980, approximately 125,000 persons fled by boat to the United States from the Cuban port of Mariel. While President Jimmy Carter welcomed the Marielitos, as the refugees came to be called, he chastised Cuban

President Fidel Castro for the disorderly nature of the boatlift and for the significant number of common criminals, released from Cuban jails, among the refugees. What follows is a series of statements issued by the White House, or by President Carter directly, about the emerging refugee crisis.

White House Announcement, May 2, 1980

The White House announced today that the Federal Government is taking additional actions to respond to the current emergency precipitated by the Cuban Government. More than 5,000 Cubans have already arrived in Florida in more than 170 small boats, and the Coast Guard estimates that as many as 2,000 additional boats are either loading passengers in Cuba or are en route to the Florida coast.

The President has directed Jack Watson, his Assistant for Intergovernmental Affairs and Secretary to the Cabinet, to work with Ambassador Victor Palmieri, U.S. Coordinator for Refugee Affairs, in managing the Federal Government's overall response to the emergency. Watson outlined the following actions:

- A processing and screening center will be established at Eglin Air Force Base in Fort Walton Beach, Fla., to supplement the receiving and processing facilities already located in Key West and Miami. The Eglin facility will accommodate approximately 1,000 persons within 24 hours and will be expanded to accommodate between 5,000 and 10,000 within 10 days. Additional facilities will be added as needed.

- Reception facilities at Key West are being expanded to accommodate daily flows of between 2,500 and 3,000, and other Federal services are being made available there, including those of a Public Health Service medical assistance team.

- Several hundred Federal personnel have been directed to the Miami/Key West area, so that more than 1,000 personnel from eight Federal agencies are now actively engaged with volunteer organizations and State and local governments in receiving, processing, and assisting the arriving Cubans. Tom Casey, Deputy Associate Director of the Federal Emergency Management Agency, has been assigned responsibility for on-site coordination of all Federal Government activities.

- The Coast Guard has expanded its capability to provide rescue and assistance missions between the Florida and Cuban coasts and, within the last few days, has performed approximately 300 rescue missions in the area. As announced earlier this week by the Department of Defense, U.S. naval vessels which had been intended for Operation Solid Shield are now being made available to assist the Coast Guard in rescue operations.

- Because the Cuban Government is including individuals with criminal records in the boatloads of departing Cubans, careful screening of all arrivals is being conducted by appropriate Federal officials. Under U.S. immigration laws, individuals with records of criminal activity who represent a threat to the country or whose presence would not be in the best interests of the United States are subject to arrest, detention, and deportation to their countries of origin. The United States will enforce these laws.

- State Department officials will be working with national voluntary organizations to provide additional reception and resettlement assistance to Cuban, Haitian, and other groups seeking political asylum, which are so heavily affecting the Miami area.

The President appreciates the extraordinarily effective efforts of the State and local governments in Florida in dealing with this extremely difficult situation . . .

President Carter's Statement, May 14, 1980

The President. I'd like to make a statement to you and to the Nation about the extremely critical problem with the Cuban citizens who are escaping from their country and coming to our shores in a very haphazard and dangerous way.

Tens of thousands of Cubans are fleeing the repression of the Castro regime under chaotic and perilous conditions. Castro himself has refused to permit them a safe and orderly passage to the United States and to other countries who are also willing to receive them. Repeated international efforts to resolve this crisis have been rejected or ignored by the Cuban Government. At least seven people have died on the high seas. The responsibility for those deaths and the threat of further loss of life rests on the shoulders of Fidel Castro, who has so far refused to cooperate with us, with those escaping his regime, or with other countries in establishing a legal and orderly procedure for dealing with this Cuban problem.

In keeping with the laws and traditions of our own country, the United States has provided a safe haven for many of these people who have arrived on our shores. Since the beginning of this crisis we have been operating under three basic principles: first, to treat the escaping Cubans with decency, fairness, and humanity; second, to observe and to enforce the existing United States law; and third, to work with other countries and with international organizations to develop an orderly and legal solution to this very painful human dilemma. That is still our fundamental approach.

But now we must take additional steps to end Cuba's inhumane actions and to bring safety and order to a process that continues to threaten lives. Therefore we will implement a five-point program to permit safe and orderly passage from Cuba for those people who sought freedom in the U.S. Interest Section in Havana, first of all; for political prisoners who have been held by Castro for many years; for those who sought a haven of freedom in the Peruvian Embassy, some of whom are still being held there; and for close family members of Cuban Americans who live in this country and who have permanent resident status. Those four categories will be given priority in their authorization to come to our country.

First, we are ready to start an airlift and a sealift for these screened and qualified people to come to our country, and for no other escapees from Cuba. We will provide this airlift and sealift to our country and to other countries as well, just as soon as the Cubans accept this offer. The U.S. Government will have aircraft ready and will immediately charter ships—one of which will be standing by in Key West—to bring the first group of Cubans, after they are screened, to our country. These ships and the Key West planes will be ready to go to Cuba to receive properly screened Cubans for entry to the United States and to other countries, to help in their resettlement.

To ensure legality and order, all people will have to be screened before departure from Cuba. We will work with the Congress, the Cuban American community, interested nations, and the Cuban Government to determine the total number of people that we will receive, both on a monthly basis and during the next 12 months.

Second, tomorrow we will open a family registration center in Miami, and later perhaps in other communities, to begin receiving the names of people who are eligible for immigration to our Nation because they are close members of Cuban American families who have permanent residence here.

Third, the Coast Guard is now communicating with all boats who are en route to Cuba and those in Mariel Harbor in Cuba, to urge them to return to the United States without accepting additional passengers. No new trips to Cuba by these unauthorized boats should be started. Those who comply with this request or command will have nothing to fear from the law, but we will ensure that the law is obeyed. Persons who violate this requirement and who violate U.S. immigration custom laws by traveling to Cuba to pick up additional passengers will be subject to civil fines and to criminal prosecution. Furthermore, boats used to bring people unlawfully to this country will be seized. I have directed the various law enforcement agencies to take additional steps as necessary to assure that this policy and the law are obeyed.

Fourth, in an unprecedented and irresponsible act, Castro has taken hardened criminals out of prison and forced some of the boatowners who have gone to Cuba from our country to bring these criminals back to the United States. Thus far over 400 such persons have been detained. I have instructed the Attorney General to commence exclusion proceedings immediately for these criminals and others who represent any danger to our country. We will ask also appropriate international agencies to negotiate their return to Cuba.

These steps are fully consistent with the consensus which was reached by 22 nations and 7 international organizations in the San Jose Conference on May 8 this last week. In addition, the Secretary of State will continue consultation with other nations to determine additional steps that the international community can take to resolve this problem. We will seek the help of the United Nations, the Organization of American States, and other international organizations as well.

The Cuban American community has, of course, contributed much to Miami, to Florida, and to our own country. I respect the deep desire to reunite divided families. In the interest of that great and valiant ethnic community and in the interest of our country, we will continue to work closely with the Cuban American community to bring about a safe and orderly resolution of this crisis.

I continue to be greatly concerned about the treatment of Haitians who have also come to this country recently on small boats. I've instructed all appropriate Federal agencies to treat the Haitians now here in the same, exact, humane manner as we treat Cubans and others who seek asylum in this country. Our laws never contemplated and do not adequately provide for people coming to our shores directly for asylum the way the Cubans and the Haitians have done recently. I will work closely with the Congress to formulate a long-term solution to this problem and to determine the legal status of the boat people once this current emergency is under control.

White House Statement, May 14, 1980

After consultations with senior advisers and with Congress, and in the spirit of the San Jose Conference, the President has decided to take the following steps to welcome the Cuban refugees in a legal and orderly process:

1. We are prepared to start an airlift or a sealift immediately as soon as President Castro accepts this offer. Our Government is chartering two large, seaworthy ships, which will go to Key West to stand by, ready to go to Cuba. To ensure a legal and orderly process, all people will have to be screened before departure from Cuba. Priority will be given to political prisoners, to close relatives of U.S. permanent residents, and to persons who sought freedom in the Peruvian Embassy and in our Interest Section last month. In the course of our discussions with the Congress and with the Cuban American community, the international community, and the Cuban Government, we will determine the number of people to be taken over the next 12 months. We will fulfill our humanitarian responsibilities, and we hope other governments will adjust their previous pledges to resettle Cuban refugees to take into account the larger problem that has developed. This will provide a safe and orderly way to accommodate Cubans wishing to enter the United States.

2. Tomorrow, we will open a Family Registration Office in Miami to receive the names of close Cuban relatives of U.S. permanent residents who will be eligible for immigration.

3. The Coast Guard is now communicating with these vessels illegally enroute to or from Cuba and those already in Mariel Harbor to tell them to return to the United States without taking Cubans on board. If they follow this directive, they have nothing to fear from the law. We will do everything possible to stop these illegal trips to Cuba. We will take the following steps to ensure that the law is obeyed:

    (a) The Immigration and Naturalization Service (INS) will continue to issue notices of intent to fine those unlawfully bringing Cubans to this country. As fines become due, they will be collected.
    (b) All vessels currently and unlawfully carrying Cubans to this country will henceforth be seized by the Customs Service.
    (c) Anyone who tampers with or seeks to move a ship to Cuba which has been seized will be subject to separate criminal prosecution.
    (d) The Coast Guard will continue to review each vessel that returns to the United States for violations of boat safety law. Those found to be in gross violation of the law will be subject to criminal prosecution and additional fines. Furthermore, boats which are found to be safety hazards will be detained.
    (e) Any individual who has been notified by INS for unlawfully bringing Cubans into the coun-

try and who makes another trip will be subject to criminal prosecution, and the boat used for such a repeat trip will be seized for forfeiture proceedings.
    (f) Law enforcement agencies will take additional steps, as necessary, to implement this policy and to discourage the unlawful boat traffic to Cuba.

4. Castro has taken hardened criminals out of prison and mental patients out of hospitals and has forced boatowners to take them to the United States. Thus far, over 400 such prisoners have been detained. We will not permit our country to be used as a dumping ground for criminals who represent a danger to our society, and we will begin exclusion proceedings against these people at once.

5. These steps will make clear to the Government of Cuba our determination to negotiate an orderly process. This is the mission of the three-government delegation established by the San Jose Conference last week. Our actions are intended to promote an international solution to this problem. We intend to continue our consultations with the participants of the San Jose Conference and consider additional steps the international community should take to resolve this problem.

In summary, the United States will welcome Cubans, seeking freedom, in accordance with our laws, and we will pursue every avenue to establish an orderly and regular flow.

The President continues to be greatly concerned about the Haitians who have been coming to this country on small boats. He has instructed appropriate Federal agencies to receive the Haitians in the same manner as others seeking asylum. However, our laws never contemplated and do not provide adequately for people coming to our shores in the manner the Cubans and Haitians have. We will work closely with the Congress to formulate a long-term solution to this problem and to determine the legal status of these "boat people" after the current emergency situation is controlled.

The Cuban American community has contributed much to Miami, the State of Florida, and to our country. The President understands the deep desire to reunite families which has led to this situation. He calls upon the Cuban American community to end the boat flotilla and help bring about a safe and orderly resolution to this crisis.

President Carter's Announcement, June 7, 1980

Among the tens of thousands of people fleeing oppression in Cuba and seeking to reunite with their families and to seek freedom in the United States, Fidel Castro has very cynically thrown in several hundred hardened criminals from Cuban jails. These criminals will not be resettled or relocated in American communities under any circumstances. The administration will take the legal and necessary steps to make sure that this will not happen.

There is evidence that the Cuban Government exported these undesirable elements to the United States in a calculated effort to disguise the fact that the vast majority of those Cubans who have come to this country were and are law-abiding citizens whose only purpose was to seek freedom and to seek reunification with their families.

This action by the Cuban Government, in addition to its cynical and inhumane characteristics, is a direct and serious violation of international law. It would be an equally serious violation if the Government of Cuba should refuse to perform its obligations under international law to accept the return of these criminals. The President has directed the Secretary of State to press this issue urgently through diplomatic channels and in the appropriate international forum.

Unfortunately, a few of those who came to the United States seeking the right to live here in this country, to join a democratic and law-abiding society, have created disturbances and have violated the laws of the country in which they seek to live. These individuals will be dealt with in strict accordance with those laws.

The President has directed the Attorney General to take the following actions:

First, Cubans identified as having committed serious crimes in Cuba are to be securely confined. Exclusion proceedings will be expedited to the maximum extent consistent with constitutional requirements for due process of law.

Second, exclusion proceedings will also be started against those who have violated American law while waiting to be reprocessed or relocated. The Justice Department will investigate all serious violations of the law, and the Justice Department will bring prosecutions where justified. Those responsible for the disturbances at Fort Chaffee are confined and will be confined until fair decisions can be made on criminal prosecution or exclusion from this country or both. Similar measures will be taken in the event of any future disturbances.

Source: Congressional Quarterly. *Historic Documents of 1980* (Washington, DC: Congressional Quarterly, 1981).

Plyler v. Doe (1982)

On June 15, 1982, the U.S. Supreme Court declared unconstitutional a Texas law that required the children of illegal aliens to pay tuition for public schooling. The Court's 5–4 ruling in Plyler v. Doe *represented the first time the Equal Protection Clause of the U.S. Constitution was applied to illegal aliens. Writing for the majority, Associate Justice William Brennan, Jr., dismissed Texas's argument that illegal immigrants were not "persons within the jurisdiction" of the state and thus had no right to equal protection under the Fourteenth Amendment. The text that follows contains excerpts from Brennan's majority decision, as well as Chief Justice Warren Burger's dissent.*

Brennan's Majority Decision

Justice Brennan delivered the opinion of the Court:

The question presented by these cases is whether, consistent with the Equal Protection Clause of the Fourteenth Amendment, Texas may deny to undocumented school-age children the free public education that it provides to children who are citizens of the United States or legally admitted aliens.

I

Since the late nineteenth century, the United States has restricted immigration into this country. Unsanctioned entry into the United States is a crime, 8 U.S.C. § 1325, and those who have entered unlawfully are subject to deportation, 8 U.S.C. §§ 1251–1252. But despite the existence of these legal restrictions, a substantial number of persons have succeeded in unlawfully entering the United States, and now live within various States, including the State of Texas.

In May 1975, the Texas legislature revised its education laws to withhold from local school districts any state funds for the education of children who were not "legally admitted" into the United States. The 1975 revision also authorized local school districts to deny enrollment in their public schools to children not "legally admitted" to the country. These cases involve constitutional challenges to those provisions.

This is a class action, filed in the United States District Court for the Eastern District of Texas in September 1977, on behalf of certain school-age children of Mexican origin residing in Smith County, Texas, who could not establish that they had been legally admitted into the United States. The action complained of the exclusion of plaintiff children from the public schools of the Tyler Independent School District. The Superintendent and members of the Board of Trustees of the School District were named as defendants; the State of Texas intervened as a party-defendant. After certifying a class consisting of all undocumented school-age children of Mexican origin residing within the School District, the District Court preliminarily enjoined defendants from denying a free education to members of the plaintiff class. In December 1977, the Court conducted an extensive hearing on plaintiffs' motion for permanent injunctive relief.

In considering this motion, the District Court made extensive findings of fact. The court found that neither § 21.031 [of Texas' education code] nor the School District policy implementing it had "either the purpose or effect of keeping illegal aliens out of the State of Texas." Respecting defendants' further claim that § 21.031 was simply a financial measure designed to avoid a drain on the State's finances, the court recognized that the increases in population resulting from the immigration of Mexican nationals into the United States had created problems for the public schools of the State, and that these problems were exacerbated by the special educational needs of immigrant Mexican children. The court noted, however, that the increase in school enrollment was primarily attributable to the admission of children who were legal residents. It also found that while the "exclusion of all undocumented children from the public schools in Texas would eventually result in economies at some level," funding from both the state and federal governments was based primarily on the number of children enrolled. In net effect then, barring undocumented children from the schools would save money, but it would "not necessarily" improve "the quality of education." The court further observed that the impact of § 21.031 was borne primarily by a very small sub-class of illegal aliens, "entire families who have migrated illegally and—for all practical purposes—permanently to the United States." Finally, the court noted that under current laws and practices "the illegal alien of today may well be the legal alien of tomorrow," and that without an education, these undocumented children, "[a]lready disadvantaged as a result of poverty, lack of English-speaking ability, and undeniable racial prejudices, . . . will become permanently locked into the lowest socio-economic class."

The District Court held that illegal aliens were entitled to the protection of the Equal Protection Clause of the Fourteenth Amendment, and that § 21.031 violated that Clause. Suggesting that "the state's exclusion of undocumented children from its public schools . . . may well be the type of invidiously motivated state action for which the suspect classification doctrine was designed," the court held that it was unnecessary to decide whether the statute would survive a "strict scrutiny" analysis because, in any event, the discrimination embodied in the statute was not supported by a rational basis. The District

Court also concluded that the Texas statute violated the Supremacy Clause.

The Court of Appeals for the Fifth Circuit upheld the District Court's injunction. (1980). The Court of Appeals held that the District Court had erred in finding the Texas statute preempted by federal law. With respect to equal protection, however, the Court of Appeals affirmed in all essential respects the analysis of the District Court, concluding that § 21.031 was "constitutionally infirm regardless of whether it was tested using the mere rational basis standard or some more stringent test." We noted probable jurisdiction. (1981).

In re Alien Children Education Litigation
During 1978 and 1979, suits challenging the constitutionality of § 21.031 and various local practices undertaken on the authority of that provision were filed in the United States District Courts for the Southern, Western, and Northern Districts of Texas. Each suit named the State of Texas and the Texas Education Agency as defendant, along with local officials. In November 1979, the Judicial Panel on Multidistrict Litigation, on motion of the State, consolidated the claims against the State officials into a single action to be heard in the District Court for the Southern District of Texas. A hearing was conducted in February and March 1980. In July 1980, the court entered an opinion and order holding that § 21.031 violated the Equal Protection Clause of the Fourteenth Amendment. The court held that "the absolute deprivation of education should trigger strict judicial scrutiny, particularly when the absolute deprivation is the result of complete inability to pay for the desired benefit." The court determined that the State's concern for fiscal integrity was not a compelling state interest, that exclusion of these children had not been shown to be necessary to improve education within the State, and that the educational needs of the children statutorily excluded was not different from the needs of children not excluded. The court therefore concluded that § 21.031 was not carefully tailored to advance the asserted state interest in an acceptable manner. While appeal of the District Court's decision was pending, the Court of Appeals rendered its decision in No. 81-1538. Apparently on the strength of that opinion, the Court of Appeals, on February 23, 1981, summarily affirmed the decision of the Southern District. We noted probable jurisdiction (1981) and consolidated this case with No. 81-1538 for briefing and argument.

II

The Fourteenth Amendment provides that "No State shall . . . deprive any person of life, liberty, or property, without due process of law; nor deny to any person within its jurisdiction the equal protection of the laws." Appellants argue at the outset that undocumented aliens, because of their immigration status, are not "persons within the jurisdiction" of the State of Texas, and that they therefore have no right to the equal protection of Texas law. We reject this argument. Whatever his status under the immigration laws, an alien is surely a "person" in any ordinary sense of that term. Aliens, even aliens whose presence in this country is unlawful, have long been recognized as "persons" guaranteed due process of law by the Fifth and Fourteenth Amendments. *Shaughnessy v. Mezei* (1953); *Wong Wing v. United States* (1896); *Yick Wo v. Hopkins* (1886). Indeed, we have clearly held that the Fifth Amendment protects aliens whose presence in this country is unlawful from invidious discrimination by the Federal Government. *Mathews v. Diaz* (1976).

Appellants seek to distinguish our prior cases, emphasizing that the Equal Protection Clause directs a State to afford its protection to persons within its jurisdiction while the Due Process Clauses of the Fifth and Fourteenth Amendments contain no such assertedly limiting phrase. In appellants' view, persons who have entered the United States illegally are not "within the jurisdiction" of a State even if they are present within a State's boundaries and subject to its laws. Neither our cases nor the logic of the Fourteenth Amendment supports that constricting construction of the phrase "within its jurisdiction." We have never suggested that the class of persons who might avail themselves of the equal protection guarantee is less than coextensive with that entitled to due process. To the contrary, we have recognized that both provisions were fashioned to protect an identical class of persons, and to reach every exercise of State authority.

"The Fourteenth Amendment to the Constitution is not confined to the protection of citizens. It says: 'Nor shall any state deprive any persons of life, liberty or property without due process of law; nor deny to any persons within its jurisdiction the equal protection of the laws.' *These provisions are universal in their application, to all persons within the territorial jurisdiction,* without regard to any differences of race, color, or of nationality; and the protection of the laws is a pledge of the protection of equal laws." *Yick Wo* (emphasis added).

In concluding that "all persons within the territory of the United States," including aliens unlawfully present, may invoke the Fifth and Sixth Amendment to challenge actions of the Federal Government, we reasoned from the understanding that the Fourteenth Amendment was designed to afford its protection to all within the boundaries of a State. *Wong Wing.* Our cases applying the Equal Protection Clause reflect the same territorial theme:

"Manifestly, the obligation of the State to give the protection of equal laws can be performed only where its laws operate, that is, within its own jurisdiction. It is there that the equality of legal right must be maintained. That obligation is imposed by the Constitution upon the States severally as governmental entities,—each responsible for its own laws establishing the rights and duties of persons within its borders." *Missouri ex rel. Gaines v. Canada* (1938).

There is simply no support for appellants' suggestion that "due process" is somehow of greater stature than "equal protection" and therefore available to a larger class of persons. To the contrary, each aspect of the Fourteenth Amendment reflects an elementary limitation on state power. To permit a State to employ the phrase "within its jurisdiction" in order to identify subclasses of persons whom it would define as beyond its jurisdiction, thereby relieving itself of the obligation to assure that its laws are designed and applied equally to those persons, would undermine the principal purpose for which the Equal Protection Clause was incorporated in the Fourteenth Amendment. The Equal Protection Clause was intended to work nothing less than the abolition of all caste- and invidious class-based legislation. That objective is fundamentally at odds with the power the State asserts here to classify persons subject to its laws as nonetheless excepted from its protection. . . .

Use of the phrase "within its jurisdiction" . . . does not detract from, but rather confirms, the understanding that the protection of the Fourteenth Amendment extends to anyone, citizen or stranger, who is subject to the laws of a State, and reaches into every corner of a State's territory. That a person's initial entry into a State, or into the United States, was unlawful, and that he may for that reason be expelled, cannot negate the simple fact of his presence within the State's territorial perimeter. Given such presence, he is subject to the full range of obligations imposed by the State's civil and criminal laws. And until he leaves the jurisdiction— either voluntarily, or involuntarily in accordance with the Constitution and laws of the United States—he is entitled to the equal protection of the laws that a State may choose to establish.

Our conclusion that the illegal aliens who are plaintiffs in these cases may claim the benefit of the Fourteenth Amendment's guarantee of equal protection only begins the inquiry. The more difficult question is whether the Equal Protection Clause has been violated by the refusal of the State of Texas to reimburse local school boards for the education of children who cannot demonstrate that their presence within the United States is lawful, or by the imposition by those school boards of the burden of tuition on those children. It is to this question that we now turn.

III

The Equal Protection Clause directs that "all persons similarly circumstanced shall be treated alike." *F.S. Royster Guano Co. v. Virginia* (1920). But so too, "The Constitution does not require things which are different in fact or opinion to be treated in law as though they were the same." *Tigner v. Texas* (1940). The initial discretion to determine what is "different" and what is "the same" resides in the legislatures of the States. A legislature must have substantial latitude to establish classifications that roughly approximate the nature of the problem perceived, that accommodate competing concerns both public and private, and that account for limitations on the practical ability of the State to remedy every ill. In applying the Equal Protection Clause to most forms of state action, we thus seek only the assurance that the classification at issue bears some fair relationship to a legitimate public purpose.

But we would not be faithful to our obligations under the Fourteenth Amendment if we applied so deferential a standard to every classification. The Equal Protection Clause was intended as a restriction on state legislative action inconsistent with elemental constitutional premises. Thus we have treated as presumptively invidious those classifications that disadvantage a "suspect class," or that impinge upon the exercise of a "fundamental right." With respect to such classifications, it is appropriate to enforce the mandate of equal protection by requiring the State to demonstrate that its classification has been precisely tailored to serve a compelling governmental interest. In addition, we have recognized that certain forms of legislative classification, while not facially invidious, nonetheless give rise to recurring constitutional difficulties; in these limited circumstances we have sought the assurance that the classification reflects a reasoned judgment consistent with the ideal of equal protection by inquiring whether it may fairly be viewed as furthering a substantial interest of the State. We turn to a consideration of the standard appropriate for the evaluation of § 21.031.

A

Sheer incapability or lax enforcement of the laws barring entry into this country, coupled with the failure to establish an effective bar to the employment of undocumented aliens, has resulted in the creation of a substantial "shadow population" of illegal migrants—numbering in the millions—within our borders. This situation raises the specter of a permanent caste of undocumented resident aliens, encouraged by some to remain here as a source of cheap labor, but nevertheless denied the benefits that our society makes available to citizens and lawful residents. The existence of such an underclass presents most difficult problems for a Nation that prides itself on adherence to principles of equality under law.

The children who are plaintiffs in these cases are special members of this underclass. Persuasive arguments support the view that a State may withhold its beneficence from those whose very presence within the United States is the product of their own unlawful conduct. These arguments do not apply with the same force to classifications imposing disabilities on the minor children of such illegal entrants. At the least, those who elect to enter our territory by stealth and in violation of our law should be prepared to bear the consequences, including, but not limited to, deportation. But the children of those illegal entrants are not comparably situated. Their "parents have the ability to conform their conduct to societal norms," and presumably the ability to remove themselves from the State's jurisdiction; but the children who are plaintiffs in these cases "can affect neither their parents' conduct nor their own status." *Trimble v. Gordon* (1977). Even if the State found it expedient to control the conduct of adults by acting against their children, legislation directing the onus of a parent's misconduct against his children does not comport with fundamental conceptions of justice.

"[V]isiting . . . condemnation on the head of an infant is illogical and unjust. Moreover, imposing disabilities on the . . . child is contrary to the basic concept of our system that legal burdens should bear some relationship to individual responsibility or wrongdoing. Obviously, no child is responsible for his birth and penalizing the . . . child is an ineffectual—as well as unjust—way of deterring the parents." *Weber v. Aetna Casualty & Surety Co.* (1972).

Of course, undocumented status is not irrelevant to any proper legislative goal. Nor is undocumented status an absolutely immutable characteristic since it is the product of conscious, indeed unlawful, action. But § 21.031 is directed against children, and imposes its discriminatory burden on the basis of a legal characteristic over which children can have little control. It is thus difficult to conceive of a rational justification for penalizing these children for their presence within the United States. Yet that appears to be precisely the effect of § 21.031.

Public education is not a "right" granted to individuals by the Constitution. *San Antonio School District.* But neither is it merely some governmental "benefit" indistinguishable from other forms of social welfare legislation. Both the importance of education in maintaining our basic institutions, and the lasting impact of its deprivation on the life of the child, mark the distinction. The "American people have always regarded education and the acquisition of knowledge as matters of supreme importance." *Meyer v. Nebraska* (1923). We have recognized "the public school as a most vital civic institution for the preservation of a democratic system of government."

Abington School District v. Schempp (1963) (BRENNAN, J., concurring) and as the primary vehicle for transmitting "the values on which our society rests." *Ambach v. Norwick* (1979). As noted early in our history, "some degree of education is necessary to prepare citizens to participate effectively and intelligently in our open political system if we are to preserve freedom and independence." *Wisconsin v. Yoder* (1972). And these historic "perceptions of the public schools as inculcating fundamental values necessary to the maintenance of a democratic political system have been confirmed by the observations of social scientists." *Ambach v. Norwick.* In addition, education provides the basic tools by which individuals might lead economically productive lives to the benefit of us all. In sum, education has a fundamental role in maintaining the fabric of our society. We cannot ignore the significant social costs borne by our Nation when select groups are denied the means to absorb the values and skills upon which our social order rests.

In addition to the pivotal role of education in sustaining our political and cultural heritage, denial of education to some isolated group of children poses an affront to one of the goals of the Equal Protection Clause: the abolition of governmental barriers presenting unreasonable obstacles to advancement on the basis of individual merit. Paradoxically, by depriving the children of any disfavored group of an education, we foreclose the means by which that group might raise the level of esteem in which it is held by the majority. But more directly, "education prepares individuals to be self-reliant and self-sufficient participants in society." *Wisconsin v. Yoder.* Illiteracy is an enduring disability. The inability to read and write will handicap the individual deprived of a basic education each and every day of his life. The inestimable toll of that deprivation on the social, economic, intellectual, and psychological well-being of the individual, and the obstacle it poses to individual achievement, makes it most difficult to reconcile the cost or the principle of a status-based denial of basic education with the framework of equality embodied in the Equal Protection Clause. What we said 28 years ago in *Brown v. Board of Education* (1954), still holds true:

"Today, education is perhaps the most important function of state and local governments. Compulsory school attendance laws and the great expenditures for education both demonstrate our recognition of the importance of education to our democratic society. It is required in the performance of our most basic public responsibilities, even service in the armed forces. It is the very foundation of good citizenship. Today it is a principal instrument in awakening the child to cultural values, in preparing him for later professional training, and in helping him to adjust normally to his environment. In these days, it is doubtful that any child may reasonably be expected to succeed in life if he is denied the opportunity of an education. Such an opportunity, where the state has undertaken to provide it, is a right which must be made available to all on equal terms."

B

These well-settled principles allow us to determine the proper level of deference to be afforded § 21.031. Undocumented aliens cannot be treated as a suspect class because their presence in this country in violation of federal law is not a "constitutional irrelevancy." Nor is education a fundamental right; a State need not justify by compelling necessity every variation in the manner in which education is provided to its population. See *San Antonio School Dist. v. Rodriguez* (1973). But more is involved in this case than the abstract question whether § 21.031 discriminates against a suspect class, or whether education is a fundamental right. Section 21.031 imposes a lifetime hardship on a discrete class of children not accountable for their disabling status. The stigma of illiteracy will mark them for the rest of their lives. By denying these children a basic education, we deny them the ability to live within the structure of our civic institutions, and foreclose any realistic possibility that they will contribute in even the smallest way to the progress of our Nation. In determining the rationality of § 21.031, we may appropriately take into account its costs to the Nation and to the innocent children who are its victims. In light of these countervailing costs, the discrimination contained in § 21.031 can hardly be considered rational unless it furthers some substantial goal of the State.

IV

It is the State's principal argument, and apparently the view of the dissenting Justices, that the undocumented status of these children *vel non* establishes a sufficient rational basis for denying them benefits that a State might choose to afford other residents. The State notes that while other aliens are admitted "on an equality of legal privileges with all citizens under non-discriminatory laws," *Takahashi v. Fish & Game Comm'n* (1948), the asserted right of these children to an education can claim no implicit congressional imprimatur. Indeed, on the State's view, Congress' apparent disapproval of the presence of these children within the United States, and the evasion of the federal regulatory program that is the mark of undocumented status, provides authority for its decision to impose upon them special disabilities. Faced with an equal protection challenge respecting the treatment of aliens, we agree that the courts must be attentive to congressional policy; the exercise of congressional power might well affect the State's prerogatives to afford differential treatment to a particular class of aliens. But we are unable to find in the congressional immigration scheme any statement of policy that might weigh significantly in arriving at an equal protection balance concerning the State's authority to deprive these children of an education.

The Constitution grants Congress the power to "establish a uniform Rule of Naturalization." Art. I., § 8. Drawing upon this power, upon its plenary authority with respect to foreign relations and international commerce, and upon the inherent power of a sovereign to close its borders, Congress has developed a complex scheme governing admission to and status within our borders. See *Mathews v. Diaz* (1976); *Harrisades v. Shaughnessy* (1952). The obvious need for delicate policy judgments has counseled the Judicial Branch to avoid intrusion into this field. *Mathews.* But this traditional caution does not persuade us that unusual deference must be shown the classification embodied in § 21.031. The States enjoy no power with respect to the classification of aliens. See *Hines v. Davidowitz* (1941). This power is "committed to the political branches of the Federal Government." *Mathews.* Although it is "a routine and normally legitimate part" of the business of the Federal Government to classify on the basis of alien status and to "take into account the character of the relationship between the alien and this country," only rarely are such matters relevant to legislation by a State. *Nyquist v. Mauclet* (1977). . . .

To be sure, like all persons who have entered the United States unlawfully, these children are subject to deportation. But there is no assurance that a child subject to deportation will ever be deported. An illegal entrant might be granted federal permission to continue to reside in this country, or even to become a citizen. In light of the discretionary federal power to grant relief from deportation, a State cannot realistically determine that any particular undocumented child will in fact be deported until after deportation proceedings have been completed. It would of course be most difficult for the State to justify a denial of education to a child enjoying an inchoate federal permission to remain.

We are reluctant to impute to Congress the intention to withhold from these children, for so long as they are present in this country through no fault of their own, access to a basic education. In other contexts, undocumented status, coupled with some articulable federal policy, might enhance State authority with respect to the treatment of undocumented aliens. But in the area of special constitutional sensitivity presented by this case, and in the absence of any contrary indication fairly discernible in the present legislative record, we perceive no national policy that supports the State in denying these children an elementary education. The State may

borrow the federal classification. But to justify its use as a criterion for its own discriminatory policy, the State must demonstrate that the classification is reasonably adapted to *"the purposes for which the state desires to use it." Oyama v. California* (1948) (Murphy, J., concurring) (emphasis added). We therefore turn to the state objectives that are said to support § 21.031.

V

Appellants argue that the classification at issue furthers an interest in the "preservation of the state's limited resources for the education of its lawful residents." Of course, a concern for the preservation of resources standing alone can hardly justify the classification used in allocating those resources. *Graham v. Richardson.* The State must do more than justify its classification with a concise expression of an intention to discriminate. *Examining Board v. Flores de Otero* (1976). Apart from the asserted state prerogative to act against undocumented children solely on the basis of their undocumented status—an asserted prerogative that carries only minimal force in the circumstances of this case—we discern three colorable state interests that might support § 21.031.

First, appellants appear to suggest that the State may seek to protect the State from an influx of illegal immigrants. While a State might have an interest in mitigating the potentially harsh economic effects of sudden shifts in population, § 21.031 hardly offers an effective method of dealing with an urgent demographic or economic problem. There is no evidence in the record suggesting that illegal entrants impose any significant burden on the State's economy. To the contrary, the available evidence suggests that illegal aliens underutilize public services, while contributing their labor to the local economy and tax money to the State fisc. The dominant incentive for illegal entry into the State of Texas is the availability of employment; few if any illegal immigrants come to this country, or presumably to the State of Texas, in order to avail themselves of a free education. Thus, even making the doubtful assumption that the net impact of illegal aliens on the economy of the State is negative, we think it clear that "[c]harging tuition to undocumented children constitutes a ludicrously ineffectual attempt to stem the tide of illegal immigration," at least when compared with the alternative of prohibiting the employment of illegal aliens.

Second, while it is apparent that a state may "not . . . reduce expenditures for education by barring [some arbitrarily chosen class of] children from its schools," *Shapiro v. Thompson* (1969), appellants suggest that undocumented children are appropriately singled out for exclusion because of the special burdens they impose on the State's ability to provide high quality public education. But the record in no way supports the claim that exclusion of undocumented children is likely to improve the overall quality of education in the State. As the District Court in No. 80-1934 noted, the State failed to offer any "credible supporting evidence that a proportionately small diminution of the funds spent on each child [which might result from devoting some State funds to the education of the excluded group] will have a grave impact on the quality of education." And, after reviewing the State's school financing mechanism, the District Court in No. 80-1538 concluded that barring undocumented children from local schools would not necessarily improve the quality of education provided in those schools. Of course, even if improvement in the quality of education were a likely result of barring some *number* of children from the schools of the State, the State must support its selection of *this* group as the appropriate target for exclusion. In terms of educational cost and need, however, undocumented children are "basically indistinguishable" from legally resident alien children.

Finally, appellants suggest that undocumented children are appropriately singled out because their unlawful presence within the United States renders them less likely than other children to remain within the boundaries of the State, and to put their education to productive social or political use within the State. Even assuming that such an interest is legitimate, it is an interest that is most difficult to quantify. The State has no assurance that any child, citizen or not, will employ the education provided by the State within the confines of the State's borders. In any event, the record is clear that many of the undocumented children disabled by this classification will remain in this country indefinitely, and that some will become lawful residents or citizens of the United States. It is difficult to understand precisely what the State hopes to achieve by promoting the creation and perpetuation of a sub-class of illiterates within our boundaries, surely adding to the problems and costs of unemployment, welfare, and crime. It is thus clear that whatever savings might be achieved by denying these children an education, they are wholly insubstantial in light of the costs involved to these children, the State, and the Nation.

VI

If the State is to deny a discrete group of innocent children the free public education that it offers to other children residing within its borders, that denial must be justified by a showing that it furthers some substantial state interest. No such showing was made here. Accordingly, the judgment of the Court of Appeals in each of these cases is

Affirmed.

Chief Justice Burger, with whom Justice White, Justice Rehnquist, and Justice O'Connor join, dissenting.

Were it our business to set the Nation's social policy, I would agree without hesitation that it is senseless for an enlightened society to deprive any children—including illegal aliens—of an elementary education. I fully agree that it would be folly—and wrong—to tolerate creation of a segment of society made up of illiterate persons, many having a limited or no command of our language. However, the Constitution does not constitute us as "Platonic Guardians" nor does it vest in this Court the authority to strike down laws because they do not meet our standards of desirable social policy, "wisdom," or "common sense." See *Tennessee Valley Authority v. Hill* (1978). We trespass on the assigned function of the political branches under our structure of limited and separated powers when we assume a policymaking role as the Court does today.

The Court makes no attempt to disguise that it is acting to make up for Congress' lack of "effective leadership" in dealing with the serious national problems caused by the influx of uncountable millions of illegal aliens across our borders. The failure of enforcement of the immigration laws over more than a decade and the inherent difficulty and expense of sealing our vast borders have combined to create a grave socio-economic dilemma. It is a dilemma that has not yet even been fully assessed, let alone addressed. However, it is not the function of the judiciary to provide "effective leadership" simply because the political branches of government fail to do so.

The Court's holding today manifests the justly criticized judicial tendency to attempt speedy and wholesale formulation of "remedies" for the failures—or simply the laggard pace—of the political processes of our system of government. The Court employs, and in my view abuses, the Fourteenth Amendment in an effort to become an omnipotent and omniscient problem solver. That the motives for doing so are noble and compassionate does not alter the fact that the Court distorts our constitutional function to make amends for the defaults of others.

I

In a sense, the Court's opinion rests on such a unique confluence of theories and rationales that it will likely stand for little beyond the results in these particular cases. Yet the extent to which the Court departs from principled constitutional adjudication is nonetheless disturbing.

I have no quarrel with the conclusion that the Equal Protection Clause of the Fourteenth Amendment *applies* to aliens who, after the illegal entry into this country, are indeed physically "within the jurisdiction" of a State. However, as the Court concedes, this "only begins the inquiry." The Equal Protection Clause does not mandate identical treatment of different categories of persons. *Jefferson v. Hackney* (1972); *Reed v. Reed* (1971); *Tigner v. Texas* (1940).

The dispositive issue in these cases, simply put, is whether, for purposes of allocating its finite resources, a State as a legitimate reason to differentiate between persons who are lawfully within the State and those who are unlawfully there. The distinction the State of Texas has drawn—based not only upon its own legitimate interests but on classifications established by the federal government in its immigration laws and policies—is not unconstitutional.

A

The Court acknowledges that, except in those cases when state classifications disadvantage a "suspect class" or impinge upon a "fundamental right," the Equal Protection Clause permits a State "substantial latitude" in distinguishing between different groups of persons. Moreover, the Court expressly—and correctly—rejects any suggestion that illegal aliens are a suspect class, or that education is a fundamental right. Yet by patching together bits and pieces of what might be termed quasi-suspect-class and quasi-fundamental-rights analysis, the Court spins out a theory custom-tailored to the facts of these cases.

In the end, we are told little more than that the level of scrutiny employed to strike down the Texas law applies only when illegal alien children are deprived of a public education. If ever a court was guilty of an unabashedly result-oriented approach, this case is a prime example.

(1)

The Court first suggests that these illegal alien children, although not a suspect class, are entitled to special solicitude under the Equal Protection Clause because they lack "control" over or "responsibility" for their unlawful entry into this country. Similarly, the Court appears to take the position that § 21.031 is presumptively "irrational" because it has the effect of imposing "penalties" on "innocent" children. However, the Equal Protection Clause does not preclude legislators from classifying among persons on the basis of factors and characteristics over which individuals may be said to lack "control." Indeed, in some circumstances persons generally, and children in particular, may have little control over or responsibility for such things as their ill-health, need for public assistance, or place of residence. Yet a state legislature is not barred from considering, for example, relevant differences between the mentally-healthy and the mentally-ill, or between the residents of different counties, simply because these may be factors unrelated to individual choice or to

any "wrongdoing." The Equal Protection Clause protects against arbitrary and irrational classifications, and against invidious discrimination stemming from prejudice and hostility; it is not an all-encompassing "equalizer" designed to eradicate every distinction for which persons are not "responsible." . . .

. . . This Court has recognized that in allocating governmental benefits to a given class of aliens, one "may take into account the character of the relationship between the alien and this country." *Mathews v. Diaz* (1976). When that "relationship" is a federally-prohibited one, there can, of course, be no presumption that a State has a constitutional duty to include illegal aliens among the recipients of its governmental benefits.

(2)

The second strand of the Court's analysis rests on the premise that, although public education is not a constitutionally-guaranteed right, "neither is it merely some governmental 'benefit' indistinguishable from other forms of social welfare legislation." Whatever meaning or relevance this opaque observation might have in some other context, it simply has no bearing on the issues at hand. Indeed, it is never made clear what the Court's opinion means on this score.

The importance of education is beyond dispute. Yet we have held repeatedly that the importance of a governmental service does not elevate it to the status of a "fundamental right" for purposes of equal protection analysis. *San Antonio School District v. Rodriguez* (1973); *Lindsey v. Normet* (1972). In *San Antonio School District,* JUSTICE POWELL, speaking for the Court, expressly rejected the proposition that state laws dealing with public education are subject to special scrutiny under the Equal Protection Clause. Moreover, the Court points to no meaningful way to distinguish between education and other governmental benefits in this context. Is the Court suggesting that education is more "fundamental" than food, shelter, or medical care?

The Equal Protection Clause guarantees similar treatment of similarly situated persons, but it does not mandate a constitutional hierarchy of governmental services. JUSTICE POWELL, speaking for the Court in *San Antonio School District,* put it well in stating that to the extent this Court raises or lowers the degree of "judicial scrutiny" in equal protection cases according to a transient Court majority's view of the societal importance of the interest affected, we "assum[e] a legislative role and one for which the Court lacks both authority and competence." Yet that is precisely what the Court does today. . . .

The central question in these cases, as in every equal protection case not involving truly fundamental rights "explicitly or implicitly guaranteed by the Constitution,"

San Antonio School District, is whether there is some legitimate basis for a legislative distinction between different classes of persons. The fact that the distinction is drawn in legislation affecting access to public education—as opposed to legislation allocating other important governmental benefits, such as public assistance, health care, or housing—cannot make a difference in the level of scrutiny applied.

B

Once it is conceded—as the Court does—that illegal aliens are not a suspect class, and that education is not a fundamental right, our inquiry should focus on and be limited to whether the legislative classification at issue bears a rational relationship to a legitimate state purpose. *Vance v. Bradley* (1979); *Dandridge v. Williams* (1970).

The State contends primarily that § 21.031 serves to prevent undue depletion of its limited revenues available for education, and to preserve the fiscal integrity of the State's school financing system against an ever-increasing flood of illegal aliens—aliens over whose entry or continued presence it has no control. Of course such fiscal concerns alone could not justify discrimination against a suspect class or an arbitrary and irrational denial of benefits to a particular group of persons. Yet I assume no member of this Court would argue that prudent conservation of finite state revenues is *per se* an illegitimate goal. . . .

Without laboring what will undoubtedly seem obvious to many, it simply is not "irrational" for a State to conclude that it does not have the same responsibility to provide benefits for persons whose very presence in the State and this country is illegal as it does to provide for persons lawfully present. By definition, illegal aliens have no right whatever to be here, and the State may reasonably, and constitutionally, elect not to provide them with governmental services at the expense of those who are lawfully in the State. In *DeCamas v. Bica* (1976), we held that a State may protect its "fiscal interests and lawfully resident labor force from the deleterious effects on its economy resulting from the employment of illegal aliens." . . .

It is significant that the federal government has seen fit to exclude illegal aliens from numerous social welfare programs, such as the food stamp program, the old age assistance, aid to families with dependent children, aid to the blind, aid to the permanently and totally disabled, and supplemental security income programs, the Medicare hospital insurance benefits program, and the Medicaid hospital insurance benefits for the aged and disabled program. Although these exclusions do not conclusively demonstrate the constitutionality of the State's use of the same classification for comparable purposes, at the very least they tend to support the rationality of excluding illegal alien residents of a State from such programs so as to preserve the State's finite revenues for the benefit of lawful residents. See *Mathews v. Diaz* (1976).

The Court maintains—as if this were the issue—that "barring undocumented children from local schools would not necessarily improve the quality of education provided in those schools." . . . However, the legitimacy of barring illegal aliens from programs such as Medicare or Medicaid does not depend on a showing that the barrier would "improve the quality" of medical care given to persons lawfully entitled to participate in such programs. Modern education, like medical care, is enormously expensive, and there can be no doubt that very large added costs will fall on the State or its local school districts as a result of the inclusion of illegal aliens in the tuition-free public schools. . . .

Denying a free education to illegal alien children is not a choice I would make were I a legislator. Apart from compassionate considerations, the long-range costs of excluding any children from the public schools may well outweigh the costs of educating them. But that is not the issue; the fact that there are sound policy arguments against the Texas legislature's choice does not render that choice an unconstitutional one.

Source: Plyler v. Doe, 457 U.S. 202 (1982).

U.S.–Cuba Agreement on *Marielito* Refugees (1984)

In the wake of the Mariel boatlift of 1980, most of the Cuban refugees were quickly released from U.S. holding centers and integrated into Cuban American communities, largely in Florida. At the same time, thousands were held in custody. These were predominantly nonpolitical criminals whom Cuban President Fidel Castro had released from prison and sent away with the other refugees. In 1984, hundreds of these detainees rioted at the federal penitentiary in Atlanta where they were being held. Meanwhile, Cuban and American authorities were negotiating the terms under which the criminals would be returned to Cuba. In December 1984, the two sides reached an agreement, as outlined in this joint communiqué.

Discussions between representatives of the United States of America and of the Republic of Cuba on immigration matters concluded today with the adoption of agreements for the normalization of immigration procedures between the two countries and to put an end to the abnormal situation which has existed since 1980.

The United States will resume issuance of preference

immigrant visas to Cuban nationals residing in Cuba up to the number of 20,000 each year, in particular to close family relatives of United States citizens and of Cuban permanent residents in the United States.

The United States side expressed its willingness to implement—with the cooperation of the Cuban authorities—all necessary measures to ensure that Cuban nationals residing in Cuba wishing to emigrate to the United States and who qualify under United States law to receive immigrant visas, may enter the United States, taking maximum advantage of the number of up to 20,000 immigrants per year.

For its part, the United States will continue granting immigrant visas to residents of Cuba who are parents, spouses, and unmarried children under 21 years of age of United States citizens. These immigrants will not be counted against the annual limit indicated above.

Cuba will accept the return of those Cuban nationals who came to the United States in 1980 via the port of Mariel and who have been declared ineligible to enter the United States legally. The number of such persons is 2,746 and their names appear on an approved list. The return of these persons will be carried out by means of an orderly program of returns with the cooperation of the immigration authorities of both countries. The returns will proceed in a phased and orderly manner until all the identified individuals who appear on the approved list have been returned. The returns will be effected at a rate of 100 each calendar month, but if the figure of 100 is not met in a given month, the remaining numbers may be used in subsequent months, provided that no more than 150 will be returned in any calendar month. The United States stated that measures were being taken so that the Cuban nationals who came to the United States in 1980 via the port of Mariel may acquire, beginning now and with retroactive effect of approximately 30 months, legal status as permanent residents of the United States.

Both delegations expressed their concern in regard to the situation of those persons who, having been released after serving sentences for acts which Cuban penal legislation defines as "Offenses against the Security of the State," wish to reside permanently in the United States. The United States will facilitate the admission of such persons and their immediate family members by means of a program to be carried out under applicable United States law. The United States delegation stated that to this end the necessary steps have been taken for admission during Fiscal Year 1985 of up to 3,000 such persons, including immediate family members. The size of the program and any possible increase in subsequent fiscal years will be determined in the light of experience with the process and the desire expressed by both parties to carry out this program in such a way as to allow its ongoing implementation until fully completed in the shortest possible time.

Source: U.S. Department of State.

California Proposition 63 (1986)

On November 4, 1986, Californians voted 73 percent to 26 percent in favor of Proposition 63, a controversial ballot initiative on adding an amendment to the state constitution that would make English the "official language" of the state. The campaign to do so was part of a broader English-language–only movement, the modern incarnation of which began with a Virginia statute six years before. Latinos and other immigrant groups claimed that the amendment would prevent non-English-speaking residents from getting access to government services and the court system. Opponents of Proposition 63 immediately launched legal challenges, but the U.S. Court of Appeals upheld the state constitutional amendment in January 1988.

California Vote on English as Official Language, November 4, 1986

SEC. 6. (a) Purpose. English is the common language of the people of the United States of America and the State of California. This section is intended to preserve, protect and strengthen the English language, and not to supersede any of the rights guaranteed to the people by this Constitution.

(b) English as the Official Language of California. English is the official language of the State of California.

(c) Enforcement. The Legislature shall enforce this section by appropriate legislation. The Legislature and officials of the State of California shall take all steps necessary to insure that the role of English as the common language of the State of California is preserved and enhanced. The Legislature shall make no law which diminishes or ignores the role of English as the common language of the State of California.

(d) Personal Right of Action and Jurisdiction of Courts. Any person who is a resident of or doing business in the State of California shall have standing to sue the State of California to enforce this section, and the Courts of record of the State of California shall have jurisdiction to hear cases brought to enforce this section. The Legislature may provide reasonable and appropriate limitations on the time and manner of suits brought under this section.

Source: California State Ballot, Proposition 63, November 4, 1986.

Immigration Reform and Control Act (1986)

With the heavy influx of immigrants following the Immigration and Nationality Act of 1965, public sentiment against open immigration began to turn, especially during the conservative ascendancy of the Ronald Reagan era in the 1980s. In 1986, Congress passed and President Reagan signed the Immigration Reform and Control Act, which featured efforts to punish employers who knowingly hired illegal immigrants and a major amnesty program for undocumented aliens who had lived in the United States for a number of years.

Title I—Control of Illegal Immigration

Part A—Employment

Sec. 101. Control of Unlawful Employment of Aliens

(a) In General

(1) New Provision.—Chapter 8 of title II is amended by inserting after section 274 the following new section:

"Unlawful employment of aliens

"Sec. 274A. (a) Making Employment of Unauthorized Aliens Unlawful.—

"(1) In General—It is unlawful for a person or other entity to hire, or to recruit or refer for a fee, for employment in the United States—

"(A) an alien knowing the alien is an unauthorized alien (as defined in subsection (h)(3)) . . .

"(B) an individual without complying with the requirements of subsection (b).

"(2) Continuing Employment—It is unlawful for a person or other entity, after hiring an alien for employment in accordance with paragraph (1), to continue to employ the alien in the United States knowing the alien is (or has become) an unauthorized alien with respect to such employment.

"(3) Defense—A person or entity that establishes that it has complied in good faith with the requirements of subsection (b) with respect to the hiring, recruiting, or referral for employment of an alien in the United States who has established an affirmative defense that the person or entity has not violated paragraph (1)(A) with respect to such hiring, recruiting, or referral.

"(4) Use of Labor Through Contract—For the purposes of this section, a person or other entity who uses a contract, subcontract, or exchange, entered into, renegotiated, or extended after the date of the enactment of this section, to obtain the labor of an alien in the United States knowing that the alien is an unauthorized alien . . . with respect to performing such labor, shall be considered to have hired the alien for employment in the United States in violation of paragraph (1)(A).

"(5) Use of State Employment Agency Documentation—For the purposes of paragraph (1)(B) and (3), a person or entity shall be deemed to have complied with the requirements of subsection (b) with respect to the hiring of an individual who was referred for such employment by a State employment agency. . . .

"(b) Employment Verification System.—The requirements referred to in paragraphs (1)(B) and (3) are, in the case of a person or other entity hiring, recruiting, or referring an individual for employment in the United States, the requirements specified in the following three paragraphs:

"(1) Attestation After Examination of Documentation—

"(A) In General—The person or entity must attest, under penalty of perjury and on a form designated or established by the Attorney General by regulation, that it has verified that the individual is not an unauthorized alien by examining—

"(i) a document described in subparagraph (B), or

"(ii) a document described in subparagraph (C) and (D).

"(B) Documents Establishing Both Employment Authorization and Identity—A document described in this subparagraph is an individual's—

"(i) United States passport;

"(ii) certificate of United States Citizenship;

"(iii) certificate of naturalization;

"(iv) unexpired foreign passport, if the passport has an appropriate, unexpired endorsement of the Attorney General authorizing the individual's employment in the United States; or

"(v) resident alien card or other alien registration, if the card—

"(I) contains a photograph of the individual . . .

"(II) is evidence of authorization of employment in the United States

"(C) Documents Evidencing Employment Authorization—A document described . . . is [a]

"(i) social security account number card . . .

"(ii) certificate of birth in the United States or establishing United States nationality at birth;

"(iii) other documents evidencing authorization of employment in the United States which Attorney General finds, by regulation, to be acceptable for the purposes of this section.

"(D) Documents establishing identity of individual—A document described in this subparagraph is an individual's

"(i) driver's license or similar document issued for the purpose of identification by a State, if it contains a photograph of the individual . . .

"(ii) in the case of individuals under 16 years of age or in a State which does not provide for issuance of an identification document . . . referred to in clause (ii), documentation of personal identity of such type as the Attorney General finds, by regulation, provides a reliable means of identification. . . .

"(h) Miscellaneous Provisions. . . .

"(3) Definition of Unauthorized Alien—As used in this section, the term 'unauthorized alien' means, with respect to the employment of an alien at a particular time, that the alien is not at that time either (A) an alien lawfully admitted for permanent residence, or (B) authorized to be so employed by this Act or by the Attorney General. . . .

"(i) Effective Dates. . . .

"(3) Deferral of Enforcement with Respect to Seasonal Agricultural Services—

"(A) In General—Except as provided in subparagraph (B), before the end of the application period, it is unlawful for a person or entity (including a farm labor contractor) or an agent of such a person or entity, to recruit an unauthorized alien (other than an alien described in clause (ii)) who is outside the United States to enter the United States to perform seasonal agricultural services. . .

"(ii) Exception—Clause (i) shall not apply to an alien who the person or entity reasonably believes to meet the requirements of section 210(a)(2) of this Act (relating to the performance of seasonal agricultural services).

"(j) General Accounting Office Reports.—

"(1) In General—Beginning one year after the date of enactment of this Act, and at intervals of one year thereafter for a period of three years after such date, the Comptroller General of the United States shall prepare and transmit to the Congress and to the taskforce established under subsection (k) a report describing the results of a review of the implementation and enforcement of this section during the preceding twelve-month period, for the purpose of determining if—

"(A) such provisions have been carried out satisfactorily;

"(B) a pattern of discrimination has resulted against citizens or nationals of the United States or against eligible workers seeking employment; and

"(C) an unnecessary regulatory burden has been created for employers hiring such workers.

"(k) Review by Taskforce—

"(1) Establishment of Joint Taskforce—The Attorney General, jointly with the Chairman of the Commission on Civil Rights and the Chairman of the Equal Employment Opportunity Commission, shall establish a taskforce to review each report of the Comptroller General transmitted under subsection (j)(1).

"(2) Recommendations to Congress—If the report transmitted includes a determination that the implementation of this section has resulted in a pattern of discrimination in employment (against other than unauthorized aliens) on the basis of national origin, the taskforce shall, taking into consideration any recommendations in the report, report to Congress recommendations for such legislation as may be appropriate to deter or remedy such discrimination. . . .

"(1) Termination Date for Employer Sanctions—

"(1) If Report of Widespread Discrimination and Congressional Approval—The provisions of this section shall terminate 30 days after receipt of the last report required to be transmitted under subsection (j), if—

"(A) the Comptroller General determines, and so reports . . . that a widespread pattern of discrimination has resulted against citizens or nationals of the United States or against eligible workers seeking employment solely from the implementation of this section; and

"(B) there is enacted, within such period of 30 calendar days, a joint resolution stating in substance that the Congress approves the findings of the Comptroller General contained in such report.

"(2) Senate Procedures for Consideration—Any joint resolution referred to in clause (B) of paragraph (1) shall be considered in the Senate in accordance with subsection (n). . . ."

Part B—Improvement of Enforcement and Services

Sec. 111. . . .

(b) Increased Authorization of Appropriations for INS and EOIR—In addition to any other amounts authorized to be appropriated, in order to carry out this Act, there are authorized to be appropriated to the Department of Justice...

(2) for the Immigration and Naturalization Service, for fiscal year 1987, $12,000,000, and for fiscal year 1988, $15,000,000 . . . to provide for an increase in the border patrol personnel of the INS so that the average level of such personnel in each fiscal year 1987 and 1988 is at

least 50 per cent higher than such level for fiscal year 1986. . . .

Title II — Legalization

Sec. 201. Legalization of status

(a) Providing for Legalization Program—(1) Chapter 5 of title II is amended by inserting after section 245 (8 U.S.C. 1255) the following new section:

"Adjustment of Status of Certain Entrants Before January 1, 1982, to that of Person Admitted for Lawful Residence

"Sec. 245A. (a) Temporary Resident Status—The Attorney General shall adjust the status of an alien to that of an alien lawfully admitted for temporary residence if the alien meets the following requirements:

"(1) Timely Application—

"(A) During Application Period—Except as provided in subparagraph (B), the alien must apply for such adjustment during the 12-month period beginning on a date (not later than 180 days after the date of enactment of this section) designated by the Attorney General. . . .

"(2) Continuous Lawful Residence Since 1982—

"(A) In General—The alien must establish that he entered the United States before January 1, 1982, and that he has resided continuously in the United States in an unlawful status since such date and through the date the application is filed under this subsection.

"(B) Non-immigrants—In the case of an alien who entered the United States as a non-immigrant before January 1, 1982, the alien must establish that the alien's period of authorized stay as a non-immigrant expired before such date through the passage of time or the alien's unlawful status was known to the Government as of such date. . . .

"(4) Admissible as Immigrant...

For the purposes of this subsection, an alien in the status of a Cuban and Haitian entrant described in paragraph (1) or (2)(A) of section 501(e) of Public Law 96-422 shall be considered to have entered the United States and to be in an unlawful status in the United States.

"(b) Subsequent Adjustment to Permanent Residence and Nature of Temporary Resident Status—

"(1) Adjustment to Permanent Residence—The Attorney General shall adjust the status of any alien provided lawful temporary resident status under subsection (a) to that of an alien lawfully admitted for permanent residence if the alien meets the following requirements:

"(A) Timely Application After One Year's Residence—The alien must apply for such adjustment during the one-year period beginning with the nineteenth month that begins after the date the alien was granted such temporary resident status.

"(B) Continuous Residence...

"(i) The alien must establish that he has continuously resided in the United States since the date the alien was granted such temporary resident status.

"(C) Admissible as Immigrant—The alien must establish that he—

"(i) is admissible to the United States as an immigrant, except as otherwise provided under subsection (d)(2), and

"(ii) has not been convicted of any felony or three or more misdemeanors committed in the United States.

"(D) Basic Citizenship Skills.—

"(i) The alien must demonstrate that he either—

"(I) meets the requirements of section 312 (relating to minimal understanding of ordinary English and a knowledge and understanding of the history and government of the United States. . . .

"(II) is satisfactorily pursuing a course of study (recognized by the Attorney General) to achieve an understanding of English and such knowledge and understanding of the history and government of the United States. . . .

"(h) Temporary Disqualification of Newly Legalized Aliens from Receiving Certain Public Welfare Assistance—

"(1) In General—During the five year period beginning on the date an alien was granted lawful temporary resident status under subsection (a), and notwithstanding any other provision of law—

"(A) except as provided in paragraphs (2) and (3), the alien is not eligible for—

"(i) any program of financial assistance furnished under Federal law . . .

"(ii) medical assistance under a State plan approved under Title XIX of the Social Security Act; and

"(iii) assistance under the Food Stamp Act of 1977; and

"(B) a State or political subdivision therein may, to the extent consistent with subparagraph (A) and paragraphs (2) and (3), provide that an alien is not eligible for the programs of financial assistance or for medical assistance described in subparagraph (A) (ii) furnished under the law of that State or political subdivision . . .

Unless otherwise specifically provided by this section or other law, an alien in temporary lawful residence status granted under subsection (a) shall not be considered (for purposes of any law of a State or political subdivision providing for a program of financial assistance) to be permanently residing in the United States under color of law.

"(2) Exceptions.—Paragraph (1) shall not apply—
"(A) to a Cuban and Haitian entrant (as defined in paragraph (1) or (2)(A) of section 501(e) of Public Law 96-422, as in effect on April 1, 1983) . . ."

Title III—Reform of Legal Immigration

PART A—Temporary Agricultural Workers

Sec. 301. H-2A Agricultural Workers

(a) Providing New "H-2A" Nonimmigrant Classification for Temporary Agricultural Labor—Paragraph (15) (H) of section 101 (a) (8 U.S.C. 1101(a)) is amended by striking out "to perform temporary services or labor," in clause (ii) and inserting in lieu thereof, "(a) to perform agricultural labor or services, as defined by the Secretary of Labor in regulations and including agricultural labor defined in section 3121(g) of the Internal Revenue Code of 1954 and agriculture as defined in section 3(f) of the Fair Labor Standards Act of 1938 . . . of a temporary or seasonal nature, or (b) to perform other temporary service or labor."

(b) Involvement of Departments of Labor and Agriculture in H-2A Program—Section 214(c) (8 U.S.C. 1184(c)) is amended by adding to the end the following: "For purposes of this subsection with respect to non-immigrants described in section 101(a)(15)(H)(ii)(a), the term 'appropriate agencies of Government' means the Department of Labor and includes the Department of Agriculture. The provisions of section 216 shall apply to the question of importing any alien as non-immigrant under section 101(a)(15)(H)(ii)(a)."

(c) Admission of H-2A Workers—Chapter 2 of Title II is amended by adding after section 215 the following new section:

Admission of Temporary H-2a Workers

"Sec. 216(a) Conditions for Approval of H-2A Petitions—(1) A petition to import an alien as an H-2A worker . . . may not be approved by the Attorney General unless the petitioner has applied to the Secretary of Labor for a certification that—
"(A) there are not sufficient workers who are able, willing, and qualified, and who will be available at the time and place needed, to perform the labor or services involved in the petition, and
"(B) the employment of the alien in such labor or services will not adversely affect the wages and working conditions of workers in the United States similarly employed."

[Title IV of the act specifies various reports to Congress over the next three years dealing with comprehensive reports on immigration, unauthorized alien employment, the H-2A program, the legalization program, evidence of discrimination, and the visa waiver pilot program.]

Source: Act of November 6, 1986, 100 Stat. 3360.

Statement on Signing Immigration Reform and Control Act of 1986, President Ronald Reagan

On November 6, 1986, President Ronald Reagan signed the Immigration Reform and Control Act, arguably the most important piece of U.S. immigration legislation since the Immigration and Nationality Act of 1965. As reflected in his signing statement, President Reagan strongly believed that amnesty, along with sanctions against employers illegally hiring undocumented workers, was an important component of any legislation addressing the problem of illegal aliens. Despite Reagan's support, the concept of amnesty became anathema to conservative lawmakers, who blocked all further efforts to grant legal status to undocumented immigrants into the twenty-first century.

The Immigration Reform and Control Act of 1986 is the most comprehensive reform of our immigration laws since 1952. In the past 35 years our nation has been increasingly affected by illegal immigration. This legislation takes a major step toward meeting this challenge to our sovereignty. At the same time, it preserves and enhances the Nation's heritage of legal immigration. I am pleased to sign the bill into law.

In 1981 this administration asked the Congress to pass a comprehensive legislative package, including employer sanctions, other measures to increase enforcement of the immigration laws, and legalization. The act provides these three essential components. The employer sanctions program is the keystone and major element. It will remove the incentive for illegal immigration by eliminating the job opportunities which draw illegal aliens here.

We have consistently supported a legalization program which is both generous to the alien and fair to the countless thousands of people throughout the world who seek legally to come to America. The legalization provisions in this act will go far to improve the lives of a class of individuals who now must hide in the shadows, without access to many of the benefits of a free and open society. Very soon many of these men and women will be able to step into the sunlight and, ultimately, if they choose, they may become Americans.

Section 102(a) of the bill adds section 274B to the Immigration and Nationality Act. This new section relates to certain kinds of discrimination in connection with employment in the United States. Section 274B(a) provides that it is an "unfair immigration-related employment practice" to "discriminate against" any individual in hiring, recruitment or referral for a fee, or discharging from employment "because of" such individual's national origin or—if such individual is a United States citizen or an alien who is a lawful permanent resident, refugee admitted under INA section 296, or asylee granted asylum under section 208, and who has taken certain steps evidencing an intent to become a United States citizen—because of such individual's citizenship status. Employers of fewer than four employees are expressly exempted from coverage. Discrimination against an "unauthorized alien," as defined in section 274A(h)(3), is also not covered. Other exceptions include cases of discrimination because of national origin that are covered by title VII of the Civil Rights Act of 1964, discrimination based on citizenship status when lawfully required under government authority, and discrimination in favor of a United States citizen over an alien if the citizen is at least "equally qualified."

The major purpose of section 274B is to reduce the possibility that employer sanctions will result in increased national origin and alienage discrimination and to provide a remedy if employer sanctions enforcement does have this result. Accordingly, subsection (k) provides that the section will not apply to any discrimination that takes place after a repeal of employer sanctions if this should occur. In the light of this major purpose, the Special Counsel should exercise the discretion provided under subsection (d)(1) so as to limit the investigations conducted on his own initiative to cases involving discrimination apparently caused by an employer's fear of liability under the employer sanctions program.

I understand section 274B to require a "discriminatory intent" standard of proof: The party bringing the action must show that in the decisionmaking process the defendant's action was motivated by one of the prohibited criteria. Thus, it would be improper to use the "disparate impact" theory of recovery, which was developed under paragraph (2) of section 793(a) of title VII, in a line of Supreme Court cases over the last 15 years. This paragraph of title VII does not have a counterpart in section 274B. Section 274B tracks only the language of paragraph (1) of section 703(a), the basis of the "disparate treatment" (discriminatory intent) theory of recovery under title VII. Moreover, paragraph (d)(2) refers to "knowing and intentional discrimination" and "a pattern or practice

of discriminatory activity." The meaning of the former phrase is self-evident, while the latter is taken from the Supreme Court's disparate treatment jurisprudence and thus includes the requirement of a discriminatory intent.

Thus, a facially neutral employee selection practice that is employed without discriminatory intent will be permissible under the provisions of section 274B. For example, the section does not preclude a requirement of English language skill or a minimum score on an aptitude test even if the employer cannot show a "manifest relationship" to the job in question or that the requirement is a "bona fide occupational qualification reasonably necessary to the normal operation of that particular business or enterprise," so long as the practice is not a guise used to discriminate on account of national origin or citizenship status. Indeed, unless the plaintiff presents evidence that the employer has intentionally discriminated on proscribed grounds, the employer need not offer *any* explanation for his employee selection procedures.

Section 274B(c) provides that the President shall appoint, with the advice and consent of the Senate, a Special Counsel for Immigration-Related Unfair Employment Practices within the Justice Department, to serve for a term of 4 years. I understand this subsection to provide that the Special Counsel shall serve at the pleasure and with the policy guidance of the President, but for no longer than for a 4-year term (subject to reappointment by the President with the advice and consent of the Senate).

In accordance with the provisions of section 174B(h) and (j)(4), a requirement to pay attorneys' fees may be imposed against non-prevailing parties—including alleged victims or persons who file on their behalf as well as employers—if claims or defenses are made that do not have a reasonable foundation in both law and fact. The same standard for the imposing of attorneys' fees applies to all nonprevailing parties. It is therefore expected that prevailing defendants would recover attorneys' fees in all cases for which this standard is satisfied, not merely in cases where the claim of the victim or person filing on their behalf is found to be vexatious or frivolous.

The provisions of new INA section 245A(a)(4)(B) and (b)(1)(C)(ii), added by section 201(a) of the bill, state that no alien would qualify for the lawful temporary or the permanent residence status provided in that section if he or she has been convicted of *any* felony or three or more misdemeanors committed in the United States.

New INA section 245A(d)(2) states that no alien would qualify for the lawful temporary or permanent residence status provided in that section if "likely to become [a] public charge []." This disqualification could be waived by the Attorney General under certain circumstances. A likelihood that an applicant would become a public charge would exist, for example, if the applicant had failed to demonstrate either a history of employment in the United States of a kind that would provide sufficient means without public cash assistance for the support of the alien and his likely dependents who are not United States citizens or the possession of independent means sufficient by itself for such support for an indefinite period.

New INA section 245A(a)(3) requires that an applicant for legalization establish that he has been "continuously physically present in the United States since the date of the enactment" but states that "brief, casual, and innocent absences from the United States" will not be considered a break in the continuous physical presence. To the extent that the INS has made available a procedure by which aliens can obtain permission to depart and re-enter the United States after a brief, casual, and innocent absence by establishing a *prima facie* case of eligibility for adjustment of status under this section, I understand section 245A(a)(3) to require that an authorized departure and illegal reentry will constitute a break in "continuous physical presence."

New INA section 210(d), added by section 302(a) of the bill, provides that an alien who is "apprehended" before or during the application period for adjustment of status for certain "special agricultural workers," may not under certain circumstances related to the establishment of a nonfrivolous case of eligibility for such adjustment of status be excluded or deported. I understand this subsection not to authorize any alien to apply for admission to or to be admitted to the United States in order to apply for adjustment of status under this section. Aliens outside the United States may apply for adjustment of status under this section at an appropriate consular office outside the United States pursuant to the procedures established by the Attorney General, in cooperation with the Secretary of State, as provided in section 210(b)(1)(B).

Section 304 of the bill establishes the Commission on Agricultural Workers, half of whose 12 members are appointed by the executive branch and half by the legislative branch. This hybrid Commission is not consistent with constitutional separation of powers. However, the Commission's role will be entirely advisory.

Section 304(g) provides that upon request of the Commission's Chairman, the head of "any department or agency of the United States" must supply "information necessary to enable it to carry out [the] section." Although I expect that the executive branch will cooperate closely with the Commission, its access to executive branch information will be limited in accordance with established principles of law, including the constitutional separation of powers.

Section 601 establishes a Commission for the Study of International Migration and Cooperative Economic Development, all of whose members are appointed by the legislative branch. Section 601(d)(1) states that the access to executive branch information required under section 304(g) must be provided to this Commission also. Accordingly, the comments of the preceding paragraph are appropriate here as well.

New INA section 274A(a)(5) provides that a person or entity shall be deemed in compliance with the employment verification system in the case of an individual who is referred for employment by a State employment agency if that person or entity retains documentation of such referral certifying that the agency complied with the verification system with respect to the individual referred. I understand this provision not to mandate State employment agencies to issue referral documents certifying compliance with the verification system or to impose any additional affirmative duty or obligation on the offices or personnel of such agencies.

Distance has not discouraged illegal immigration to the United States from all around the globe. The problem of illegal immigration should not, therefore, be seen as a problem between the United States and its neighbors. Our objective is only to establish a reasonable, fair, orderly, and secure system of immigration into this country and not to discriminate in any way against particular nations or people.

The act I am signing today is the product of one of the longest and most difficult legislative undertakings of recent memory. It has truly been a bipartisan effort, with this administration and the allies of immigration reform in the Congress, of both parties, working together to accomplish these critically important reforms.

Future generations of Americans will be thankful for our efforts to humanely regain control of our borders and thereby preserve the value of one of the most sacred possessions of our people: American citizenship.

Source: Ronald Reagan. *Statement on Signing Immigration Bill,* November 6, 1986 (Washington, DC: U.S. Government Printing Office, 1986).

Debate on Reparations for Japanese American Internees, U.S. Senate (1988)

On February 19, 1942, some two months after the Japanese attack on Pearl Harbor, President Franklin D. Roosevelt issued an executive order, later upheld by the U.S. Supreme Court, that led to the internment of more than 120,000 Japanese Americans living *in the Western United States. Many of the internees lost property and savings accumulated over a lifetime. Forty-six years later—on August 10, 1988—President Ronald Reagan signed legislation providing an apology and reparations of $20,000 to each of about 60,000 survivors of the camps. While most all Americans agreed that the apology was warranted and most supported some level of monetary compensation for survivors, a few conservative Republicans disagreed with the reparations, whose total cost exceeded $1.2 billion. The following excerpts of the Senate debate over the reparations legislation on April 20, 1988, capture the general tenor of contemporary public opinion on the matter.*

Senator [Daniel K.] Inouye [D-HI]: . . . The measure before us is the source of much anguish and much controversy. Because of the commitment and dedication of Senator [Spark M.] Matsunaga [D-HI], he has been able to convince 72 of his colleagues to join him in this endeavor.

Many fellow Americans, including my colleague from Nevada, have asked: "Why should Japanese Americans be compensated?" During times of war, especially in times of fear, all people suffer. That is a very common argument made against this measure.

[W]hile it is true that all people of this Nation suffer during wartime, the Japanese-American internment experience is unprecedented in the history of American civil rights deprivation. I think we should recall, even if painful, that Americans of Japanese ancestry were determined by our Government to be security risks without any formal allegations or charges of disloyalty or espionage. They were arbitrarily branded disloyal solely on the grounds of racial ancestry.

No similar mass internment was deemed necessary for Americans of German or Italian ancestries, and I think we should recall and remind ourselves that in World War II, the Japanese were not our only enemies.

These Japanese Americans who were interned could not confront their accusers or bring their case before a court. These are basic rights of all Americans. They were incarcerated, forced to live in public communities with no privacy, and stripped of their freedom to move about as others could.

Japanese Americans wishing to fight for this country were initially declared ineligible. However, once allowed to volunteer, they volunteered in great numbers. In fact, proportionately and percentagewise, more Japanese Americans put on the uniform of this country during World War II, more were wounded and more were killed, even if they were restricted to serving in ethnically restricted military units.

The individual payments acknowledge the unjust deprivation of liberty, the infliction of mental and physical suffering, and the stigma of being branded disloyal, losses not compensable under the Japanese Evacuation Claims Act of 1948. . . .

The Presidentially appointed Commission on Wartime Relocation and Internment of Civilians found no documented acts of espionage, sabotage, or fifth column activity by any identifiable American citizen of Japanese ancestry or resident Japanese aliens on the west coast.

This was supposed to have been the rationale for this mass evacuation and mass incarceration, that these Americans were not to be trusted, that these Americans were agents of an enemy country, that these Americans would spy and carry out espionage, and this Presidentially appointed Commission, which incidentally was made up of leading citizens throughout this land—and only one member of that Commission was of Japanese ancestry—declared that there were no acts of espionage whatsoever. And sadly, the Commission in its 1983 report concluded that internment was motivated by racial prejudice, war hysteria, and a failure of political leadership. . . .

[T]he goal of [this bill] S. 1009 is to benefit all citizens of our Nation by educating our citizens to preclude this event from occurring again to any other ethnic or religious group or any person suspected of being less than a loyal citizen. This bill reinforces the strength of our Constitution by reaffirming our commitment to upholding the constitutional rights of all our citizens. So, respectfully, I strongly urge its passage and in so doing once again commend and congratulate my distinguished colleague from Hawaii. . . .

Senator [Spark M.] Matsunaga [D-HI]: I congratulate the senior Senator from Hawaii for his excellent statement. Coming from one who served in the 442d Regimental Combat Team, the most highly decorated military unit in the entire history of the United States, and having been highly decorated with the second highest award, the Distinguished Service Cross, and having sacrificed an arm in that war, I believe what the senior Senator from Hawaii has to say should be taken most seriously. . . .

Senator [Ted] Stevens [R-AK]: . . . As recounted yesterday what happened when the United States military removed 900 American citizens—Aleuts, who lived on the Aleutian chain and the Pribilof Islands—from their homes and took them to abandoned canneries and gold mining camps in southeastern Alaska.

Not many people understand the distances in our State. Attu and Kiska, which the Japanese invaded, are the most western islands in the Aleutian chain. The military saw fit to remove all Aleuts from all of the islands. Alaskans believed they did that because they wanted to occupy the islands and just did not want any local people in their way.

The Pribilof Islands were over 1,000 miles from the

two islands the Japanese had taken. The Japanese never attempted to move further up along the Aleutian chain. They made an invasion of those two islands and fortified them. But there was really no necessity to remove these people. . . . Let us assume that the Japanese came to Baltimore. The action of the United States military removing the Aleuts would be like going to Chicago and then going west from Chicago about 1,000 miles and taking everyone between Chicago and Denver and moving them out of harm's way.

The record is clear that in terms of this internment—and it was an internment—was for the convenience of the Government. And these people, because they were of native descent, were taken and interned. They were kept for 2 to 3 years in those camps. In those days, Alaska was a territory, under wartime conditions, and it was not possible to travel.

I related yesterday how one of my friends, Flore Lekanoff, was taken from one of those camps in southeastern Alaska back to the Pribilof Islands to hunt for seals for the military. He was never paid for that. He was never recognized as being in the service of the Government. None of these people were treated as though they were in the service of the Government. They were literally just shoved aside. . . .

They have waited a long, long time. Most of them never recovered financially, particularly the people I represent in the Aleutian chain. Many are still destitute. This settlement is the final act to close this chapter of history and try to make restitution for that period of hysteria.

The people who made those decisions were good Americans. They were defending the country. They made mistakes. . . .

Senator [Daniel J.] Evans [D-WA]: As a Senator from the State of Washington, I have a special interest in this legislation. The first group of Japanese citizens to be removed from their homes under President Roosevelt's Executive Order were from Bainbridge Island, WA. They were the first of nearly 13,000 Japanese Americans from the State of Washington to be funneled into assembly centers and eventually into relocation facilities.

Victims of Executive Order 9066 were given very short notice that they would be sent to relocation facilities. Most were granted just a few days to abandon their homes and belongings. As a result they were forced to sell or lease their property and businesses at prices reflecting only a fraction of their worth. Substantial economic losses were incurred. Once they arrived at the relocation centers they found a quality of life which was atrocious. They were overcrowded and families suffered from an acute lack of privacy with no borders or walls to separate them from others.

Opponents of this legislation choose to ignore raw, racial prejudice woven in what was supposed to be legitimate national security justification for internment. The evacuees, however, were guilty of no crime other than the apparent crime of being of Japanese ancestry. Japanese Americans left their homes in an atmosphere of racial prejudice and returned to the same.

What is perhaps most alarming about the Japanese internment is that it took place in the United States of America. This is the same country which has prided itself on freedom, justice, and the preservation and protection of individual rights.

Thirty-four years after the last citizens were released from captivity, Congress established the Commission on the Wartime Relocation and Internment of Japanese-American Citizens to assess the decision to intern and relocate Japanese Americans. Two years after its inception, the Commission issued certain factual findings and subsequent recommendations. I have cosponsored legislation to implement these recommendations throughout my tenure in the U.S. Senate.

The $20,000 compensation that would be allotted to each victim, and the educational fund established by this legislation are a modest attempt to redress wrongs against loyal Americans. Although we cannot restore completely what already has been lost, the legislation would serve as a symbol to all that the United States can come to terms with its own tragic mistake. . . .

Senator [Jesse A.] Helms [R-NC]: . . . Nobody is, in retrospect, proud of the relocation of the Japanese Americans during World War II, but as I said earlier, we lived in a time of terror in this country immediately after the attack on Pearl Harbor. Nobody knew what was coming next. . . . We had just been attacked by a totalitarian regime which had enjoyed a virtually unbroken string of military successes, both before and immediately after the Government of Japan attacked the United States of America. . . .

I think it is only fair to look back to that time, and recall the fact that our intelligence community told the then President of the United States, Franklin Delano Roosevelt, that there was great risk. Now we can see that it was a mistake.

I have no vision problem with respect to that. We will have 20–20 vision by hindsight, and I am perfectly willing for this Senate and this Congress to declare that this kind of thing must never happen again.

But the Senate has just voted to give the priority emphasis to money, $1.3 billion. So I think we ought to look at our priorities. . . .

. . . The U.S. Government, contrary to suggestions otherwise, has not ignored the suffering that occurred as a result of the relocation and internment during the war. The Government has officially recognized that much unjustified personal hardship was, in fact, caused. Previous Congresses, Presidents, and Attorneys General have taken steps to acknowledge and compensate Japanese Americans for the injuries they suffered.

For example, in 1948, Congress enacted the American Japanese Claims Act, which authorized compensation for "any claim" for damages to or loss of real or personal property "as a reasonable consequence of the evacuation or exclusion of" persons of Japanese ancestry as a result of governmental action during World War II.

I might add that this act of 1948 was subsequently amended to liberalize its compensation provisions.

Under the amended act, the Justice Department received claims seeking approximately $147 million. Ultimately, 26,568 settlements were achieved. . . . True enough, the American Japanese Claims Act did not include every item of damage that was or could have been suggested. It did, however, address the hardships visited upon persons of Japanese ancestry in a comprehensive, considered manner taking into account individual needs and losses, and this effort to correct injustice to individuals was in keeping with our Nation's best tradition of individual rather than collective response, and it was far more contemporaneous with the injuries to the claimants than would be any payments at this late date. . . .

Senator [Alan K.] Simpson [R-WY]: It has been a very interesting debate for me. I have been paying attention to it on the monitor. It has made me recall some most interesting and memorable parts of my own life because I was a young boy in Cody, WY, in 1941 when the war started. I was 10 then.

Two years later, at the age of 12, somewhere between the years of 12 and 13, the third largest community in Wyoming was constructed between the communities of Powell and Cody, WY, a city of 15,000 people which really literally went up overnight. And the name of it, of course, was Heart Mountain War Relocation Center, known to the people of the area simply as the "Jap Camp," a term which may be hard for us to believe now but that is what it was referred to then; swiftly built by those who had not been drafted into the war, or older men in their 40's who were not able to be taken into the war effort.

And so came into being Heart Mountain, WY, War Relocation Center. There was barbed wire around it. There were guard towers at the edges of it. It was a very imposing area. . . . I remember one night very distinctly when the scoutmaster—I was a Boy Scout, a rather nominal one, but I enjoyed the activities of the group. And he said, "We are going to go out to the War Relocation Center and have a scout meeting." I said, "Well, I mean, are there any of them out there?" . . . He said, "Yes, yes,

these are American citizens, you see." And that put a new twist on it because we thought of them as something else—as aliens; we thought of them as spies; we thought of them as people who were behind wire because they were trying to do in our country.

So I shall not forget going to the Boy Scout meeting and meeting Boy Scouts from California, most of them, I recall, same merit badges, same scout sashes, same clothing.

And why not? Some of them were second- or third-generation American citizens. . . . I also remember those other nights we would go into the compound—which it was in every sense, with searchlights and with wire—visiting with some of the older people. There were very few young men there from the ages of 17 through 28, because many of them were in the armed services of the United States. But I do remember visiting with the older people and there were many of them there.

The younger and the older were there. Those were the principal inhabitants. I remember a woman, a very old woman to me at that age, said "Do you have grandparents?"

I said, "Yes, I do."

She said, "Where do they live?"

I said, "In Cody, down the road there."

She said, "Well, what kind of a house do they have?"

I thought, well, that is interesting to ask. I described it.

"What do they do?"

And then I remember she showed me pictures of her family.

She said, "This is my son. He is in Italy now fighting for this country, the United States of America."

Then we would go downtown in Cody, WY, and there would be a sign on the restaurant that said, "No Japs allowed here." And then you would go down to another place of business, it might be a sign that said, "My son was killed at Iwo Jima. How do you think I feel?"

And the trustees would come into town. They were remarkable people. Usually the best and the brightest. Maybe those who had been involved in agriculture and whose lands had been taken from them—confiscated.

So I really had a lot of trouble sorting that all out at the age of 13. I maybe have some of the same kind of trouble sorting it all out at the age of 56. But let me just say that I preserve it as a very formative part of my life. . . . There is no question about it being the gravest of injustices. And it may be hardly a repayable one. How do you ever really repay these people for the wages, the property, the opportunity, the education, the part of their lives lost during this period? And this taxpayer expenditure is a troubling part of the bill for me.

I have trouble with the money. An apology may be long overdue and may be so appropriate. But, coupled with money, it takes away some of the sincerity of the apology, somehow. If you did that with a friend, a lovely friend, and you said: I am sorry for what I did. I know that was very harmful to you and hurtful. But I am sorry and I apologize and I want to give you some money.

I think that that somehow is unbecoming. It may not be to some. It is a troubling aspect of it to me. . . . So we will conclude this, and I think probably we will revisit this issue again, not with this situation but in other populations of our country, and we best know indeed, that will likely take place.

There is not one of us here today with what we have been through with our civil rights activities in 1964 and Selma that probably thinks: "How could this have ever occurred?" And yet at the time it occurred, it seemed at that time of our lives to be the most important step that could be taken.

That decision was made by people with much greater wisdom than I had at the age of 13 in Cody, WY.

Hopefully, we will conclude this debate shortly and move on to other issues of the day because this is an old and sad and very painful thing that we have reopened here in this debate. The sooner we close that wound and suture it with love and understanding and affection, we will be better off. And suturing it with money does not seem like the best way to conclude the issue.

Source: Congressional Record, April 20, 1988.

Immigration Act of 1990

On November 29, 1990, Congress passed legislation to modify the Immigration Reform and Control Act of 1986. The changes applied largely to the preference system of admission, increasing the number of family members of resident aliens and citizens allowed entry. In addition, the new legislation increased immigration levels for persons with specialized skills and occupations. Finally, it added an entirely new category, intended to increase ethnic and geographic diversity among immigrants, by allowing unused visas to be shifted to immigrants from countries and regions underrepresented in previous years.

Title I — Immigrants

Subtitle A—Worldwide and Per Country Levels

Sec. 101. Worldwide Levels.
(a) In General.—Section 201 (8 U.S.C. 1151) is amended to read as follows:

"Worldwide Level of Immigration
"Sec. 201. (a) In General—Exclusive of aliens described in subsection (b), aliens born in a foreign state or dependent area who may be issued immigrant visas or who may otherwise acquire the status of an alien lawfully admitted to the United States for permanent residence are limited to—

"(1) family-sponsored immigrants described in section 203(a) . . . in a number not to exceed in any fiscal year the number specified in subsection (c) for that year, and not to exceed in any of the first three quarters of any fiscal year 27 percent of the worldwide level under such subsection for all such fiscal year;

"(2) employment-based immigrants described in subsection 203(b) . . . in a number not to exceed in any fiscal year the number specified in subsection (d) for that year, and not exceed in any of the first 3 quarters of any fiscal year 27 percent of the worldwide level under such subsection for all of such fiscal year; and

"(3) for fiscal years beginning with fiscal year 1995, diversity immigrants described in section 203(c) . . . in a number not to exceed in any fiscal year the number specified in subsection (e) for that year, and not to exceed in any of the first three quarters of any fiscal year 27 percent of the worldwide level under such subsection for all such fiscal year. . .

"(b)Aliens not subject to direct numerical limitations.—
"(2)(A)(i) Immediate Relatives—For purposes of this subsection, the term 'immediate relatives' means the children, spouses, and parents of a citizen of the United States, except that, in the case of parents, such citizens be at least 21 years of age. In the case of an alien who was the spouse of a citizen of the United States for at least 2 years at the time of the citizen's death and was not legally separated from the citizen at the time of the citizen's death, the alien shall be considered, for the purpose of this subsection, to remain an immediate relative after the date of the citizen's death but only if the spouse files a petition under section 204(a)(1)(A) within 2 years after such date and only until the date the spouse remarries.

"(c) Worldwide Level of Family-Sponsored Immigrants—(1)(A) The worldwide level of family-sponsored immigrants under this subsection for a fiscal year is, subject to subparagraph (B) equal to—
"(i) 480,000 minus
"(ii) the number computed under paragraph (2), plus
"(iii) the number (if any) computed under paragraph (3).

"(B)(i) For each of fiscal years 1992, 1993, and 1994, 465,000 shall be substituted for 480,000 in subparagraph (A)(i).

"(ii) In no case shall the number computed under subparagraph (A) be less than 226,000 . . .

"(d) Worldwide Level of Employment-Based Immigrants—(1) The worldwide level of employment-based immigrants under this subsection for a fiscal year is equal to—

"(A) 140,000 plus

"(B) the number computed under paragraph (2).

"(2) The number computed under this paragraph for a fiscal year is the difference (if any) between the maximum number of visas which may be issued in section 203(a) . . . during the previous fiscal year and the number of visas issued under that section during that year.

"(e) Worldwide Level of Diversity Immigrants—The worldwide level of diversity immigrants is equal to 55,000 for each fiscal year."

Sec. 102. Per Country Levels.

Sec. 202 (8 U.S.C. 1152) is amended—

(1) by amending subsection (a) to read as follows:

"(a) Per Country Level—

"(1) Nondiscrimination—Except as specifically provided in paragraph (2) and in sections 101(a)(27), 201(b)(2)(A)(i), and 203, no person shall receive any preference or priority or be discriminated against in the issuance of an immigrant visa because of a person's race, sex, nationality, place of birth, or place of residence...

"(2) Per Country Levels for Family-Sponsored and Employment-Based Immigrants—Subject to paragraphs (3) and (4), the total number of immigrant visas made available to natives of any single foreign state or dependent area under subsections (a) and (b) of section 203 in any fiscal year may not exceed 7 percent (in the case of a single foreign state) or 2 percent (in the case of a dependent area) of the total number of such visas made available under such subsection in that fiscal year. . . ."

Subtitle B—Preference System
Part 1—Family-Sponsored Immigrants

Sec. 111. Family-Sponsored Immigrants

Sec. 203 (8 U.S.C. 1153) is amended—

(1) by redesignating subsections (b) and (e) as subsections (d) through (g), respectively, and

(2) by striking subsection (a) and inserting the following:

"(a) Preference Allocation for Family-Sponsored Immigrants—Aliens subject to the worldwide level specified in section 201(c) for family-sponsored immigrants shall be allotted visas as follows:

"(1) Unmarried sons and daughters of citizens . . . in a number not to exceed 23,400 plus any visas required for the class specified in paragraph (4).

"(2) Spouses and unmarried sons and unmarried daughters of permanent resident aliens . . . shall be allocated visas in a number not to exceed 114,200 plus the number (if any) by which such worldwide level exceeds 226,000 plus any visas not required for the class specified in paragraph (1); except that not less than 77 percent of such visa numbers shall be allocated to aliens described in subparagraph (A).

"(3) Married sons and married daughters of immigrants—in a number not to exceed 23,400, plus any visas not required for the classes specified in paragraphs (1) and (2).

"(4) Brothers and sisters of citizens—in a number not to exceed 65,000, plus any visas not required for the classes specified in paragraphs (1) through (3) . . . ."

Sec. 112. Transition for Spouses and minor children of legalized aliens...

"(c) Legalized Alien Defined—In this section, the term 'legalized alien' means an alien lawfully admitted for temporary or permanent residence who was provided—

"(1) temporary or permanent residence status under section 210 of the Immigration and Nationality Act,

"(2) temporary or permanent residence status under section 245A of the Immigration and Nationality Act, or

"(3) permanent residence status under section 202 of the Immigration Reform and Control Act of 1986. . . ."

Part 2—Employment-Based Immigrants

Sec. 121. Employment-Based Immigrants

(a) In General—Section 203 (8 U.S.C. 1153) is amended by inserting after subsection (a), as inserted by section 111, the following new subsection:

"(b) Preference Allocation for Employment-Based Immigrants—Aliens subject to the worldwide level specified in section 201(d) for employment-based immigrants in a fiscal year shall be allocated visas as follows:

"(1) Priority Workers—Visas shall first be made available in a number not to exceed 40,000, plus any visas not required for the classes specified in paragraphs (4) and (5), to qualified immigrants who are aliens described in any of the following subparagraphs (A) through (C):

"(A) Aliens with extraordinary ability—in sciences, arts, education, business, or athletics which has been demonstrated by sustained national or international acclaim and whose achievements have been recognized in the field through extensive documentation.

"(B) Outstanding Professors and Researchers. . . .

"(C) Certain Multinational Executives and Managers. . . .

"(2) Alien members of Professions holding advanced degrees or aliens of exceptional ability. . . .

"(3) Skilled workers, professionals, and other workers. . . .

"(4) Certain special immigrants—Visas shall be made available, in a number not to exceed 10,000 to qualified special immigrants described in section 101 (a)(27) . . . of which not more than 5,000 may be made available in any fiscal year to special immigrants described in subclause (II) or (III) of section 101 (a) (27)(C)(ii).

"(5) Employment Creation—
"(A) In General—Visas shall be made available, in a number not to exceed 10,000, to qualified immigrants seeking to enter the United States for the purpose of engaging in a new commercial enterprise—
"(i) which the alien has established,
"(ii) in which such alien has invested . . . or is actively in the process of investing, capital in an amount not less than the amount specified in subparagraph (C), and
"(iii) which will benefit the United States economy and create full-time employment for not fewer than 10 United States citizens or aliens lawfully admitted for permanent residence or other immigrants lawfully authorized to be employed in the United States (other than the immigrant and the immigrant's spouse, sons, or daughters). . . ."

Part 3—Diversity Immigrants

Sec. 131. Diversity Immigrants
Sec. 203, as amended by sections 111 and 121 of this Act, is further amended by inserting after subsection (b) the following new subsection:
"(c) Diversity Immigrants—
"(1) In General—Except as provided in paragraph (2), aliens subject to the worldwide level specified in section 201(e) for diversity immigrants shall be allotted visas each fiscal year as follows:

"(A) Determination of Preference Immigration—The Attorney General shall determine for the most recent previous 5-year period for which data are available, the total number of aliens who are natives of each foreign state and who (i) were admitted or otherwise provided lawful permanent resident status . . . and (ii) were subject to the numerical limitations of section 201(a) . . . or who were admitted or otherwise provided lawful permanent resident status as an immediate relative or other alien described in section 201(b)(2) . . . (iv) Redistribution of Unused Visa Numbers—If the Secretary of State estimates that the number of immigrant visas to be issued to natives in any region for the fiscal year under this paragraph is less than the number of immigrant visas made available to such natives under this paragraph for the fiscal year, subject to clause (v), the excess visa numbers shall be made available to natives (other than the natives of a high-admission state) of the other regions in proportion to the percentages otherwise specified in clauses (ii) and (iii). . . ."

Subtitle C—Commission and Information

Sec. 141. Commission of Legal Immigration Reform
(a) Establishment and Composition of Commission—(1) Effective October 1, 1991, there is established a Commission on Legal Immigration Reform . . . which shall be composed of 9 members . . .

Title III—Family Unity and Temporary Protected Status

Sec. 301. Family Unity
(a) Temporary Stay of Deportation and Work Authorization for Certain Eligible Immigrants—The Attorney General shall provide that in the case of an alien who is an eligible immigrant . . . who has entered the United States before [May 5, 1988], who has resided in the United States on such date, and who is not lawfully admitted for permanent residence, the alien—. . . .

(2) The term "legalized alien" means an alien lawfully admitted for temporary or permanent residence who was provided—
(A) such under section 210 of the Immigration and Nationality Act;
(B) temporary or permanent residence status under section 245A of the Immigration and Nationality Act, or
(C) permanent residence status under section 202 of the Immigration Reform and Control Act of 1986. . . .

Sec. 302. Temporary Protected Status.
(a) In General—The Immigration and Nationality Act

is amended by inserting after section 244 the following new section:

"Temporary Protected Status
"Sec. 244 A. (a) Granting of Status—
"(1) In General—In the case of an alien who is a national of a foreign state . . . under subsection (b) and who meets the requirements of subsection (c), the Attorney General—
"(A) may grant the alien temporary protected status in the U.S. and shall not deport the alien from the U.S. during the period in which such status is in effect, and
"(B) shall authorize the alien to engage in employment in the U.S. and to provide the alien with an 'employment authorized' endorsement or other appropriate work permit.

"(b) Designations—

"(1) In General—The Attorney General, after consultation with appropriate agencies . . . may designate any foreign state . . . under this subsection only if—
"(A) the Attorney General finds that there is an ongoing armed conflict within the state, and, due to such conflict, requiring the return of aliens who are nationals of that state . . . would pose a serious threat to their personal safety.
"(B) the Attorney General finds that—
"(i) there has been an earthquake, flood, drought, epidemic, or other environmental disaster in the state resulting in a substantial, but temporary, disruption of living conditions in the area affected,
"(ii) the foreign state is unable, temporarily, to handle adequately the return to the state of aliens who are nationals of the state, and
"(iii) the foreign state officially has requested designation under this paragraph; or
"(C) the Attorney General finds that there exists extraordinary and temporary conditions in a foreign state that prevent aliens who are nationals from the state from returning to the state safely. . . ."

(c) No effect on Executive Order 12711—Notwithstanding subsection (g) of section 244 A of the Immigration and Nationality Act . . . such section shall not supersede or affect Executive Order 12711 (April 11, 1990), relating to policy implementation with respect to nationals of the People's Republic of China.

Sec. 303. Special Temporary Protected Status for Salvadorans.
(a) Designation—
(1) In General.—El Salvador is hereby designated under

section 244(b) of the Immigration and Nationality Act, subject to the provisions of this section.

(2) Period of Designation.—Such designation shall take effect on the date of the enactment of this section and shall remain in effect until the end of the 18-month period beginning January 1, 1991.

Title IV — Naturalization
Sec. 401. Administrative Naturalization
(a) Naturalization Authority.—Section 310 (8 U.S.C. 1421) is amended to read as follows:

"Naturalization Authority
"Sec. 310. (a) Authority in Attorney General—The sole authority to naturalize persons as citizens of the United States is conferred upon the Attorney General.

"(b) Administration of Oaths.—An applicant for naturalization may choose to have the oath of allegiance under section 337 (a) administered by the Attorney General or by any District Court of the United States for any State or by any court of record in any State having a seal, clerk, and jurisdiction in actions in law or equity, or law and equity, in which the amount in controversy is unlimited. . . ."

Sec. 402. Substituting 3 Months residence in INS District or State for 6 months residence in a State.
Section 316(a)(1) (8 U.S.C. 1427(a)(1)) is amended by striking "and who has resided within the State in which the petitioner filed the petition for at least six months" and inserting "and who has resided within the State or within the district of the Service in the United States in which the applicant filed the application for at least three months."

Sec. 403. Waiver of English Language Requirement for Naturalization.
Section 312(1) (8 U.S.C. 1423(1)) is amended by striking "is over fifty years of age and has been living in the United States for periods totaling at least twenty years subsequent to a lawful admission for permanent residence" and inserting "either (A) is over fifty years of age and has been living in the United States for periods totaling at least 20 years subsequent to a lawful admission for permanent residence, or (B) is over 55 years of age and has been living in the U.S. for periods totaling at least 15 years subsequent to a lawful admission for permanent residence."

Sec. 405. Naturalization of Natives of the Philippines Through Certain Active Duty Service During World War II.

(a) Waiver of Certain Requirements.—(1) Clauses (1) and (2) of section 329(a) of the Immigration and Nationality Act . . . shall not apply to the naturalization of any person—

(A) who was born in the Philippines and who was residing in the Philippines before the service described in subparagraph (B);

(B) who served honorably—

(i) in an active-duty status under the command of the United States Armed Forces in the Far East, or

(ii) within the Philippine Army, the Philippine Scouts, or recognized guerilla units, at any time during the period beginning September 1, 1939, and ending December 31, 1946;

(C) who is otherwise eligible for naturalization under section 329 of such Act; and

(D) who applies for naturalization during the 2-year period beginning on the date of the enactment of this Act.

Sec. 406. Public Education regarding naturalization benefits.

Section 332 (8 U.S.C. 1443) is amended by adding at the end the following subsection:

"(h) In order to promote the opportunities and responsibilities of United States citizenship, the Attorney General shall broadly distribute information concerning the benefits which persons may receive under this title and the requirements to obtain such benefits. In carrying out this subsection, the Attorney General shall seek the assistance of appropriate community groups, private voluntary agencies, and other relevant organizations. . . ."

Source: Act of November 29, 1990, 104 Stat. 4981.

New York State Report on Multicultural Textbooks (1991)

The public school system of New York State is among the largest and most ethnically diverse in the country. In 1991, facing criticism that its curriculum placed excessive emphasis on European culture and history, a review committee appointed by the state commissioner of education issued a report that called for a more multicultural approach to social studies instruction, emphasizing the contributions of diverse cultures to American and world civilization. Critics expressed concern that the new approach would "balkanize" education along ethnic lines and undermine the role of public schools in molding a common national heritage. The text that follows includes excerpts of the original committee report—titled One Nation, Many Peoples: A Declaration of Cultural Independence—*and dissenting views by Professor Kenneth T. Jackson and historian Arthur Schlesinger, Jr.*

Preamble

The United States is a microcosm of humanity today. No other country in the world is peopled by a greater variety of races, nationalities, and ethnic groups. But although the United States has been a great asylum for diverse peoples, it has not always been a great refuge for diverse cultures. The country has opened its doors to a multitude of nationalities, but often their cultures have not been encouraged to survive or, at best, have been kept marginal to the mainstream.

Since the 1960s, however, a profound reorientation of the self-image of Americans has been under way. Before this time the dominant model of the typical American had been conditioned primarily by the need to shape a unified nation out of a variety of contrasting and often conflicting European immigrant communities. But following the struggles for civil rights, the unprecedented increase in non-European immigration over the last two decades and the increasing recognition of our nation's indigenous heritage, there has been a fundamental change in the image of what a resident of the United States is.

With this change, which necessarily highlights the racial and ethnic pluralism of the nation, previous ideals of assimilation to an Anglo-American model have been put in question and are now slowly and sometimes painfully being set aside. Many people in the United States are no longer comfortable with the requirement, common in the past, that they shed their specific cultural differences in order to be considered American. Instead, while busily adapting to and shaping mainstream cultural ideals commonly identified as American, in recent decades many in the United States—from European and non-European backgrounds—have been encouraging a more tolerant, inclusive, and realistic vision of American identity than any that has existed in the past.

This identity, committed to the democratic principles of the nation and the nation-building in which all Americans are engaged, is progressively evolving from the past model toward a new model marked by respect for pluralism and awareness of the virtues of diversity. This situation is a current reality, and a multicultural education, anchored to the shared principles of a liberal democracy, is today less an educational innovation than a national priority.

It is fitting for New York State, host to the Statue of Liberty, to inaugurate a curriculum that reflects the rich cultural diversity of the nation. The beacon of hope welcomes not just the "wretched and poor" individuals of the world, but also the dynamic and rich cultures all people bring with them.

Two centuries after this country's founders issued a Declaration of Independence, focused on the political independence from which societies distant from the United

States have continued to draw inspiration, the time has come to recognize cultural interdependence. We propose that the principle of respect for diverse cultures is critical to our nation, and we affirm that a right to cultural diversity exists. We believe that the schoolroom is one of the places where this cultural interdependence must be reflected.

It is in this spirit that we have crafted this report, "One Nation, Many Peoples." We see the social studies as the primary avenue through which the school addresses our cultural diversity and interdependence. But the study of cultural diversity and interdependence is only one goal. It is through such studies that we seek to strengthen our national commitment and world citizenship, with the development of intellectual competence in our students as the foundation. We see the social studies as directed at the development of intellectual competence in learners, with the capacity to view the world and understand it from multiple perspectives as one of the main components of such competence. Multicultural knowledge in this conception of the social studies becomes a vehicle and not a goal. Multicultural content and experience become instruments by which we enable students to develop their intelligence and to function as human and humane persons.

I. Introduction: Affirmation of Purpose

This Committee affirms that multicultural education should be a source of strength and pride. Multicultural education is often viewed as divisive and even as destructive of the values and beliefs which hold us together as Americans. Certainly, contemporary trends toward separation and dissolution in such disparate countries as the Soviet Union, South Africa, Canada, Yugoslavia, Spain, and the United Kingdom remind us that different ethnic and racial groups have often had extraordinary difficulty remaining together in nation-states. But national unity does not require that we eliminate the very diversity that is the source of our uniqueness and, indeed, of our adaptability and viability among the nations of the world. *If the United States is to continue to prosper in the 21st century, then all of its citizens, whatever their race or ethnicity, must believe that they and their ancestors have shared in the building of the country and have a stake in its success.* Thus, multicultural education, far from being a source of dissolution, is necessary for the cultural health, social stability, and economic future of New York State and the nation.

The Committee believes that to achieve these ends, the teaching of social studies should emphasize the following:

First, beginning in the earliest grades social studies should be taught from a global perspective. The earth is humankind's common home. Migration is our common history. The earth's peoples, cultures, and material resources are our common wealth. Both humankind's pain and humankind's triumphs must be shared globally. The uniqueness of humankind is our many ways of being human, our remarkable range of cultural and physical diversity within a common biological unity.

Second, the social studies will very likely continue to serve nation-building purposes, among others, even as we encourage global perspectives. With efforts to respect and honor the diverse and pluralistic elements in our nation, special attention will need to be given to those values, characteristics, and traditions which we share in common. Commitment to the presentation of multiple perspectives in the social studies curriculum encourages attention to the traditional and dominant elements in our society, even as we introduce and examine minority elements which have been neglected or those which are emerging as a result of new scholarship and newly recognized voices.

Third, the curriculum must strive to be informed by the most up-to-date scholarship. It must be open to all relevant input, to new knowledge, to fresh perspectives. Human history is to be seen as ongoing, often contradictory, and subject to reasonable differences based on contrasting perceptions and distinct viewpoints.

Fourth, students need to see themselves as active makers and changers of culture and society; they must be helped to develop the tools by which to judge, analyze, act, and evaluate.

Fifth, the program should be committed to the honoring and continuing examination of democratic values as an essential basis for social organization and nation-building. The application of democracy to social organization should be viewed as a continuing process which sometimes succeeds and sometimes fails, and thus requires constant effort.

Sixth, one of the central aims of the social studies is the development of the intellect; thus, the social studies should be taught not solely as information, but rather through the critical examination of ideas and events rooted in time and place and responding to social interests. The social studies should be seen not as some dreary schoolroom task of fact mastery to be tested and forgotten, but as one of the best curricular vehicles for telling the story of humanity in a way that motivates and inspires all of our children to continue the process of responsible nation-building in a world context. . . .

Background: The Social Studies and the Changing Society

Recent debate concerning change in New York State's social studies curriculum often implies that the curriculum stands as a fixed and unchanging prescription for the classroom, its stability protecting the inculcation of basic values from shifting political and economic winds. Closer examination, however, reveals that the curriculum has grown and been transformed over time in response to societal change, as a few examples will show. . . .

Unlike literature and languages, the social studies and their parent disciplines of history and geography were not a major part of the mainstream of the school curriculum until the present century. In 1899, a Committee of Seven of the American Historical Association (founded in 1884) made a recommendation which led to the study of European and American history and government in schools, including those of New York State. Other subject-matter organizations, as they were formed, also began to press for inclusion in the school curriculum (the American Political Science Association and the American Sociological Association, for example, founded respectively in 1903 and 1905).

In the second decade of this century, the need to accommodate the surge of immigration led to the view that the schools should help students develop the attitudes and skills necessary for good citizenship. In 1916 a Committee on the Social Studies of the American Historical Association declared this to be the goal of schooling, bringing the term "social studies" into formal use. In 1951, responding to the mood of national insecurity reflected in McCarthyism, New York State dropped the term "social studies" in favor of "citizenship education," and the amount of American history in the secondary curriculum was greatly increased ("social studies" re-emerged in 1960). Between 1965 and the late 1980s, as international communication and commerce increased, the curriculum was enlarged to include more global studies, such as year-long courses in Asian and African Studies (grade 9) and European Studies (grade 10). Since 1987, these in turn have been replaced by a two-year global studies sequence.

Indeed, the processes of contest, debate, and transformation are integral parts of the rich history of education in the United States. That history has reflected the society of which it is a part, and societal changes over the past 30 years have brought with them rising interest in the study of diverse cultures in the United States and the world. In the universities, scholarly attention has turned to previously neglected groups (those that have historically been minorities in the United States and women) and topics (social history, ethnic and cultural studies). Such scholarship has brought to light much that had been omitted from U.S. and world history, as traditionally studied.

In the 1970s and early 1980s, elementary and secondary schools, like colleges and universities, were faced with the recognition that much of the experience, cultural values, and collective pasts of their students was not identified or represented in the curriculum. Corresponding to what James A. Banks has termed the "demographic imperative" of increasing numbers of minority students enrolled in public schools, parents, students, and communities served by the schools became more forceful in demanding that their children learn about their own pasts. There was a new recognition that the teaching of social studies as a single officially sanctioned story was inaccurate as to the facts of conflict in American history, and further, that it was limiting for white students and students of color alike.

Much of the heat of debate concerning the importance of valuing cultural difference in the schools arises from divergent opinions on whether preparing students to become members of U.S. society necessarily means assimilation. While the goal of assimilation has historically been relatively explicit in American schooling, in recent years many thoughtful writers and educators have argued against assimilation when interpreted as erasure of distinctive cultural identities. Education must respond to the joint imperatives of educating toward citizenship in a common polity while respecting and taking account of continuing distinctiveness. Even more, as we have argued, the perspectives of a number of major groups in American society must be recognized and incorporated. Nor is assimilation essential to educate citizens who value this country's ideals and participate in its polity and economy. . . .

Over the past two decades, elementary, middle, and secondary schools and post-secondary institutions have seen efforts to restructure the curriculum in order to represent more adequately the diverse cultures of the student body and the world in which students must eventually function. Shifts in curriculum design in such states as California, Oregon, Iowa, Ohio, and Florida reflect an increasing awareness that children and society are inadequately served when study is limited to the intellectual monuments of Western civilization. Comprehensive study of multiple cultures is increasingly recognized as having critical relevance for students who will face a national economy and political structures that grow more globally interdependent and increasingly diverse. . . .

A Dissenting Comment: Kenneth T. Jackson, Jacques Barzun Professor of History and the Social Sciences, Columbia University

The purpose of this Committee is a good one. Certainly, we should celebrate the cultural diversity which has made the United States almost unique among the world's nations. Certainly, we should acknowledge that heterogeneity has made this land rich and creative. Certainly, we should give our students a varied and challenging multicultural education. . . .

. . . I would argue that it is politically and intellectually unwise for us to attack the traditions, customs, and values which attracted immigrants to these shores in the first place. The people of the United States will recognize, even if this Committee does not, that every viable nation has to have a common culture to survive in peace. As our own document indicates, one need look no further than Yugoslavia, the Soviet Union, or Canada to see the accuracy of this proposition. We might want to add India after the events of the past two weeks. The dominant American culture might have been German or French or Chinese or Algonquin or African, but for various historical reasons the English language and British political and legal traditions prevailed. Whether or not we would have been better off if Montcalm had defeated Wolfe on the Plains of Abraham is beside the point. . . .

A better strategy for this Committee would have been to argue in a positive rather than a negative way. Because we are made up of many peoples and cultures, because all these peoples and cultures have contributed to national greatness, and because the United States has typically done a better job of integrating newcomers into its social and political fabric (with racial prejudice being a glaring and persistent exception) than other places, its educational system should reflect that experience. We have been multicultural, we are multicultural, and we hope that we will always be multicultural. Moreover, the enemies of multiculturism are not teachers, textbooks, or curricular guides, but shopping centers, fast food outlets, and situation comedies, all of which threaten to turn us into an amorphous mass.

The report highlights the notion that all cultures are created equal. This may be true in the abstract, and I have no problem with the philosophical concept. But I cannot endorse a "Declaration of Cultural Independence," which is the subtitle of our Committee report. Within any single country, one culture must be accepted as the standard. Unfortunately, our document has virtually nothing to say about the things which hold us together. . . .

A Dissenting Opinion: Arthur M. Schlesinger, Jr.

I agree with many of the practical recommendations in the report. It is unquestionably necessary to diversify the syllabus in order to meet the needs of a more diversified society. It is unquestionably necessary to provide for global education in an increasingly interdependent world. Our students should by all means be better acquainted with women's history, with the history of ethnic and racial minorities, with Latin American, Asian, and African his-

tory. Debate, alternative interpretations, "multiple perspectives" are all essential to the educational enterprise. I welcome changes that would adapt the curriculum to these purposes. If that is what the report means by multicultural education, I am all for it.

But I fear that the report implies much more than this. The underlying philosophy of the report, as I read it, is that ethnicity is the defining experience for most Americans, that ethnic ties are permanent and indelible, that the division into ethnic groups establishes the basic structure of American society and that a main objective of public education should be the protection, strengthening, celebration, and perpetuation of ethnic origins and identities. Implicit in the report is the classification of all Americans according to ethnic and racial criteria.

These propositions are assumed rather than argued in the report. They constitute an ethnic interpretation of American history that, like the economic interpretation, is valid up to a point but misleading and wrong when presented as the whole picture.

The ethnic interpretation, moreover, reverses the historic theory of America—which has been, not the preservation and sanctification of old cultures and identities, but the creation of a new national culture and a new national identity. . . .

Of course students should learn more about the rich variety of peoples and cultures that have forged this new American identity. They also should understand the curse of racism—the great failure of the American experiment, the glaring contradiction of American ideals and the still-crippling disease of American society. But we should also be alert to the danger of a society divided into distinct and immutable ethnic and racial groups, each taught to cherish its own apartness from the rest.

While I favor curricular changes that make for more inclusive interpretations of past and present, I do not believe that we should magnify ethnic and racial themes at the expense of the unifying ideals that precariously hold our highly differentiated society together. The republic has survived and grown because it has maintained a balance between *pluribus* and *unum*. The report, it seems to me, is saturated with *pluribus* and neglectful of *unum*. . . .

Obviously the reason why the United States, for all its manifest failure to live up to its own ideals, is still the most successful large multi-ethnic nation is precisely because, instead of emphasizing and perpetuating ethnic separatism, it has assimilated immigrant cultures into a new American culture. . . .

. . . If the ethnic subcultures had genuine vitality, they would be sufficiently instilled in children by family, church, and community. It is surely not the office of the public school to promote ethnic separatism and heighten ethnic tensions.

Should public education move in this direction, it will only increase the fragmentation, resegregation, and self-ghettoization of American life. The bonds of national cohesion in the republic are sufficiently fragile already. Public education should aim to strengthen those bonds, not to weaken them. . . .

What has held Americans together in the absence of a common ethnic origin has been the creation of a new American identity—a distinctive American culture based on a common language and common adherence to ideals of democracy and human rights, a culture to which many nationalities and races have made emphatic contributions in the past and will (one hopes) make emphatic contributions in the future. Our democratic ideals have been imperfectly realized, but the long labor to achieve them and to move the American experiment from exclusion to participation has been a central theme of American history. It should be a central theme of the New York social studies curriculum.

And it is important for students to understand where these democratic ideals come from. They come of course from Europe. Indeed, Europe is the unique source of these ideals—ideals that today empower people in every continent and to which today most of the world aspires. That is why it is so essential (in my view) to acquaint students with the western history and tradition that created our democratic ideals—and why it is so wrong to tell students of non-European origin that western ideals are not for them.

I regret the note of Europhobia that sometimes emerges in vulgar attacks on "Eurocentric" curriculums. Certainly Europe, like every other culture, has committed its share of crimes. But, unlike most cultures, it has also generated ideals that have opposed and exposed those crimes.

The report, however, plays up the crimes and plays down the ideals. Thus, when it talks about the European colonization of Africa and India, it deplores "the eradication of many varieties of traditional culture and knowledge." Like infanticide? slavery? polygamy? subjection of women? suttee? veil-wearing? foot-binding? clitorectomies? Nothing is said about the influence of European ideas of democracy, human rights, self-government, rule of law. . . .

I also am doubtful about the note occasionally sounded in the report that "students must be taught social criticism" and "see themselves as active makers and changers of culture and society" and "promote economic fairness and social justice" and "bring about change in their communities, the nation, and the world." I very much hope that, as citizens, students will do all these things, but I do not think it is the function of the schools to teach students to become reformers any more than I

ever thought it the function of the schools to teach them the beauty of private enterprise and the sanctity of the status quo. I will be satisfied if we can teach children to read, write, and calculate. If students understand the nature of our western democratic tradition, they will move into social criticism of their own. But let us not politicize the curriculum on behalf either of the left or of the right. . . .

Source: Congressional Quarterly. *Historic Documents of 1991* (Washington, DC: Congressional Quarterly, 1992).

Executive Order and Press Release on U.S. Repatriation of Haitian Refugees, President George H.W. Bush (1992)

Following a military coup against President Jean-Bertrand Aristide in September 1991, tens of thousands of Haitians fled the worsening lawlessness and violence in their island nation. Citing concerns that refugees were using dangerous and unseaworthy boats to escape, President George H.W. Bush issued an executive order on May 24, 1992, that called on the U.S. Coast Guard to repatriate the Haitian "boat people." Advocates for the refugees won a temporary halt to the repatriation in federal appeals court, but the U.S. Supreme Court ultimately overturned the ruling. Many in the Haitian American community and others noted the different treatment of the 1980 Marielito refugees from communist Cuba, most of whom were welcomed into the United States, and the 1992 Haitians, who were repatriated. The following documents include the text of President Bush's executive order and a White House press release explaining it.

Executive Order 12807—Interdiction of Illegal Aliens

By the authority vested in me as President by the Constitution and the laws of the United States of America, including sections 212(f) and 215(a)(1) of the Immigration and Nationality Act [INA], as amended (8 U.S.C. 1182(f) and 1185(a)(1)), and whereas:

(1) The President has authority to suspend the entry of aliens coming by sea to the United States without necessary documentation, to establish reasonable rules and regulations regarding, and other limitations on, the entry or attempted entry of aliens into the United States, and to repatriate aliens interdicted beyond the territorial sea of the United States;

(2) The international legal obligations of the United States under the United Nations Protocol Relating to the Status of Refugees (U.S. T.I.A.S. 6577; 19 U.S.T. 6223) to apply Article 33 of the United National Convention Relating to the Status of Refugees do not extend to persons located outside the territory of the United States;

(3) Proclamation No. 4865 suspends the entry of all undocumented aliens into the United States by the high seas; and

(4) There continues to be a serious problem of persons attempting to come to the United States by sea without necessary documentation and otherwise illegally;

I, GEORGE BUSH, President of the United States of America, hereby order as follows:

Section 1. The Secretary of State shall undertake to enter into, on behalf of the United States, cooperative arrangements with appropriate foreign governments for the purpose of preventing illegal migration to the United States by sea.

Sec. 2. (a) The Secretary of the Department in which the Coast Guard is operating, in consultation, where appropriate, with the Secretary of Defense, the Attorney General, and the Secretary of State, shall issue appropriate instructions to the Coast Guard in order to enforce the suspension of the entry of undocumented aliens by sea and the interdiction of any defined vessel carrying such aliens.

(b) Those instructions shall apply to any of the following defined vessels:

(1) Vessels of the United States, meaning any vessel documented or numbered pursuant to the laws of the United States, or owned in whole or in part by the United States, a citizen of the United States, or a corporation incorporated under the laws of the United States or any State, Territory, District, Commonwealth, or possession thereof, unless the vessel has been granted nationality by a foreign nation in accord with Article 5 of the Convention on the High Seas of 1958 (U.S. T.I.A.S. 5200; 13 U.S.T. 2312).

(2) Vessels without nationality or vessels assimilated to vessels without nationality in accordance with paragraph (2) of Article 6 of the Convention on the High Seas of 1958 (U.S. T.I.A.S. 5200; 13 U.S.T. 2312).

(3) Vessels of foreign nations with whom we have arrangements authorizing the United States to stop and board such vessels.

(c) Those instructions to the Coast Guard shall include appropriate directives providing for the Coast Guard:

(1) To stop and board defined vessels, when there is reason to believe that such vessels are engaged in the irregular transportation of persons or violations of United States law or the law of a country with which the United States has an arrangement authorizing such action.

(2) To make inquiries of those on board, examine documents and take such actions as are necessary to carry out this order.

(3) To return the vessel and its passengers to the country from which it came, or to another country, when there is reason to believe that an offense is being committed against the United States immigration laws, or appropriate laws of a foreign country with which we have an arrangement to assist; provided, however, that the Attorney General, in his unreviewable discretion, may decide that a person who is a refugee will not be returned without his consent.

(d) These actions, pursuant to this section, are authorized to be undertaken only beyond the territorial sea of the United States.

Sec. 3. This order is intended only to improve the internal management of the Executive Branch. Neither this order nor any agency guidelines, procedures, instructions, directives, rules or regulations implementing this order shall create, or shall be construed to create, any right or benefit, substantive or procedural (including without limitation any right or benefit under the Administrative Procedure Act), legally enforceable by any party against the United States, its agencies or instrumentalities, officers, employees, or any other person. Nor shall this order be construed to require any procedures to determine whether a person is a refugee.

Sec. 4. Executive Order No. 12324 is hereby revoked and replaced by this order.

Sec. 5. This order shall be effective immediately.

The White House Press Release

President Bush has issued an executive order which will permit the U.S. Coast Guard to begin returning Haitians picked up at sea directly to Haiti. This action follows a large surge in Haitian boat people seeking to enter the United States and is necessary to protect the lives of the Haitians, whose boats are not equipped for the 600-mile sea journey.

The large number of Haitian migrants has led to a dangerous and unmanageable situation. Both the temporary processing facility at the U.S. Naval base Guantanamo and the Coast Guard cutters on patrol are filled to capacity. The President's action will also allow continued orderly processing of more than 12,000 Haitians presently at Guantanamo.

Through broadcasts on the Voice of America and public statements in the Haitian media we continue to urge Haitians not to attempt the dangerous sea journey to the United States. Last week alone eighteen Haitians perished when their vessel capsized off the Cuban coast.

Under current circumstances, the safety of Haitians is best assured by remaining in their country. We urge any Haitians who fear persecution to avail themselves of our refugee processing service at our Embassy in Port-au-Prince. The Embassy has been processing refugee claims since February. We utilize this special procedure in only four countries in the world. We are prepared to increase the American embassy staff in Haiti for refugee processing if necessary.

The United States Coast Guard has picked up over 34,000 since the coup in Haiti last September 30. Senior U.S. officials are seeking the assistance of other countries and the United Nations to help deal with the plight of Haitian boat people, and we will continue our intensive efforts to find alternative solutions to avoid further tragedies on the high seas.

The President has also directed an intensification of our ongoing humanitarian assistance efforts in Haiti. Our current programs total 47 million dollars and provide food for over 600,000 Haitians and health care services which reach nearly two million. We hope other nations will also increase their humanitarian assistance as called for in the resolution on Haiti passed by the OAS [Organization of American States] Foreign Ministers on May 17.

Source: U.S. Government Printing Office.

District Court Ruling on Admission of Haitian Refugees (1993)

In 1990, amid widespread fear about a disease for which there was little effective treatment, Congress passed a law banning HIV-positive persons from entering the United States. President George H.W. Bush used the law to keep more than 150 Haitian refugees in confinement at the U.S. military base at Guantánamo Bay, Cuba. Bill Clinton, who criticized Bush's decision during the presidential campaign of 1992, maintained the ban after coming to office in January 1993. Later that year, however, a

U.S. district court declared the confinement unconstitutional on grounds that the detainees were being denied their rights to legal counsel and due process. Excerpts from the district court's ruling on June 8, 1993, follow.

Statement of Facts

In 1981, the United States commenced the Alien Migration Interdiction Operation ("AMIO"), formerly known as the Haitian Migrant Interdiction Operation. A cooperative agreement between the United States and Haiti dated September 23, 1981 ("Haiti-U.S. Agreement") allows the United States Coast Guard ("Coast Guard") to board Haitian-flagged vessels on the high seas in order to inquire into the condition and destination of the vessel and the status of those on board. While the Agreement explicitly provides that the "United States does not intend to return to Haiti any Haitian migrants whom the United States authorities determine to qualify for refugee status," a vessel and its passengers were subject to return or repatriation to Haiti if the Coast Guard determined that a violation of United States or Haitian law had occurred. Between 1981 and 1991, the United States interdicted approximately 25,000 Haitians. The United States conducted refugee or asylum prescreening aboard Coast Guard cutters for interdicted Haitians as well as for interdicted nationals of 39 other countries including the Dominican Republic, the Bahamas, Pakistan, Iran, India, Colombia, and Chile during that period.

On September 30, 1991, Jean Bertrand Aristide ("Aristide"), the first democratically elected president in Haiti's history, was overthrown in a military coup. Fearing political persecution, thousands of Haitians fled the country by crossing the border into the Dominican Republic or taking to the high seas. Within a month of the coup, a large number of overcrowded, unseaworthy boats began departing from Haiti, and the United States Coast Guard began interdicting an increasing number of such vessels in international waters.

Prior to interdicting a vessel, the Coast Guard inquired about the vessel's destination. Except when effecting a rescue at sea, the Coast Guard would not remove the passengers or master of a Haitian boat unless it was determined that the vessel was bound for the United States. However, the Coast Guard made no effort to determine the intended destination of each passenger on a particular vessel. If the Coast Guard believed that the vessel was headed for the United States, the Coast Guard interdicted all passengers, even if the passengers were willing to go to locations other than the United States. Because of their lack of seaworthiness, most of the interdicted Haitian vessels, if not all, would not have made it to the United States. In fact, some of the Haitian vessels landed in Cuba, Jamaica, and the Bahamas. When the Coast Guard detained a Haitian vessel, it boarded the vessel and required all passengers to disembark. After all of the passengers had complied, the Coast Guard destroyed the Haitian vessel. Interdicted Haitians were thus given no option but to be detained on the Coast Guard cutter and to be taken to whatever location the Coast Guard elected.

Asylum Screening and Pre-Screening Procedures

Following the coup, the United States temporarily suspended its repatriation program while the Immigration and Naturalization Service ("INS") consulted with the United States Department of State ("State Department") on the procedures for handling the Haitian refugees. While the INS awaited a decision from Washington, the Coast Guard cutters with Haitian refugees aboard circled in international waters. For health and safety reasons, the cutters docked at Guantanamo Bay Naval Base, Cuba ("Guantanamo") on or about November 13, 1991, and the Haitians disembarked. A few days later, the decision making authority for determining whether interdicted Haitians were screened in or screened out was delegated back to INS officers in the field.

On November 22, 1991, the Office of the Deputy Commissioner of INS issued a memorandum stating that a "credible fear of return" standard was to be utilized in asylum pre-screening procedures. Under this "credible fear" standard, Haitians with only one or two "refugee-like" characteristics would be screened in, and thus determined to be eligible for political asylum. Interdicted Haitians with no "refugee-like" characteristics would be "screened out," and thus determined to be ineligible for political asylum and subject to repatriation. The "credible fear of return" standard was designed to be far more generous than the "well-founded fear of return" standard generally applied to asylum seekers.

As the number of interdicted Haitians rose, the INS transferred their interviewing operations from the Coast Guard cutters to Guantanamo. The interviews were conducted by highly trained members of the INS asylum corps which included INS officers, immigration lawyers, and human rights monitors. No attorneys representing the refugees were present during the "credible fear of return" interviews. Since October 1991, the INS screened in 10,500 Haitians found to have a "credible fear of return" and transported them to the United States to apply for asylum. An additional 25,000 interdictees were returned to Haiti by the Coast Guard after undergoing INS prescreening. A very small number were accepted by third countries.

Rescreening HIV+ Haitian Detainees

Soon after the INS began its Guantanamo operation, the United States began to seek third countries in which the Haitians could be relocated. The State Department pursued this with various countries in the region. Two countries, Belize and Honduras, offered to provide limited assistance, but prior to accepting the Haitians asked that they be tested for the HIV virus. The results of those tests disclosed the presence of the virus in a number of the Haitian detainees at Guantanamo leading the Government to conduct HIV testing for all screened-in Haitians. The Haitians are the only group of asylum seekers to be medically tested for HIV.

Prior to September 1991, all screened-in Haitian refugees were brought to the United States before receiving medical screening. As Gene McNary, then INS Commissioner, [stated] in a memorandum dated May 30, 1991, entitled "Asylum Pre-Screening of Interdicted Aliens and Asylum Seekers in INS Custody": "[i]nterdicted asylum seekers identified at sea for transfer to the United States will be properly inspected and medically screened *upon arrival* into the United States."

Then in a memorandum dated February 29, 1992, Grover Joseph Rees, INS General Counsel, stated a new INS policy requiring second or "well-founded fear" interviews of screened-in persons who tested positive for the Human Immunodeficiency Virus ("HIV"). . . .

By letter dated March 11, 1992, attorneys for the Haitian Service Organizations requested permission to communicate with the screened-in Haitians held on Guantanamo. The request was denied. The Screened In Plaintiffs detained on Guantanamo themselves repeatedly requested counsel. Their requests were also denied. The military did not oppose visits from counsel and when such visits have been permitted, the military has not found any disruption to the operation of the camp. Other groups, including the press, clergy, and non-U.S. contract workers (e.g., Cubans, Jamaicans, and Filipinos) have been permitted access to Guantanamo. In the absence of attorneys, the Haitians have received legal advice from the military, INS, Community Relations Service representatives, ministers, and even military doctors.

Notwithstanding the fact that attorneys are regularly present during nearly identical asylum interviews in the United States, the INS refused to permit the Screened In Plaintiffs to have counsel present at their "well-founded fear" interview. At trial, an INS official expressed the agency's concern with the presence of attorneys at asylum interviews saying that lawyers would only stress the positive element of an applicant's case and deemphasize the negative aspects. This Court finds that lawyers serve a necessary and useful purpose in representing an asylum seeker in connection with the well-founded fear of return interview. Their presence at these interviews is also clearly feasible. The Government's decision to deny Plaintiff Haitian Service Organizations access to Camp Bulkeley is based solely on the content of what they had to say and the viewpoint they would express.

The second interviews, like the first interviews, were conducted in the absence of attorneys. Of the HIV+ Screened In Plaintiffs who underwent the second interview, 115 Haitians were found to have a well-founded fear of return. A number of HIV+ Haitians who had been screened in were repatriated to Haiti after having failed the second interview or having declined to undergo the second interview. Haitians who received an adverse determination did not have the opportunity to appeal the decision.

Guantanamo Operation

. . . When the first group of Haitians arrived in November 1991, the existing facilities at Guantanamo were not sufficient to provide housing for all interdictees. A special Joint Task Force ("JTF") comprised of several branches of the Armed Services, was sent to Guantanamo to provide temporary humanitarian assistance to the Haitians including housing, food, and medical care from military physicians. In order to house the Haitians, the JTF evicted U.S. military personnel from the cinder-block quarters at Camp Bulkeley on the eastern edge of the base. Tents were also erected at Camp Bulkeley to temporarily house the several thousand migrants who arrived at Guantanamo at the outset. When Camp Bulkeley's capacity proved inadequate, the JTF opened a new series of camps at the unused McCalla air field. These McCalla camps were all tent facilities except for the large hangar at the airfield.
. . .

In March 1992, after the prevalence of the HIV virus among the refugee population was ascertained, the JTF created a separate camp for them. Camp Bulkeley was chosen for that purpose. The then existing population of HIV negative Haitians at Camp Bulkeley remained until they were processed and departed Guantanamo. As "screened in" HIV+ Haitians were identified, they were transferred to Camp Bulkeley, eventually making it predominantly an HIV+ facility. The camp also contained HIV negative relatives of the HIV+ Haitians.

Today there are approximately 200 "screened in" HIV+ Haitians remaining at Guantanamo. They live in camps surrounded by razor barbed wire. They tie plastic garbage bags to the sides of the building to keep the rain out. They sleep on cots and hang sheets to create some semblance of privacy. They are guarded by the military and are not permitted to leave the camp, except under military escort. The Haitian detainees have been subjected to pre-dawn military sweeps as they sleep by as many as 400 soldiers dressed in full riot gear. They are confined like prisoners and are subject to detention in the brig without a hearing for camp rule infractions. Although the Haitian detainees have a chapel, weight room, bicycle repair shop, beauty parlor, and other amenities at their disposal, none of these things are currently available to them, as they are now confined to Camp Alpha, a small section of Camp Bulkeley, or to the brig.

Medical Care at Guantanamo

. . . The two physicians [at the Haitian clinic] are assisted by a medical staff of four registered nurses, three independent duty corpsmen, a family practice nurse practitioner, 20 general duty corpsmen, and a preventive medicine technician whose duties include spraying standing water against insects, and rodent control. The clinic is a cinderblock, air conditioned building with four examining rooms, a large waiting area, a laboratory, and a pharmacy. The clinic, open generally from 7:30 a.m. to 4:00 p.m. daily, has 11 beds, but its capacity is expandable to about 55.

The Haitians do not need an appointment to come to the clinic, however, they may make appointments to see physicians as needed. The clinic is staffed 24 hours a day, seven days a week either by general duty corpsmen or physicians. . . .

Despite the ability of military doctors and facilities to treat routine illnesses, the Government acknowledges that the medical facilities on the Guantanamo Naval Base are inadequate to provide medical care to those Haitians who have developed AIDS, particularly patients with T-cell counts of 200 or below or a percentage of 13 or less. The military doctors believe that the medical facilities on Guantanamo are inadequate to treat such AIDS patients. . . . The military doctors first raised these concerns at least as early as May 1992. The military has requested that certain HIV+ Haitians be medically evacuated from Guantanamo because the military does not believe it can provide adequate medical care to those patients on Guantanamo. Certain of these requests have been denied by the INS on more than one occasion.

At trial the Government did not offer any evidence which would prove the facilities at Guantanamo to be adequate. In fact, defendants' counsel admitted that "the medical facilities at Guantanamo are not presently sufficient to provide treatment for such AIDS patients under the medical care standard applicable within the United States itself." But when asked whether the Government was "prepared to send those [patients] to the United States for treatment," Defendants' counsel responded,

"The government does not intend at this point to do that." . . .

Although the defendants euphemistically refer to its Guantanamo operation as a "humanitarian camp," the facts disclose that it is nothing more than an HIV prison camp presenting potential public health risks to the Haitians held there. There is no dispute that because HIV+ individuals are immunosuppressed, they are more susceptible to a variety of infections, many of which can be transmitted from one person to the next. No major outbreak of infectious disease has occurred yet, but by segregating HIV+ individuals, the Government places the Haitian detainees at greater risk of contracting infections, including tuberculosis, measles and other life-threatening diseases, than if they were permitted to live in the general population. . . .

In addition, the prison camp environment created by the Government is not conducive to an effective doctor-patient relationship. . . .

The seriously impaired doctor-patient relationship makes it more difficult for defendants to provide adequate medical care at the camp. Even if Defendants continue to provide medical services, many of the Haitian detainees will grow increasingly sick because they do not trust their diagnosis or the medication prescribed for them.

Conclusions of Law

Haitian Service Organizations' First Amendment Rights

Plaintiff Haitian Service Organizations' First Claim for Relief is that the Government has violated their First Amendment right by denying them and their attorneys access to the Screened In Plaintiffs for the purpose of counseling, advocacy, and representation. . . .

The First Amendment says that "Congress shall make no Law . . . abridging the freedom of speech." U.S. Const. amend. 1. That provision applies on Guantanamo Bay Naval Base, which is under the complete control and jurisdiction of the United States government, and where the government exercises complete control over all means of delivering communications. . . . The Government has violated the Haitian Service Organization's First Amendment rights to free speech and to associate for the purpose of providing legal counsel by denying them equal access to the screened-in Haitians held on Guantanamo. Defendants have permitted press, clergy, politicians and other non-lawyers to meet with the Haitians and have permitted many others, including non-citizen contract workers, onto the base. In addition, the Haitians have received legal advice, which has often been erroneous, from the military, the INS, the Community Relations Service and even military doctors. The legal

rights and options of Haitian detainees are discussed on Guantanamo, but only from the viewpoint of which the Government approves. . . .

[T]he Haitian Service Organizations have been retained by the Screened In Plaintiffs and have asserted a right to speak with their clients, the screened-in Haitians. The lawyers here seek only to communicate, at their own expense, with clients who have specifically sought them out. The Court thus finds that the lawyers for the Haitian Service Organizations have been barred because of the viewpoint of the message they seek to convey to the Haitians, in violation of the First Amendment. Such Government discrimination against disfavored viewpoints strikes at the heart of the First Amendment. . . .

Due Process

Plaintiffs' Third Claim for Relief in the Amended Complaint states that the Government has violated the Screened In Plaintiffs' due process rights under the Fifth Amendment. . . .

The Supreme Court has long held that aliens outside the United States are entitled to due process in civil suits in United States courts. . . .

The United States government has already bound itself by treaty not to "impose penalties" on persons it has recognized as refugees who flee to the United States "directly from a territory where their life or freedom was threatened" on account of political persecution. . . .

The Haitian detainees are imprisoned in squalid, prison-like camps surrounded by razor barbed wire. They are not free to wander about the base. Guarded by the military day and night, the Screened In Plaintiffs are subject to surprise pre-dawn military sweeps conducted by soldiers outfitted in full riot gear searching for missing detainees. Haitian detainees have been punished for rule infractions by being flexicuffed and sent to "administrative segregation camp" (Camp Alpha or Camp 7) or the brig. Such conditions cannot be tolerated when, as here, the detainees have a right to due process.

Access to Counsel During "Well-Founded" Interviews

The Screened In Plaintiffs have a protected liberty interest in not being wrongly repatriated to Haiti, . . . and to due process before defendants alter their screened in status. . . .

. . . [T]he private interest of the Screened In Plaintiffs not to be returned to Haiti is of the highest order. Based on the INS's own findings, the screened-in Haitians have already been found to have at least a credible fear of return. This showing exceeds that of an unscreened asylum applicant in the United States whose interest in applying for asylum is constitutionally protected. . . .

Medical Care

Constitutional due process mandates both provision of adequate medical care to persons in official custody.... As persons in coercive, nonpunitive, and indefinite detention, the Haitian detainees on Guantanamo are constitutionally entitled to medically adequate conditions of confinement. ...

The military's own doctors have made INS aware that Haitian detainees with T-cell counts of 200 or below or percentages of 13 or below should be medically evacuated to the United States because of a lack of facilities and specialists at Guantanamo. Despite this knowledge, Defendant INS has repeatedly failed to act on recommendations and deliberately ignored the medical advice of U.S. military doctors that all persons with T-cell count below 200 or percentages below 13 be transported to the United States for treatment. Such actions constitute deliberate indifference to the Haitians' medical needs in violation of their due process rights....

Indefinite Detention

As individuals held in custody by the United States, the Screened In Plaintiffs also have a liberty interest in not being arbitrarily or indefinitely detained....

Here, the Screened In Plaintiffs continued detention is the result of the Defendants' actions, not the aliens' own choices. The Government stopped processing the cases of these and other screened-in Haitians in June 1992, after the Second Circuit upheld this Court's injunction entitling the Haitians to be represented by counsel. One-hundred and fifteen Haitians at Guantanamo have met the well-founded fear standard in the second interviews and have remained in detention for almost two years....

... [T]he detained Haitians are neither criminals nor national security risks. Some are pregnant mothers and others are children. Simply put, they are merely the unfortunate victims of a fatal disease. The Government has failed to demonstrate to this Court's satisfaction that the detainees' illness warrants the kind of indefinite detention usually reserved for spies and murderers.... Where detention no longer serves a legitimate purpose, the detainees must be released. The Haitian camp at Guantanamo is the only known refugee camp in the world composed entirely of HIV+ refugees. The Haitians' plight is a tragedy of immense proportion and their continued detainment is totally unacceptable to this Court....

Violations of Administrative Procedure Act

For their Fifth Claim for Relief, Plaintiffs allege that a) the Government violated the APA by conducting unauthorized "well-founded fear" interviews and b) the Attorney General abused her discretion by denying parole for the screened-in Haitian Plaintiffs....

Plaintiffs allege that the Attorney General's refusal to parole them from detention due to their HIV+ status constitutes an abuse of discretion. For the reason set forth below, the Court agrees and sets aside her denial of parole....

By effectively denying the plaintiffs release from detention, defendant Attorney General has abused her discretion.... Haitians remain in detention solely because they are Haitian and have tested HIV-positive. The Government has admitted that the ban on the admission of aliens with communicable diseases has not been strictly enforced against every person seeking entry. Each year many "non-immigrants" enter the United States, are legally entitled to remain for years, and are not subject to HIV testing. To date, the Government has only enforced the ban against Haitians....

The Attorney General has abused her discretion in failing to parole the HIV+ Haitian detainees on Guantanamo. Her decision to detain these Haitians deviates from established parole policy and is illegally based upon a statute which is selectively enforced against Haitian nationals and merely makes persons carrying the HIV virus excludable from "admission" or permanent residence. For foregoing reasons, the Court hereby sets aside the Attorney General's denial of parole....

Relief

For the reasons stated above,

1. The following class is hereby certified:

(a) all Haitian citizens who have been or will be "screened in" who are, have been or will be detained on Guantanamo Bay Naval Base, or any other territory subject to United States jurisdiction, or on Coast Guard cutters, including those who have been or will be subject to post-screening processing (or who have resisted such processing) (hereinafter "Screened In Plaintiffs");

2. It is hereby,

(a) DECLARED that the "Well-Founded Fear" Processing by Defendants set forth in the Rees Memorandum is in excess of Defendants' statutory authority, and

(b) ORDERED that such "Well-Founded Fear" Processing be permanently enjoined, held unlawful and set aside pursuant to the Administrative Procedure Act: and

3. It is hereby further

(a) DECLARED that defendant Attorney General's exercise of the statutory parole power under INA § 212(d)(5) to deny Screened In Plaintiffs parole out of detention constitutes an abuse of discretion; and

(b) ORDERED that defendant Attorney General's exercise of the statutory parole power under INA § 212(d)(5) to deny Screened In Plaintiffs parole out of detention be permanently enjoined, held unlawful and set aside pursuant to the Administrative Procedure Act; and

4. It is hereby further

(a) DECLARED that the "Well-Founded Fear" Processing, Disciplinary Proceedings, Arbitrary and Indefinite Detention, Medical Care and Camp Conditions to which Screened In Plaintiffs are being subjected by Defendants denies those plaintiffs Due Process of Law; and

(b) ORDERED that such "Well-Founded Fear" Processing, Disciplinary Proceedings, Arbitrary and Indefinite Detention, Medical Care and Camp Conditions be permanently enjoined pursuant to the Fifth Amendment of the United States Constitution; and that Screened In Plaintiffs be immediately released (to anywhere but Haiti) from such processing, proceedings, detention, medical care and camp conditions; and

5. It is hereby further

(a) DECLARED that denying plaintiff Haitian Service Organizations immediate access to Guantanamo to communicate and associate with their detained Screened-In Plaintiff clients violates the First Amendment; and

(b) ORDERED that Defendants are permanently enjoined from denying plaintiff Haitian Service Organizations immediate access at Guantanamo, on Coast Guard Cutters, or at any other place subject to U.S. jurisdiction to any member of the class of Screened In Plaintiffs (regardless of whether any such screened-in plaintiff has been furnished with an exact date and time for an interview), subject to reasonable time, place, and manner limitations for the purpose of providing class members legal counsel, advocacy, and representation; and

6. It is hereby finally

(a) DECLARED that Plaintiffs are entitled to such other and further relief as the Court may deem just and proper, including reasonable attorneys' fees and costs, to be determined at a future hearing.

So ordered.
Sterling Johnson, Jr.
United States District Judge
Dated: Brooklyn, New York
June 8, 1993

Source: U.S. District Court for the Eastern District of New York. *Ruling on Admission of Haitians.* June 8, 1993.

"Report Under the International Covenant on Civil and Political Rights," U.S. Immigration and Naturalization Service (1994)

As a signatory to the 1966 International Covenant on Civil and Political Rights, the United States is obliged to adhere to certain international rules concerning the exclusion and deportation of refugees. In the report excerpted below, issued in July 1994 by the Immigration and Naturalization Service, the U.S. government explains its policy and practice regarding the acceptance, exclusion, and deportation of refugees of various sorts. The report declares that U.S. policy is humane and fair, that deportation proceedings follow strict rules, and that prospective deportees have effective rights of appeal.

Article 13—Expulsion of Aliens

The United States has a strong tradition of supporting immigration and has adopted immigration policies reflective of the view that immigrants make invaluable contributions to the fabric of American society. At present, the United States provides annually for the legal immigration of over 700,000 aliens each year, with special preferences granted for family reunification and employment skills purposes. In addition, the United States grants admission to some 120,000 refugees from abroad annually, and accords political asylum to many others within the United States. Notwithstanding these large programs for legal immigration to the United States, illegal immigration to the United States continues in substantial numbers. The total number of aliens illegally in the United States is currently estimated to be over 3 million. Due to the ease of travel and relative lack of residence controls within the United States, as well as the extensive procedural guarantees accompanying deportation, aliens who enter the continental United States illegally, or who stay on illegally after an initial lawful entry, are often able to remain for many years.

Aliens who have entered the United States, whether legally or illegally, may be expelled only pursuant to deportation proceedings, as described below. (Different procedures apply to diplomatic representatives, who may be declared persona non grata.) The legal protection for such persons includes the extensive procedural safeguards provided by the Immigration and Nationality Act (INA), U.S.C. 1101 et seq., and rests fundamentally on the constitutional rights of due process afforded to all. As the Supreme Court has stated:

Aliens who have once passed through our gates, even

illegally, may be expelled only after proceedings conforming to traditional standards of fairness encompassed in due process of law. *Shaughnessy v. United States*, 206 U.S. 206, 212 (1953).

Whatever his status under the immigration laws, an alien is surely a "person" [for purposes of certain constitutional guarantees] in any ordinary sense of that term. Aliens, even aliens whose presence in this country is unlawful, have long been recognized as "persons" guaranteed due process of law by the Fifth and Fourteenth Amendments. *Plyler v. Doe*, 457 U.S. 202, 210 (1981).

The term "entry" is generally defined under INA 101(a)(13) as "any coming of an alien into the United States from a foreign port or place." Aliens within the United States who were inspected and admitted as well as those who evaded inspection and came into the United States illegally are considered to have effected an "entry." Persons who attempt illegal entry but are detected at the border prior to entry are occasionally allowed into the United States for further processing of their entry claims (in lieu of return to their home country or detention at the border), or under the Attorney General's discretionary parole authority. Such excludable aliens, whose presence in the United States results solely from the limited, conditional permission of the United States Government, are not considered to have entered the United States for immigration purposes. They generally are subject to exclusion proceedings, as described below, which provide some due process protections, although not as extensive as those provided in deportation proceedings.

Deportation

Aliens who have entered the United States and who violate U.S. immigration laws are subject to deportation proceedings. Grounds for deportation include: (1) excludability at time of entry or adjustment of status; (2) entry without inspection; (3) alien smuggling; (4) marriage fraud; (5) criminal offenses; (6) falsification of documents; (7) security grounds; (8) public charge grounds. . . .

Generally, an alien "is not and should not be detained or required to post bond except on a finding that he is a threat to the national security . . . or that he is a poor bail risk." Matter of Patel, 15 I&N Dec. 666 (BIA 1976). The Attorney General is, however, obligated to take into custody any alien convicted of an aggravated felony, but may release the alien, if the alien demonstrates that the alien "is not a threat to the community and that the alien is likely to appear before any scheduled hearings." INA 242(a)(2)(B); 8 C.F.R. 3.19(h).

Custody and bond determinations made by the Immigration and Naturalization Service (INS) may be reviewed by an immigration judge and may be appealed to the Board of Immigration Appeals (BIA). An alien's release on bond or parole may be revoked at any time in the discretion of the Attorney General. INA 242(a). . . .

During deportation proceedings, the immigration judge has the authority to determine deportability, to grant discretionary relief, and to determine the country to which an alien's deportation will be directed. The immigration judge must also: (1) advise the alien of the alien's right to representation, at no expense to the Government, by qualified counsel of his choice; (2) advise the alien of the availability of local free legal services programs; (3) ascertain that the alien has received a list of such programs and a copy of INS Form I-618, Written Notice of Appeal Rights; (4) advise the alien that the alien will have a reasonable opportunity to examine and object to adverse evidence, to present evidence, and to cross-examine witnesses presented by the Government; (5) place the alien under oath; (6) read the factual allegations and the charges in the order to show cause to the alien and explain them in nontechnical language, and enter the order to show cause as an exhibit in the record. 8 C.F.R. 242.16(a).

The INA mandates that the "alien shall have a reasonable opportunity to be present" at the deportation proceeding. INA 242(b). The BIA has held that aliens "must be given a reasonable opportunity to present evidence on their own behalf, including their testimony." Matter of Tomas, 19 I&N Dec. 464, 465 (BIA 1987). The BIA has further noted that in most cases, "all that need be translated are the immigration judge's statements to the alien, the examination of the alien by his counsel, the attorney for the Service, and the immigration judge, and the alien's responses to their questions." Matter of Exilus, 18 I&N 276, 281 (BIA 1982). However, "the immigration judge may determine . . . that the alien's understanding of other dialogue is essential to his ability to assist in the presentation of his case." Id.

If the alien concedes deportability and the alien has not applied for discretionary relief other than voluntary departure (discussed below), the immigration judge may enter a summary decision ordering deportation or granting voluntary departure with an alternate order of deportation. 8 C.F.R. 242.18(b). The immigration judge may not accept an admission of deportability "from an unrepresented respondent who is incompetent or under age 16 and is not accompanied by a guardian, relative, or friend; nor from an officer of an institution in which [an alien] is an inmate or patient." 8 C.F.R. 242.16(b).

In cases where deportability is at issue and/or where the alien has applied for discretionary relief, the immigration judge receives evidence on the issues. The Government must establish an alien's deportability by clear, convincing, and unequivocal evidence and must establish that the person is an alien. 8 C.F.R. 242.14(a). If deportability is based on an entry violation, such as entry without inspection, however, after the INS establishes identity and alienage of the person, the burden shifts to the alien to show the time, place, and manner of his entry into the United States. If this burden of proof "is not sustained, such person shall be presumed to be in the United States in violation of law." INA 291.

Relief from Deportation. . .

Waivers. Waivers are available for some of the grounds of deportation.

Suspensions of Deportation. Under INA 244(a), the Attorney General may "suspend deportation and adjust the status to that of an alien lawfully admitted for permanent residence, in the case of an alien . . . , who applies for suspension of deportation" and (1) is deportable; (2) subject to certain exceptions, has been physically present in the United States for a continuous period of not less than seven years immediately preceding the date of such application; (3) proves that during all of such period he was and is a person of good moral character; and (4) is a person whose deportation would in the opinion of the Attorney General result in extreme hardship to the alien or to his spouse, parent, or child, who is a citizen of the United States or an alien lawfully admitted for permanent residence. INA 244(a)(1).

Voluntary Departure. The Attorney General may permit an alien to "depart voluntarily from the United States at his own expense in lieu of deportation" if such alien (1) is not deportable for criminal offenses, falsification of documents or on security grounds; (2) is not an aggravated felon; and (3) establishes "to the satisfaction of the Attorney General that he is, and has been, a person of good moral character for at least five years immediately preceding his application for voluntary departure." INA 244(e)(1).

Registry. INA 249 generally provides that the Attorney General may create a record of lawful admission for permanent residence for an alien, as of the date of the approval of his application, if (1) such alien is (a) not excludable as [a] participant in Nazi persecutions or genocide and (b) not excludable under INA 212(a) "as it relates to criminals, procurers, and other immoral persons, subversives, violators of the narcotic laws or smugglers of aliens"; and (2) the alien establishes that he (a) entered the United States prior to January 1, 1972; (b) has had residence in the United States continuously since such entry; (c) is a person of good moral character; and (d) is not ineligible for citizenship. INA 249; see also 8 C.F.R. 249.1 (discussing waivers of inadmissibility for

certain exclusion grounds in conjunction with registry applications).

Decisions and Appeals. A decision of an immigration judge in a deportation hearing may be written or oral. Appeal from the decision lies with the BIA. 8 C.F.R. 242.21. A final order of deportation may be reviewed by federal courts, but will not be reviewed "if the alien has not exhausted the administrative remedies available to him as of right under the immigration laws and regulations or if he has departed from the United States after the issuance of the order." INA 106 (c). The immigration judge may upon the judge's own motion, or upon motion of the trial attorney, or the alien, reopen any case which the judge decided, "unless jurisdiction in the case is vested in the Board of Immigration Appeals." 8 C.F.R. 242.22. A motion to reopen "will not be granted unless the immigration judge is satisfied that evidence sought to be offered is material and was not available and could not have been discovered or presented at the hearing." 8 C.F.R. 242.22.

Exclusion

An alien has the burden of satisfying the INS officer at the border point of entry that the alien is entitled to enter the United States and not subject to exclusion. If the officer concludes the alien is not clearly entitled to enter, the officer must detain the alien for further inspection. INA 235(b). The alien may be released on bond or parole; the standards for release are essentially the same as they are in deportation proceedings. . . .

The immigration judge must inform the alien of the nature and purpose of the hearing; advise the alien that the alien has a statutory right to have an attorney at no cost to the government, and of the availability of free legal services programs; ascertain that the applicant has received a list of such programs; request the alien to determine then and there whether the alien desires representation; and advise the alien that the alien will have a reasonable opportunity to present evidence, to examine and object to adverse evidence, and to cross-examine witnesses presented by the government.

Except for aliens previously admitted to the United States for lawful permanent residence, aliens have the burden of proving their admissibility in exclusion proceedings. The immigration judge can grant various forms of relief, including waivers, adjustment of status under certain conditions, and political asylum and withholding of exclusion. Suspension of deportation and voluntary departure are not available. . . .

Following a final determination of exclusion, an alien may surrender himself to the custody of the INS, or may be notified to surrender to custody. An alien taken into custody either upon notice to surrender or by arrest may not be deported less than 72 hours thereafter unless the alien consents in writing. 8 C.F.R. 237.2. An alien detained pending or during exclusion proceedings may seek further review in federal court under a writ of habeas corpus.

United States Refugee and Asylum Policy

The refugee and asylum policy of the United States, set forth primarily in the Refugee Act of 1980 and the Immigration and Nationality Act (the INA), was created in accordance with the strong, historical commitment of the United States to the protection of refugees and in compliance with the 1967 United Nations Protocol Relating to the Status of Refugees. The Protocol, to which the United States has acceded, adopted the operative provisions of the 1951 United Nations Convention Relating to the Status of Refugees.

Under the INA, persons within the United States may seek refugee protection through a grant of asylum or withholding of deportation. The standard for such determinations is that provided in the Protocol, defining a refugee as: "any person who is outside of any country of such person's nationality or, in the case of a person having no nationality, is outside any country in which such person last habitually resided, and who is unable or unwilling to return to, and is unable or unwilling to avail himself or herself of the protection of, that country because of persecution or a well-founded fear of persecution on account of race, religion, nationality, membership in a particular social group, or political opinion." INA 101(a)(42)(A); 8 U.S.C. 1101(a)(42)(A). Refugee status is not available to "any person who ordered, incited, assisted, or otherwise participated in the persecution of any person on account of race, religion, nationality, membership in a particular social group, or political opinion," or for aliens who have been convicted of an aggravated felony. INA 101(a)(42)(B) and 208(d); 8 U.S.C. 1101(a)(42)(B) and 1158(d).

At present, there are some 300,000 asylum claims pending in various stages of adjudication; over 100,000 new claims were filed in Fiscal Year 1992. A related form of protection, temporary protected status, is available to persons already within the United States when the Attorney General determines that certain extreme and temporary conditions in their country of nationality (such as ongoing armed conflict or an environmental disaster) generally do not permit the United States to return them to that country in safety.

In addition, the United States maintains a substantial program for providing assistance to refugees overseas. The United States overseas refugee admissions program, which also uses the Protocol definition of refugee, provides for the admission and resettlement in the United States of over 120,000 refugees of special humanitarian concern to the United States each year from throughout the world. In addition, the United States provides on-site assistance, primarily through relevant international organizations such as the United Nations High Commissioner for Refugees, the International Committee of the Red Cross, and the International Organization for Migration, in the amount of over $300 million dollars each year, not only to "Protocol refugees" but also to others who are suffering from the disruptive effects of conflict or other forms of dislocation. In the last three years alone, the United States has contributed over $1 billion in assistance to refugees throughout the world.

Refugee Admissions. The INA provides for the admission of refugees outside the United States. Each year the President, after appropriate consultation with Congress, determines an authorized admission level for refugees. For example, the admission ceiling for refugees in 1994 was 121,000. This annual ceiling represents the maximum number of refugees allowed to enter the United States each year, allocated by world geographical region. INA 207(a). The President may accommodate an emergency refugee situation by increasing the refugee admissions ceiling for a twelve-month period. INA 207(b); 8 U.S.C. 1157(b).

Persons applying in overseas offices for refugee protection in the United States must satisfy four criteria. They must: (1) fall within the definition of a refugee set forth in the INA; (2) be among the types of refugees determined to be of special humanitarian concern to the United States; (3) be admissible under the Immigration and Nationality Act; and (4) not be firmly resettled in any foreign country.

The refugee application process originates either at a United States embassy or at a designated consular office, if distance makes direct filing at an embassy impracticable. 8 C.F.R. 207.1(a). Interviews are then conducted by employees of the Immigration and Naturalization Service. There exists no formal procedure for either administrative appeal or judicial review of adverse decisions. The applicant has the burden of showing entitlement to refugee status. 8 C.F.R. 208.8(d).

Asylum. Asylum applications may be submitted by persons who are physically present in the United States. Asylum may be granted without regard to the applicant's immigration status or country of origin. There are two paths for an alien present in the United States seeking asylum. First, the alien may come forward to the INS to apply "affirmatively." Second, the alien may seek asylum as a defense to exclusion or deportation proceedings, even after a denial of asylum through the affirmative process. . . .

Affirmative Asylum. Affirmative asylum claims are heard and decided by a corps of INS asylum officers located in seven regional offices. The asylum officer conducts an interview with the applicant "in a nonadversarial manner . . . to elicit all relevant and useful information bearing on the applicant's eligibility." 8 C.F.R. 208.9(b). The applicant may have counsel present at the interview and may submit the affidavits of witnesses. In addition, the applicant may supplement the record within thirty days of the interview. 8 C.F.R. 208.9. Upon completion of the interview, the asylum officer must forward a copy of the asylum application to the Bureau of Human Rights and Humanitarian Affairs (BHRHA) (recently renamed the Bureau of Democracy Rights and Labor) of the Department of State. The BHRHA may comment on the application within 45 days. The asylum officer may make a final decision if no response from the BHRHA arrives within 60 days. 8 C.F.R. 208.11.

The asylum officer's decision must be in writing and, if asylum is denied, the decision must include a credibility assessment. 8 C.F.R. 208.17. The alien has the right to specific reasons for denial and the right to both factually and legally rebut the denial. 8 C.F.R. 103.3(a) and 103.2(b)(2). The decision of the asylum officer is reviewed by the INS's Office of Refugees, Asylum, and Parole (CORAP), but the applicant has no right to appeal. 8 C.F.R. 208.18(a).

Asylum claims must be denied when: (1) the alien has been convicted of a particularly serious crime in the United States and constitutes a danger to the community; (2) the alien has been firmly resettled in a third country; or (3) there are reasonable grounds for regarding the alien as a threat to the security of the United States. 8 C.F.R. 208.14(c). In addition, asylum officers may use discretion in asylum denials.

Asylum officers also have limited power to revoke asylum and relief under the "withholding of deportation" provision of the INA (243(h)). This power may be exercised when: (1) the alien no longer has a well-founded fear of persecution or is no longer entitled to relief under 243(h) because of changed country conditions; (2) there existed fraud in the application such that the alien was not eligible for asylum at the time it was granted; or (3) the alien has committed any act that would have been grounds for denial. 8 C.F.R. 208.24(a)(b). Once an affirmative asylum application is denied, the asylum officer is empowered, if appropriate, to initiate the alien's exclusion or deportation proceedings.

Asylum and Withholding of Exclusion/Deportation in Exclusion or Deportation Proceedings. If an alien has been served with an Order to Show Cause to appear at a deportation hearing or a notice to appear at an exclusion hearing, he must appear before an immigration judge, with whom he may file an asylum application. The filing of an asylum application is also considered a request for withholding of deportation or exclusion under INA 243(h).

Relief under INA 243(h) differs from a request for asylum in three ways. First, 243(h) provides relief from deportation or exclusion to a specific country where the applicant's "life or freedom would be threatened," while asylum protects the alien from deportation generally and only requires a well-founded fear of persecution. Second, relief under 243(h) cannot result in permanent residence, while asylees are eligible for permanent residence after one year. Third, relief under 243(h) is mandatory while asylum is a discretionary grant. . . .

The alien will be denied 243(h) relief and will remain subject to exclusion or deportation if the alien: (1) engaged in persecution of others; (2) has been convicted of a particularly serious crime that constitutes a danger to the community of the United States; (3) has committed a serious nonpolitical crime outside of the United States; or (4) may represent a danger to the security of the United States. INA 243(h)(2). . . .

Parole Under INA 212(d)(5)(B). A refugee may be paroled into the United States by the Attorney General only if there exist "compelling reasons in the public interest with respect to that particular alien" to parole rather than admit the person as a refugee under INA 207. INA 212(d)(5)(B). Parole allows an alien to remain in the United States temporarily until a final status decision is made. Parole is not equivalent to an "admission," and thus leaves the alien subject to exclusion.

The Attorney General has created a "special interest parole" process "on an exceptional basis only for an unspecified but limited period of time" pursuant to the Lautenberg Amendment of the Foreign Operations Appropriations Act. Pub. L. No. 101-167. Under this provision, certain persons from Cambodia, Laos, Vietnam, and the former Soviet Union (specifically Jews, Evangelical Christians, Ukrainian Catholics, and Ukrainian Orthodox Christians), who were inspected and paroled into the United States between August 15, 1988 and September 30, 1994 after being denied refugee status, are eligible for adjustment of status.

Temporary Protected Status. Under INA 244A, the Attorney General has the authority to grant temporary protected status to aliens in the United States, temporarily allowing foreign nationals to live and work in the

United States without fear of being sent back to unstable or dangerous conditions. The United States thus may become, at the Attorney General's discretion, a temporary safe haven for foreign nationals already in this country if one of three conditions exists: (1) there is an ongoing conflict within the state, which would pose a serious threat to the personal safety of returned nationals; (2) there has been an earthquake, flood, drought, epidemic, or other environmental disaster in the state resulting in a substantial but temporary disruption of living conditions; the state is temporarily unable to accept the return of nationals; and the state officially asks the Attorney General for a designation of temporary protected status; or (3) there exist extraordinary and temporary conditions in the state that prevent nationals from returning in safety, as long as the grant of temporary protected status is not contrary to the national interest of the United States. INA 244A(b)(1). Designation of temporary protected status may last for six to eighteen months, with the possibility of extension.

An alien is ineligible for temporary protected status if he has been convicted of at least one felony or two or more misdemeanors. 8 C.F.R. 240.4. Ineligibility is also based upon the grounds for denial of relief under INA 243(h)(2), as stated above. Temporary protected status may be terminated if: (1) the Attorney General finds that the alien was not eligible for such status; (2) the alien was not continuously physically present, except for brief, casual, and innocent departures or travel with advance permission; (3) the alien failed to register annually; or (4) the Attorney General terminates the program. INA 244A(c)(3).

An alien granted temporary protected status cannot be deported during the designated period and shall be granted employment authorization. The alien may also travel abroad with advance permission. Temporary protected status also allows the alien to adjust or change status. . . .

Rights of Refugees and Asylees. Certain benefits are available to an alien applying for asylum. First, as long as the asylum claim appears nonfrivolous, the applicant may be granted employment authorization while the asylum application is pending. Second, the applicant may be granted advance parole to travel abroad to a third country for humanitarian reasons.

In April 1992, the INS created a "pre-screening" procedure to identify genuine asylum seekers whose parole from detention might be appropriate while their asylum claims are pending. Specially trained asylum pre-screening officers interview applicants in detention and evaluate asylum claims. If the claimant is deemed to have a "credible fear of persecution," then the alien may be released pending the asylum claim. The alien must, however, agree to check in periodically with the INS and appear at all relevant hearings.

The immediate family (spouse and children) of the person granted refugee admission or political asylum can accompany or follow such person without having to apply for protection independently. INA 207(c)(2) and 208(c).

Finally, one who entered the United States as a refugee is eligible for permanent resident status after one year of continuous physical presence in the United States. The number of refugees adjusting to permanent resident status is not subject to the annual limitation on immigrants into the United States. INA 209. An asylee may also apply for permanent resident status after being continuously present in the United States for at least one year after being granted asylum. There are 10,000 visas set aside each year for asylees applying for residency.

Source: U.S. Immigration and Naturalization Service. *U.S. Report Under the International Covenant on Civil and Political Rights* (Washington, DC: U.S. Immigration and Naturalization Service, 1994).

Report to Congress, U.S. Commission on Immigration Reform (1994)

In 1990, Congress created the U.S. Commission on Immigration Reform to examine national immigration policy and recommend appropriate changes. Four years later, the commission issued its first report. The document advocated, among other things, stronger border controls, prompt deportation of illegal aliens, no access to nonemergency public services for illegal aliens, and, most controversially, a national computer registry that all employers would be required to check before hiring to ensure that potential employees are residing legally in the United States. Some of the commission's recommendations pertaining to deportation were included in the Illegal Immigration Reform and Immigrant Responsibility Act of 1996, and some of its proposals concerning public services were written into the Personal Responsibility and Work Opportunity Act of the same year. All in all, the 1994 report and the legislation that followed reflected an increasingly harsh attitude toward illegal immigrants in the 1990s and 2000s.

Executive Summary

Introduction

The U.S. Commission on Immigration Reform was created by Congress to assess U.S. immigration policy and make recommendations regarding its implementation and effects. Mandated in the Immigration Act of 1990 to submit an interim report in 1994 and a final report in 1997, the Commission has undertaken public hearings, fact-finding missions, and expert consultations to identify the major immigration-related issues facing the United States today.

This process has been a complex one. Distinguishing fact from fiction has been difficult, in some cases because of what has become a highly emotional debate on immigration. We have heard contradictory testimony, shaky statistics, and a great deal of honest confusion regarding the impacts of immigration. Nevertheless, we have tried throughout to engage in what we believe is a systematic, non-partisan effort to reach conclusions drawn from analysis of the best data available.

Underlying Principles

Certain basic principles underlie the Commission's work. The Commission decries hostility and discrimination against immigrants as antithetical to the traditions and interests of the country. At the same time, we disagree with those who would label efforts to control immigration as being inherently anti-immigrant. Rather, it is both a right and a responsibility of a democratic society to manage immigration so that it serves the national interest.

Challenges Ahead

The Commission believes that legal immigration has strengthened and can continue to strengthen this country. While we will be reporting at a later date on the impacts of our legal immigration system, and while there may even be disagreements among us as to the total number of immigrants that can be absorbed into the United States or the categories that should be given priority for admission, the Commission members agree that immigration presents many opportunities for this nation. Immigrants can contribute to the building of the country. In most cases, they have been actively sought by family members or businesses in the U.S. The tradition of welcoming newcomers has become an important element of how we define ourselves as a nation.

The Commission is mindful of the problems that also emanate from immigration. In particular, we believe that unlawful immigration is unacceptable. Enforcement efforts have not been effective in deterring unlawful immigration. This failure to develop effective strategies to control unlawful immigration has blurred the public perception of the distinction between legal and illegal immigrants.

For the Commission, the principal issue at present is how to manage immigration so that it will continue to be in the national interest.

- How do we ensure that immigration is based on and supports broad national economic, social, and humanitarian interests, rather than the interests of those who would abuse our laws?
- How do we gain effective control over our borders while still encouraging international trade, investment, and tourism?
- How do we maintain a civic culture based on shared values while accommodating the large and diverse population admitted through immigration policy?

The credibility of immigration policy can be measured by a simple yardstick: people who should get in, do get in; people who should not get in are kept out; and people who are judged deportable are required to leave.

During the decade from 1980 to 1990, three major pieces of legislation were adopted to govern immigration policy—the Refugee Act of 1980, the Immigration Reform and Control Act of 1986, and the Immigration Act of 1990. The Commission supports the broad framework for immigration policy that these laws represent: a legal immigration system that strives to serve the national interest in helping families to reunify and employers to obtain skills not available in the U.S. labor force; a refugee system that reflects both our humanitarian beliefs and international refugee law; and an enforcement system that seeks to deter unlawful immigration through employer sanctions and tighter border control.

The Commission has concluded, however, that more needs to be done to guarantee that the stated goals of our immigration policy are met. The immediate need is more effective prevention and deterrence of unlawful immigration. This report to Congress outlines the Commission's recommendations in this area.

In the long term, immigration policies for the 1990s and beyond should anticipate the challenges of the next century. These challenges will be substantially influenced by factors such as the restructuring of our own economy, the establishment of such new trade relationships as the North American Free Trade Agreement [NAFTA], and changing geopolitical relations. No less importantly, immigration policy must carefully take into account social concerns, demographic trends, and the impact of added population on the country's environment.

Finally, current immigration is the first to occur in what economists call a post-industrial economy, just as it is the first to occur after the appearance of the modern welfare state. The Commission's report to Congress in 1997 will cover these issues in assessing the impact of the Immigration Act of 1990. The present report reviews the progress of the beginning implementation of this legislation.

Recommendations

Serious problems undermine present immigration policies, their implementation, and their credibility: people who should get in find a cumbersome process that often impedes their entry; people who should not get in find it all too easy to enter; and people who are here without permission remain with impunity.

The Commission is convinced that unlawful immigration can be controlled consistent with our traditions, civil rights, and civil liberties. As a nation with a long history of immigration and commitment to the rule of law, this country must set limits on who can enter and then must credibly enforce our immigration law. Unfortunately, no quick and easy solutions are available. The United States can do a more effective job, but only with additional financial resources and the political will to take action. Our recommendations for a comprehensive, effective strategy follow.

Border Management

The Commission believes that significant progress has been made during the past several years in identifying and remedying some of the weaknesses in U.S. border management. Nevertheless, we believe that far more can and should be done to meet the twin goals of border management: preventing illegal entries while facilitating legal ones.

Land Borders

Credibility is a problem at U.S. land borders, given the ease of illegal entry and various obstacles to legal entry. These problems are particularly prevalent at the U.S.-Mexico border, as the Commission's visit to San Diego and El Paso demonstrated. The Commission believes that an underlying principle of border management is that prevention is far more effective and cost-efficient than the apprehension and removal of illegal aliens after entry. At the same time, the Commission believes that legal entry should be facilitated in order for the country to benefit from cross-border trade and tourism.

The Commission supports the strategy, now being tested as "Operation Hold the Line" in El Paso, that emphasizes prevention of illegal entry at the border, rather than apprehension following illegal entry. Prevention holds many advantages: it is more cost-effective than apprehension and removal; it eliminates the cycle of voluntary return and reentry that has characterized unlawful border crossings; and it reduces potentially violent confrontations on the border. The Commission recommends:

- Increased resources for prevention, including additional staff, such improved technology as sensors and infrared scopes, data systems that permit expeditious identification of repeat offenders, and such additional equipment as vehicles and radios.

- Increased training for border control officers to execute strategies that emphasize prevention of illegal entry.

- Formation of a mobile, rapid response team to improve Border Patrol anticipation of new smuggling sites and to augment their capacity at these locations. The Immigration and Naturalization Service [INS] must develop a capacity to respond quickly to changing patterns of unlawful immigration along the land border. Also, contingency plans should be developed to address increased boat arrivals that may arise from improved land border enforcement.

- Use of fences to reduce border violence and facilitate enforcement. However, the Commission does not support the erection of extraordinary physical barriers, such as unscalable walls, unless needed as a last resort to stop violence when other means have proved ineffective. Fences have been used effectively in San Diego to reduce border violence, deter illegal aliens from running across the interstate highway that leads from Mexico, and facilitate enforcement.

- Systematic evaluation of the effectiveness of any new border strategies by INS. The typical measurements of Border Patrol effectiveness—apprehension rates—have little meaning in assessing a prevention strategy. INS should develop new evaluation techniques that measure the effects of border management efforts in terms of the flow of unauthorized aliens and their impacts on U.S. communities.

The Commission supports efforts to reduce potentially violent confrontations between Border Patrol officers and those believed to be seeking illegal entry into the U.S. Such confrontations were reduced, for example, during "Operation Hold the Line," in terms of both reported human rights violations against suspected illegal aliens and attacks on Border Patrol officers.

The Commission supports efforts already underway to address complaints about human rights violations, including:

- Increased training and professionalism of Border Patrol officers to enable them to respond appropriately to potentially violent situations;
- Improved procedures for adjudicating complaints of Border Patrol abuses;

- Mechanisms to provide redress or relief to those subjected to improper actions; and
- More effective protection of Border Patrol officers from violence directed at them.

The Commission believes that port entry operations can be improved. Legal entry at the border should be facilitated as the United States benefits from trade, tourism, family visits, and consumer spending. More specifically, the Commission supports:

- Additional resources for inspections at land border ports of entry.
- An expedited adjudication and issuance process for the Border Crossing Card [BCC]. Mexican nationals are required to have a visa (unlike Canadians). Because of the volume of BCC applications on the Mexican border, the Commission encourages negotiations between the U.S. and Mexico to amend the bilateral treaty to permit collection of fees to be used exclusively to expedite the issuance and adjudication of the card.
- Further steps to better ensure that the BCC is not misused by legal crossers who engage in unauthorized employment after entry. Each BCC should contain the legend indicating it is "not for work authorization," as currently appears on INS-issued cards.
- Development of a land border user fee to pay for needed improvements in the inspection of border crossers, with fees to be used exclusively to facilitate land border management.

The Commission supports increased coordination on border issues between the governments of the U.S. and Mexico. The Commission views favorably the discussions underway between the U.S. and Mexican governments. These discussions promote greater cooperation . . . in solving problems of mutual concern. In particular, the Commission encourages:

- Continued cooperation in antismuggling efforts to reduce smuggling of people and goods across the U.S.-Mexico border.
- Bilateral discussions that take into account both U.S. entry and Mexican exit laws in devising a cooperative approach to regulating the movements of people across the U.S.-Mexican land border. Mexican law requires that Mexican nationals exit Mexico through official inspection stations. Thus, unauthorized migration into the United States generally violates not only U.S. law, but Mexican law as well.

- Cross border discussions and cooperative law enforcement efforts among federal, state, and local officials of both countries to develop cooperative approaches to combat violent crimes and auto and cargo theft along the border.
- Continued U.S. cooperation and support for Mexican efforts to address the problem of third-country nationals crossing Mexico to come to the United States.

Airports
Each year about 50 million citizens and aliens enter the country through airports.

The Commission supports a combined facilitation and enforcement strategy that would prevent the entry of unauthorized aliens while facilitating legal admissions at U.S. airports as efficiently as possible, including:

- The use of new technologies to expedite the inspections process and improve law enforcement, including more efficient processing of travelers with Machine Readable Documents.
- Programs that enhance the capacity of airline carriers to identify and refuse travel to aliens seeking to enter the U.S. on fraudulent documents, including the Carrier Consultant Program and other coordinated efforts to maintain complete, accurate, and reliable Advance Passenger Information System [APIS] data and improved lookout data systems.
- Continued government-airline industry discussions on improving inspections that have led to innovative proposals.
- Development of a system for mitigation of penalties or fines for those carriers that cooperate in screening and other programs and demonstrate success in reducing the number of unauthorized aliens they carry.
- Making INS, not the carrier, responsible for the actual physical custody of inadmissible air passengers.

Interagency Coordination
The Commission expresses its dissatisfaction with the past lack of coordination between the Customs Service and the INS at ports of entry. This has hampered effective border management by both agencies.

The Commission recommends implementation of initiatives to improve coordination between INS and Customs, as recommended by the General Accounting Office {GAO} and the National Performance Review. The Commission will monitor these efforts to improve coordination of border management, particularly as they relate to immigration matters.

If these efforts prove ineffective, the Commission will recommend more extensive action, such as creating a new immigration and customs agency or designating one agency as the lead agency on inspections.

Alien Smuggling

Organized smuggling operations undermine the credibility of U.S. enforcement efforts and pose dangers to the smuggled aliens.

The Commission recommends an effective prevention strategy that requires enhanced capacities to combat organized smuggling for commercial gain. Possible enhancements include:

- Expanded enforcement authorities, such as Racketeer Influenced and Corrupt Organizations Act [RICO] provisions, wire-tap authority, and expanded asset forfeiture for smuggling aliens; and
- Enhanced intelligence gathering and diplomatic efforts to deter smuggling.

Worksite Enforcement

The Commission believes that reducing the employment magnet is the linchpin of a comprehensive strategy to reduce illegal immigration. The ineffectiveness of employer sanctions, prevalence of fraudulent documents, and continued high numbers of unauthorized workers, combined with confusion for employers and reported discrimination against employees, have challenged the credibility of current worksite enforcement efforts.

Verification

A better system for verifying work authorization is central to effective enforcement of employer sanctions.

The Commission recommends development and implementation of a simpler, more fraud-resistant system for verifying work authorization. The current system is doubly flawed: it is too susceptible to fraud, particularly through the counterfeiting of documents; and it can lead to increased discrimination against foreign-looking or foreign-sounding authorized workers.

In examining the options for improving verification, *the Commission believes that the most promising option for secure, non-discriminatory verification is a computerized registry* using data provided by the Social Security Administration [SSA] and the INS.

The key to this process is the social security number. For decades all workers have been required to provide employers with their social security number. The computer registry would add only one step to this existing requirement: an employer check that the social security number is valid and has been issued to someone authorized to work in the United States.

The Commission believes the computerized system is the most promising option because it holds great potential for accomplishing the following:

- Reduction in the potential for fraud. Using a computerized registry, rather than only an identification card, guards against counterfeiting of documents. It provides more reliable information about work authorization.
- Reduction in the potential for discrimination based on national origin and citizenship status, as well as inappropriate demands for specific or additional documents, given that employers will not be required to ascertain whether a worker is a citizen or an immigrant and will have no reason to reject documents they believe to be counterfeit. The only relevant question will be: "What is your social security number?"
- Reduction in the time, resources, and paperwork spent by employers in complying with the Immigration Reform and Control Act of 1986 [IRCA] and corresponding redirection of enforcement activities from paperwork violations to knowing hire of unauthorized workers.

The Commission recommends that the President immediately initiate and evaluate pilot programs using the proposed computerized verification system in the five states with the highest levels of illegal immigration as well as several less affected states. The President has the authority to do so under Section 274A(d)(4) of the Immigration and Nationality Act. A pilot program will: permit the testing of various approaches to using the proposed verification system; provide needed information about the advantages, disadvantages, and costs of the various approaches; develop and evaluate measures to protect civil rights and civil liberties; and ensure that any potential obstacles, such as the quality of the data used in the registry, are addressed prior to national implementation. Assuming the successful results of the pilot program, Congress should pass the necessary statutory authorities to support more effective verification. Pilot program features should include:

- A means by which employers will access the verification system to validate the accuracy of information given by workers. We have received conflicting testimony about the best way to check the applicant's identity. We have heard proposals for a more secure social security card, a counterfeit-resistant driver's license, and a telephone verification system that does not rely on any document. The pilot program presents an opportunity to determine the most cost-effective, fraud-resistant, and nondiscriminatory method available.

- Measures to ensure the accuracy of and access to the specific data needed to ensure that employers have timely and reliable information when seeking verification of work authorization. Improvements in the Social Security Administration and INS databases must be made to ensure that these data are available. Procedures must be developed to ensure timely and accurate entry, update, extraction, and correction of data. The Commission strongly urges INS and the Social Security Administration to cooperate in this endeavor, as the proposed registry would be built upon and—once implemented—would support the primary missions of those agencies.

- Measures to ensure against discrimination and disparate treatment of foreign-looking or -sounding persons. The Commission believes that the least discriminatory system would have the same requirements for citizens and aliens alike. To reduce the potential for discrimination and increase the security of the system, the Commission also believes that employers should not be required to ascertain immigration status in the process of verifying authorization for employment. Their only requirement should be to check the social security number presented by each employee against the registry and record an authorization number to prove that they have done so.

- Measures to protect civil liberties. It is essential that explicit protections be devised against use of the database—and any card or any other means used to gain access to it—for purposes other than those specified in law. The uses to be made of the verification system must be clearly specified. We believe the worksite verification system could be used, without damage to civil liberties, for verifying eligibility to receive public benefits. However, it should be stipulated that no one should be required to carry a card, if one is used, or to present it for routine identification purposes. There also should be penalties for inappropriate use of the verification process.

- Measures to protect the privacy of the information included in the database. The Commission is aware of the proliferation of databases and the potential for the invasion of privacy by both government and private agencies. There need to be explicit provisions for protecting privacy; the resultant system should incorporate appropriate safeguards regarding authorized users' access to individual information. In establishing privacy safeguards, it is important to take into account that, while access to any one piece of information may not be intrusive, in combination with other information such access may violate privacy.

- Estimates of the start-up time and financial and other costs of developing, implementing, and maintaining a national system in such a manner that verification is reliable.

- Specification of the rights, responsibilities, and impact on individual workers and employers, for example: what individuals must do; how long it will take for newly authorized workers to get on the system and to correct inaccurate data; and what will be required of employers and at what expense. Provisions must also be developed to protect both workers from denial of employment and employers from penalties in cases where the information provided by the computer registry may be missing or inaccurate.

- A plan for phasing in of the system. The Commission recognizes that the proposed verification system will result in financial costs. The system should be phased in to lessen the immediate impact. The pilot programs should test various phase-in procedures. Given the required levels of accuracy, reliability, and convenience required, the evaluation should help measure the cost of phasing in the system nationally.

The Commission recommends evaluation of the pilot programs to assess the effectiveness of the verification system. The evaluation should include objective measures and procedures to determine whether current problems related to fraud, discrimination, and excessive paperwork requirements for employers are effectively overcome without imposing undue costs on the government, employers, or employees. The evaluation should pay particular attention to the effectiveness of the measures used to protect civil liberties and privacy.

The Commission supports INS efforts to improve its Telephone Verification System/SAVE {TVS/SAVE} database but only as an interim measure. The improvements are essential for improving the data needed for the new, more effective verification process. The Commission is aware of the inadequacies of the current INS data that would be used in the proposed system. The Commission does not endorse the TVS/SAVE program as a long-term solution to the verification problem because use of TVS/SAVE requires the inadequate mechanism of self-attestation by workers as to their citizenship or alienage, thus making it easy for aliens to fraudulently claim U.S. citizenship. It also imposes requirements on legal immigrants that do not apply to citizens. Nevertheless, improvements in this database, as well as the Social Security Administration database, are essential to the development of a more secure, less potentially discriminatory verification system.

The Commission also recommends action that would reduce the fraudulent access to so-called "breeder documents," particularly birth certificates, that can be used to establish an identity in this country, including:

- Regulation of requests for birth certificates through standardized application forms;
- A system of interstate and intrastate matching of birth and death records;
- Making certified copies of birth certificates issued by states or state-controlled vital records offices the only forms accepted by federal agencies;
- Using a standard design and paperstock for all certified copies of birth certificates to reduce counterfeiting; and
- Encouraging states to computerize birth records repositories.

To address the abuse of fraudulent documents, the Commission recommends an imposition of greater penalties on those producing or selling such documents. Document fraud and counterfeiting has become a lucrative and well-organized operation that may involve international networks that conspire to produce and sell the resulting fraudulent products. These documents are used in smuggling and terrorist operations, as well as for work authorization. RICO provisions designed to facilitate racketeering investigations should cover conspiracy to produce and sell fraudulent documents. Criminal penalties should also be increased for large-scale counterfeiting activities.

Antidiscrimination Strategies

The Commission is concerned about unfair immigration-related employment practices against both citizens and noncitizens that may occur under the current system of employer sanctions. A more reliable, simpler verification system holds great potential to reduce any such discrimination because employers will no longer have to make any determination as to immigration status. Nevertheless, mechanisms must effectively prevent and redress discrimination.

The Commission recommends that the Office of the Special Counsel {OSC} for Immigration-Related Unfair Employment Practices in the Department of Justice initiate more proactive strategies to identify and combat immigration-related discrimination at the workplace. OSC should target resources on independent investigations and on programs to assess the incidence and prevalence of unfair immigration-related employment practices.

The Commission also recommends a methodologically sound study to document the nature and extent of unfair immigration-related employment practices that have occurred since GAO's {General Accounting Office} 1990 report. The new study should measure the effects of immigration policy—as distinct from other factors—on discrimination at the worksite. As noted above, the pilot programs should be evaluated to determine if they substantially reduce immigration-related discrimination at the workplace.

Employer Sanctions and Labor Standards Enforcement

The Commission believes that enforcement of employer sanctions, wage/hour, child labor, and other labor standards can be an effective tool in reducing employment of unauthorized workers. The Commission finds, however, that current enforcement efforts are inadequate. In addition, the Commission expresses its concern that current coordination efforts between the Immigration and Naturalization Service and the Department of Labor are insufficient.

The Commission supports vigorous enforcement of labor standards and enforcement against knowing hire of unauthorized workers as an integral part of the strategy to reduce illegal immigration. Labor standards and employer sanctions should be seen as mutually reinforcing. Specifically, the Commission recommends:

- Allocation of increased staff and resources to the enforcement of labor standards to complement employer sanctions enforcement.
- Vigorous enforcement, increased staff and resources, and full use of current penalties against those who knowingly hire unauthorized workers. If the new verification system proposed by the Commission substantially reduces inadvertent hiring of unauthorized workers—as we believe will occur—Congress should discontinue paperwork penalties and evaluate the need for increased penalties against violators and businesses that knowingly hire or fail to verify work authorization for all employees.
- Targeting of investigations to industries that have a history of using illegal alien labor.
- Enhanced enforcement efforts targeted at farm labor and other contractors who hire unauthorized workers on behalf of agricultural growers and other businesses.
- Application of employer sanctions to the federal government. At a minimum, the President should issue an Executive Order requiring federal agencies to abide by the procedures required of other employers. Alternatively, legislation should stipulate that federal agencies follow the verification procedures required of other employers and be subject to penalties if they fail to verify work authorization.

The Commission urges the Attorney General and the Secretary of Labor to review the current division of responsibilities between the Departments of Justice and Labor in the enforcement of employer sanctions and labor standards. INS and the Department of Labor have signed a Memorandum of Understanding [MOU] that spells out each agency's responsibility for enforcing employer sanctions and labor standards. Preliminary evidence indicates that few warnings have been issued to employers under the MOU. The implementation of the MOU should be closely monitored over the next twelve months. Should the monitoring demonstrate that the joint efforts have not resulted in effective enforcement, it may be necessary to designate a single agency to enforce employer sanctions.

The Commission recommends enhanced coordination mechanisms to promote cooperation among all of the agencies responsible for worksite enforcement. Strategies to promote coordination at headquarters and in field operations include:

- Establishment of a taskforce in Washington, D.C., to review and set policy;
- Local taskforces of worksite investigators to coordinate field operations; and
- Continued joint training for worksite investigators from all applicable agencies.

Education
Thousands of new businesses begin operations each year. New workers enter the labor force each year as well.

The Commission recommends coordination and continuance of educational efforts by the Immigration and Naturalization Service, the Office of Special Counsel, and the Department of Labor regarding employer sanctions, antidiscrimination provisions, and labor standards. The Commission calls upon these agencies to develop and communicate a single message to all employers and employees. The Commission also recommends the development of new strategies, including the enhanced use of technology, to inform employers and workers of their rights and responsibilities under the law.

Source: U.S. Commission on Immigration Reform. *Report by U.S. Commission on Immigration Reform,* September 30, 1994 (Washington, DC: U.S. Government Printing Office, 1994).

California Proposition 187 (1994)

In November 1994, the voters of California approved Proposition 187, popularly known as the "Save Our State" initiative. Facing unprecedented waves of legal and illegal immigration, the state's largely native white electorate passed a referendum intended to reduce the economic, educational, and social welfare benefits said to be attracting the large numbers of immigrants. Federal courts later ruled that the proposition violated, among other things, the Equal Protection Clause of the Fourteenth Amendment by discriminating against one class of persons—immigrants.

Section 1. Findings and Declaration
The People of California find and declare as follows:

That they have suffered and are suffering economic hardship by the presence of illegal aliens in the state. That they have suffered and are suffering personal injury and damage by the criminal conduct of illegal aliens in the state. That they have a right to the protection of their government from any person or persons entering this country unlawfully.

Therefore, the People of California declare their intention to provide for cooperation between their agencies of state and local government with the federal government, and to establish a system of required notification by and between such agencies to prevent illegal aliens in the United States from receiving benefits or public services in the State of California.

Section 2. Manufacture, Distribution or Sale of False Citizenship or Resident Alien Documents: Crime and Punishment.
Section 113 is added to the Penal Code, to read:
"Section 113. Any person who manufactures, distributes or sells false documents to conceal the true citizenship or resident alien status of another is guilty of a felony and shall be punished by imprisonment in the state prison for five years or by a fine of seventy-five thousand dollars."

Section 3. Use of False Citizenship or Resident Alien Documents: Crime and Punishment.
Section 114 is added to the Penal Code, to read:
"Section 114. Any person who uses false documents to conceal his or her true citizenship or resident alien status is guilty of a felony, and shall be punished by imprisonment in a state prison for five years or by a fine of twenty-five thousand dollars."

Section 4. Law Enforcement Cooperation with INS [Immigration and Naturalization Service].
Section 834b is added to the Penal Code, to read:
"Section 834b. (a) Every law enforcement agency in California shall fully cooperate with the United States Immigration and Naturalization Service regarding any person who is arrested if he or she is suspected of being present in the United States in violation of federal immigration laws.

"(b) With respect to any such person who is arrested, and suspected of being present in the United States in violation of federal immigration laws, every law enforcement agency shall do the following:

"(1). Attempt to verify the legal status of such person as a citizen of the United States, an alien lawfully admitted as a permanent resident, an alien lawfully admitted for a temporary period of time or as an alien who is present in the United States in violation of immigration laws. The verification process may include, but shall not be limited to, questioning the person regarding his or her date and place of birth and entry into the United States, and demanding documentation to indicate his or her legal status.

"(2). Notify the person of his or her apparent status as an alien who is present in the United States in violation of federal immigration laws and inform him or her that, apart from any criminal justice precedings [*sic*], he or she must obtain legal status or leave the United States.

"(3). Notify the Attorney General of California and the United States Immigration and Naturalization Service of the apparent illegal status and provide any additional information that may be requested by any other public entity.

"(c) Any legislative, administrative, or other action by a city, county, or other legally authorized local governmental entity with jurisdictional boundaries, or by a law enforcement agency, to prevent or limit the cooperation required by subdivision (a) is expressly prohibited."

Section 5. Exclusion of Illegal Aliens from Public Social Services.

Section 10001.5. Is added to the Welfare and Institutions Code, to read:

"Section 10001.5 (a) In order to carry out the intention of the People of California that only citizens of the United States and aliens lawfully admitted to the United States may receive the benefits of public social services and to ensure that all persons employed in the providing of those services shall diligently protect public funds from misuse, the provisions of this section are adopted.

"(b) A person shall not receive any public social services to which he or she may not otherwise be entitled until the legal status of that person has been verified as one of the following:

"(1) A citizen of the United States.

"(2) An alien lawfully admitted as a permanent resident.

"(3) An alien lawfully admitted for a temporary period of time . . ."

Section 6. Exclusion of Illegal Aliens from Publicly Funded Health Care.

Chapter 1.3 (commencing with Section 130) is added to Part 1 of Division 1 of the Health and Safety Code, to read:

"Chapter 1.3. Publicly Funded Health Care Services.
"Section 130. (a) In order to carry out the intention of the People of California that, excepting emergency medical care as required by federal law, only citizens of the United States and aliens lawfully admitted to the United States may receive the benefits of publicly funded health care, and to ensure that all persons employed in the providing of those services shall diligently protect public funds from misuse, the provisions of this section are adopted. . . .

"(c) If any publicly funded health care facility in this state from whom a person seeks health care services, other than emergency medical care as required by federal law, determines or reasonably suspects, based on the information provided it, that the person is an alien in the United States in violation of the federal law. . . . [Services will not be forthcoming and the Immigration and Naturalization Service will be notified.]"

Section 7. Exclusion of Illegal Aliens from Public Elementary and Secondary Schools.

Section 48215 is added to the Education Code to read:
"Section 48215. (a) No public elementary or secondary school shall admit, or permit the attendance of, any child who is not a citizen of the United States, an alien lawfully admitted as a permanent resident, or a person who is otherwise authorized under federal law to be present. . . .

"(b) Commencing January 1, 1995, each school district shall verify the legal status of each child enrolling in the school district for the first time. . . .

"(d) By January 1, 1996, each school district shall also have verified the legal status of each parent or guardian of each child. . . .

"(e) Each school district shall provide information to the State Superintendent of Public Instruction, the Attorney General of California and the United States Immigration and Naturalization Service regarding any enrollee or pupil, or parent or guardian, attending a public elementary or secondary school in the school district determined or reasonably suspected to be in violation of federal immigration laws within forty-five days after becoming aware of an apparent violation. . . .

"(f) For each child who cannot establish legal status in the United States each school district shall continue to provide education for a period of ninety days from the date of the notice. . . ."

Section 8. Exclusion of Illegal Aliens from Public Postsecondary Educational Institutions.

Section 66010.8. is added to the Education Code to read:

"Section 66010.8. (a) No public institution of postsecondary education shall admit, enroll, or permit the attendance of any person who is not a citizen of the United States, an alien lawfully admitted as a permanent resident, in the United States, or a person who is otherwise authorized under federal law to be present in the United States.

"(c) Commencing with the first term or semester that begins after January 1, 1996, and at the end of each term or semester thereafter, each public postsecondary educational institution shall verify the status of each person enrolled or in attendance at that institution. . . ."

Section 9. Attorney General Cooperation with the INS.

Section 53609.65. Is added to the Government Code, to read:

"Section 53609.65. Whenever the state or a city, or a county, or any other legally authorized local government entity with jurisdictional boundaries reports the presence of a person who is suspected of being present in the United States in violation of federal immigration laws to the Attorney General of California, that report shall be transmitted to the United States Immigration and Naturalization Service. The Attorney General shall be responsible for maintaining on-going and accurate records of such reports, and shall provide any additional information that may be requested by any other government entity."

Source: League of United Latin American Citizens v. Wilson, 908 F. Supp. 755 (C.D. California 1995).

Revised Guidelines on Asylum for Women, U.S. Immigration and Naturalization Service (1995)

In May 1995, the Immigration and Naturalization Service (INS) issued revised guidelines that recognized sexual violence as potential grounds for granting refugee status to female asylum seekers. INS Commissioner Doris Meissner was quick to point out, however, that the new guidelines did not change the standard that women seeking asylum must meet. Instead, she said, the guidelines were issued simply to "educate Asylum officers about gender-based discrimination" and to provide them with the appropriate "procedures and methods for evaluating whether individual claims meet the refugee standard."

Background

Human rights violations against women are not a new phenomenon in the world. Yet, only recently have they risen to the forefront of the international agenda.

- In 1979, the Convention on the Elimination of All Forms of Discrimination Against Women (CEDAW) recommended the eradication of violations against women.
- In June 1993, the United Nations World Conference on Human Rights emphasized the need to incorporate the rights of women, and called upon the General Assembly to adopt the Declaration on the Elimination of Violence against Women. On December 20, 1993, the United Nations General Assembly adopted the Declaration.
- There have also been Conclusions from the United Nations High Commissioner for Refugees (UNHCR). For example, in 1985 the UNHCR Executive Committee adopted Conclusion No. 39, noting that refugee women and girls constitute the majority of the world population and that many of them are exposed to special problems.

All of these international initiatives underscored and contributed to the development of guidance related to women refugee claimants.

The Canadian Immigration and Refugee Board (IRB) issued its asylum gender guidelines over two years ago, in March 1993. The UNHCR issued a set of guidelines in 1991, and faculty members at Harvard Law School also submitted a proposed set of guidelines in 1994. Despite the increased attention to gender-based asylum claims, they are still relatively new developments in refugee protection.

INS Implementation

Because gender issues are novel, and adjudicators of asylum claims are guided by recent (and still developing) U.S. case law, INS felt that guidance to all Asylum Officers would be appropriate to ensure uniformity in adjudications, and would allow Asylum Officers to be more responsive to bona fide asylum claims.

Women asylum applicants, like all applicants, must satisfy the refugee definition provided for by statute. Under U.S. law, the term *refugee* means " . . . any person who is outside any country of such person's nationality," and who is "unable or unwilling to return to . . . that country because of persecution or a well-founded fear of persecution on account of race, religion, nationality, membership in a particular social group, or political opinion. . . ."

The U.S. refugee definition is a narrow one. Individuals cannot qualify for asylum in the United States unless the persecution is on account of one of the protected grounds specified by Congress. There must also be a favorable credibility finding by an Asylum Officer. The INS Guidelines summarize recent decisions from the courts and the Board of Immigration Appeals, which provide appropriate analysis for gender-related and other asylum claims. The INS Gender Guidelines do not enlarge or expand on the grounds that were specified by Congress and the understandings the courts have reached about those grounds.

Not all women who apply for asylum under this new guidance will be granted asylum. INS asylum decisions are individualized, case-by-case determinations. For example, INS sometimes encounters women asylum applicants who come from countries where domestic or sexual abuse is tolerated. However, to qualify for asylum these women must show, for example, that:

- The domestic violence cannot be purely "personal." It must relate to one of the grounds enumerated in the statute.
- The harm feared must rise to the level of "persecution." The courts have uniformly held that "persecution" denotes extreme conduct and does not include every sort of treatment our society regards as offensive, unfair, unjust, or even unlawful or unconstitutional.
- Also, both U.S. law and the UN Protocol require that the fear of persecution must normally extend to the entire country of origin; that is, in order for an applicant to meet the definition of a refugee she must do more than show a well-founded fear of persecution in a particular place or abode within a "country"—she must show that the threat of persecution exists for her countrywide. For example, some battered women may be denied asylum because they could have sought safety from the batterer simply by moving to another town or province in their country of origin. National protection should take precedence over international protection.

In sum, every asylum applicant is carefully interviewed. No applicant can be approved unless all the definitional elements of the statute are satisfied.

INS does not expect the rate of asylum applications to increase because of the Gender Guidelines. That was not the experience of the Canadians who issued their guidelines more than 2 years ago.

Asylum Interviews/Officers: All INS Asylum Officers—men and women—will be expected to conduct interviews of women with gender based claims. To the extent that personnel resources permit, however, Asylum Officers may allow women Asylum Offices to interview these cases. An interview will not generally be canceled because of the unavailability of a woman Asylum Officer. But INS also recognizes that, because of the very delicate and personal issues arising from sexual abuse, some women claimants may understandably have inhibitions about disclosing past experiences to male interviewers.

Interpreters/Presence of Family Members: Testimony on sensitive issues such as sexual abuse can be diluted when received through the filter of a male interpreter. While INS encourages the use of female interpreters, interviews will not generally be canceled and rescheduled because women with gender-based asylum claims have brought male interpreters.

Interviewing Asylum Officers will provide women with the opportunity to be interviewed outside the hearing of other members of their family, especially male family members and children. There is a greater likelihood that a woman applicant may more freely communicate a claim involving sexual abuse when family members are not present.

Generally, the new Guidelines will assist Asylum Officers in the attentive examination of cases, and the approval of legitimate claimants.

Source: U.S. Bureau of Citizenship and Immigration Services, *Considerations for Asylum Officers Adjudicating Asylum Claims from Women ("INS Gender Guidelines")*, May 26, 1995.

Personal Responsibility and Work Opportunity Reconciliation Act, Summary (1996)

In summer 1996, Congress passed and President Bill Clinton signed the Personal Responsibility and Work Opportunity Reconciliation Act, also known as the Welfare Reform Act. While the legislation revised the welfare system for all Americans, it also included various provisions aimed specifically at immigrants. In effect, these provisions of the bill closely reflected the intent of California Proposition 187, passed two years earlier. Essentially, the law severely limited the access of legal and illegal immigrants to social welfare and other benefit programs of the federal government. The text that follows is a summary, produced by Congressional Quarterly Almanac, *of the immigrant-related portions of the Personal Responsibility and Work Opportunity Reconciliation Act of 1996.*

The new welfare law imposed new restrictions on both legal and illegal immigrants, including provisions to:

Illegal Aliens

1. Restrictions. Restrict the federal benefits for which illegal aliens and legal non-immigrants, such as travelers and students, could qualify. The benefits denied were those provided by a federal agency or federal funds for:

—Any grant, contract, loan, professional license or commercial license.

—Any retirement, welfare, health, disability, food assistance or unemployment benefit.

2. Exceptions. Allow illegal aliens and legal non-immigrants to receive:

—Emergency medical services under Medicaid, but denied coverage for pre-natal or delivery assistance that was not an emergency.

—Short-term, non-cash emergency disaster relief.

—Immunizations and testing for treatment for the symptoms of communicable diseases.

—Non-cash programs identified by the attorney general that were delivered by community agencies such as soup kitchens, counseling, and short-term shelter, that were not conditioned on the individual's income or resources and were necessary for the protection of life and safety.

—Certain housing benefits (for existing recipients only).

—Licenses and benefits directly related to work for which a non-immigrant had been authorized to enter the United States.

—Certain Social Security retirement benefits protected by treaty or statute.

3. State and local programs. Prohibit states from providing state or local benefits to most illegal aliens, unless a state law was enacted after August 22, 1996, the day the bill was enacted, that explicitly made illegal aliens eligible for the aid. However, illegal aliens were entitled to receive a school lunch and/or breakfast if they were eligible for a free public education under state or local law. A state could also opt to provide certain other benefits related to child nutrition and emergency food assistance.

Legal Immigrants

4. Current immigrants. Make most legal immigrants, including those already in the United States, ineligible for SSI and food stamps until they became citizens; existing recipients to have an eligibility review by August 1997. This ban was exempt for:

—Refugees, those granted asylum and aliens whose deportation was being withheld.

—Those who had worked in the United States for ten years.

—Veterans and those on active military duty, as well as their spouses and unmarried children.

5. Future immigrants. Bar legal immigrants who arrived in the United States after August 22, 1996, from receiving most low-income federal benefits for five years after their arrival. Individuals exempt from this ban were:

—Refugees and those granted asylum and aliens whose deportation had been withheld, as well as Cuban and Haitian entrants.

—Veterans and those on active military duty, their spouses and minor children.

—Programs exempt from this ban were:

—Emergency medical service under Medicaid.

—Short-term, non-cash emergency disaster relief.

—Child nutrition, including school lunch programs, WIC [Women, Infant, and Children program], etc.

—Immunization and testing for treatment of symptoms of communicable diseases.

—Foster care and adoption assistance.

—Non-cash programs identified by Attorney General [soup kitchens, etc.].

—Loans and grants for higher education.

—Elementary and secondary education.

—Head Start program for pre-school children.

—Assistance from the Job Training Partnership Act.

6. State options. Allow states to deny benefits from the welfare block grant, Medicaid and social service block grants to most legal immigrants, with exemptions the same as for SSI and Food Stamps; future immigrants subject to the five-year ban noted above.

—Existing recipients to be continued until January 1, 1997.

—Exemptions granted to refugees, those granted asylum, etc.; those who worked in U.S. for ten years;

veterans and those on active military duty, their spouses and minor children.

7. Sponsors. Expand circumstances under which an immigrant's sponsor would be financially responsible for that individual, generally affecting those entering the United States sponsored by a member of their immediate family. Affidavits of support would be legally enforceable for up to ten years after the immigrant last received benefits. Programs exempted were the same as those exempted from the five-year ban on benefits to future immigrants.

8. Reporting and verifying. Requires agencies that administer SSI, housing assistance or the welfare block grant to report quarterly to the INS the names and addresses of people they knew were unlawfully in the United States. Charged the Attorney General to issue regulations requiring within 18 months that anyone applying for federal benefits be in the United States legally and that States administering federal benefits would have to comply with the verification system within 24 months after they were issued.

Source: Congressional Quarterly Almanac, vol. 52 (1996). Washington, DC: Congressional Quarterly, 1997.

Illegal Immigration Reform and Immigrant Responsibility Act, Summary (1996)

Even as Congress was grappling with welfare reform legislation in 1996, it was working on new legislation concerning immigration. The restrictions on legal immigrants' access to social services contained in welfare reform created a political uproar. Less sensitive—and largely unprotested—was the Illegal Immigration Reform and Immigrant Responsibility Act of 1996, aimed at curbing illegal immigration and illegal immigrants' rights to social services. It also called for tougher border enforcement, imposed sanctions against employers who knowingly hire undocumented workers, and removed legal barriers to the deportation of illegal immigrants. The document that follows is a summary, prepared by Congressional Quarterly Almanac, *of the 1996 Illegal Immigration Reform and Immigrant Responsibility Act.*

1. Border agents. Authorize funding to increase the number of Border Patrol agents by 1,000 per year through fiscal 2001, doubling the total force from 5,000 to 10,000. The bill also authorized funds to increase the number of

clerical workers and other support personnel at the border by 300 per year through fiscal 2001.

The bill ordered the INS [Immigration and Naturalization Service] to relocate as many agents as possible to border areas with the largest number of illegal immigrants and to coordinate relocation plans with local law enforcement agencies. The INS was required to report to Congress on these activities within six months of enactment.

2. Other INS employees. Authorize funding of 900 additional INS agents to investigate and prosecute cases of smuggling, harboring or employing illegal aliens and 300 new agents to investigate people who overstay their visas.

3. Border fence. Authorize $12 million for the second and third tiers of a triple fence along a 14-mile strip at the U.S.-Mexico border south of San Diego, and for roads surrounding the fence. The project was exempt from the strictures of the 1973 Endangered Species Act and the 1969 Environmental Policy Act if either would prevent expeditious construction. It allowed the Attorney General to acquire land through condemnation for the fence.

4. Border Crossing Cards. Require the INS to develop alien identification cards that include a biometric identifier, such as a fingerprint, that could be read by machine, and for future cards that could use such devices as retina scanners.

5. Fleeing through checkpoints. Create a penalty up to five years in prison for fleeing through an INS checkpoint and deportation of those convicted.

6. Entry-Exit system. Order the Attorney General, within two years of enactment, to create a data base of information gathered from the documents people filled out as they legally entered and left the country which would allow the INS to match entry and exit records to identify people who overstayed their visas.

7. Pre-inspection. Require the INS to establish "pre-inspection" stations at five of the 10 foreign airports that were the departure points for the largest number of inadmissible immigrants to screen people who did not have proper documents.

8. State-federal cooperation. Allow the INS to enter into agreements with state and local governments for help in investigating, arresting, detaining and transporting illegal immigrants.

Document Fraud and Alien Smuggling

9. Wiretaps. Grant wiretap authority to the criminal division of the Justice Department for investigating cases of immigration document fraud.

10. Penalties for alien smuggling. Create felonies for alien smuggling for up to 10 years in prison for the first and second offenses, and 15 years for subsequent offenses; and make it a crime with up to five years in prison for employers who knowingly hired 10 people or more who were smuggled into the United States.

11. Prosecutors. Create 25 positions for Assistant United States Attorneys to prosecute cases of alien smuggling and document fraud.

12. Undercover operations. Grant broad authority for the INS to conduct undercover operations to track organized illegal immigration rings, including allowing the INS to establish or acquire companies, deposit funds in bank accounts without regard to federal regulations, and use profits from such front companies to offset expenses.

13. Document fraud. Increase penalty for document fraud from 5 years to 10 or 15 years in most cases; and, if fraud was used in facilitating a drug trafficking crime, a new penalty of 20 years in prison, and if involving terrorism, the penalty is 25 years.

14. Assisting in document fraud. Create a civil penalty for hiring someone to make a false application for public benefits such as food stamps. It further created a criminal penalty for "knowingly and willfully" failing to disclose it. This offense is punishable by up to 15 years.

15. False attestation of citizenship. Create a criminal penalty of up to five years in prison for falsely claiming U.S. citizenship.

16. Illegal voting. Create a criminal penalty for up to one year in prison for unlawfully voting in a federal election.

17. Seizure of assets. Allow courts in imposing sentences against violators of immigration statutes, to seize vehicles, boats, airplanes, and real estate if they were used in the commission of a crime or profit from the proceeds of a crime.

18. Involuntary servitude. Increase the penalty from five years in prison to 10 years for employers who kept workers in a state of involuntary servitude.

19. Subpoenas and evidence. Allow INS agents to subpoena witnesses and to videotape testimony at deportation proceedings.

Detention and Deportation

20. Readmission of deported aliens. Bar any alien who had been deported from re-entry into the United States for five years; and up to 10 years if the alien left while deportation proceedings were in progress or attempted to re-enter the country unlawfully; and bar repeat offenders for two years, as well as people convicted of aggravated felonies.

21. Status of illegal aliens. Deny legal status to anyone who resided in the United States unlawfully for at least 180 days; and persons so convicted could not gain legal status for three years. People in the country illegally for a year or more could not become legal for ten years, except for minors or persons with a pending application for asylum, or were battered women and children, or were people granted protection under the family unity provision of the 1990 Act, or spouses and minor children granted amnesty under the Immigration Reform and Control Act of 1986 to stay in the United States even if they entered illegally, while their application for legal status was pending.

22. Inadmissibility of arriving aliens. Allow people who arrived in the United States without legitimate documentation to be detained and deported without hearing unless they could demonstrate a credible fear of persecution back home. An asylum officer was to screen each case. An officer who decided there was no credible fear could deport the applicant. The applicant could request a review by an immigration judge within seven days, during which time the applicant had to remain in detention. The review could take place by telephone or teleconference.

23. Detention of certain aliens. Require the detention of most illegal aliens serving criminal sentences after their prison terms were completed. The attorney general could release certain illegal immigrants from detention centers if there was insufficient space if he determined their release did not pose a security risk or a risk of fleeing, or who came from countries that would not take them back.

24. Deportation proceeding. Streamline deportation by replacing multiple proceedings with one, allowing proceedings by telephone or teleconference, and after 10 day notice of a hearing.

25. Departure. Require aliens be deported within 90 days of a deportation order, with mandatory detention during

that period. Violent criminals would have to complete their prison terms before being deported; some non-violent criminal aliens could be deported before their term was up.

26. Deportation appeals. Limit judicial review of deportation orders. The state department could discontinue all visas for countries that declined to take back their deported nationals.

27. Criminal alien tracking. Authorize $5 million for a criminal alien tracking center using criminal alien data base authorized in the 1994 crime law (PL 103-322) to be used to assist local governments in identifying criminals who might be deportable.

28. Prisoner transfer treaties. Advise the president to negotiate bilateral prisoner transfer treaties to allow criminals to serve their terms in their home countries; and for the Secretary of State and Attorney General to report to Congress by April 1, 1997, on the potential for such treaties.

29. Vaccinations. Make a potential immigrant who did not have proof of proper vaccinations inadmissible to the United States.

30. Stalking. Add stalking, domestic violence, and child abuse to the list of crimes that made someone deportable.

31. Benedict Arnold's language. Permanently bar from entry anyone who renounced his or her citizenship to avoid taxes.

32. Delegation of authority. Allow the attorney general to authorize local law enforcement officials to perform the duties of an immigration officer in the event of a mass influx of immigrants.

33. Judicial deportation. Broaden authority of judges to issue deportation orders, allowing someone deported as part of probation or a plea agreement.

34. Military bases. Create a pilot program on the use of closed military bases as INS detention centers.

Employee Verification

35. Employment verification programs. Order the attorney general to create three pilot programs—a basic pilot program, a Citizen Attestation Program, and the so-called Machine-Readable Document Pilot Program—

to test the effectiveness of workplace verification systems, participation in which by employers would be voluntary; and the attorney general was to choose the states where each program would be tested, though in some cases employers in non-selected states could participate. All federal departments and agencies within the chosen states were required to participate in the program.

36. Basic pilot program. Allow participating employers to contact the INS via telephone, fax, or e-mail, to check job applicant's immigration status. INS to maintain a data base of names, Social Security numbers, and other information useful to verify an applicant's eligibility to work; and the INS to respond to inquiries within 3 days, and if the tentative response was that the person was not legal, the INS to have 10 days to confirm that determination. The program was to be tested in five of the seven states with the largest number of illegal immigrants.

37. Citizen attestation program. Create a similar program that would allow applicants to bypass the check if they attested that they were U.S. citizens; the penalty for false claims set at up to five years in prison being presumed sufficient to prevent widespread abuse.

38. Machine-readable documentation program. Allow employers to scan a card into a machine, which would verify the owner's Social Security number with the INS data base; to be placed in states selected by the attorney general in which driver's licenses or other state documents included Social Security numbers that could be read by machine.

39. Non-discrimination. Make it harder for the government to sue employers who used immigration laws to discriminate against certain workers, job applicants or other individuals by placing the burden on the government to show that the employer "acted for the purpose, or with the intent to discriminate" against the individual.

Public Benefits

40. Public charges. Allow any consular agent to deny an immigrant visa on the basis that the person was likely to become a public charge.

41. Income requirement. Require sponsors of legal immigrants to earn at least 25 percent more than the federal poverty level and to sign an affidavit that they would be financially responsible for the people they sponsored.

42. Driver's license pilot program. Allow states to create pilot programs to explore the feasibility of denying

driver's licenses to illegal immigrants; the attorney general to report to Congress on these programs after three years.

43. Social Security. Clarify that Social Security benefits were not to be paid to illegal immigrants.

44. Student aid. Order the General Accounting Office to study the use of student aid by illegal immigrants and to report on such to Congress within one year of enactment.

45. Welfare. Require the GAO to report to Congress within 180 days on the unlawful use of means-tested benefits—such as food stamps and cash welfare—by illegal immigrants.

46. Battered women and children. Amend the new welfare law to permit certain illegal immigrants who were victims of domestic violence to qualify for public benefits.

47. Nonprofit organizations. Amend the welfare law so that non-profit charitable organizations were no longer required to verify the immigration status of applicants to determine their eligibility for benefits.

48. Food stamps. Allow legal immigrants who were receiving food stamps, and who would lose them under provisions of the new welfare law, to continue receiving them until April 1, 1997, and as long as August 22, 1997—when the process of certifying people for food stamps was complete.

49. Falsely applying for benefits. Allow judges to double the monetary penalty and triple the prison terms for anyone who forged or counterfeited any United States seal to make a false application for public benefits.

50. Reimbursement for medical care. Allow reimbursement to states and localities for emergency medical care of illegal immigrants, if the care was not already reimbursed via existing federal programs in an amount subject to appropriations.

51. Assisted housing. Require the Secretary of Housing and Urban Development to deny financial assistance through subsidized housing programs to families in which all members were illegal immigrants. If families were split between legal and illegal immigrants, HUD could adjust the size of the benefit to match the percentage of family members who were in the United States legally.

Other Provisions

52. Forced population control. Stipulate that anyone who had been forced to undergo sterilization or an abortion, or who had been persecuted for failure to do so, could be eligible for asylum or refugee status—up to 1,000 persons per year to be admitted to the United States under the program.

53. Parole. Limit the ability of the INS to use parole of detainees to facilitate mass immigration. When the government did use parole to facilitate immigration, the parolees would count toward caps on legal immigration.

54. Asylum. Require that asylum applications from people already in the United States be filed no later than one year after entry; asylum interviews to take place within 45 days of application; a ruling within 180 days, and an appeal to be filed within 30 days of the ruling. The provision allowed asylum to be denied for many reasons, and asylum could be rescinded if the circumstances changed, such as if a new government came to power in the home country of the person granted asylum.

55. Public education. Deny visas to immigrants whose intention was to attend a public elementary or secondary school for more than one year.

56. Visas. Clarify that a short-term visa was void as soon as the person stayed longer than its term; requiring a new visa to be issued in the home country of the applicant.

57. Buddhist monks. Allow the State Department unlimited authority to determine the procedures and locations for processing immigrant visa applications—allowing them to require Vietnamese monks and nuns of the An Quang Buddhist sect in Thailand to return to Vietnam to apply for visas to the United States.

58. Genital mutilation. Create a crime punishable by prison for performing female genital mutilation.

59. Mail-order brides. Require "international matchmaking organizations" to disseminate to their clients information about U.S. immigration laws under penalty of a $20,000 fine for failure to do so; and require the Attorney General to prepare a report to Congress on the mail-order bride business within a year of enactment.

60. Temporary agriculture workers. Require the INS to report by the end of 1996 whether or not the United States had an adequate number of temporary agricultural workers.

61. State issued documents. Set national standards for birth certificates, driver's licenses and other identification documents. The Department of Transportation was to set standards for IDs which had to include Social Security numbers, and agencies issuing them had to keep these numbers on file and confirm their accuracy with the Social Security Administration. The standards were intended to make such documents more tamper-resistant; were to be issued within one year; and to be complied with by October 1, 2000.

62. Tamper-proof Social Security cards. Require the Social Security Administration to develop a prototype tamper-proof identity card.

Source: Congressional Quarterly Almanac, vol. 52 (1996). Washington, DC: Congressional Quarterly, 1997.

Amerasian Children Act (1997)

During the Vietnam War, U.S. military personnel fathered tens of thousands of children with Vietnamese women. Many of these so-called Amerasian children, unknown to or neglected by their fathers, faced discrimination from their fellow Vietnamese. In 1997, the U.S. Congress passed legislation—excerpted below— that exempted many of these individuals (then young adults), along with their spouses and children, from certain restrictions on immigration. The result was that they could enter the United States more easily and in greater numbers.

Sec. 584 of Pub. L. 100-202, in part, as amended by Pub. L. 101-167, Pub. L. 101-513 and Pub. L. 101-649, and Pub. L. 102-232

Sec. 584. Amerasian Immigration

(a)(1) Notwithstanding any numerical limitations specified in the Immigration and Nationality Act, the Attorney General may admit aliens described in subsection (b) to the United States as immigrants if—
(A) they are admissible (except as otherwise provided in paragraph (2)) as immigrants, and
(B) they are issued an immigrant visa and depart from Vietnam on or after March 22, 1988.

(2) The provisions of paragraphs (4), (5), and (7)(A) of section 212(a) of the Immigration and Nationality Act shall not be applicable to any alien seeking admission to the United States under this section, and the Attorney General on the recommendation of a consular officer may waive any other provision of such section (other than paragraph (2)(C) or subparagraph (A), (B), (C), or

(E) of paragraph (3)) with respect to such an alien for humanitarian purposes, to assure family unity, or when it is otherwise in the public interest. Any such waiver by the Attorney General shall be in writing and shall be granted only on an individual basis following an investigation by a consular officer.

(3) Notwithstanding section 221(c) of the Immigration and Nationality Act, immigrant visas issued to aliens under this section shall be valid for a period of one year.

(b)(1) An alien described in this section is an alien who, as of the enactment of this Act, is residing in Vietnam and who establishes to the satisfaction of a consular officer or an officer of the Immigration and Naturalization Service after a face-to-face interview, that the alien—
(A) (i) was born in Vietnam after January 1, 1962, and before January 1, 1976, and (ii) was fathered by a citizen of the United States (such an alien in this section referred to as a "principal alien");
(B) is the spouse or child of a principal alien and is accompanying, or following to join, the principal alien; or
(C) subject to paragraph (2), either (i) is the principal alien's natural mother (or is the spouse or child of such mother), or (ii) has acted in effect as the principal alien's mother, father, or next-of-kin (or is the spouse or child of such an alien), and is accompanying, or following to join, the principal alien.

(2) An immigrant visa may not be issued to an alien under paragraph (1) (C) unless the officer referred to in paragraph (1) has determined, in the officer's discretion, that (A) such an alien has a bona fide relationship with the principal alien similar to that which exists between close family members and (B) the admission of such an alien is necessary for humanitarian purposes or to assure family unity. If an alien described in paragraph (1)(C)(ii) is admitted to the United States, the natural mother of the principal alien involved shall not, thereafter, be accorded any right, privilege, or status under the Immigration and Nationality Act by virtue of such parentage.
(3) For purposes of this section, the term "child" has the meaning given such term in section 101(b)(1) (A), (B), (C), (D), and (E) of the Immigration and Nationality Act.

(c) Any alien admitted (or awaiting admission) to the United States under this section shall be eligible for benefits under chapter 2 of title IV of the Immigration and Nationality Act to the same extent as individuals admitted (or awaiting admission) to the United States under section 207 of such Act are eligible for benefits under such chapter. . . .

(e) Except as otherwise specifically provided in this section, the definitions contained in the Immigration and Nationality Act shall apply in the administration of this section and nothing contained in this section shall be held to repeal, amend, alter, modify, effect, or restrict the powers, duties, functions, or authority of the Attorney General in the administration and enforcement of such Act or any other law relating to immigration, nationality, or naturalization. The fact that an alien may be eligible to be granted the status of having been lawfully admitted for permanent residence under this section shall not preclude the alien from seeking such status under any other provision of law for which the alien may be eligible.

Source: U.S. Department of State Foreign Affairs Manual, vol. 9, 9 Fam. 42.24, Related Statutory Provisions.

America's New Deficit: The Shortage of Information Technology Workers, U.S. Department of Commerce (1997)

The software and information technology (IT) industry in the United States grew rapidly in the boom economy of the mid- to late 1990s, as did the need for highly skilled workers in the field. Industry leaders insisted that the only way to satisfy the shortfall in skilled technicians was through immigration—specifically, the easing of visa restrictions on IT workers. American unions cried foul, arguing that the industry simply wanted to hire cheaper labor and that there were plenty of American workers able or trainable to perform the same functions. The issue has persisted into the twenty-first century, as high-tech firms continue to push for more visas for workers with high-value skills and unions continue to argue for the hiring of American workers and for federal training programs. The document that follows is an excerpt from a report on the subject issued by the U.S. Department of Commerce on September 29, 1997.

I. Introduction

The sweep of digital technologies and the transformation to a knowledge-based economy have created robust demand for workers highly skilled in the use of information technology. In the past ten years alone, employment in the U.S. computer and software industries has almost tripled. The demand for workers who can create, apply, and use information technology goes beyond these industries, cutting across manufacturing and services, transportation, health care, education and government.

Having led the world into the Information Age, there is substantial evidence that the United States is having trouble keeping up with the demand for new information technology workers. A recent survey of mid- and large-size U.S. companies by the Information Technology Association of America (ITAA) concluded that there are about 190,000 unfilled information technology (IT) jobs in the United States today due to a shortage of qualified workers. In another study, conducted by Coopers and Lybrand, nearly half the CEOs [Chief Executive Officers] of America's fastest growing companies reported that they had inadequate numbers of information technology workers to staff their operations.

Evidence suggests that job growth in information technology fields now exceeds the production of talent. Between 1994 and 2005, more than a million new computer scientists and engineers, systems analysts, and computer programmers will be required in the United States—an average of 95,000 per year. One difficulty is that the formal, four-year education system is producing a small proportion of the workers required. Only 24,553 U.S. students earned bachelor's degrees in computer information sciences in 1994. While many IT workers acquire the needed skills through less formal training paths, it is difficult to determine whether such training can be adequately expanded to meet the demand for IT skills.

This shortage of IT workers is not confined within the borders of the United States. Other studies, including work by the Stanford Computer Industry Project, document that there is a world wide shortage of IT workers. That industries in other nations are facing similar problems exacerbates the U.S. problem since the geographic location of such workers is of decreasing importance to the conduct of the work. U.S. employers will face tough competition from employers around the world in a tight global IT labor pool. Thus, the United States cannot expect to meet its long-term needs through increased immigration or foreign outsourcing, and must rely on retaining and updating the skills of today's IT workers as well as educating and training new ones.

Since information technology is an enabling technology that affects the entire economy, our failure to meet the growing demand for IT professionals could have severe consequences for America's competitiveness, economic growth, and job creation. . . .

II. The Demand for Workers in the Information Technology-Driven Economy

The Office of Technology Policy analyzed Bureau of Labor Statistics' [BLS] growth projections for the three core occupational classifications of IT workers—computer scientists and engineers, systems analysts, and computer programmers—to assess future U.S. demand. BLS projections for occupational growth are given in three bands—low, moderate, and high. The following analysis uses the moderate growth figures.

BLS projections indicate that between 1994 and 2005, the United States will require more than one million new IT workers in these three occupations to fill newly created jobs (820,000) and to replace workers who are leaving these fields (227,000) as a result of retirement, change of professions, or other reasons.

Of the three occupations, the largest job growth is accounted for by systems analysts, which are projected to increase from 483,000 in 1994 to 928,000 in 2005, a 92 percent jump. This compares to a projected increase of 14.5 percent for all occupations. The number of computer engineers and scientists is expected to grow by 90 percent, from 345,000 to 655,000 over the same period, while the number of computer programmer positions is expected to grow at a much slower 12 percent rate, from 537,000 in 1994 to 601,000 in 2005. However, while only 65,000 new computer programmer jobs are projected to be created during this period, 163,000 new programmers will be required to replace those exiting the occupation.

The service sector (not including transportation, communications, finance, insurance, real estate, and wholesale and retail trade) is expected to absorb the lion's share of all increases in these core information technology occupations. By 2005, the service sector is expected to increase its employment of computer scientists and engineers by 142 percent, systems analysts by 158 percent, and computer programmers by 37 percent. In contrast, the number of computer scientists and engineers and systems analysts in the manufacturing sector is expected to grow much more slowly (approximately 26 percent and 48 percent, respectively), while the number of computer programmers is expected to decrease by about 26 percent.

Rapid technological change and the growing complexity of information technologies and their applications are accelerating the trend toward outsourcing some computer-functions. Companies recognize the need to rely on outside experts to keep up with the technologies and to assemble multidisciplinary teams to meet the unique needs of each company. This is contributing to the growth of IT workers in services.

Certain industries are more IT worker intensive than others and thus, would be more severely affected by serious shortages of these workers. And these industries are only growing in their IT worker intensity. In the most IT worker intensive industry—computer and data processing services—it is projected that, by 2005,

43 percent of the industry's employees will be computer programmers, systems analysts, and computer scientists and engineers.

However, IT worker intensity does not tell the whole story. The size of an industry's IT work force is an important consideration. For example, while the Federal government is projected to be less IT worker intensive in 2005 than many other industries, the sheer size of its IT work force would make shortages of computer programmers, systems analysts, and computer scientists and engineers a troubling problem. When IT worker intensity and size of IT work force are taken together, a picture emerges as to which industries' competitive performance would be most adversely affected by severe IT worker shortages. The computer and data processing services industry stands out starkly as an industry with much at stake in the supply of IT workers.

III. Is There an Adequate Supply of IT Workers?

Current statistical frameworks and mechanisms for measuring labor supply do not allow for precise identification of IT workers shortages. However, evidence does suggest a problem may be emerging.

Upward Pressure of Salaries

The strongest evidence that a shortage exists is upward pressure on salaries. The competition for skilled IT workers has contributed to substantial salary increases in many IT professions. A compensation survey conducted by William M. Mercer showed that average hourly compensation for operating systems/software architects and consultants rose nearly 20 percent from 1995 to 1996. A survey conducted by the Deloitte & Touche Consulting Group revealed that salaries for computer network professionals rose an average of 7.4 percent from 1996 to 1997. Computerworld's annual survey found that in 11 of 26 positions tracked, average salaries increased more than 10 percent from 1996 to 1997. For example, systems analysts' salaries were up 15 percent, programmer/analysts' salaries were up 11 percent, and directors of systems development received an average increase of 10 percent. Starting salaries for graduates with bachelor's degrees in computer science have nudged up to an average of $36,666, while experienced programmers can command salaries ranging from $45,000–$75,000.

ITAA Survey

A recent survey of mid- and large-size companies, both information technology-related and non-information technology-related, conducted by the Information Technology Association of America found approximately

190,000 unfilled information technology jobs in the United States due to a shortage of qualified workers. According to this survey, shortages are likely to worsen. ITAA found that 82 percent of the information technology companies responding to the survey expect to increase their IT staffing in the coming year, while more than half of the non-information technology companies planned IT staff increases.

The Education Pipeline for IT Workers

Over the last ten years, there has been a decline in the number of students receiving university degrees in computer science. These graduates come from four-year degree-granting universities which focus on computer theory; that is, operating systems, languages, distributed systems, computer architecture and compilers. According to the U.S. Department of Education, the number of bachelor-level computer science degrees awarded by U.S. universities declined more than 40 percent between 1986 and 1994, from 42,195 to 24,553. The significant decline in bachelor-level computer science degrees is, however, an imperfect indicator of declining labor supply, given that many IT workers acquire their skills through alternative education and training paths. While there have been some increases in the award of computer science masters and doctoral degrees, overall computer science degrees awarded have dropped from a high of 50,000 in 1986 to 36,000 in 1994.

In addition, students make up a significant share of U.S. computer science graduates. Of the 36,000 individuals awarded graduate and undergraduate computer science degrees in 1994, about 18 percent were foreign nationals. For advanced degrees, the proportion of foreign nationals increases, reaching more than 50 percent for doctorates. The Computer Research Association estimates that foreign nationals comprise nearly 50 percent of computer engineering students in the United States. The high proportion of foreign nationals in the graduate population would indicate that American industry cannot count on capturing all new IT workers [who] also obtain their skills from training providers other than four-year degree-granting universities. These include:

- two-year associate-degree-granting community colleges which provide grounding in applications (especially in new computer programs and hot areas such as "the year 2000" problem) as well as basic theory, and vocational technical education programs
- special university/community college one-year programs designed to upgrade the skills of IT workers already in the work force (new applications) or those with backgrounds in other technical

fields who are looking for a fast track entry into the IT profession
- private-sector computer learning centers which typically offer courses to people with little or no computer background who are interested in discovering whether they have the aptitude to make it in the computer-related professions
- in-house company training to upgrade employee skills (e.g., client/server-based tools and architectures, C++ and Visual Basic) or to assist in the transition from one skill set (e.g., computer hardware engineers) to another (e.g., computer software engineers)
- computer user groups, Internet forums, and company-sponsored help sites also offer knowledge that can help expand or update computer skills

In addition to those earning four-year degrees in computer and information sciences, in 1994, 15,187 degrees and awards in computer and information sciences below the bachelor's level were earned.

Offshore Sourcing and Recruiting

Some companies are drawing upon talent pools outside the United States to meet their demands for IT workers. India, with more than 200,000 programmers, in conjunction with predominantly U.S. partners, has developed into one of the world's largest exporters of software. In 1996–97, out-sourced software development accounted for 41 percent of India's software exports. Companies are also searching for IT workers in foreign labor markets—in Russia, Eastern Europe, East Asia, and South Africa—using direct recruiting efforts, Internet techniques, and international recruiting agencies.

IV. Competitiveness Issues

Information technologies are the most important enabling technologies in the economy today. They affect every sector and industry in the United States, in terms of digitally-based products, services, and production and work processes. Thus, severe shortages of workers who can apply and use information technologies could undermine U.S. innovation, productivity, and competitiveness in world markets.

Productivity and the Cost of Doing Business

Competitive pressures have driven businesses to adopt a wide range of computer systems to improve productivity, manage production, improve both internal and external communications and to offer customers new services. Private sector investment in enterprise-wide applications alone was estimated to be $42 billion in 1996. The service sector, now representing 70 percent of U.S. GDP [gross domestic product], is increasingly information technology intensive. Manufacturing also relies heavily on information technology from computer aided design and computer numerically controlled machine tools to computer-based systems for inventory control, production planning, and statistical process control. In short, computer-based information systems have become an indispensable part of managing information, workflow, and transactions in both the public and private sector. Therefore, a shortage of IT workers affects directly the ability to develop and implement systems that a wide variety of users need to enhance their performance and control costs. A recent survey by Deloitte & Touche Consulting reported that worker shortages are causing many companies to delay information technology projects.

As competition for IT workers heats up, rising salary levels increase the cost of doing business. For example, Electronic Data Systems Corp. (EDS) recently reported that IT worker shortages have contributed to pushing workers' compensation up by 15 to 20 percent annually. The company reported in April 1997 that it may reduce its work force by thousands to cut labor costs and maintain profits. Many computer companies faced with rising labor costs have passed those increases along to their customers. However, EDS and similar companies rely on long-term fixed contracts to develop and manage large computer systems and have less flexibility to pass increased costs to customers.

Shortage-driven increases in salaries for both skilled IT managers and IT workers also increase the amount of venture capital investment required by start-up companies in information technology-related businesses. For example, new software technology start-ups—which have benefited substantially from private venture capital and are IT worker intensive—could require greater venture capital investment in the future to cover salary costs. These rising labor costs could result in venture capital seeking growth opportunities elsewhere, constraining the emergence and growth of many promising new companies.

Government and non-profit organizations may increasingly be squeezed out of the competition for IT talent. For example, while average starting salaries for graduates with bachelor's degrees in computer engineering grew to more than $34,000 in 1995, the Federal government's entry level salary for computer professionals with bachelor's degrees ranged from about $18,700 to $23,200 that year. The Department of Defense is already having difficulty retaining IT employees; it appears industry is offering them more attractive compensation packages. The U.S. Air Force Communications Agency reports a loss rate of 42 to 45 percent of systems administrators from 1993–1995.

Industry Growth

High-tech industries, particularly leading-edge electronics and information technology industries, are driving economic growth not only in the United States but around the world. According to industry estimates, the markets for computer and communications hardware and services, and for software have grown to one trillion dollars. With the current annual growth rate estimated at 10 percent, the global market for these products and services may be growing by $100 billion annually. These industries are IT worker intensive and shortages of critical skills would inhibit their performance and growth potential.

In the ITAA survey, 50 percent of the information technology company executives cited lack of skilled/trained workers as "the most significant barrier" to their companies' growth during the next year—a problem viewed as significantly greater than economic conditions, profitability, lack of capital investment, taxes, or regulation. An additional 20 percent of the IT company executives identified the shortage of these workers as "a barrier" to their companies' growth during the next year.

Innovation

The United States is a leader in the development of new products and services, and many important consumer and industrial innovations—from computers, consumer electronic products, and telecommunications services to automotive electronics, aerospace products, and advanced industrial systems—have been made possible by information technologies. Information technologies are expected to continue to form the basis of many of the most important products, services, and processes of the future. For example, it is expected that in less than a decade, electronics will account for about one-fifth of an automobile's value. Shortages of IT workers could inhibit the nation's ability to develop leading-edge products and services, and raise their costs, which, in turn, would reduce U.S. competitiveness and constrain economic growth.

Trade

The shortage of IT workers could undermine U.S. performance in global markets. The global market for computer software and computer services reached $277 billion in 1994. The United States is both the predominant supplier of and the primary consumer for these goods and services. Ranked in terms of global market share in 1994, eight of the world's top ten applications software vendors and seven of the top ten systems software vendors are U.S. firms. Both of these markets are growing rapidly, with the computer software market growing 12 percent annually, and the computer services market growing 11 percent annually, reaching $420 billion by 1998, a 50 percent increase just between 1994 and 1998. Aerospace, another IT worker intensive industry, is also a global market leader for the United States, and is the Nation's leading net exporter of manufactured goods. An adequate supply of IT workers is essential to America's continued strength in these markets.

High-Wage Jobs

A shortage of qualified IT workers could also prevent the United States from taking full advantage of high-wage job creation. Many information technology jobs are high-wage jobs. Workers in the software industry earn more than twice the national average. A William M. Mercer compensation study shows that the average hourly compensation in 1996 for an intermediate customer support technician was $40.80; software development architect, $77.70; operating systems software architect/consultant, $85.60, and operating systems/software programming analyst manager, $92.20. Even if shortages ease and upward pressure on salaries is reduced, the IT professions have traditionally been high-wage jobs.

Source: U.S. Department of Commerce. *Report on the Shortage of Technology Workers* (Washington, DC: U.S. Department of Commerce, 1997).

California Proposition 227 (1998)

On June 2, 1998, Californians voted by a margin of 61 percent to 39 percent in favor of Proposition 227, a referendum requiring that nearly all of the state's 1.4 million "Limited English Proficient" students be taught exclusively in English. Backed by businessman and maverick Republican politician Ron Unz, the initiative ended California's twenty-five-year experiment with bilingual education based on dual-language instruction. Facing court challenges almost immediately after, the measures enacted by the initiative remain on the books and have sparked similar legislation in other states. The following document includes text from Proposition 227—also known as the Unz initiative—as well as sample ballot arguments for and against.

SECTION 1. Chapter 3 (commencing with Section 300) is added to Part 1 of the Educational Code, to read:

Chapter 3. English Language Education for Immigrant Children

ARTICLE 1. Findings and Declarations

300. The People of California find and declare as follows:

(a) WHEREAS the English language is the national public language of the United States of America and of the state of California, is spoken by the vast majority of California residents, and is also the leading world language for science, technology, and international business, thereby being the language of economic opportunity; and

(b) WHEREAS immigrant parents are eager to have their children acquire a good knowledge of English, thereby allowing them to fully participate in the American Dream of economic and social advancement; and

(c) WHEREAS the government and the public schools of California have a moral obligation and a constitutional duty to provide all of California's children, regardless of their ethnicity or national origins, with the skills necessary to become productive members of our society, and of these skills, literacy in the English language is among the most important; and

(d) WHEREAS the public schools of California currently do a poor job of educating immigrant children, wasting financial resources on costly experimental language programs whose failure over the past two decades is demonstrated by the current high drop-out rates and low English literacy levels of many immigrant children; and

(e) WHEREAS young immigrant children can easily acquire full fluency in a new language, such as English, if they are heavily exposed to that language in the classroom at an early age.

(f) THEREFORE it is resolved that: all children in California public schools shall be taught English as rapidly and effectively as possible.

ARTICLE 2. English Language Education

305. Subject to the exceptions provided in Article 3 (commencing with Section 310), all children in California public schools shall be taught English by being taught in English. In particular, this shall require that all children be placed in English language classrooms. Children who are English learners shall be educated through sheltered English immersion during a temporary transition period not normally intended to exceed one year. Local schools shall be permitted to place in the same classroom English learners of different ages but whose degree of English proficiency is similar. Local schools shall be encouraged to mix together in the same classroom English learners from different native-language groups but with the same degree of English fluency. Once English learners have acquired a good working knowledge of English, they shall be transferred to English language mainstream classrooms. As much as possible, current supplemental funding for English learners shall be maintained, subject to possible modification under Article 8 (commencing with Section 335) below.

306. The definitions of the terms used in this article and in Article 3 (commencing with Section 310) are as follows:

(a) "English learner" means a child who does not speak English or whose native language is not English and who is not currently able to perform ordinary classroom work in English, also known as a Limited English Proficiency or LEP child.

(b) "English language classroom" means a classroom in which the language of instruction used by the teaching personnel is overwhelmingly the English language, and in which such teaching personnel possess a good knowledge of the English language.

(c) "English language mainstream classroom" means a classroom in which the students either are native English language speakers or already have acquired reasonable fluency in English.

(d) "Sheltered English immersion" or "structured English immersion" means an English language acquisition process for young children in which nearly all classroom instruction is in English but with the curriculum and presentation designed for children who are learning the language.

(e) "Bilingual education/native language instruction" means a language acquisition process for students in which much or all instruction, textbooks, and teaching materials are in the child's native language.

ARTICLE 3. Parental Exceptions

310. The requirements of Section 305 may be waived with the prior written informed consent, to be provided annually, of the child's parents or legal guardian under the circumstances specified below and in Section 311. Such informed consent shall require that said parents or legal guardian personally visit the school to apply for the waiver and that they there be provided a full description of the educational materials to be used in the different educational program choices and all the educational opportunities available to the child. Under such parental waiver conditions, children may be transferred to classes where they are taught English and other subjects through bilingual education techniques or other generally recognized educational methodologies permitted by law. Individual schools in which 20 students or more of a given grade level receive a waiver shall be required to offer such a class; otherwise, they must allow the students to transfer to a public school in which such a class is offered.

311. The circumstances in which a parental exception waiver may be granted under Section 310 are as follows:

(a) Children who already know English: the child already possesses good English language skills, as measured by standardized tests of English vocabulary comprehension, reading, and writing, in which the child scores at or above the state average for his grade level or at or above the 5th grade average, whichever is lower; or (b) Older children: the child is age 10 years or older, and it is the informed belief of the school principal and educational staff that an alternate course of educational study would be better suited to the child's rapid acquisition of basic English language skills; or. . .

(c) Children with special needs: the child already has been placed for a period of not less than thirty days during that school year in an English language classroom and it is subsequently the informed belief of the school principal and educational staff that the child has such special physical, emotional, psychological, or educational needs that an alternate course of educational study would be better suited to the child's overall educational development. A written description of these special needs must be provided and any such decision is to be made subject to the examination and approval of the local school superintendent, under guidelines established by and subject to the review of the local Board of Education and ultimately the State Board of Education. The existence of such special needs shall not compel issuance of a waiver, and the parents shall be fully informed of their right to refuse to agree to a waiver.

ARTICLE 4. Community-Based English Tutoring

315. In furtherance of its constitutional and legal requirement to offer special language assistance to children coming from backgrounds of limited English proficiency, the state shall encourage family members and others to provide personal English language tutoring to such children, and support these efforts by raising the general level of English language knowledge in the community. Commencing with the fiscal year in which this initiative is enacted and for each of the nine fiscal years following thereafter, a sum of fifty million dollars ($50,000,000) per year is hereby appropriated from the General Fund for the purpose of providing additional funding for free or subsidized programs of adult English language instruction to parents or other members of the community who pledge to provide personal English language tutoring to California school children with limited English proficiency.

316. Programs funded pursuant to this section shall be provided through schools or community organizations. Funding for these programs shall be administered by the Office of the Superintendent of Public Instruction, and shall be disbursed at the discretion of the local school boards, under reasonable guidelines established by, and subject to the review of, the State Board of Education.

ARTICLE 5. Legal Standing and Parental Enforcement

320. As detailed in Article 2 (commencing with Section 305) and Article 3 (commencing with Section 310), all California school children have the right to be provided with an English language public education. If a California school child has been denied the option of an English language instructional curriculum in public school, the child's parent or legal guardian shall have legal standing to sue for enforcement of the provisions of this statute, and if successful shall be awarded normal and customary attorney's fees and actual damages, but not punitive or consequential damages. Any school board member or other elected official or public school teacher or administrator who willfully and repeatedly refuses to implement the terms of this statute by providing such an English language educational option at an available public school to a California school child may be held personally liable for fees and actual damages by the child's parents or legal guardian.

ARTICLE 6. Severability

325. If any part or parts of this statute are found to be in conflict with federal law or the United States or the California State Constitution, the statute shall be implemented to the maximum extent that federal law, and the United States and the California State Constitution permit. Any provision held invalid shall be severed from the remaining portions of this statute.

ARTICLE 7. Operative Date

330. This initiative shall become operative for all school terms which begin more than sixty days following the date at which it becomes effective.

ARTICLE 8. Amendment

335. The provisions of this act may be amended by a statute that becomes effective upon approval by the electorate or by a statute to further the act's purpose passed by a two-thirds vote of each house of the Legislature and signed by the Governor.

ARTICLE 9. Interpretation

340. Under circumstances in which portions of this statute are subject to conflicting interpretations, Section 300 shall be assumed to contain the governing intent of the statute.

English Language in Public Schools Initiative Statute: Argument in Favor of Proposition 227

Why Do We Need to Change California's Bilingual Education System?

- Begun with the best of intentions in the 1970s, bilingual education has failed in actual practice, but the politicians and administrators have refused to admit this failure.

- For most of California's non-English speaking students, bilingual education actually means monolingual, SPANISH-ONLY education for the first 4 to 7 years of school.

- The current system fails to teach children to read and write English. Last year, only 6.7 percent of limited-English students in California learned enough English to be moved into mainstream classes.

- Latino immigrant children are the principal victims of bilingual education. They have the lowest test scores and the highest dropout rates of any immigrant group.

- There are 140 languages spoken by California's schoolchildren. To teach each group of children in their own native language before teaching them English is educationally and fiscally impossible. Yet this impossibility is the goal of bilingual education.

Common Sense About Learning English

- Learning a new language is easier the younger the age of the child.

- Learning a language is much easier if the child is immersed in that language.

- Immigrant children already know their native language; they need the public schools to teach them English.

- Children who leave school without knowing how to speak, read, and write English are injured for life economically and socially.

What "English for the Children" Will Do:

- Require children to be taught English as soon as they start school.

- Provide "sheltered English immersion" classes to help non-English speaking students learn English; research shows this is the most effective method.

- Allow parents to request a special waiver for children with individual educational needs who would benefit from another method.

What "English for the Children" Won't Do:
It will:

- NOT throw children who can't speak English into regular classes where they would have to "sink or swim."

- NOT cut special funding for children learning English.

- NOT violate any federal laws or court decisions.

Who Supports the Initiative?

- Teachers worried by the undeniable failure of bilingual education and who have long wanted to implement a successful alternative—sheltered English immersion.
- Most Latino parents, according to public polls. They know that Spanish-only bilingual education is preventing their children from learning English by segregating them into an educational dead-end.
- Most Californians. They know that bilingual education has created an educational ghetto by isolating non-English speaking students and preventing them from becoming successful members of society.

Who Opposes the Initiative?

- Individuals who profit from bilingual education. Bilingual teachers are paid up to $5,000 extra annually and the program provides jobs to thousands of bilingual coordinators and administrators.
- Schools and school districts which receive HUNDREDS OF MILLIONS of extra dollars for schoolchildren classified as not knowing English and who, therefore, have a financial incentive to avoid teaching English to children.
- Activist groups with special agendas and the politicians who support them.

ALICE CALLAGHAN
Director, Las Familias del Pueblo
RON UNZ
Chairman, English for the Children
FERNANDO VEGA
Past Redwood City School Board Member

English Language in Public Schools Initiative Statute: Argument against Proposition 227

Proposition 227 imposes one untested method for teaching English on every local school district in California.

Proposition 227 puts limited English speaking children of all ages and languages into one classroom.

The California PTA opposes Proposition 227 because it takes away parents' right to choose what's best for their children.

The California School Boards Association opposes Proposition 227 because it outlaws the best local programs for teaching English.

California's teachers oppose Proposition 227—teachers can be sued personally for teaching in the children's language to help them learn English.

Outlawing decisions by parents, teachers, and school boards on how to teach children English is wrong.

Children in California must learn English.

In thousands of classrooms all over California, they are. Good teachers. Good local school boards. Good parent involvement.

Those successes are not the result of one instructional method imposed on every school by state government.

Sadly, there have been failures too. However, these failures can best be remedied by reasonable program changes that maximize local control.

California should be returning more decisions to parents, teachers, principals, and local school boards.

A growing number of school districts are working with new English teaching methods. Proposition 227 stops them.

The San Diego Union-Tribune Editorial said it best: "School districts should decide for themselves."

We urge you to join us, the California PTA, the California School Boards Association, and California's teachers in voting "NO" on Proposition 227.

JOHN D'AMELIO
President, California School Boards Association
MARY BERGAN
President, California Federation of Teachers, AFL–CIO
LOIS TINSON
President, California Teachers Association

Source: California State Ballot, Proposition 227, June 2, 1998. *1998 California Primary Election Voter Information Guide/Ballot Pamphlet.*

"Recommendations for Prevention and Control of Tuberculosis Among Foreign-Born Persons," Centers for Disease Control and Prevention (1998)

While the incidence of tuberculosis in the United States dropped by 75 percent between the 1950s and the 1980s, the decade from 1985 to 1995 saw an increase of approximately 20 percent. As indicated in this 1998 report by the Centers for Disease Control and Prevention (CDC), much of the growth in tuberculosis rates was due to increases in immigration from countries where the disease remained widespread, particularly in the developing world. The CDC report offers a portrait of tuberculosis in the immigrant population, as well as recommendations for control-ling the disease.

Summary

During 1986–1997, the number of tuberculosis (TB) cases among foreign-born persons in the United States increased by 56%, from 4,925 cases (22% of the national total) to 7,702 cases (39% of the national total). As the percentage of reported TB cases among foreign-born persons continues to increase, the elimination of TB in the United States will depend increasingly on the elimination of TB among foreign-born persons.

On May 16–17, 1997, CDC [Centers for Disease Control and Prevention] convened a working group of state and city TB-control program staff, as well as representatives from CDC's Division of TB Elimination and Division of Quarantine, to outline problems and propose solutions for addressing TB among foreign-born persons. The Working Group's deliberations and the resulting recommendations for action by federal agencies, state and local TB-control programs, community-based organizations (CBOs) and private health-care providers form the basis of this report. For each of the five topics of discussion, the group identified key issues, problems, and constraints and suggested solutions in the form of recommendations, which are detailed in this report. The Working Group made the following recommendations:

- The epidemiology of TB among foreign-born populations differs considerably from area to area. To tailor TB-control efforts to local needs, TB-control programs should develop epidemiologic profiles to identify groups of foreign-born persons in their jurisdictions who are at high risk for TB.
- The priorities of TB control among the foreign born should be the same as those for control of TB among other U.S. populations—completion of treatment by persons infected with active TB, contact tracing, and screening and provision of preventive therapy for groups at high risk. Screening and preventive therapy should be limited to areas where completion of therapy rates and contact-tracing activities are currently adequate.
- Based on local epidemiologic profiles, selective screening should be conducted among populations identified as being at high risk for TB. Screening should target groups of persons who are at the highest risk for TB infection and disease, accessible for screening, and likely to complete preventive therapy. The decision to screen for infection, disease, or both should be based on the person's age and time in the United States, prior screening, and locally available resources for the provision of preventive therapy.
- TB-control programs should direct efforts towards identifying impediments to TB diagnosis and care among local foreign-born populations, devising strategies to address these barriers, and maximizing activities to ensure completion of treatment.
- Providing TB preventive therapy and other TB-related services for foreign-born persons is often impeded by linguistic, cultural, and health-services barriers. TB-control programs can help overcome these barriers by establishing partnerships with CBOs and by strengthening training and education efforts. Collaborations with health-service CBOs should center on developing more complementary roles, more effective coordination of services, and better use of existing resources for serving the foreign born. TB-related training should be linked to overall TB-control strategies for the foreign born. Training and education should be targeted to providers, patients, and community workers.

Introduction

In 1986, CDC began collecting information on place of birth for those persons residing in the United States who have been reported to be infected with tuberculosis (TB). National surveillance data for the decade that followed indicate that the number of TB cases among persons born in other countries increased from 4,925 in 1986 to 7,702 in 1997, and that the percentage of foreign-born cases increased from 22% to 39% of the national total. In Canada and several European countries, foreign-born persons now account for more than half of TB cases. If current U.S. trends continue through the next decade, more than half of TB cases are likely to occur among the foreign born.

Background: Immigration Trends

The increase in TB cases among foreign-born persons over the past decade is partly attributable to increased immigration. The largest wave of immigration in U.S. history occurred in the early 1900s; by 1910, 14% of all U.S. residents were foreign born. Immigration declined during the next two decades, reached a low during the Great Depression (1929–1939), and then gradually increased until the mid-1980s. A peak occurred in 1986, when the Immigration Reform and Control Act was passed and persons who had entered the country illegally were allowed to legalize their status. In 1996, the most recent year for which immigration figures are available, 915,900 persons were granted permanent residence

(1). In addition, an estimated 275,000 undocumented aliens arrive annually. In 1996, an estimated 24.6 million foreign-born persons resided in the United States, representing 9% of the total population (2).

Another factor in the increase in TB cases among foreign-born persons is changing trends in countries of origin. Immigration has been increasing from Asia and the Latin Americas, where TB rates are 5–20 times higher than those in the United States. In 1994, 25% of the 24 million foreign-born persons in the United States were from Asia and 42% from Latin America, including 6 million persons from Mexico (2). In recent years, Asian-born persons have accounted for an increasing percentage of new immigrants; in 1995, 37% of new arrivals were from Asia (3). After Mexico, the top two countries of birth among immigrants in that year were the Philippines and Vietnam. . . .

Characteristics of TB Cases Among Foreign-Born Persons

The composition of TB cases among foreign-born persons reflects immigration patterns and trends. In 1997, Mexico was the country of origin for 22% of immigrants with TB, with the Philippines (14%) and Vietnam (11%) the next most common countries of birth. India, China, Haiti, and Korea each accounted for 3%-6% of the total. Together, these seven countries accounted for two thirds of TB cases among foreign-born persons in the United States.

As expected, most TB cases among foreign-born persons are reported from the states with the most immigrants. In 1997, 66% of all TB cases among foreign-born persons were reported from California (36% of the national total), New York (15%), Texas (8%), Florida (5%), New Jersey (4%), Illinois (3%), Washington (2%), Massachusetts (2%), Virginia (2%), and Hawaii (2%). In 1997, TB cases among foreign-born persons were examined as a proportion of total TB cases in each state. A total of 66% of TB cases occurred among foreign-born persons in California and 51% in New York. Even in states with relatively few cases among the foreign born (e.g., Minnesota and Rhode Island), approximately 60% of TB cases in 1997 were among persons born outside the United States.

Most TB cases among foreign-born persons are likely the result of reactivation of remotely acquired infection, although some transmission is probably occurring in the United States. . . . For all immigrant groups, the disease risk appears highest in the first years after U.S. arrival. . . . The risk for disease among the foreign born also appears related to chronological age and age at immigration; younger persons and those who immigrated at younger ages are at lower risk for subsequent infection with TB.

The number of foreign-born persons in the United States with TB infection is unknown. However, based on the World Health Organization (WHO) estimate that one third of the world's population is infected, more than 7 million foreign-born persons in the United States might be at risk for reactivation of remotely acquired infection.

Source: Morbidity and Mortality Weekly Report, vol. 47, no. 16 (September 18, 1998): 1–26 (weekly report of the Centers for Disease Control and Prevention).

"Renunciation of U.S. Citizenship," U.S. Immigration and Naturalization Service (1998)

While often referred to as a "nation of immigrants," the United States also sees thousands of residents emigrate each year to other countries. Many of them are former immigrants to America who return to their land of origin but would like to retain their U.S. citizenship as well. In general, however, the United States discourages dual citizenship, whether for naturalized or native-born Americans. In the document that follows, the U.S. Immigration and Naturalization Service (the predecessor agency of today's Immigration and Customs Enforcement) explains the process of citizenship renunciation.

United States citizens have the right to remain citizens until they intend to give up citizenship. It is also the right of every citizen to relinquish United States citizenship. Section 349(a) of the Immigration and Nationality Act [8 U.S.C. 1481] states:

a person who is a national of the United States whether by birth or naturalization, shall lose his nationality by voluntarily performing any of the following acts with the intention of relinquishing United States nationality;

making a formal renunciation of nationality before a diplomatic or consular officer of the United States in a foreign state, in such form as may be prescribed by the Secretary of State; or

making in the United States a formal written renunciation of nationality in such form as may be prescribed by, and before such officer as may be designated by, the Attorney General, whenever the United States shall be in a state of war and the Attorney General shall approve such renunciation as not contrary to the interests of national defense.

Renunciation is the most unequivocal way in which a person can manifest an intention to relinquish U.S.

citizenship. In order for a renunciation under Section 349(a)(5) to be effective, all of the conditions of the statute must be met. In other words, a person wishing to renounce American citizenship must appear in person and sign an oath of renunciation before a U.S. consular or diplomatic officer abroad, generally at an American Embassy or Consulate. Renunciations which are not in the form prescribed by the Secretary of State have no legal effect. Because of the way in which Section 349(a)(5) is written and interpreted, Americans cannot effectively renounce their citizenship by mail, through an agent, or while in the United States.

Section 349(a)(6) provides for renunciation of United States citizenship under certain circumstances in the United States when the United States is in a state of war. Such a state does not currently exist. Questions concerning renunciation of American citizenship under Section 349(a)(6) should be addressed to the Attorney General.

Parents cannot renounce United States citizenship on behalf of their children. Before an oath of renunciation will be administered under Section 349(a)(5), persons under the age of eighteen must convince a U.S. diplomatic or consular officer that they fully understand the nature and consequences of the oath of renunciation and are voluntarily seeking to renounce their citizenship. United States common law establishes an arbitrary limit of age fourteen under which a child's understanding must be established by substantial evidence.

Under Section 351(b) of the Immigration and Nationality Act [8 U.S.C. 1483(b)], a person who renounced U.S. citizenship before the age of eighteen years and "who within six months after attaining the age of eighteen years asserts his claim to United States nationality in such manner as the Secretary of State shall by regulation prescribe, shall not be deemed to have expatriated himself. . . ." The relevant regulation is Section 50.20(b) of Title 22 of the Code of Federal Regulations which requires that the person take an oath of allegiance to the United States before a diplomatic or consular officer in order to retain U.S. citizenship.

Persons who contemplate renunciation of U.S. nationality should be aware that, unless they already possess a foreign nationality or are assured of acquiring another nationality shortly after completing their renunciation, severe hardship to them could result. In the absence of a second nationality, those individuals would become stateless. As stateless persons, they would not be entitled to the protection of any government. They might also find it difficult or impossible to travel as they would probably not be entitled to a passport from any country. Further, a person who has renounced U.S. nationality will be required to apply for a visa to travel to the United States, just as other aliens do. If found ineligible for a visa, a renunciant could be permanently barred from the United States. Renunciation of American citizenship does not necessarily prevent a former citizen's deportation from a foreign country to the United States.

Renunciation of U.S. Citizenship and Taxation

P.L. 104-191 contains changes in the taxation of U.S. citizens who renounce or otherwise lose U.S. citizenship. In general, any person who lost U.S. citizenship within 10 years immediately preceding the close of the taxable year, whose principal purpose in losing citizenship was to avoid taxation, will be subject to continued taxation. For the purposes of this statute, persons are presumed to have a principal purpose of avoiding taxation if 1) their average annual net income tax for a five year period before the date of loss of citizenship is greater than $100,000, or 2) their net worth on the date of the loss of U.S. nationality is $500,000 or more (subject to cost of living adjustments). The effective date of the law is retroactive to February 6, 1995. Copies of approved Certificates of Loss of Nationality are provided by the Department of State to the Internal Revenue Service pursuant to P.L. 104-191. Questions regarding United States taxation consequences upon loss of U.S. nationality, should be addressed to the U.S. Internal Revenue Service.

Other Obligations

Persons considering renunciation should also be aware that the fact that they have renounced U.S. nationality may have no effect whatsoever on their U.S. military service obligations. Nor will it allow them to escape possible prosecution for crimes which they may have committed in the United States, or repayment of financial obligations previously incurred in the United States. Questions about these matters should be directed to the government agency concerned.

Finally, those contemplating a renunciation of U.S. citizenship should understand that renunciation is irrevocable, except as provided in Section 351 of the Immigration and Nationality Act, and cannot be canceled or set aside absent successful administrative or judicial appeal.

Source: U.S. Department of State. *Renunciation of U.S. Citizenship,* July 1998 (Washington DC: Department of State, 1998).

Report of the National Commission on Terrorist Attacks Upon the United States (9/11 Commission) (2004)

In 2002, President George W. Bush established the National Commission on Terrorist Attacks Upon the United States—

commonly referred to as the 9/11 Commission—a group of high-level advisers charged with investigating what had led to the 9/11 terrorist attacks on New York City and Washington, D.C., and to offer recommendations on how to avoid future attacks. In this excerpt from its 2004 report, the commission outlines the failure of America's immigration and border security system in stopping the nineteen hijackers from entering the country. The commission's recommendations included improvements in the screening system for travelers and better coordination of data among the various agencies overseeing intelligence-gathering, law enforcement, immigration, and border security.

Terrorist Travel

More than 500 million people annually cross U.S. borders at legal entry points, about 330 million of them noncitizens. Another 500,000 or more enter illegally without inspection across America's thousands of miles of land borders or remain in the country past the expiration of their permitted stay. The challenge for national security in an age of terrorism is to prevent the very few people who may pose overwhelming risks from entering or remaining in the United States undetected.

In the decade before September 11, 2001, border security—encompassing travel, entry, and immigration—was not seen as a national security matter. Public figures voiced concern about the "war on drugs," the right level and kind of immigration, problems along the southwest border, migration crises originating in the Caribbean and elsewhere, or the growing criminal traffic in humans. The immigration system as a whole was widely viewed as increasingly dysfunctional and badly in need of reform. In national security circles, however, only smuggling of weapons of mass destruction carried weight, not the entry of terrorists who might use such weapons or the presence of associated foreign-born terrorists.

For terrorists, travel documents are as important as weapons. Terrorists must travel clandestinely to meet, train, plan, case targets, and gain access to attack. To them, international travel presents great danger, because they must surface to pass through regulated channels, present themselves to border security officials, or attempt to circumvent inspection points.

In their travels, terrorists use evasive methods, such as altered and counterfeit passports and visas, specific travel methods and routes, liaisons with corrupt government officials, human smuggling networks, supportive travel agencies, and immigration and identity fraud. These can sometimes be detected.

Before 9/11, no agency of the U.S. government systematically analyzed terrorists' travel strategies. Had they done so, they could have discovered the ways in which the terrorist predecessors to al Qaeda had been systematically but detectably exploiting weaknesses in our border security since the early 1990s.

We found that as many as 15 of the 19 hijackers were potentially vulnerable to interception by border authorities. Analyzing their characteristic travel documents and travel patterns could have allowed authorities to intercept 4 to 15 hijackers and more effective use of information available in U.S. government databases could have identified up to 3 hijackers.

Looking back, we can also see that the routine operations of our immigration laws—that is, aspects of those laws not specifically aimed at protecting against terrorism—inevitably shaped al Qaeda's planning and opportunities. Because they were deemed not to be bona fide tourists or students as they claimed, five conspirators that we know of tried to get visas and failed, and one was denied entry by an inspector. We also found that had the immigration system set a higher bar for determining whether individuals are who or what they claim to be—and ensuring routine consequences for violations—it could potentially have excluded, removed, or come into further contact with several hijackers who did not appear to meet the terms for admitting short-term visitors.

Our investigation showed that two systemic weaknesses came together in our border system's inability to contribute to an effective defense against the 9/11 attacks: a lack of well-developed counterterrorism measures as a part of border security and an immigration system not able to deliver on its basic commitments, much less support counterterrorism. These weaknesses have been reduced but are far from being overcome.

Recommendation: Targeting travel is at least as powerful a weapon against terrorists as targeting their money. The United States should combine terrorist travel intelligence, operations, and law enforcement in a strategy to intercept terrorists, find terrorist travel facilitators, and constrain terrorist mobility.

Since 9/11, significant improvements have been made to create an integrated watchlist that makes terrorist name information available to border and law enforcement authorities. However, in the already difficult process of merging border agencies in the new Department of Homeland Security—"changing the engine while flying" as one official put it—new insights into terrorist travel have not yet been integrated into the front lines of border security.

The small terrorist travel intelligence collection and analysis program currently in place has produced disproportionately useful results. It should be expanded. Since officials at the borders encounter travelers and their documents first and investigate travel facilitators, they must work closely with intelligence officials.

Internationally and in the United States, constraining terrorist travel should become a vital part of counterterrorism strategy. Better technology and training to detect terrorist travel documents are the most important immediate steps to reduce America's vulnerability to clandestine entry. Every stage of our border and immigration system should have as a part of its operations the detection of terrorist indicators on travel documents. Information systems able to authenticate travel documents and detect potential terrorist indicators should be used at consulates, at primary border inspection lines, in immigration services offices, and in intelligence and enforcement units. All frontline personnel should receive some training. Dedicated specialists and ongoing linkages with the intelligence community are also required. The Homeland Security Department's Directorate of Information Analysis and Infrastructure Protection should receive more resources to accomplish its mission as the bridge between the frontline border agencies and the rest of the government counterterrorism community.

Source: National Commission on Terrorist Attacks Upon the United States (9/11 Commission).

Secure Fence Act (2006)

Signed into law by President George W. Bush on October 26, 2006, the Secure Fence Act authorized the construction of an elaborate security system along the entire length of the U.S.–Mexican border. The purpose of the legislation was to reduce the flow of drugs and illegal aliens from entering the country, as well as to prevent infiltration by terrorists. A former governor of Texas and its large Latino population, Bush had wanted to reform America's immigration system and allow some kind of legal status for illegal aliens already in the country. But conservatives on both sides of the aisle insisted on border security first. In the end, only the Secure Fence Act was passed, while more comprehensive immigration reform was never enacted during Bush's term in office.

An Act
To establish operational control over the international land and maritime borders of the United States . . .

Be it enacted by the Senate and House of Representatives of the United States of America in Congress assembled,

Section 1. Short Title.
This Act may be cited as the "Secure Fence Act of 2006."

Sec. 2. Achieving Operational Control on the Border.
(a) In General.—Not later than 18 months after the date of the enactment of this Act, the Secretary of Homeland Security shall take all actions the Secretary determines necessary and appropriate to achieve and maintain operational control over the entire international land and maritime borders of the United States, to include the following—

(1) systematic surveillance of the international land and maritime borders of the United States through more effective use of personnel and technology, such as unmanned aerial vehicles, ground-based sensors, satellites, radar coverage, and cameras; and

(2) physical infrastructure enhancements to prevent unlawful entry by aliens into the United States and facilitate access to the international land and maritime borders by United States Customs and Border Protection, such as additional checkpoints, all weather access roads, and vehicle barriers.

(b) Operational Control Defined.—In this section, the term "operational control" means the prevention of all unlawful entries into the United States, including entries by terrorists, other unlawful aliens, instruments of terrorism, narcotics, and other contraband.

(c) Report.—Not later than one year after the date of the enactment of this Act and annually thereafter, the Secretary shall submit to Congress a report on the progress made toward achieving and maintaining operational control over the entire international land and maritime borders of the United States in accordance with this section.

Sec. 3. Construction of Fencing and Security Improvements in Border Area from Pacific Ocean to Gulf of Mexico.
Section 102(b) of the Illegal Immigration Reform and Immigrant Responsibility Act of 1996 (Public Law 104-208; 8 U.S.C. 1103 note) is amended—
(1) in the subsection heading by striking "Near San Diego, California"; and

(2) by amending paragraph (1) to read as follows:
"(1) Security features.—
"(A) Reinforced fencing.—In carrying out subsection (a), the Secretary of Homeland Security shall provide for least 2 layers of reinforced fencing, the installation of additional physical barriers, roads, lighting, cameras, and sensors—
"(i) extending from 10 miles west of the Tecate, California, port of entry to 10 miles east of the Tecate, California, port of entry;

"(ii) extending from 10 miles west of the Calexico, California, port of entry to 5 miles east of the Douglas, Arizona, port of entry;

"(iii) extending from 5 miles west of the Columbus, New Mexico, port of entry to 10 miles east of El Paso, Texas;

"(iv) extending from 5 miles northwest of the Rio, Texas, port of entry to 5 miles southeast of the Eagle Pass, Texas, port of entry; and

"(v) extending 15 miles northwest of the Laredo, Texas, port of entry to the Brownsville, Texas, port of entry.

"(B) Priority areas.

With respect to the border described—

"(i) in subparagraph (A)(ii), the Secretary shall ensure that an interlocking surveillance camera system is installed along such area by May 30, 2007, and that fence construction is completed by May 30, 2008; and

"(ii) in subparagraph (A)(v), the Secretary shall ensure that fence construction from 15 miles northwest of the Laredo, Texas, port of entry to 15 southeast of the Laredo, Texas, port of entry is completed by December 31, 2008.

"(C) Exception.—If the topography of a specific area has an elevation grade that exceeds 10 percent, the Secretary may use other means to secure such area, including the use of surveillance and barrier tools."

Sec. 4. Northern Border Study.

(a) In General.—The Secretary of Homeland Security shall conduct a study on the feasibility of a state of-the-art infrastructure security system along the northern international land and maritime border of the United States and shall include in the study—

(1) the necessity of implementing such a system;

(2) the feasibility of implementing such a system; and

(3) the economic impact implementing such a system will have along the northern border.

(b) Report.—Not later than one year after the date of the enactment of this Act, the Secretary of Homeland Security shall submit to the Committee on Homeland Security of the House of Representatives and the Committee on Homeland Security and Governmental Affairs of the Senate a report that contains the results of the study conducted under subsection (a).

Sec. 5. Evaluation and Report Relating to Customs Authority to Stop Certain Fleeing Vehicles.

(a) Evaluation.—Not later than 30 days after the date of the enactment of this Act, the Secretary of Homeland Security shall—

(1) evaluate the authority of personnel of United States Customs and Border Protection to stop vehicles that enter the United States illegally and refuse to stop when ordered to do so by such personnel, compare such Customs authority with the authority of the Coast Guard to stop vessels under section 637 of title 14, United States Code, and make an assessment as to whether such Customs authority should be expanded;

(2) review the equipment and technology available to United States Customs and Border Protection personnel to stop vehicles described in paragraph (1) and make an assessment as to whether or not better equipment or technology is available or should be developed; and

(3) evaluate the training provided to United States Customs and Border Protection personnel to stop vehicles described in paragraph (1).

(b) Report.—Not later than 60 days after the date of the enactment of this Act, the Secretary of Homeland Security shall submit to the Committee on Homeland Security of the House of Representatives and the Committee on Homeland Security and Governmental Affairs of the Senate a report that contains the results of the evaluation conducted under subsection (a).

Approved October 26, 2006.

Source: Public Law 109-367.

Illegal Immigration Relief Act Ordinance, City of Hazleton, Pennsylvania (2006)

On September 8, 2006, the council for the City of Hazleton, Pennsylvania, passed an anti–illegal immigration statute that barred employers from hiring undocumented aliens and landlords from renting property to them. The statute, regarded by many on both sides of the illegal immigration debate as one of the toughest in the country, created widespread controversy and led to a series of court challenges. In 2007, the U.S. Court of Appeals declared the ordinance unconstitutional, as it infringed on the federal government's exclusive right to regulate immigration. In June 2011, however, the U.S. Supreme Court voided the lower court's ruling and instructed it to revisit the case.

Be it ordained by the Council of the City of Hazleton as follows:

Section 1. Title

This chapter shall be known and may be cited as the "City of Hazleton Illegal Immigration Relief Act Ordinance."

Section 2. Findings and Declaration of Purpose

The People of the City of Hazleton find and declare:

A. That state and federal law require that certain conditions be met before a person may be authorized to work or reside in this country.

B. That unlawful workers and illegal aliens, as defined by this ordinance and state and federal law, do not normally meet such conditions as a matter of law when present in the City of Hazleton.

C. That unlawful employment, the harboring of illegal aliens in dwelling units in the City of Hazleton, and crime committed by illegal aliens harm the health, safety and welfare of authorized US workers and legal residents in the City of Hazleton. Illegal immigration leads to higher crime rates, subjects our hospitals to fiscal hardship and legal residents to substandard quality of care, contributes to other burdens on public services, increasing their cost and diminishing their availability to legal residents, and diminishes our overall quality of life.

D. That the City of Hazleton is authorized to abate public nuisances and empowered and mandated by the people of Hazleton to abate the nuisance of illegal immigration by diligently prohibiting the acts and policies that facilitate illegal immigration in a manner consistent with federal law and the objectives of Congress.

E. That United States Code Title 8, subsection 1324(a)(1)(A) prohibits the harboring of illegal aliens. The provision of housing to illegal aliens is a fundamental component of harboring.

F. This ordinance seeks to secure to those lawfully present in the United States and this City, whether or not they are citizens of the United States, the right to live in peace free of the threat crime, to enjoy the public services provided by this city without being burdened by the cost of providing goods, support and services to aliens unlawfully present in the United States, and to be free of the debilitating effects on their economic and social well being imposed by the influx of illegal aliens to the fullest extent that these goals can be achieved consistent with the Constitution and Laws of the United States and the Commonwealth of Pennsylvania.

G. The City shall not construe this ordinance to prohibit the rendering of emergency medical care, emergency assistance, or legal assistance to any person.

Section 3. Definitions . . .

G. "Basic Pilot Program" means the electronic verification of work authorization program of the Illegal Immigration Reform and Immigration Responsibility Act of 1996, P.L. 104-208, Division C, Section 403(a); United States Code Title 8, subsection 1324a, and operated by the United States Department of Homeland Security (or a successor program established by the federal government.)

Section 4. Business Permits, Contracts, or Grants

A. It is unlawful for any business entity to recruit, hire for employment, or continue to employ, or to permit, dispatch, or instruct any person who is an unlawful worker to perform work in whole or part within the City. Every business entity that applies for a business permit to engage in any type of work in the City shall sign an affidavit, prepared by the City Solicitor, affirming that they do not knowingly utilize the services or hire any person who is an unlawful worker.

B. Enforcement: The Hazleton Code Enforcement Office shall enforce the requirements of this section.

(1) An enforcement action shall be initiated by means of a written signed complaint to the Hazleton Code Enforcement Office submitted by any City official, business entity, or City resident. A valid complaint shall include an allegation which describes the alleged violator(s) as well as the actions constituting the violation, and the date and location where such actions occurred.

(2) A complaint which alleges a violation solely or primarily on the basis of national origin, ethnicity, or race shall be deemed invalid and shall not be enforced.

(3) Upon receipt of a valid complaint, the Hazleton Code Enforcement Office shall, within three business days, request identity information from the business entity regarding any persons alleged to be unlawful workers. The Hazleton Code Enforcement Office shall suspend the business permit of any business entity which fails, within three business days after receipt of the request, to provide such information. In instances where an unlawful worker is alleged to be an unauthorized alien, as defined in United States Code Title 8, subsection 1324a(h)(3), the Hazleton Code Enforcement Office shall submit identity data required by the federal government to verify, pursuant to United States Code Title 8, section 1373, the immigration status of such person(s), and shall provide the business entity with written confirmation of that verification.

(4) The Hazleton Code Enforcement Office shall suspend the business permit of any business entity which fails correct a violation of this section within three business days after notification of the violation by the Hazleton Code Enforcement Office.

(5) The Hazleton Code Enforcement Office shall not suspend the business permit of a business entity if, prior to the date of the violation, the business entity had verified the work authorization of the alleged unlawful worker(s) using the Basic Pilot Program.

(6) The suspension shall terminate one business day after a legal representative of the business entity submits, at a City office designated by the City Solicitor, a sworn affidavit stating that the violation has ended.

(a) The affidavit shall include a description of the specific measures and actions taken by the business entity to end the violation, and shall include the name, address and other adequate identifying information of the unlawful workers related to the complaint.

(b) Where two or more of the unlawful workers were verified by the federal government to be unauthorized aliens, the legal representative of the business entity shall submit to the Hazleton Code Enforcement Office, in addition to the prescribed affidavit, documentation acceptable to the City Solicitor which confirms that the business entity has enrolled in and will participate in the Basic Pilot Program for the duration of the validity of the business permit granted to the business entity.

(7) For a second or subsequent violation, the Hazleton Code Enforcement Office shall suspend the business permit of a business entity for a period of twenty days. After the end of the suspension period, and upon receipt of the prescribed affidavit, the Hazleton Code Enforcement Office shall reinstate the business permit. The Hazleton Code Enforcement Office shall forward the affidavit, complaint, and associated documents to the appropriate federal enforcement agency, pursuant to United States Code Title 8, section 1373. In the case of an unlawful worker disqualified by state law not related to immigration, the Hazleton Code Enforcement Office shall forward the affidavit, complaint, and associated documents to the appropriate state enforcement agency.

C. All agencies of the City shall enroll and participate in the Basic Pilot Program.

D. As a condition for the award of any City contract or grant to a business entity for which the value of employment, labor or, personal services shall exceed $10,000, the business entity shall provide documentation confirming its enrollment and participation in the Basic Pilot Program.

E. Private Cause of Action for Unfairly Discharged Employees

(1) The discharge of any employee who is not an unlawful worker by a business entity in the City is an unfair business practice if, on the date of the discharge, the business entity was not participating in the Basic Pilot program and the business entity was employing an unlawful worker.

(2) The discharged worker shall have a private cause of action in the Municipal Court of Hazleton against the business entity for the unfair business practice. The business entity found to have violated this subsection shall be liable to the aggrieved employee for:

(a) three times the actual damages sustained by the employee, including but not limited to lost wages or compensation from the date of the discharge until the date the employee has procured new employment at an equivalent rate of compensation, up to a period of one hundred and twenty days; and

(b) reasonable attorney's fees and costs.

Section 5. Harboring Illegal Aliens

A. It is unlawful for any person or business entity that owns a dwelling unit in the City to harbor an illegal alien in the dwelling unit, knowing or in reckless disregard of the fact that an alien has come to, entered, or remains in the United States in violation of law, unless such harboring is otherwise expressly permitted by federal law.

(1) For the purposes of this section, to let, lease, or rent a dwelling unit to an illegal alien, knowing or in reckless disregard of the fact that an alien has come to, entered, or remains in the United States in violation of law, shall be deemed to constitute harboring. To suffer or permit the occupancy of the dwelling unit by an illegal alien, knowing or in reckless disregard of the fact that an alien has come to, entered, or remains in the United States in violation of law, shall also be deemed to constitute harboring.

(2) A separate violation shall be deemed to have been committed on each day that such harboring occurs, and for each adult illegal alien harbored in the dwelling unit, beginning one business day after receipt of a notice of violation from the Hazleton Code Enforcement Office.

(3) A separate violation of this section shall be deemed to have been committed for each business day on which the owner fails to provide the Hazleton Code Enforcement Office with identity data needed to obtain a federal verification of immigration status, beginning three days after the owner receives written notice from the Hazleton Code Enforcement Office.

B. Enforcement: The Hazleton Code Enforcement Office shall enforce the requirements of this section.

(1) An enforcement action shall be initiated by means of a written signed complaint to the Hazleton Code Enforcement Office submitted by any official, business entity, or resident of the City. A valid complaint shall include an allegation which describes the alleged violator(s) as well as the actions constituting the violation, and the date and location where such actions occurred.

(2) A complaint which alleges a violation solely or primarily on the basis of national origin, ethnicity, or race shall be deemed invalid and shall not be enforced.

(3) Upon receipt of a valid written complaint, the Hazleton Code Enforcement Office shall, pursuant to United States Code Title 8, section 1373(c), verify with the federal government the immigration status of a person

seeking to use, occupy, lease, or rent a dwelling unit in the City. The Hazleton Code Enforcement Office shall submit identity data required by the federal government to verify immigration status. The City shall forward identity data provided by the owner to the federal government, and shall provide the property owner with written confirmation of that verification.

(4) If after five business days following receipt of written notice from the City that a violation has occurred and that the immigration status of any alleged illegal alien has been verified, pursuant to United States Code Title 8, section 1373(c), the owner of the dwelling unit fails to correct a violation of this section, the Hazleton Code Enforcement Office shall deny or suspend the rental license of the dwelling unit.

(5) For the period of suspension, the owner of the dwelling unit shall not be permitted to collect any rent, payment, fee, or any other form of compensation from, or on behalf of, any tenant or occupant in the dwelling unit.

(6) The denial or suspension shall terminate one business day after a legal representative of the dwelling unit owner submits to the Hazleton Code Enforcement Office a sworn affidavit stating that each and every violation has ended. The affidavit shall include a description of the specific measures and actions taken by the business entity to end the violation, and shall include the name, address and other adequate identifying information for the illegal aliens who were the subject of the complaint.

(7) The Hazleton Code Enforcement Office shall forward the affidavit, complaint, and associated documents to the appropriate federal enforcement agency, pursuant to United States Code Title 8, section 1373.

(8) Any dwelling unit owner who commits a second or subsequent violation of this section shall be subject to a fine of two hundred and fifty dollars ($250) for each separate violation. The suspension provisions of this section applicable to a first violation shall also apply.

(9) Upon the request of a dwelling unit owner, the Hazleton Code Enforcement Office shall, pursuant to United States Code Title 8, section 1373(c), verify with the federal government the lawful immigration status of a person seeking to use, occupy, lease, or rent a dwelling unit in the City. The penalties in this section shall not apply in the case of dwelling unit occupants whose status as an alien lawfully present in the United States has been verified.

Section 6. Construction and Severability

A. The requirements and obligations of this section shall be implemented in a manner fully consistent with federal law regulating immigration and protecting the civil rights of all citizens and aliens.

B. If any part of provision of this Chapter is in conflict or inconsistent with applicable provisions of federal or state statutes, or is otherwise held to be invalid or unenforceable by any court of competent jurisdiction, such part of provision shall be suspended and superseded by such applicable laws or regulations, and the remainder of this Chapter shall not be affected thereby.

Source: Ordinance 2006-18, City of Hazleton, Pennsylvania.

Hearing Before a Subcommittee of the U.S. House of Representatives on a Federal Immigration Raid in Postville, Iowa (2008)

On May 12, 2008, U.S. Immigration and Customs Enforcement (ICE) conducted its largest-ever raid on an American workplace—a kosher meatpacking plant in Postville, Iowa, called Agriprocessors Inc.—in search of undocumented workers. Of the nearly 400 people arrested as a result of the raid, about three-quarters received five-month prison sentences for identity theft, document fraud, and use of stolen Social Security numbers and then were then deported. Supporters of a tough approach to illegal immigration, such as U.S. Representative Steve King (R-IA), hailed the raid as a necessary tactic in the fight against illegal immigration. Defenders of the workers, such as Professor Erik Camayd-Freixas of Florida International University, who also served as a court interpreter for some of the workers, argued that the raid and subsequent prosecutions, and others like them, were unnecessarily cruel and denied undocumented workers their basic civil liberties. In May 2009, the U.S. Supreme Court ruled that the convictions for identity theft be vacated because the workers were not aware that the false identities they used belonged to other people—a requirement of the law.

Representative Steve King (R-IA): . . . I wasn't present at the Agriprocessors Incorporated plant in Postville, on May 12, when 389 illegal immigrant workers were arrested and detained by ICE. Nor was I present during the prosecution of those workers a short while later.

But what I have heard from parties who were present is that the workers were in this country illegally. They used false identification documents and stolen Social Security numbers to get their job. They were provided competent criminal defense attorneys and interpreters during the prosecution process and were given a choice of pleading guilty or going to trial.

If this is the case, I see no reason for this hearing other than to try to lend credence to the arguments of those who want amnesty and believe that working illegally in the United States is a victimless crime. When an illegal immigrant gets a job in this country using the identification documents or Social Security number of another person, it is a crime, and the other person is the victim of that crime.

The FTC [Federal Trade Commission] estimates that 8.3 million Americans were victims of identity fraud in the year 2005, and that number is on the rise. We will hear today from Mrs. Lora Costner. Both she and her husband had their identify stolen by illegal immigrants, and she will tell us how it ruined their lives.

With respect to Agriprocessors—the enforcement action—the allegations are that the illegal immigrant defendants somehow did not receive due process. But each defendant was provided a criminal defense attorney, and it was up to those defense attorneys to ensure due process. They were also provided interpreters.

According to one of the defense attorneys present, the client did get due process. According to a July 11, 2008, *New York Times* article, attorney Sarah Smith stated, "I think they understood what their options were. I tried to make it very clear." And according to the article, Mrs. Smith said she was convinced, after examining the prosecutor's evidence, that it was not in her client's best interest to go to trial. So a defense attorney, who was an advocate for her client, believed her clients made the right choice by accepting the plea agreements offered by the U.S. Attorney's Office.

For far too many years, employers have gotten the message that they can hire illegal immigrant workers with few or no consequences. ICE worksite enforcement actions, like the ones in the Postville, put these employers and the illegal workers themselves on notice that, if they chose to violate the law, they are subject to prosecution.

And listening to the gentlelady [Representative Zoe Lofgren (D-CA)] from California's opening statement about the defendants being coerced into guilty pleas, I think that is a presumption that I would—if we can hear that confirmed here today, I would be quite interested.

But if you have an attorney—if you come into the United States illegally, and you go to get a job, and you are breaking the law, and then you are rounded up in an ICE raid, and this country and the taxpayers fund to the tune of $4 million your attorney and your interpreter, and then you plead guilty because it is in your best interest—and by the way, in a plea bargain agreement, as well—I mean, that is the equivalent of—this is on a far-higher scale for those of you who will choose to misinterpret my intent here.

But let us just say that law enforcement arrests someone on suspicion of murder, and they say, "Tell us

where the body is, we will plea agreement that down, and we won't go for the death penalty." If that defendant tells where the body is, they get a plea agreement for a life sentence rather than a death penalty. That is not in proportion, obviously, but that illustrates for you what a plea agreement really is. And if they have to hand them a piece of paper so that they can answer in English in America, that is not what I call confusion.

So in group hearings, by the way, we are looking at 12 to 20 or more million people in the United States unlawfully, and I don't know how we process 12 to 20 million in an individual fashion. If you do it in group, they consent to that, I believe their rights were protected. I am willing to listen to the arguments to the contrary here today . . .

Mr. Erik Camayd-Freixas: I was 1 of 16 interpreters who served both weeks of the Postville hearing. Unlike judges, prosecutors or attorney, I was present at every step of the process. It is my duty as an impartial expert witness, an officer of the court, to ensure that the court is not misled and to bring to its attention any impediments to due process. I have done so in the best interest of the Federal court I am proud to serve and with the conviction that, if our honorable judges had known how this judicial experiment would turn out, they would have never allowed it.

In my statement submitted for congressional record, I document the flaws. Detainees' quarters were not certified. The court failed to maintain physical and operational independence from ICE prosecution and a level playing field for the defense.

There was inadequate access to counsel, no meaningful presumption of innocence. Defendants appear not to understand their rights and charges. Bail hearings and other due process rights were denied. The charge of identity theft used to force a plea lacked foundation and was never tested for probable cause.

Defendant did not know what a Social Security number was and were not guilty of intent crime. Guilty pleas were obtained under duress. Judges had no sentencing discretion pursuant to a binding plea agreement. Sole providers whose families are in jeopardy now endure a cruel and unusual psychological punishment, the foreseeable effect of a prison time on common [words missing].

Abridgement of process produced wholesaling justice at the other end. Parents begging to be deported put in jail at public expense. Proud working mothers branded like cattle with the scarlet letter of an ankle monitor dehumanized and reduced to begging at the doors of the church as they were released on humanitarian grounds.

The town of Postville devastated. The kinship ties

our noble people are quick to forge with all newcomers painfully severed. Families and friends separated.

I saw the Bill of Rights denied and democratic values threatened by the breakdown of checks and balances, and it all appeared to be within the framework of the law pursuant to a broken immigration system.

Postville lays bare a grave distortion in the legal structure of government. Post 9-11, ICE was granted power to wage the war on terror, but since 2006, it has diverted resources even from disaster relief to an escalating and unauthorized war on immigration.

Yet the men and women of ICE are not to be faulted for doing their duty. It is unrealistic in our adversarial system to ask prosecutors to exercise restraint and not use all legal mean to win convictions. The fact is our laws have not kept up with this growth in enforcement.

Congress failed to pass immigration reform, and ICE has filled the legal void with its own version of it. Now we have a serious contradiction, the growth of authoritarian rule inside a democratic government. This entity can simultaneously wield immigration and criminal codes plus issue administrative rules, leaving no room for constitutional guarantees.

It co-ops other branches of government—Social Security, U.S. Attorney, Federal court—and uses appropriations to recruit local police for immigration enforcement, setting neighbor against neighbor and dangerously dividing the Nation.

With the help of local sheriffs, Postville repeats itself daily while the harshness of border enforcement is reenacted in the American Heartland with great collateral damage to our citizens and community. It is a rush to raid as much as possible before Congress regains the vision and courage to restore the law of the land.

Part of immigration reform is redefining jurisdiction over—ICE jurisdiction over immigration and criminal matters without impairing the agency's ability to defend us from terrorist threats. Since 2006, families have been separated on a scale unseen in the Americas since the Spanish Conquest, when it led to the extinction of Ameri-Indian nations. In Postville, we have the added moral burden posed by the presence of ethnic Mayan, testimonial people who constitute and endanger patrimony of humanity.

I bring to this forum three requests from the people of Postville.

First, our government has left a humanitarian crisis for Sister Mary McCauley and her good neighbors to cure. I call on all to contribute to St. Bridget's Church and on the Federal Government to respond with aid that guarantees survival for their schools, businesses and institutions. It is time for America to adopt Postville.

Second, with regard to the imprisoned aliens, govern-ment says they have 300 criminals. The people say, "Show us one victim of their crime or send them home."

Third, our national unity requires that Congress pass not only comprehensive but compassionate immigration reform as would befit the dignity of this great country built upon the shoulders of immigrants by their children.

Source: U.S. House Committee on the Judiciary, Subcommittee on Immigration, Citizenship, Refugees, Border Security, and International Law. *Immigration Raids: Postville and Beyond,* July 24, 1998 (Washington, DC: U.S. Government Printing Office, 1998).

Support Our Law Enforcement and Safe Neighborhoods Act (SB 1070) of Arizona (2010)

In April 2010, Arizona Governor Jan Brewer signed the Support Our Law Enforcement and Safe Neighborhoods Act (widely known as SB 1070, or Senate Bill 1070). The legislation included a number of provisions pertaining to aliens within the state, including one requiring all of them over the age of fourteen to carry legal status documentation at all times and requiring state and local law enforcement officers during a "lawful stop, detention or arrest" to determine the immigration status of those whom they reasonably suspect of being in the country illegally. The law stirred immediate controversy, with critics arguing that it was a form of legalized racial profiling. The Barack Obama administration contended that SB 1070 violated the U.S. Constitution, which gives exclusive immigration enforcement powers to the federal government.

Article 8. Enforcement of Immigration Laws

A. No official or agency of this state or a county, city, town or other political subdivision of this state may adopt a policy that limits or restricts the enforcement of federal immigration laws to less than the full extent permitted by federal law.

B. For any lawful contact made by a law enforcement official or agency of this state or a county, city, town or other political subdivision of this state where reasonable suspicion exists that the person is an alien who is unlawfully present in the United States, a reasonable attempt shall be made, when practicable, to determine the immigration status of the person. The person's immigration status shall be verified with the federal government pursuant to 8 United States code section 1373(c).

C. If an alien who is unlawfully present in the United States is convicted of a violation of state or local law, on discharge from imprisonment or assessment of any fine that is imposed, the alien shall be transferred immediately to the custody of the United States immigration and customs enforcement or the United States customs and border protection.

D. Notwithstanding any other law, a law enforcement agency may securely transport an alien who is unlawfully present in the United States and who is in the agency's custody to a federal facility in this state or to any other point of transfer into federal custody that is outside the jurisdiction of the law enforcement agency.

E. A law enforcement officer, without a warrant, may arrest a person if the officer has probable cause to believe that the person has committed any public offense that makes the person removable from the United States.

F. Except as provided in federal law, officials or agencies of this state and counties, cities, towns and other political subdivisions of this state may not be prohibited or in any way be restricted from sending, receiving or maintaining information relating to the immigration status of any individual or exchanging that information with any other federal, state or local governmental entity for the following official purposes:

    1. Determining eligibility for any public benefit, service or license provided by any federal, state, local or other political subdivision of this state.

    2. Verifying any claim of residence or domicile if determination of residence or domicile is required under the laws of this state or a judicial order issued pursuant to a civil or criminal proceeding in this state.

    3. Confirming the identity of any person who is detained.

    4. If the person is an alien, determining whether the person is in compliance with the federal registration laws prescribed by title II, chapter 7 of the federal immigration and nationality act.

G. A person may bring an action in superior court to challenge any official or agency of this state or a county, city, town or other political subdivision of this state that adopts or implements a policy that limits or restricts the enforcement of federal immigration laws to less than the full extent permitted by federal law. If there is a judicial finding that an entity has violated this section, the court shall order any of the following:

    1. That the person who brought the action recover court costs and attorney fees.

    2. That the entity pay a civil penalty of not less than one thousand dollars and not more than five thousand dollars for each day that the policy has remained in effect after the filing of an action pursuant to this subsection.

H. A court shall collect the civil penalty prescribed in subsection G and remit the civil penalty to the department of public safety for deposit in the gang and immigration intelligence team enforcement mission fund established by section 41-1724.

I. A law enforcement officer is indemnified by the law enforcement officer's agency against reasonable costs and expenses, including attorney fees, incurred by the officer in connection with any action, suit or proceeding brought pursuant to this section to which the officer may be a party by reason of the officer being or having been a member of the law enforcement agency, except in relation to matters in which the officer is adjudged to have acted in bad faith.

J. This section shall be implemented in a manner consistent with federal laws regulating immigration, protecting the civil rights of all persons and respecting the privileges and immunities of United States citizens.

Source: Senate Bill 1070, Arizona State Legislature.

Arizona et al. v. United States (2012)

On June 25, 2012, the U.S. Supreme Court issued its ruling in the case of Arizona et al. v. United States, *regarding the constitutionality of certain provisions in Arizona's Support Our Law Enforcement and Safe Neighborhoods Act (commonly known as Senate Bill 1070, or SB 1070). Writing for the majority, Associate Justice Anthony Kennedy declared most of the law unconstitutional, including its controversial requirement that aliens in the state at all times carry documentation attesting to their legal presence in the country. At the same time, the Court did uphold another provision opposed by immigration advocates—one requiring state and local law enforcement to check a person's legal status if the officer has stopped, detained, or arrested a person on suspicion of a non-immigration-related legal infraction. However, the Court did say that it would monitor the situation to make sure that such documentation requests are handled in ways that do not violate constitutional protections (in other words, to ensure that law enforcement officers do not engage in racial profiling). The excerpts that follow reflect the legal reasoning of Kennedy and the majority of the Court on these provisions. (The abbreviation "ICE" in the document refers to U.S. Immigration and Customs Enforcement.)*

IV

A

Section 3

Section 3 of S.B. 1070 creates a new state misdemeanor. It forbids the "willful failure to complete or carry an alien registration document . . . in violation of 8 United States Code section 1304(e) or 1306(a)." *Ariz. Rev. Stat. Ann.* §11-1509(A) (West Supp. 2011). In effect, §3 adds a state-law penalty for conduct proscribed by federal law. The United States contends that this state enforcement mechanism intrudes on the field of alien registration, a field in which Congress has left no room for States to regulate. See Brief for United States 27, 31.

The Court discussed federal alien-registration requirements in *Hines v. Davidowitz*, 312 U.S. 52. In 1940, as international conflict spread, Congress added to federal immigration law a "complete system for alien registration." Id., at 70. The new federal law struck a careful balance. It punished an alien's willful failure to register but did not require aliens to carry identification cards. There were also limits on the sharing of registration records and fingerprints. The Court found that Congress intended the federal plan for registration to be a "single integrated and all-embracing system." Id., at 74. Because this "complete scheme . . . for the registration of aliens" touched on foreign relations, it did not allow the States to "curtail or complement" federal law or to "enforce additional or auxiliary regulations." Id., at 66–67. As a consequence, the Court ruled that Pennsylvania could not enforce its own alien-registration program. See id., at 59, 74.

The present regime of federal regulation is not identical to the statutory framework considered in Hines, but it remains comprehensive. Federal law now includes a requirement that aliens carry proof of registration. 8 U.S.C. §1304(e). Other aspects, however, have stayed the same. Aliens who remain in the country for more than 30 days must apply for registration and be fingerprinted. Compare §1302(a) with id., §452(a) (1940 ed.). Detailed information is required, and any change of address has to be reported to the Federal Government. Compare §§1304(a), 1305(a) (2006 ed.), with id., §§455(a), 456 (1940 ed.). The statute continues to provide penalties for the willful failure to register. Compare §1306(a) (2006 ed.), with id., §457 (1940 ed.).

The framework enacted by Congress leads to the conclusion here, as it did in Hines, that the Federal Government has occupied the field of alien registration. See *American Ins. Assn. v. Garamendi,* 539 U.S. 396, 419, n. 11 (2003) (characterizing Hines as a field preemption case); *Pennsylvania v. Nelson,* 350 U.S. 497, 504 (1956) (same); see also Dinh, Reassessing the Law of Preemption, 88 Geo. L. J. 2085, 2098–2099, 2107 (2000) (same). The federal statutory directives provide a full set of standards governing alien registration, including the punishment for noncompliance. It was designed as a "'harmonious whole.'" Hines, supra, at 72. Where Congress occupies an entire field, as it has in the field of alien registration, even complementary state regulation is impermissible. Field preemption reflects a congressional decision to foreclose any state regulation in the area, even if it is parallel to federal standards. *See Silkwood v. Kerr-McGee Corp.,* 464 U.S. 238, 249 (1984).

Federal law makes a single sovereign responsible for maintaining a comprehensive and unified system to keep track of aliens within the Nation's borders. If §3 of the Arizona statute were valid, every State could give itself independent authority to prosecute federal registration violations, "diminish[ing] the [Federal Government]'s control over enforcement" and "detract[ing] from the 'integrated scheme of regulation' created by Congress." Wisconsin *Dept. of Industry v. Gould Inc.,* 475 U.S. 282, 288–289 (1986). Even if a State may make violation of federal law a crime in some instances, it cannot do so in a field (like the field of alien registration) that has been occupied by federal law. See *California v. Zook,* 336 U.S. 725, 730–731, 733 (1949); see also In re Loney, 134 U.S. 372, 375–376 (1890) (States may not impose their own punishment for perjury in federal courts).

Arizona contends that §3 can survive preemption because the provision has the same aim as federal law and adopts its substantive standards. This argument not only ignores the basic premise of field preemption—that States may not enter, in any respect, an area the Federal Government has reserved for itself—but also is unpersuasive on its own terms. Permitting the State to impose its own penalties for the federal offenses here would conflict with the careful framework Congress adopted. *Cf. Buckman Co. v. Plaintiffs' Legal Comm.,* 531 U.S. 341, 347–348 (2001) (States may not impose their own punishment for fraud on the Food and Drug Administration); Wisconsin Dept., supra, at 288 (States may not impose their own punishment for repeat violations of the National Labor Relations Act). Were §3 to come into force, the State would have the power to bring criminal charges against individuals for violating a federal law even in circumstances where federal officials in charge of the comprehensive scheme determine that prosecution would frustrate federal policies.

There is a further intrusion upon the federal scheme. Even where federal authorities believe prosecution is appropriate, there is an inconsistency between §3 and federal law with respect to penalties. Under federal law, the failure to carry registration papers is a misdemeanor that may be punished by a fine, imprisonment, or a term of probation. See 8 U.S.C. §1304(e) (2006 ed.); 18 U.S.C. §3561. State law, by contrast, rules out probation as a possible sentence (and also eliminates the possibility of a pardon). See *Ariz. Rev. Stat. Ann.* §13-1509(D) (West Supp. 2011). This state framework of sanctions creates a conflict with the plan Congress put in place. See Wisconsin Dept., supra, at 286 ("[C]onflict is imminent whenever two separate remedies are brought to bear on the same activity" (internal quotation marks omitted)).

These specific conflicts between state and federal law simply underscore the reason for field preemption. As it did in Hines, the Court now concludes that, with respect to the subject of alien registration, Congress intended to preclude States from "complement[ing] the federal law, or enforc[ing] additional or auxiliary regulations." 312 U.S., at 66–67. Section 3 is preempted by federal law. . . .

D

Section 2(B)

Section 2(B) of S. B. 1070 requires state officers to make a "reasonable attempt . . . to determine the immigration status" of any person they stop, detain, or arrest on some other legitimate basis if "reasonable suspicion exists that the person is an alien and is unlawfully present in the United States." *Ariz. Rev. Stat. Ann.* §11-1051(B) (West 2012). The law also provides that "[a]ny person who is arrested shall have the person's immigration status determined before the person is released." Ibid. The accepted way to perform these status checks is to contact ICE, which maintains a database of immigration records.

Three limits are built into the state provision. First, a detainee is presumed not to be an alien unlawfully present in the United States if he or she provides a valid Arizona driver's license or similar identification. Second, officers "may not consider race, color or national origin . . . except to the extent permitted by the United States [and] Arizona Constitution[s]." Ibid. Third, the provisions must be "implemented in a manner consistent with federal law regulating immigration, protecting the civil rights of all persons and respecting the privileges and immunities of United States citizens." §11-1051(L) (West 2012).

The United States and its amici contend that, even with these limits, the State's verification requirements pose an obstacle to the framework Congress put in place. The first concern is the mandatory nature of the status checks. The second is the possibility of prolonged detention while the checks are being performed.

1

Consultation between federal and state officials is an important feature of the immigration system. Congress has made clear that no formal agreement or special training needs to be in place for state officers to "communicate with the [Federal Government] regarding the immigration status of any individual, including reporting knowledge that a par-

ticular alien is not lawfully present in the United States." 8 U.S.C. §1357(g)(10)(A). And Congress has obligated ICE to respond to any request made by state officials for verification of a person's citizenship or immigration status. See §1373(c); see also §1226(d)(1)(A) (requiring a system for determining whether individuals arrested for aggravated felonies are aliens). ICE's Law Enforcement Support Center operates "24 hours a day, seven days a week, 365 days a year" and provides, among other things, "immigration status, identity information and real-time assistance to local, state and federal law enforcement agencies." ICE, Fact Sheet: Law Enforcement Support Center (May 29, 2012), online at http://www.ice.gov/news/library/factsheets/lesc.htm. LESC responded to more than one million requests for information in 2009 alone. App. 93.

The United States argues that making status verification mandatory interferes with the federal immigration scheme. It is true that §2(B) does not allow state officers to consider federal enforcement priorities in deciding whether to contact ICE about someone they have detained. See Brief for United States 47–50. In other words, the officers must make an inquiry even in cases where it seems unlikely that the Attorney General would have the alien removed. This might be the case, for example, when an alien is an elderly veteran with significant and longstanding ties to the community. See 2011 ICE Memorandum 4-5 (mentioning these factors as relevant).

Congress has done nothing to suggest it is inappropriate to communicate with ICE in these situations, however. Indeed, it has encouraged the sharing of information about possible immigration violations. See 8 U.S.C. §1357(g)(10)(A). A federal statute regulating the public benefits provided to qualified aliens in fact instructs that "no State or local government entity may be prohibited, or in any way restricted, from sending to or receiving from [ICE] information regarding the immigration status, lawful or unlawful, of an alien in the United States." §1644. The federal scheme thus leaves room for a policy requiring state officials to contact ICE as a routine matter. Cf. Whiting, 563 U.S., at ___–___ (slip op., at 23–24) (rejecting argument that federal law preempted Arizona's requirement that employers determine whether employees were eligible to work through the federal E-Verify system where the Federal Government had encouraged its use).

2

Some who support the challenge to §2(B) argue that, in practice, state officers will be required to delay the release of some detainees for no reason other than to verify their immigration status. See, e.g., Brief for Former Arizona Attorney General Terry Goddard et al. as Amici Curiae 37, n. 49. Detaining individuals solely to verify their immigration status would raise constitutional concerns. See, e.g., *Arizona v. Johnson,* 555 U.S. 323, 333 (2009); *Illinois v. Caballes,* 543 U.S. 405, 407 (2005) ("A seizure that is justified solely by the interest in issuing a warning ticket to the driver can become unlawful if it is prolonged beyond the time reasonably required to complete that mission"). And it would disrupt the federal framework to put state officers in the position of holding aliens in custody for possible unlawful presence without federal direction and supervision. Cf. Part IV–C, *supra* (concluding that Arizona may not authorize warrantless arrests on the basis of removability). The program put in place by Congress does not allow state or local officers to adopt this enforcement mechanism.

But §2(B) could be read to avoid these concerns. To take one example, a person might be stopped for jaywalking in Tucson and be unable to produce identification. The first sentence of §2(B) instructs officers to make a "reasonable" attempt to verify his immigration status with ICE if there is reasonable suspicion that his presence in the United States is unlawful. The state courts may conclude that, unless the person continues to be suspected of some crime for which he may be detained by state officers, it would not be reasonable to prolong the stop for the immigration inquiry. See Reply Brief for Petitioners 12, n. 4 ("[Section 2(B)] does not require the verification be completed during the stop or detention if that is not reasonable or practicable"); cf. *Muehler v. Mena,* 544 U.S. 93, 101 (2005) (finding no Fourth Amendment violation where questioning about immigration status did not prolong a stop).

To take another example, a person might be held pending release on a charge of driving under the influence of alcohol. As this goes beyond a mere stop, the arrestee (unlike the jaywalker) would appear to be subject to the categorical requirement in the second sentence of §2(B) that "[a]ny person who is arrested shall have the person's immigration status determined before [he] is released." State courts may read this as an instruction to initiate a status check every time someone is arrested, or in some subset of those cases, rather than as a command to hold the person until the check is complete no matter the circumstances. Even if the law is read as an instruction to complete a check while the person is in custody, moreover, it is not clear at this stage and on this record that the verification process would result in prolonged detention. However the law is interpreted, if §2(B) only requires state officers to conduct a status check during the course of an authorized, lawful detention or after a detainee has been released, the provision likely would survive preemption—at least absent some showing that it has other consequences that are adverse to federal law and its objectives. There is no need in this case to address whether reasonable suspicion of illegal entry or another immigration crime would be a legitimate basis for prolonging a detention,

or whether this too would be preempted by federal law. See, e.g., *United States v. Di Re,* 332 U.S. 581, 589 (1948) (authority of state officers to make arrests for federal crimes is, absent federal statutory instruction, a matter of state law); *Gonzales v. Peoria,* 722 F. 2d 468, 475–476 (CA9 1983) (concluding that Arizona officers have authority to enforce the criminal provisions of federal immigration law), overruled on other grounds in *Hodgers-Durgin v. de la Vina,* 199 F. 3d 1037 (CA9 1999).

The nature and timing of this case counsel caution in evaluating the validity of §2(B). The Federal Government has brought suit against a sovereign State to challenge the provision even before the law has gone into effect. There is a basic uncertainty about what the law means and how it will be enforced. At this stage, without the benefit of a definitive interpretation from the state courts, it would be inappropriate to assume §2(B) will be construed in a way that creates a conflict with federal law. Cf. *Fox v. Washington,* 236 U.S. 273, 277 (1915) ("So far as statutes fairly may be construed in such a way as to avoid doubtful constitutional questions they should be so construed; and it is to be presumed that state laws will be construed in that way by the state courts" (citation omitted)). As a result, the United States cannot prevail in its current challenge.

See *Huron Portland Cement Co. v. Detroit,* 362 U.S. 440, 446 (1960) ("To hold otherwise would be to ignore the teaching of this Court's decisions which enjoin seeking out conflicts between state and federal regulation where none clearly exists"). This opinion does not foreclose other preemption and constitutional challenges to the law as interpreted and applied after it goes into effect.

Source: Arizona et al. v. United States, 132 S. Ct. 2492 (2012).

Implementation Guidelines for President Barack Obama's "DREAM Act" Executive Order (2012)

In June 2012, President Barack Obama issued an executive order that called on the U.S. Department of Homeland Security (DHS), which oversees Immigration and Customs Enforcement (ICE), to defer action for two years on the deportation of persons under the age of thirty who were brought to the United States illegally by their parents when they were fifteen years of age or under, as long as they met certain criteria: no felony convictions in the United States, current attendance in school or graduation from high school, and current or past service in the U.S. armed forces. The order won praise from immigration advocates frustrated by Congress's unwillingness to pass the so-called DREAM Act, giving permanent amnesty to such persons; the order elicited criticism from those opposing amnesty for any undocumented aliens on grounds that it would encourage more illegal immigration and that Obama was bypassing Congress in order to implement a policy that would help him gain Latino votes in the upcoming election. The following document includes excerpts from the DHS's official guidelines for the executive order.

On June 15, 2012, the Secretary of Homeland Security announced that certain people who came to the United States as children and meet several key guidelines may request consideration of deferred action for a period of two years, subject to renewal, and would then be eligible for work authorization. Deferred action is a discretionary determination to defer removal action of an individual as an act of prosecutorial discretion. Deferred action does not provide an individual with lawful status . . .

Guidelines

You may request consideration of deferred action for childhood arrivals if you:

1. Were under the age of 31 as of June 15, 2012;

2. Came to the United States before reaching your 16th birthday;

3. Have continuously resided in the United States since June 15, 2007, up to the present time;

4. Were physically present in the United States on June 15, 2012, and at the time of making your request for consideration of deferred action with USCIS [U.S. Citizenship and Immigration Services];

5. Entered without inspection before June 15, 2012, or your lawful immigration status expired as of June 15, 2012;

6. Are currently in school, have graduated or obtained a certificate of completion from high school, have obtained a general education development (GED) certificate, or are an honorably discharged veteran of the Coast Guard or Armed Forces of the United States; and

7. Have not been convicted of a felony, significant misdemeanor, three or more other misdemeanors, and do not otherwise pose a threat to national security or public safety.

Age Requirements

Anyone requesting consideration for deferred action under this process must have been under 31 years old as of June 15, 2012. You must also be at least 15 years or older to request deferred action, unless you are currently in removal proceedings or have a final removal or voluntary departure order, as summarized in the table below:

Your situation	Required age
I have never been in removal proceedings, or my proceedings have been terminated before making my request.	At least 15 years old at the time of submitting your request and not over 31 years of age as of June 15, 2012.
I am in removal proceedings, have a final removal order, or have a voluntary departure order, and I am not in immigration detention.	Not above the age of 31 as of June 15, 2012, but you may be younger than 15 years old at the time you submit your request.

Timeframe for Meeting the Guidelines

You must prove

That on June 15, 2012, you
- Were under 31 years old
- Had come to the United States before your 16th birthday
- Were physically present in the United States
- Entered without inspection by this date, or your lawful immigration status expired as of this date

As of the date you file your request you
- Have resided continuously in the U.S. since June 15, 2007;
- Were physically present in the United States; and
- Are in school, have graduated from high school in the United States, or have a GED; or
- Are an honorably discharged veteran of the Coast Guard or Armed Forces of the United States

Education and Military Service Guidelines

Your school or military status at the time of requesting deferred action under this process	Meet education or military service guidelines for deferred action under this process (Y/N)
I graduated from: • Public or private high school; or • Secondary school. Or • I have obtained a GED.	Yes
I am currently enrolled in school. See the Education section of the FAQs for a full explanation of who is considered currently in school.	Yes
I was in school but dropped out and did not graduate. I am not currently in school and am not an honorably discharged veteran of the Coast Guard or Armed Forces of the U.S.	No
I am an honorably discharged veteran of the Coast Guard or Armed Forces of the U.S.	Yes

Filing Process for Consideration of Deferred Action for Childhood Arrivals

If you meet the guidelines for deferred action under this process, you will need to complete the following steps to make your request to USCIS. . . .

Examples of Documents to Submit to Demonstrate you Meet the Guidelines . . .

Proof of identity

- Passport or national identity document from your country of origin
- Birth certificate with photo identification
- School or military ID with photo
- Any U.S. government immigration or other document bearing your name and photo

Proof you came to U.S. before your 16th birthday

- Passport with admission stamp
- Form I-94/I-95/I-94W
- School records from the U.S. schools you have attended
- Any Immigration and Naturalization Service or DHS document stating your date of entry (Form I-862, Notice to Appear)
- Travel records
- Hospital or medical records

Proof of immigration status

- Form I-94/I-95/I-94W with authorized stay expiration date
- Final order of exclusion, deportation, or removal issued as of June 15, 2012
- A charging document placing you into removal proceedings

Proof of presence in U.S. on June 15, 2012

- Rent receipts or utility bills
- Employment records (pay stubs, W-2 Forms, etc)
- School records (letters, report cards, etc)
- Military records (Form DD-214 or NGB Form 22)
- Official records from a religious entity confirming participation in a religious ceremony
- Copies of money order receipts for money sent in or out of the country
- Passport entries

- Birth certificates of children born in the U.S.
- Dated bank transactions
- Social Security card
- Automobile license receipts or registration
- Deeds, mortgages, rental agreement contracts
- Tax receipts, insurance policies
- Proof you continuously resided in U.S. since June 15, 2007

Proof of your student status at the time of requesting consideration of deferred action for childhood arrivals

- School records (transcripts, report cards, etc) from the school that you are currently attending in the United States showing the name(s) of the school(s) and periods of school attendance and the current educational or grade level
- U.S. high school diploma or certificate of completion
- U.S. GED certificate

Proof you are an honorably discharged veteran of the Coast Guard or Armed Forces of the U.S.

- Form DD-214, Certificate of Release or Discharge from Active Duty
- NGB Form 22, National Guard Report of Separation and Record of Service
- Military personnel records
- Military health records . . .

National Security and Public Safety Guidelines

If you have been convicted of a felony offense, a significant misdemeanor offense, or three or more other misdemeanor offenses not occurring on the same date and not arising out of the same act, omission, or scheme of misconduct, or are otherwise deemed to pose a threat to national security or public safety, you will not be considered for deferred action under this process.

What is the difference between "significant misdemeanor," "non-significant misdemeanor," and "felony"?

A minor traffic offense will not be considered a misdemeanor for purposes of this process, but it is important to emphasize that driving under the influence is a significant misdemeanor regardless of the sentence imposed. You can find detailed information in the National Security and Public Safety section of the Frequent Asked Questions.

Felony	Significant misdemeanor	Non-significant misdemeanor
A felony is a federal, state or local criminal offense punishable by imprisonment for a term exceeding one year.	A significant misdemeanor is a misdemeanor as defined by federal law (specifically, one for which the maximum term of imprisonment authorized is one year or less but greater than five days) and: 1. Regardless of the sentence imposed, is an offense of domestic violence; sexual abuse or exploitation; burglary; unlawful possession or use of a firearm; drug distribution or trafficking; or, driving under the influence; or, 2. If not an offense listed above, is one for which the individual was sentenced to time in custody of more than 90 days. The sentence must involve time to be served in custody, and therefore does not include a suspended sentence.	A crime is considered a non-significant misdemeanor (maximum term of imprisonment is one year or less but greater than five days) if it: 1. Is not an offense of domestic violence; sexual abuse or exploitation; burglary; unlawful possession or use of a firearm; drug distribution or trafficking; or, driving under the influence; and 2. Is one for which the individual was sentenced to time in custody of 90 days or less.

Renewing Deferred Action Under This Process

Individuals whose case is deferred under this process will not be placed into removal proceedings or removed from the United States for a period of two years, unless terminated. You may request consideration for a two-year extension of deferred action through a process to be detailed in the future. As long as you were under the age of 31 on June 15, 2012, you may request a renewal even after turning 31. Your request for an extension will be considered on a case-by-case basis.

Source: U.S. Department of Homeland Security.

Bipartisan Framework for Comprehensive Immigration Reform, U.S. Senate (2013)

In the wake of the 2012 national elections, immigration reform became a top priority of both the Barack Obama administration and Congress. In January 2013, the so-called Gang of Eight Democratic and Republican senators worked out a "framework" for an immigration bill, calling for tougher border and port-of-entry security, more visas for skilled and education immigrants, more effective employer verification systems to prevent illegal aliens from working, and protections for American workers from unfair competition with low-paid immigrant labor. The most controversial provision was one creating "a path to citizenship" for the estimated 11 million persons already in the country illegally, a path that would require a clean criminal record, payment of fees and back taxes, and the ability to speak English.

Senators Schumer, McCain, Durbin, Graham, Menendez, Rubio, Bennet, and Flake

Introduction

We recognize that our immigration system is broken. And while border security has improved significantly over the last two Administrations, we still don't have a functioning immigration system. This has created a situation where up to 11 million undocumented immigrants are living in the shadows. Our legislation acknowledges these realities by finally committing the resources needed to secure the border, modernize and streamline our current legal immigration system, while creating a tough but fair legalization program for individuals who are currently here. We will ensure that this is a successful permanent reform to our immigration system that will not need to be revisited.

Four Basic Legislative Pillars:

- o Create a tough but fair path to citizenship for unauthorized immigrants currently living in the United States that is contingent upon securing our borders and tracking whether legal immigrants have left the country when required;
- o Reform our legal immigration system to better recognize the importance of characteristics that will help build the American economy and strengthen American families;
- o Create an effective employment verification system that will prevent identity theft and end the hiring of future unauthorized workers; and,
- o Establish an improved process for admitting future workers to serve our nation's workforce needs, while simultaneously protecting all workers.

I. Creating a Path to Citizenship for Unauthorized Immigrants Already Here that is Contingent Upon Securing the Border and Combating Visa Overstays

- ◇ Our legislation will provide a tough, fair, and practical roadmap to address the status of unauthorized immigrants in the United States that is contingent upon our success in securing our borders and addressing visa overstays.

- ◇ To fulfill the basic governmental function of securing our borders, we will continue the increased efforts of the Border Patrol by providing them with the latest technology, infrastructure, and personnel needed to prevent, detect, and apprehend every unauthorized entrant.

- ◇ Additionally, our legislation will increase the number of unmanned aerial vehicles and surveillance equipment, improve radio interoperability and increase the number of agents at and between ports of entry. The purpose is to substantially lower the number of successful illegal border crossings while continuing to facilitate commerce.

- ◇ We will strengthen prohibitions against racial profiling and inappropriate use of force, enhance the training of border patrol agents, increase oversight, and create a mechanism to ensure a meaningful opportunity for border communities to share input, including critiques.

- ◇ Our legislation will require the completion of an entry-exit system that tracks whether all persons entering the United States on temporary visas via airports and seaports have left the country as required by law.

- ◇ We recognize that Americans living along the Southwest border are key to recognizing and understanding when the border is truly secure. Our legislation will create a commission comprised of governors, attorneys general, and community leaders living along the Southwest border to monitor the progress of securing our border and to make a recommendation regarding when the bill's security measures outlined in the legislation are completed.

- ◇ While these security measures are being put into place, we will simultaneously require those who came or remained in the United States without our permission to register with the government. This will include passing a background check and settling their debt to society by paying a fine and back taxes, in order to earn probationary legal status, which will allow them to live and work legally in the United States. Individuals with a serious criminal background or others who pose a threat to our national security will be ineligible for legal status and subject to deportation. Illegal immigrants who have committed serious crimes face immediate deportation.

- ◇ We will demonstrate our commitment to securing our borders and combating visa overstays by requiring our proposed enforcement measures be complete before any immigrant on probationary status can earn a green card.

- ◇ Current restrictions preventing non-immigrants from accessing federal public benefits will also apply to lawful probationary immigrants.

- ◇ Once the enforcement measures have been completed, individuals with probationary legal status will be required to go to the back of the line of prospective immigrants, pass an additional background check, pay taxes, learn English and civics, demonstrate a history of work in the United States, and current employment, among other requirements, in order to earn the opportunity to apply for lawful permanent residency. Those individuals who successfully complete these requirements can eventually earn a green card.

- ◇ Individuals who are present without lawful status—not including people within the two categories identified below—will only receive a green card after every individual who is already waiting in line for a green card, at the time this legislation is enacted, has received their green card. Our purpose is to ensure that no one who has violated America's immigration laws will receive preferential treatment as they relate to those individuals who have complied with the law.

- ◇ Our legislation also recognizes that the circumstances and the conduct of people without lawful status are not the same, and cannot be addressed identically.

  - ○ For instance, individuals who entered the United States as minor children did not knowingly choose to violate any immigration laws. Consequently, under our proposal these individuals will not face the same requirements as other individuals in order to earn a path to citizenship.

  - ○ Similarly, individuals who have been working without legal status in the United States agricultural industry have been performing very important and difficult work to maintain America's food supply while earning subsistence wages. Due to the utmost importance in our nation maintaining the safety of its food supply, agricultural workers who commit to the long term stability of our nation's agricultural industries will be treated differently than the rest of the undocumented population because of the role they play in ensuring that Americans have safe and secure agricultural products to sell and consume. These individuals will earn a path to citizenship through a different process under our new agricultural worker program.

II. Improving our Legal Immigration System and Attracting the World's Best and Brightest

◇ The development of a rational legal immigration system is essential to ensuring America's future economic prosperity. Our failure to act is perpetuating a broken system which sadly discourages the world's best and brightest citizens from coming to the United States and remaining in our country to contribute to our economy. This failure makes a legal path to entry in the United States insurmountably difficult for well-meaning immigrants. This unarguably discourages innovation and economic growth. It has also created substantial visa backlogs which force families to live apart, which incentivizes illegal immigration.

◇ Our new immigration system must be more focused on recognizing the important characteristics which will help build the American economy and strengthen American families. Additionally, we must reduce backlogs in the family and employment visa categories so that future immigrants view our future legal immigration system as the exclusive means for entry into the United States.

◇ The United States must do a better job of attracting and keeping the world's best and brightest. As such, our immigration proposal will award a green card to immigrants who have received a PhD or Master's degree in science, technology, engineering, or math from an American university. It makes no sense to educate the world's future innovators and entrepreneurs only to ultimately force them to leave our country at the moment they are most able to contribute to our economy.

III. Strong Employment Verification

◇ We recognize that undocumented immigrants come to the United States almost exclusively for jobs. As such, dramatically reducing future illegal immigration can only be achieved by developing a tough, fair, effective and mandatory employment verification system. An employment verification system must hold employers accountable for knowingly hiring undocumented workers and make it more difficult for unauthorized immigrants to falsify documents to obtain employment. Employers who knowingly hire unauthorized workers must face stiff fines and criminal penalties for egregious offenses.

◇ We believe the federal government must provide U.S. employers with a fast and reliable method to confirm whether new hires are legally authorized to work in the United States. This is essential to ensure the effective enforcement of immigration laws.

◇ Our proposal will create an effective employment verification system which prevents identity theft and ends the hiring of future unauthorized workers. We believe requiring prospective workers to demonstrate both legal status and identity, through non-forgeable electronic means prior to obtaining employment, is essential to an employee verification system; and,

◇ The employee verification system in our proposal will be crafted with procedural safeguards to protect American workers, prevent identity theft, and provide due process protections.

IV. Admitting New Workers and Protecting Workers' Rights

◇ The overwhelming majority of the 327,000 illegal entrants apprehended by CBP in FY2011 were seeking employment in the United States. We recognize that to prevent future waves of illegal immigration a humane and effective system needs to be created for these immigrant workers to enter the country and find employment without seeking the aid of human traffickers or drug cartels.

◇ Our proposal will provide businesses with the ability to hire lower-skilled workers in a timely manner when Americans are unavailable or unwilling to fill those jobs.

◇ Our legislation would:
  ○ Allow employers to hire immigrants if it can be demonstrated that they were unsuccessful in recruiting an American to fill an open position and the hiring of an immigrant will not displace American workers;
  ○ Create a workable program to meet the needs of America's agricultural industry, including dairy to find agricultural workers when American workers are not available to fill open positions;
  ○ Allow more lower-skilled immigrants to come here when our economy is creating jobs, and fewer when our economy is not creating jobs;
  ○ Protect workers by ensuring strong labor protections; and,
  ○ Permit workers who have succeeded in the workplace and contributed to their communities over many years to earn green cards.

Source: U.S. Senate, January 29, 2013.

Immigration Planks of Democratic Party Platforms, 1856–2012

The text that follows contains the planks on immigration from the Democratic Party platforms of 1856 through 2012. In the course of those 156 years, two recurring points stand out. First, immigration tends to be mentioned only when it becomes a pressing national issue; and, second, the Democrats generally have been more welcoming of immigrants than their Republican rivals. That has been no less true regarding undocumented aliens, the nation's central immigration issue in the late twentieth and early twenty-first centuries. As recent platforms show, the Democrats have tried to offer various forms of "amnesty" for the millions of illegal immigrants already in the country, along with some of the tougher border security measures and sanctions against employers who hire undocumented workers that Republicans support. All in all, Democratic positions have accounted for the party's long history of lopsided support from immigrant voters.

1856

Resolved, That the foundation of this union of States having been laid in, and its prosperity, expansion, and pre-eminent example in free government, built upon entire freedom in matters of religious concernments [*sic*], and no respect of person in regard to rank or place of birth; no party can justly be deemed national, constitutional, or in accordance with American principles, which bases its exclusive organization upon religious opinions and accidental birth-place. And hence a political crusade in the nineteenth century, and in the United States of America, against Catholic and foreign-born is neither justified by the past history or the future prospects of the country, nor in unison with the spirit of toleration and enlarged freedom which peculiarly distinguishes the American system of popular government.

1880

Amendment of the Burlingame Treaty. No more Chinese immigration, except for travel, education, and foreign commerce, and that even carefully guarded.

1884

In reaffirming the declaration of the Democratic platform of 1856, that, "the liberal principles embodied by Jefferson in the Declaration of Independence, and sanctioned in the Constitution, which make ours the land of liberty and the asylum of the oppressed of every Nation, have ever been cardinal principles in the Democratic faith," we nevertheless do not sanction the importation of foreign labor, or the admission of servile races, unfitted by habits, training, religion, or kindred, for absorption into the great body of our people, or for the citizenship which our laws confer. American civilization demands that against the immigration or importation of Mongolians to these shores our gates be closed.

1888

The exclusion from our shores of Chinese laborers has been effectually secured under the provisions of treaty, the operation of which has been postponed by the action of a Republican majority in the Senate.

1892

We heartily approve all legitimate efforts to prevent the United States from being used as a dumping ground for the known criminals and professional paupers of Europe; and we demand the rigid enforcement of the laws against Chinese immigration and the importation of foreign workers under contract, to degrade American labor and lessen its wages; but we condemn and denounce any and all attempts to restrict the immigration of the industrious and worthy of foreign lands.

1896

We hold that the most efficient way of protecting American labor is to prevent the importation of foreign pauper labor to compete with it in the home market, and that the value of the home market to our American farmers and artisans is greatly reduced by a vicious monetary system which depresses the prices of their products below the cost of production, and thus deprives them of the means of purchasing the products of our home manufactories; and as labor creates the wealth of the country, we demand the passage of such laws as may be necessary to protect it in all its rights.

1900

We favor the continuance and strict enforcement of the Chinese exclusion law, and its application to the same classes of all Asiatic races.

1908

We favor full protection, by both National and State governments within their respective spheres, of all foreigners residing in the United States under treaty, but we are opposed to the admission of Asiatic immigrants who cannot be amalgamated with our population, or whose presence among us would raise a race issue and involve us in diplomatic controversies with Oriental powers.

1920

The policy of the United States with reference to the non-admission of Asiatic immigrants is a true expression of the judgment of our people, and to the several states, whose geographical situation or internal conditions make this policy, and the enforcement of the laws enacted pursuant thereto, of particular concern, we pledge our support.

1924

We pledge ourselves to maintain our established position in favor of the exclusion of Asiatic immigration.

1928

Laws which limit immigration must be preserved in full force and effect, but the provisions contained in these laws that separate husbands from wives and parents from infant children are inhuman and not essential to the purpose of the efficacy of such laws.

1952

Solution of the problem of refugees from communism and over-population has become a permanent part of the foreign policy program of the Democratic Party. We pledge continued cooperation with other free nations to solve it.

We pledge continued aid to refugees from communism and the enactment of President Truman's proposals for legislation in this field. In this way we can give hope and courage to the victims of Soviet brutality and can carry on the humanitarian tradition of the Displaced Persons Act.

Subversive elements must be screened out and prevented from entering our land, but the gates must be left open for practical numbers of desirable persons from abroad whose immigration to this country provides an invigorating infusion into the stream of American life, as well as a significant contribution to the solution of the world refugee and over-population problems.

We pledge continuing revision of our immigration and naturalization laws to do away with any unjust and unfair practices against national groups which have contributed some of our best citizens. We will eliminate distinctions between native-born and naturalized citizens. We want no "second-class" citizens in free America.

1956

America's long tradition of hospitality and asylum for those seeking freedom, opportunity, and escape from oppression, has been besmirched by the delays, failures, and broken promises of the Republican Administration. The Democratic Party favors prompt revision of the immigration and nationality laws to eliminate unfair provisions under which admissions to this country depend upon quotas based upon the accident of national origin. Proper safeguards against subversive elements should be provided. Our immigration procedures must reflect the principles of our Bill of Rights.

We favor eliminating the provisions of law which charge displaced persons admitted to our shores against quotas for future years. Through such "mortgages" of future quotas, thousands of qualified persons are being forced to wait long years before they can hope for admission.

We also favor more liberal admission of relatives to eliminate the unnecessary tragedies of broken families.

We favor elimination of unnecessary distinctions between native-born and naturalized citizens. There should be no "second-class" citizenship in the United States.

The administration of the Refugee Relief Act of 1953 has been a disgrace to our country. Rescue has been denied to innocent, defenseless and suffering people, the victims of war and the aftermath of wars. The purpose of the Act has been defeated by Republican mismanagement.

1960

We shall adjust our immigration, nationality and refugee policies to eliminate discrimination and to enable members of scattered families abroad to be united with relatives already in our midst.

The national-origins quota system of limiting immigration contradicts the founding principles of this nation. It is inconsistent with our belief in the rights of man. This system was instituted after World War I as a policy of deliberate discrimination by a Republican Administration and Congress.

The revision of immigration and nationality laws we seek will implement our belief that enlightened immigration, naturalization and refugee policies and humane administration of them are important aspects of our foreign policy.

These laws will bring greater skills to our land, reunite families, permit the United States to meet its fair share of world programs of rescue and rehabilitation, and take advantage of immigration as an important factor in the growth of the American economy.

In this World Refugee Year it is our hope to achieve

admission of our fair share of refugees. We will institute policies to alleviate suffering among the homeless wherever we are able to extend our aid.

We must remove the distinctions between native-born and naturalized citizens to assure full protection of our laws to all. There is no place in the United States for "second-class citizenship."

The projections provided by due process, right of appeal, and statutes of limitation, can be extended to non-citizens without hampering the security of our nation.

We commend the Democratic Congress for the initial steps that have recently been taken toward liberalizing changes in immigration law. However, this should not be a piecemeal project and we are confident that a Democratic President in cooperation with Democratic Congresses will again implant a humanitarian and liberal spirit in our nation's immigration and citizenship policies.

1964

In 1960, we proposed to—

Adjust our immigration, nationality and refugee policies to eliminate discrimination and to enable members of scattered families abroad to be united with relatives already in our midst.

The national-origins quota system of limiting immigration contradicts the founding principles of this nation. It is inconsistent with our belief in the rights of men.

The immigration law amendments proposed by the Administration, and now before Congress, by abolishing the national-origin quota system, will eliminate discrimination based upon race and place of birth and will facilitate the reunion of families.

The Cuban Refugee Program begun in 1961 has re-settled over 81,000 refugees, who are now self-supporting members of 1,800 American communities. The Chinese Refugee Program, begun in 1962, provides for the admission to the United States of 12,000 Hong Kong refugees from Red China.

1968

A new Immigration Act removed the harsh injustice of the national-origins quota system and opened our shores without discrimination to those who can contribute to the growth and strength of America.

1972

The next Democratic Administration should: . . .
Re-establish a U.S.-Mexico border commission, with representatives, to develop a comprehensive program to desalinate and eradicate pollution of the Colorado River

and other waterways flowing into Mexico, and conduct substantial programs to raise the economic level on both sides of the border. This should remove the economic reasons which contribute to illegal immigration and discourage run-away industries. In addition, language requirements for citizenship should be removed.

1976

We support a provision in the immigration laws to facilitate acquisition of citizenship by Resident Aliens.

1980

Ethnic America
President Carter has stated that the composition of American society is analogous to a beautiful mosaic. Each separate part retains its own integrity and identity while adding to and being part of the whole.

America is a pluralistic society. Each of us must learn to live, communicate, and cooperate with persons of other cultures. Our public policies and programs must reflect this pluralism. Immigrants from every nation and their descendants have made numerous contributions to this country, economically, politically and socially. They have traditionally been the backbone of the labor movement and an integral part of the Democratic Party.

Ethnic Americans share the concerns of all Americans. They too are concerned about decent housing, health care, equal employment opportunities, care of the elderly, and education. In addition, ethnic Americans have some concerns of their own. They want to preserve the culture and language of their former homeland. They want to be integrated into the political, social and economic mainstream of American society, but at the same time they are concerned about the foreign policy issues that affect their native countries. We as a nation must be sensitive to their concerns.

President Carter established the Office of Ethnic Affairs and charged it with a broad and diverse mission. The predominant functions of the office are to link the Administration and its ethnic constituents, to foster the concept of pluralism, and to enable all Americans to partake equally in the American way of life.

Refugees and Migration
America's roots are found in the immigrants and refugees who have come to our shores to build new lives in a new world. The Democratic Party pledges to honor our historic commitment to this heritage.

The first comprehensive reform of this nation's refugee policies in over 25 years was completed with the signing in March 1980 of the Refugee Act of 1980, based on legislation submitted to Congress by the Carter Administration in March 1979.

This Act offers a comprehensive alternative to the chaotic movement and the inefficient and inequitable administration of past refugee programs in the United States. We favor the full use of refugee legislation now to cope with the flow of Cuban and Haitian refugees, and to help the states, local communities and voluntary agencies resettle them across our land. We urge that monies be distributed to voluntary agencies fairly so that aid is distributed to all refugees without discrimination.

The Administration also established the first refugee coordination office in the Department of State under the leadership of a special ambassador and coordinator for refugee affairs and programs.

The new legislation and the coordinator's office will bring common sense and consolidation to our nation's previously fragmented, inconsistent, and, in many ways, outdated refugee and immigration policies.

A Select Commission on Immigration and Refugee Policy is now at work to further reform the system. We pledge our support to the goals and purposes of the Commission, and we urge the Administration to move aggressively in this area once the Commission submits its report.

Once that report has been completed, we must work to resolve the issue of undocumented residents in a fair and humane way. We will oppose any legislation designed to allow workers into the country to undercut U.S. wages and working conditions, and which would reestablish the Bracero Program of the past.

World population projections, as well as international economic indicators—especially in the Third World—forewarn us that migration pressures will mount rapidly in many areas of the world in the decade ahead. Our own situation of undocumented workers underscores how difficult it is to deal with economic and employment forces that are beyond any nation's immediate control. Most of Europe, and many parts of Latin America and Asia, face similar dilemmas. For example, Mexico faces the pressure of migration from Central America.

We will work with other nations to develop international policies to regularize population movement and to protect the human rights of migrants even as we protect the jobs of American workers and the economic interest of the United States. In this hemisphere, such a policy will require close cooperation with our neighbors, especially Mexico and Canada.

We must also work to resolve the difficult problems presented by the immigration from Haiti and from the more recent immigration from Cuba. In doing so, we must ensure that there is no discrimination in the treatment afforded to the Cubans or Haitians. We must also

work to ensure that future Cuban immigration is handled in an orderly way, consistent with our laws. To ameliorate the impact on state and local communities and school districts of the influx of new immigrants from Cuba and Haiti, we must provide the affected areas with special fiscal assistance.

We support continued financial backing of international relief programs such as those financed by the United States, the International Red Cross, UNICEF and the private, non-profit organizations to aid the starving people of Kampuchea. We also endorse such support for the Cambodian refugees and encourage participation in the campaign of the National Cambodian Crisis Committee.

We support, through U.S. contributions to the UN High Commissioner for Refugees and other means aid for the mounting Afghan refugee population in Pakistan and other desperate refugee situations.

1988

A Fair and Humane Immigration Policy

Our nation's outdated immigration laws require comprehensive reform that reflects our national interests and our immigrant heritage. Our first priority must be to protect the fundamental human rights of American citizens and aliens. We will oppose any "reforms" that violate these rights or that will create new incentives for discrimination against Hispanic Americans and other minorities arising from the discriminatory use of employer sanctions. Specifically, we oppose employer sanctions designed to penalize employers who hire undocumented workers. Such sanctions inevitably will increase discrimination against minority Americans. We oppose identification procedures that threaten civil liberties, as well as any changes that subvert the basic principle of family unification. And we will put an end to this Administration's policies of barring foreign visitors from our country for political or ideological reasons. We strongly oppose "bracero" or guest-worker programs as a form of legalized exploitation. We firmly support a one-tiered legalization program with a 1982 cut-off date.

The Democratic Party will implement a balanced, fair, and non-discriminatory immigration and refugee policy consistent with the principle of affording all applications for admission equal protection under the law. It will work for improved performance by the Immigration and Naturalization Service in adjudicating petitions for permanent residence and naturalization. The Party will also advocate reform within the INS [Immigration and Naturalization Service] to improve the enforcement operations of the Service consistent with civil liberties protection. The correction of past and present bias in the allocation of slots for refugee admissions will be a top priority. Additionally, it will work to ensure that the Refugee Act of 1980, which prohibits discrimination on the basis of ideology and race in adjudicating asylum claims, is complied with. The Party will provide the necessary oversight of the Department of State and the Immigration and Naturalization Service so as to ensure that the unjustifiable treatment visited upon the Haitian refugees will never again be repeated.

The Democratic Party will formulate foreign policies which alleviate, not aggravate, the root causes of poverty, war, and human rights violations and instability which compel people to flee their homelands.

We support the creation of an international body on immigration to address the economic development problems affecting Mexico and Latin American countries which contribute to unauthorized immigration to the U.S. and to respond to the backlog of approved immigrant visas.

To pursue these and other goals, the Democratic Party nominee upon election shall establish the following national advisory committees to the President and the national Democratic Party: civil rights and justice; fair housing; affirmative action; equal rights for women; rights for workers; immigration policy; and voting rights. These committees shall be representative on the basis of geography, race, sex, and ethnicity.

1992

Our nation of immigrants has been invigorated repeatedly as new people, ideas and ways of life have become part of the American tapestry. Democrats support immigration policies that promote fairness, non-discrimination and family reunification, and that reflect our constitutional freedoms of speech, association and travel.

1996

Democrats remember that we are a nation of immigrants. We recognize the extraordinary contribution of immigrants to America throughout our history. We welcome legal immigrants to America. We support a legal immigration policy that is pro-family, pro-work, pro-responsibility, and pro-citizenship, and we deplore those who blame immigrants for economic and social problems. . . .

Today's Democratic Party also believes we must remain a nation of laws. We cannot tolerate illegal immigration and we must stop it. . . .

However, as we work to stop illegal immigration, we call on all Americans to avoid the temptation to use this issue to divide people from each other. We deplore

those who use the need to stop illegal immigration as a pretext for discrimination. And we applaud the wisdom of Republicans like [New York City] Mayor [Rudolph] Giuliani and Senator [Pete] Domenici [New Mexico] who oppose the mean-spirited and shortsighted effort of Republicans in Congress to bar the children of illegal immigrants from schools—it is wrong, and forcing children onto the streets is an invitation for them to join gangs and turn to crime. Democrats want to protect American jobs by increasing criminal and civil sanctions against employers who hire illegal workers, but Republicans continue to favor inflammatory rhetoric over real action. We will continue to enforce labor standards to protect workers in vulnerable industries. We continue to firmly oppose welfare benefits for illegal immigrants. We believe family members who sponsor immigrants into this country should take financial responsibility for them, and be held legally responsible for supporting them.

2000

Welcoming Our Newest Americans

Immigrants enrich the tapestry of American life, making our economy more vibrant, our workplaces more productive, and our nation stronger. We believe that all levels of government, in partnership with the private and voluntary sectors, must devise and pursue a comprehensive immigrant integration agenda that will make the newest Americans full participants in the nation's mainstream. That's why Democrats support reforming the INS to provide better services, and investing the resources needed to reduce the backlog of citizenship applications from nearly two years to three months. Democrats also support increased resources for English language courses, which not only help newcomers learn our common language but also help us promote our common values. And, we believe that family reunification should continue to be the cornerstone of our legal immigration system.

Democrats believe in an effective immigration system that balances a strong enforcement of our laws with fair and evenhanded treatment of immigrants and their families. The Clinton-Gore administration provided long overdue leadership in dramatically improving border management and law enforcement, including a major expansion of the Border Patrol and curbs on abuses of the asylum process. We also recognize that the current system fails to effectively control illegal immigration, has serious adverse impacts on state and local services, and on many communities and workers, and has led to an alarming number of deaths of migrants on the border. Democrats are committed to reexamining and fixing these failed policies.

We must punish employers who engage in a pattern and practice of recruiting undocumented workers in order to intimidate and exploit them, and provide strengthened protections for immigrant workers, including whistleblower protections. Doing so enhances conditions for everyone in the workplace. We believe that any increases in H1-B visas must be temporary, must address only genuine shortages of highly skilled workers, and must include worker protections. They must also be accompanied by other immigration fairness measures and by increased fees to train American workers for high skill jobs. The Democratic Party is committed to assuring an adequate, predictable supply of agricultural labor while protecting American farm workers who are among the poorest and more vulnerable in our society. We reject calls for guest worker programs that lead to exploitation, and instead call for adjusting the status of immigrants with deep roots in the country. We should have equitable asylum policies that treat people the same whether they have fled violence from the Right and Left. And we support restoration of basic due process protections and essential benefits for legal immigrants, so that immigrants are no longer subject to deportation for minor offenses, often committed decades ago without opportunity for any judicial review, and are eligible to receive safety net services supported by their tax dollars.

2004

We will extend the promise of citizenship to those still struggling for freedom. Today's immigration laws do not reflect our values or serve our security, and we will work for real reform. The solution is not to establish a massive new status of second-class workers; that betrays our values and hurts all working people. Undocumented immigrants within our borders who clear a background check, work hard and pay taxes should have a path to earn full participation in America. We will hasten family reunification for parents and children, husbands and wives, and offer more English-language and civic education classes so immigrants can assume all the rights and responsibilities of citizenship. As we undertake these steps, we will work with our neighbors to strengthen our security so we are safer from those who would come here to harm us. We are a nation of immigrants, and from Arab-Americans in California to Latinos in Florida, we share the dream of a better life in the country we love.

2008

America has always been a nation of immigrants. Over the years, millions of people have come here in the hope that in America, you can make it if you try. Each successive wave of immigrants has contributed to our country's rich culture, economy and spirit. Like the immigrants that came before them, today's immigrants will shape their own destinies and enrich our country.

Nonetheless, our current immigration system has been broken for far too long. We need comprehensive immigration reform, not just piecemeal efforts. We must work together to pass immigration reform in a way that unites this country, not in a way that divides us by playing on our worst instincts and fears. We are committed to pursuing tough, practical, and humane immigration reform in the first year of the next administration.

We cannot continue to allow people to enter the United States undetected, undocumented, and unchecked. The American people are a welcoming and generous people, but those who enter our country's borders illegally, and those who employ them, disrespect the rule of the law. We need to secure our borders, and support additional personnel, infrastructure, and technology on the border and at our ports of entry. We need additional Customs and Border Protection agents equipped with better technology and real-time intelligence. We need to dismantle human smuggling organizations, combating the crime associated with this trade. We also need to do more to promote economic development in migrant-sending nations, to reduce incentives to come to the United States illegally. And we need to crack down on employers who hire undocumented immigrants. It's a problem when we only enforce our laws against the immigrants themselves, with raids that are ineffective, tear apart families, and leave people detained without adequate access to counsel. We realize that employers need a method to verify whether their employees are legally eligible to work in the United States, and we will ensure that our system is accurate, fair to legal workers, safeguards people's privacy, and cannot be used to discriminate against workers.

We must also improve the legal immigration system, and make our nation's naturalization process fair and accessible to the thousands of legal permanent residents who are eager to become full Americans. We should fix the dysfunctional immigration bureaucracy that hampers family reunification, the cornerstone of our immigration policy for years. Given the importance of both keeping families together and supporting American businesses, we will increase the number of immigration visas for family members of people living here and for immigrants who meet the demand for jobs that employers cannot fill, as long as appropriate labor market protections and standards are in place. We will fight discrimination against Americans who have always played by our immigration rules but are sometimes treated as if they had not.

For the millions living here illegally but otherwise

playing by the rules, we must require them to come out of the shadows and get right with the law. We support a system that requires undocumented immigrants who are in good standing to pay a fine, pay taxes, learn English, and go to the back of the line for the opportunity to become citizens. They are our neighbors, and we can help them become full tax-paying, law-abiding, productive members of society.

2012

Democrats are strongly committed to enacting comprehensive immigration reform that supports our economic goals and reflects our values as both a nation of laws and a nation of immigrants. The story of the United States would not be possible without the generations of immigrants who have strengthened our country and contributed to our economy. Our prosperity depends on an immigration system that reflects our values and meets America's needs. But Americans know that today, our immigration system is badly broken—separating families, undermining honest employers and workers, burdening law enforcement, and leaving millions of people working and living in the shadows.

Democrats know there is broad consensus to repair that system and strengthen our economy, and that the country urgently needs comprehensive immigration reform that brings undocumented immigrants out of the shadows and requires them to get right with the law, learn English, and pay taxes in order to get on a path to earn citizenship. We need an immigration reform that creates a system for allocating visas that meets our economic needs, keeps families together, and enforces the law. But instead of promoting the national interest, Republicans have blocked immigration reform in Congress and used the issue as a political wedge.

Despite the obstacles, President Obama has made important progress in implementing immigration policies that reward hard work and demand personal responsibility. Today, the Southwest border is more secure than at any time in the past 20 years. Unlawful crossings are at a 40-year low, and the Border Patrol is better staffed than at any time in its history. We are continuing to work to hold employers accountable for whom they hire. The Department of Homeland Security is prioritizing the deportation of criminals who endanger our communities over the deportation of immigrants who do not pose a threat, such as children who came here through no fault of their own and are pursuing an education. President Obama's administration has streamlined the process of legal immigration for immediate relatives of U.S. citizens, supporting family reunification as a priority, and has enhanced opportunities for English-language learning and immigrant integration. When states sought to interfere with federal immigration law by passing local measures targeting immigrants, this administration challenged them in court.

President Obama and the Democrats fought for the DREAM Act [Development, Relief, and Education for Alien Minors Act], legislation ensuring that young people who want to contribute fully to our society and serve our country are able to become legal residents and ultimately citizens. Although this bill has a long history of bipartisan support, Republicans decided to play politics with it rather than do the right thing. So the Obama administration provided temporary relief for youth who came to the United States as children, through no fault of their own, grew up as Americans and are poised to make a real contribution to our country.

These are not permanent fixes. Only Congress can provide a permanent, comprehensive solution. But these are steps in the right direction. President Obama and the Democratic Party stand for comprehensive immigration reform that intelligently prioritizes our country's security and economic needs, while Mitt Romney and the Republicans have opposed commonsense reforms and pandered to the far right.

Source: Democratic Party.

Immigration Planks of Republican Party Platforms, 1860–2012

The text that follows contains the planks on immigration from the Republican Party platforms from 1860 through 2012. As in the Democratic Party platforms, two recurring trends stand out: Immigration tends to be mentioned only when it becomes a pressing national issue; and the Republican Party platforms are generally less welcoming of immigrants than those of their Democratic counterparts. This has been especially true of illegal immigration and border security, the hot-button immigration issues of the late twentieth and early twenty-first centuries. Since President Ronald Reagan signed the last "amnesty" bill for illegal immigrants in 1986, the GOP has avoided any talk of a new amnesty, emphasizing instead the need to secure America's borders. This hard-line position has alienated many immigrant voters, who have cast ballots for Republicans in dwindling numbers since 2004. The GOP loss in the 2012 presidential election, which many political commentators attributed in part to its poor showing among Latinos and Asian Americans, prompted a reassessment of the party's position on illegal aliens and a "path to citizenship."

1860

That the Republican Party is opposed to any change in our naturalization laws or any state legislation by which the rights of citizens hitherto accorded to immigrants from foreign lands shall be abridged or impaired; and in favor of giving a full and efficient protection of the rights of all classes of citizens, whether native or naturalized, both at home and abroad.

1864

Resolved, That foreign immigration, which in the past has added so much to the wealth, development of resources and increase of power to the nation, the asylum of the oppressed of all nations, should be fostered and encouraged by a liberal and just policy.

1880

Since the authority to regulate immigration and intercourse between the United States and foreign nations rests with the Congress of the United States and the treaty-making power, the Republican Party, regarding the unrestricted immigration of the Chinese as a matter of grave concernment [*sic*] under the exercise of both these powers, would limit and restrict that immigration by the enactment of such just, humane and reasonable laws and treaties as will produce that result.

1884

The Republican Party, having its birth in a hatred of slave labor and a desire that all men may be truly free and equal, is unalterably opposed to placing our workingmen in competition with any form of servile labor, whether at home and abroad. In this spirit, we denounce the importation of contract labor, whether from Europe or Asia, as an offense against the spirit of American institutions; and we pledge ourselves to sustain the present law restricting Chinese immigration, and to provide such further legislation as is necessary to carry out its purposes.

1888

We declare our hostility to the introduction into this country of foreign contract labor and of Chinese labor, alien to our civilization and constitution; and we demand the rigid enforcement of the existing laws against it, and favor such immediate legislation as will exclude such labor from our shores.

1896

For the protection of the equality of our American citizenship and of the wages of our workingmen, against the fatal competition of low priced labor, we demand that the immigration laws be thoroughly enforced, and so extended as to exclude from entrance to the United States those who can neither read nor write.

1912

We pledge the Republican Party to the enactment of appropriate laws to give relief from the constantly growing evil of induced or undesirable immigration, which is inimical to the progress and welfare of the people of the United States.

1920

Immigration

The standard of living and the standard of citizenship of a nation are its most precious possessions, and the preservation and the elevation of those standards is the first duty of our government. The immigration policy of the U.S. should be such as to insure that the number of foreigners in the country at any one time shall not exceed that which can be assimilated with reasonable rapidity, and to favor immigrants whose standards are similar to ours.

The selective tests that are at present applied should be improved by requiring a higher physical standard, a more complete exclusion of mental defectives and of criminals, and a more effective inspection applied as near the source of immigration as possible, as well as at the port of entry. Justice to the foreigner and to ourselves demands provision for the guidance, protection and better economic distribution of our alien population. To facilitate government supervision, all aliens should be required to register annually until they become naturalized.

The existing policy of the United States for the practical exclusion of Asiatic immigrants is sound, and should be maintained.

Naturalization

There is urgent need of improvement in our naturalization law. No alien should become a citizen until he has become genuinely American, and adequate tests for determining the alien's fitness for American citizenship should be provided for by law.

We advocate, in addition, the independent naturalization of married women. An American woman, resident in the United States, should not lose her citizenship by marriage to an alien.

1924

The unprecedented living conditions in Europe following the world war created a condition by which we were threatened with mass immigration that would have seriously disturbed our economic life. The law recently enacted is designed to protect the inhabitants of our country, not only the American citizen, but also the alien already with us who is seeking to secure an economic foothold for himself and family from the competition that would come from unrestricted immigration. The administrative features of the law represent a great constructive advance, and eliminate the hardships suffered by immigrants under emergency statute.

We favor the adoption of methods which will exercise a helpful influence among the foreign born population and provide for the education of the alien in our language, customs, ideals and standards of life. We favor the improvement of naturalization laws.

1928

The Republican Party believes that in the interest of both native and foreign-born wage earners, it is necessary to restrict immigration. Unrestricted immigration would result in widespread unemployment and in the breakdown of the American standard of living. Where, however, the law works undue hardships by depriving the immigrant of the comfort and society of those bound by close family ties, such modification should be adopted as will afford relief.

We commend Congress for correcting defects for humanitarian reasons and for providing an effective system of examining prospective immigrants in their home countries.

1940

We favor the strict enforcement of all laws controlling the entry of aliens. The activities of undesirable aliens should be investigated and those who seek to change by force and violence the American form of government should be deported.

1956

The Republican Party supports an immigration policy which is in keeping with the traditions of America in providing a haven for oppressed peoples, and which is based on equality of treatment, freedom from implications of discrimination between racial, nationality and religious groups, and flexible enough to conform to changing needs and conditions.

We believe that such a policy serves our self-interest, reflects our responsibility for world leadership and develops maximum cooperation with other nations in resolving problems in this area.

We support the President's program submitted to the 84th Congress to carry out needed modifications in existing law and to take such further steps as may be necessary to carry out our traditional policy.

In that concept, this Republican Administration sponsored the Refugee Relief Act to provide asylum for thousands of refugees, expellees and displaced persons, and undertook in the face of Democrat opposition to correct the inequities in existing law and to bring our immigration policies in line with the dynamic needs of the country and principles of equity and justice.

We believe also that the Congress should consider the extension of the Refugee Relief Act of 1953 in resolving this difficult refugee problem which resulted from world conflict. To all this we give our wholehearted support.

1960

Immigration has historically been a great factor in the growth of the United States, not only in numbers but in the enrichment of ideas that immigrants have brought with them. This Republican Administration has given refuge to over 32,000 victims of Communist tyranny from Hungary, ended needless delay in processing applications for naturalization, and has urged other enlightened legislation to liberalize existing restrictions.

Immigration has been reduced to the point where it does not provide the stimulus to growth that it should, nor are we fulfilling our obligation as a haven for the oppressed. Republican conscience and Republican policy require that:

The annual number of immigrants we accept be at least doubled.

Obsolete immigration laws be amended by abandoning the outdated 1920 census data as a base and substituting the 1960 census.

The guidelines of our immigration policy be based upon judgment of the individual merit of each applicant for admission and citizenship.

1964

We Republicans shall first rely on the individual's right and capacity to advance his own economic well-being, to control the fruits of his efforts and to plan his own and his family's future; and, where government is rightly involved, we shall assist the individual in surmounting urgent problems beyond his own power and responsibility to control. For instance, we pledge: . . . immigration legislation seeking to re-unite families and continuation of the "Fair Share" Refugee Program

1968

The principles of the 1965 Immigration [and Nationality] Act—non-discrimination against national origins, reunification of families, and selective support for the American labor market—have our unreserved backing. We will refine this new law to make our immigration policy still more equitable and non-discriminatory.

1972

Spanish-Speaking Americans
In recognition of the significant contributions to our country by our proud and independent Spanish-speaking citizens, we have developed a comprehensive program to help achieve equal opportunity.

During the last four years Spanish-speaking Americans have achieved a greater role in national affairs. More than thirty have been appointed to high Federal positions.

To provide the same learning opportunities enjoyed by other American children, we have increased bilingual education programs almost sixfold since 1969. We initiated a 16-point employment program to help Spanish-speaking workers, created the National Economic Development Association to promote Spanish-speaking business development and expanded economic development opportunities in Spanish-speaking communities.

We will work for the use of bilingual staffs in localities where this language capability is desirable for effective health care.

1976

Hispanic-Americans
When language is a cause for discrimination, there must be an intensive educational effort to enable Spanish-speaking students to become fully proficient in English while maintaining their own language and cultural heritage. Hispanic Americans must not be treated as second-class citizens in schools, employment or any other aspect of life just because English is not their first language. Hispanic Americans truly believe that individual integrity must be paramount; what they want most from government and politics is the opportunity to participate fully. The Republican Party has and always will offer this opportunity.

1980

Hispanic Americans
Hispanics are rapidly becoming the largest minority in the country and are one of the major pillars in our cultural, social, and economic life. Diverse in character, proud in heritage, they are greatly enriching the American melting pot.

Hispanics seek only the full rights of citizenship—in education, in law enforcement, in housing—and an equal opportunity to achieve economic security. Unfortunately, those desires have not always been fulfilled; as in so many other areas, the Carter Administration has been long on rhetoric and short on action in its approach to the Hispanic community.

We pledge to pursue policies that will help to make the opportunities of American life a reality for Hispanics. The economic policies enunciated in this platform will, we believe, create new jobs for Hispanic teenagers and adults and will also open up new business opportunities for them. We also believe there should be local educational programs which enable those who grew up learning another language such as Spanish to become proficient in English while also maintaining their own language and cultural heritage. Neither Hispanics nor any other American citizen should be barred from education or employment opportunities because English is not their first language.

Immigration and Refugee Policy
Residency in the United States is one of the most precious and valued of conditions. The traditional hospitality of the American people has been severely tested by recent events, but it remains the strongest in the world. Republicans are proud that our people have opened their arms and hearts to strangers from abroad and we favor an immigration and refugee policy which is consistent with this tradition. We believe that to the fullest extent possible those immigrants should be admitted who will make a positive contribution to America and who are willing to accept the fundamental American values and way of life. At the same time, United States immigration and refugee policy must reflect the interests of the nation's political and economic well-being. Immigration into this country must not be determined solely by foreign governments or even by the millions of people around the world who wish to come to America. The federal government has a duty to adopt immigration laws and follow enforcement procedures which will fairly and effectively implement the immigration policy desired by American people.

The immediate adoption of this policy is essential to an orderly approach to the great problem of oppressed people seeking entry, so that the deserving can be accepted in America without adding to their hardships.

The refugee problem is an international problem and every effort should be made to coordinate plans for absorbing refugee populations with regional bodies, such as the Organization of American States and the Association of Southeast Asian Nations, on a global basis.

1984

Our history is a story about immigrants. We are proud that America still symbolizes hope and promise to the world. We have shown unparalleled generosity to the persecuted and to those seeking a better life. In return, they have helped to make a great land greater still.

We affirm our country's absolute right to control its borders. Those desiring to enter must comply with our immigration laws. Failure to do so not only is an offense to the American people but is fundamentally unjust to those in foreign lands patiently waiting for legal entry. We will preserve the principle of family reunification.

With the estimates of the number of illegal aliens in the United States ranging as high as 12 million and better than one million more entering each year, we believe it is critical that responsible reforms of our immigration laws be made to enable us to regain control of our borders.

The flight of oppressed people in search of freedom has created pressures beyond the capacity of any one nation. The refugee problem is global and requires the cooperation of all democratic nations. We commend the President for encouraging other countries to assume greater refugee responsibilities.

1988

We welcome those from other lands who bring to America their ideals and industry. At the same time, we insist upon our country's absolute right to control its borders. We call upon our allies to join us in the responsibility shared by all democratic nations for resettlement of refugees, especially those fleeing communism in Southeast Asia.

1992

New Members of the American Family
Our Nation of immigrants continues to welcome those seeking a better life. This reflects our past, when some newcomers fled intolerance; some sought prosperity; some came as slaves. All suffered and sacrificed but hoped their children would have a better life. All searched for a shared vision—and found one in America. Today we are stronger for our diversity.

Illegal entry into the United States, on the other hand, threatens the social compact on which immigration is based. That is, the nation accepts immigrants and is enriched by their determination and values. Illegal immigration, on the other hand, undermines the integrity of border communities and already crowded urban neighborhoods. We will build on the already announced strengthening of the Border Patrol to better coordinate interdiction of illegal entrants through greater cross-border cooperation. Specifically, we will increase the size of the Border Patrol in order to meet the increasing need to stop illegal immigration and we will equip the Border Patrol with the tools, technologies, and structures necessary to secure the border.

We will seek stiff penalties for those who smuggle illegal aliens into the country, and for those who produce or sell fraudulent documents. We also will reduce incentives to enter the United States by promoting initiatives like the North American Free Trade Agreement [NAFTA]. In creating new economic opportunity in Mexico, a NAFTA removes the incentive to cross the border illegally in search of work.

1996

A Sensible Immigration Policy
As a nation of immigrants, we welcome those who follow our laws and come to our land to seek a better life. New Americans strengthen our economy, enrich our culture, and defend the nation in war and in peace. At the same time, we are determined to reform the system by which we welcome them to the American family. We must set immigration at manageable levels, balance the competing goals of uniting families of our citizens and admitting specially talented persons, and end asylum abuses through expedited exclusion of false claimants.

Bill Clinton's immigration record does not match his rhetoric. While talking tough on illegal immigration, he has proposed a reduction in the number of border patrol agents authorized by the Republicans in Congress, has opposed the most successful border control program in decades (Operation Hold the Line in Texas), has opposed Proposition 187 in California, which 60 percent of Californians supported, and has opposed Republican efforts to ensure that non-citizens do not take advantage of expensive welfare programs. Unlike Bill Clinton, we stand with the American people on immigration policy and will continue to reform and enforce our immigration laws to ensure that they reflect America's national interest.

We also support efforts to secure our borders from the threat of illegal immigration. Illegal immigration has reached crisis proportions, with more than four million illegal aliens now present in the United States. That number, growing by 300,000 each year, burdens taxpayers, strains public services, takes jobs, and increases crime. Republicans in both the House and Senate have passed bills that tighten border enforcement, speed up deportation of criminal aliens, toughen penalties for overstaying visas, and streamline the Immigration and Naturalization Service.

Illegal aliens should not receive public benefits other than emergency aid, and those who become parents while illegally in the United States should not be qualified to claim benefits for their offspring. Legal immigrants should depend for assistance on their sponsors, who are legally responsible for their financial well-being, not the American taxpayers. Just as we require "deadbeat dads" to provide for the children they bring into the world, we should require "deadbeat sponsors" to provide for the immigrants they bring into the country. We support a constitutional amendment or constitutionally valid legislation declaring that children born in the United States of parents who are not legally present in the United States or who are not long-term residents are not automatically citizens.

We endorse the Dole/Coverdell [Senators Bob Dole and Paul Coverdell] proposal to make crimes of domestic violence, stalking, child abuse, child neglect, and child abandonment committed by aliens residing in this country deportable offenses under our immigration laws.

We call for harsh penalties against exploiters who smuggle illegal aliens and for those who profit from the production of false documents. Republicans believe that by eliminating the magnet for illegal immigration, increasing border security, enforcing our immigration laws, and producing counterfeit-proof documents, we will finally put an end to the illegal immigration crisis. We oppose the creation of any national ID card.

From Many, One

. . . English, our common language, provides a shared foundation which has allowed people from every corner of the world to come together to build the American nation. The use of English is indispensable to all who wish to participate fully in our society and realize the American dream. As Bob Dole has said: "For more than two centuries now, English has been a force for unity, indispensable to the process of transforming untold millions of immigrants from all parts of the globe into citizens of the most open and free society the world has ever seen." For newcomers, learning the English language has always been the fastest route to the mainstream of American life. That should be the goal of bilingual education programs. We support the official recognition of English as the nation's common language. We advocate foreign language training in our schools and retention of heritage languages in homes and cultural institutions.

Foreign language fluency is also an essential component of America's competitiveness in the world market.

2000

From Many, One

Our country's ethnic diversity within a shared national culture is unique in all the world. We benefit from our differences, but we must also strengthen the ties that bind us to one another. Foremost among those is the flag. Its deliberate desecration is not "free speech" but an assault against both our proud history and our greatest hopes. We therefore support a constitutional amendment that will restore to the people, through their elected representatives, their right to safeguard Old Glory.

Another sign of our unity is the role of English as our common language. It has enabled people from every corner of the world to come together to build this nation. For newcomers, it has always been the fastest route to the mainstream of American life. English empowers. That is why fluency in English must be the goal of bilingual education programs. We support the recognition of English as the nation's common language. At the same time, mastery of other languages is important for America's competitiveness in the world market. We advocate foreign language training in our schools and the fostering of respect for other languages and cultures throughout our society.

We have reaped enormous human capital in the genius and talent and industry of those who have escaped nations captive to totalitarianism. Our country still attracts the best and brightest to invent here, create wealth here, improve the quality of life here. As a nation of immigrants, we welcome all new Americans who have entered lawfully and are prepared to follow our laws and provide for themselves and their families. In their search for a better life, they strengthen our economy, enrich our culture, and defend the nation in war and in peace. To ensure fairness for those wishing to reside in this country, and to meet the manpower needs of our expanding economy, a total overhaul of the immigration system is sorely needed.

The administration's lax enforcement of our borders has led to tragic exploitation of smuggled immigrants, and untold suffering, at the hands of law-breakers. We call for harsh penalties against smugglers and those who provide fake documents. We oppose the creation of any national ID card.

Because free trade is the most powerful force for the kind of development that creates a middle class and offers opportunity at home, the long-term solution for illegal immigration is economic growth in Mexico, Central America, and the Caribbean. In the short run, however, decisive action is needed. We therefore endorse the recommendations of the U.S. Commission on Immigration Reform:

- Restore credibility to enforcement by devoting more resources both to border control and to internal operations.
- Reorganize family unification preferences to give priority to spouses and children, rather than extended family members.
- Emphasize needed skills in determining eligibility for admission.
- Overhaul the failed Labor Certification Program to end the huge delays in matching qualified workers with urgent work.
- Reform the Immigration and Naturalization Service by splitting its functions into two agencies, one focusing on enforcement and one exclusively devoted to service.

The education reforms we propose elsewhere in this platform will, over time, greatly increase the number of highly qualified workers in all sectors of the American economy. To meet immediate needs, however, we support increasing the number of H-1B visas to ensure high-tech workers in specialized positions, provided such workers do not pose a national security risk; and we will expand the H-2A program for the temporary agricultural workers so important to the nation's farms.

2004

Border Security
Our nation has been enriched by immigrants seeking a better life. In many cases, immigrants of the past fled violence and oppression searching for peace and freedom. All suffered and sacrificed but hoped for a better future for their children in America. Our nation has been enriched by their determination, energy, and diversity.

Ensuring the integrity of our borders is vital to ensuring the safety of our citizens. We must know the identity of all visitors who enter the United States, and we must know when they leave. The US-VISIT system, which uses biometric data to better track the entry and exit of foreign travelers, has been implemented at more than 115 airports and is presently being implemented at land border crossings. Reconnaissance cameras, border patrol agents, and unmanned aerial flights have all been increased at our borders.

We must strengthen our Border Patrol to stop illegal crossings, and we will equip the Border Patrol with the tools, technologies, structures, and sufficient force necessary to secure the border. We will seek stiff penalties for

those who smuggle illegal aliens into the country and for those who sell fraudulent documents. We urge continued support for state, local, and federal law enforcement to work in a cohesive manner in securing our borders to prevent illegal entry.

Supporting Humane and Legal Immigration
The Republican Party supports reforming the immigration system to ensure that it is legal, safe, orderly and humane. It also supports measures to ensure that the immigration system is structured to address the needs of national security. America is a stronger and better nation because of the hard work and entrepreneurial spirit of immigrants, and the Republican Party honors them. A growing economy requires a growing number of workers, and President Bush has proposed a new temporary worker program that applies when no Americans can be found to fill the jobs. This new program would allow workers who currently hold jobs to come out of the shadows and to participate legally in America's economy. It would allow men and women who enter the program to apply for citizenship in the same manner as those who apply from outside the United States. There must be strong workplace enforcement with tough penalties against employees and employers who violate immigration laws. We oppose amnesty because it would have the effect of encouraging illegal immigration and would give an unfair advantage to those who have broken our laws.

To better ensure that immigrants enter the United States only through legal means that allow for verification of their identity, reconnaissance cameras, border patrol agents, and unmanned aerial flights have all been increased at the border. In addition, Border Patrol agents now have sweeping new powers to deport illegal aliens without having first to go through the cumbersome process of allowing the illegal alien to have a hearing before an immigration judge. We support these efforts to enforce the law while welcoming immigrants who enter America through legal avenues.

2008

Immigration, National Security, and the Rule of Law
Immigration policy is a national security issue, for which we have one test: Does it serve the national interest? By that standard, Republicans know America can have a strong immigration system without sacrificing the rule of law.

Enforcing the Rule of Law at the Border and Throughout the Nation
Border security is essential to national security. In an age

of terrorism, drug cartels, and criminal gangs, allowing millions of unidentified persons to enter and remain in this country poses grave risks to the sovereignty of the United States and the security of its people. We simply must be able to track who is entering and leaving our country.

Our determination to uphold the rule of law begins with more effective enforcement, giving our agents the tools and resources they need to protect our sovereignty, completing the border fence quickly and securing the borders, and employing complementary strategies to secure our ports of entry. Experience shows that enforcement of existing laws is effective in reducing and reversing illegal immigration.

Our commitment to the rule of law means smarter enforcement at the workplace, against illegal workers and lawbreaking employers alike, along with those who practice identity theft and traffic in fraudulent documents. As long as jobs are available in the United States, economic incentives to enter illegally will persist. But we must empower employers so they can know with confidence that those they hire are permitted to work. That means that the E-Verify system—which is an internet-based system that verifies the employment authorization and identity of employees—must be reauthorized. A phased in requirement that employers use the E-Verify system must be enacted.

The rule of law means guaranteeing to law enforcement the tools and coordination to deport criminal aliens without delay—and correcting court decisions that have made deportation so difficult. It means enforcing the law against those who overstay their visas, rather than letting millions flout the generosity that gave them temporary entry. It means imposing maximum penalties on those who smuggle illegal aliens into the U.S., both for their lawbreaking and for their cruel exploitation. It means requiring cooperation among federal, state and local law enforcement and real consequences, including the denial of federal funds, for self-described sanctuary cities, which stand in open defiance of the federal and state statutes that expressly prohibit such sanctuary policies, and which endanger the lives of U.S. citizens. It does not mean driver's licenses for illegal aliens, nor does it mean that states should be allowed to flout the federal law barring them from giving in-state tuition rates to illegal aliens, nor does it mean that illegal aliens should receive social security benefits, or other public benefits, except as provided by federal law.

We oppose amnesty. The rule of law suffers if government policies encourage or reward illegal activity. The American people's rejection of en masse legalizations is especially appropriate given the federal government's past failures to enforce the law.

Embracing Immigrant Communities

Today's immigrants are walking in the steps of most other Americans' ancestors, seeking the American dream and contributing culturally and economically to our nation. We celebrate the industry and love of liberty of these fellow Americans.

Both government and the private sector must do more to foster legally present immigrants' integration into American life to advance respect for the rule of law and a common American identity. It is a national disgrace that the first experience most new Americans have is with a dysfunctional immigration bureaucracy defined by delay and confusion; we will no longer tolerate those failures.

In our multi-ethnic nation, everyone—immigrants and native-born alike—must embrace our core values of liberty, equality, meritocracy, and respect for human dignity and the rights of women.

One sign of our unity is our English language. For newcomers, it has always been the fastest route to prosperity in America. English empowers. We support English as the official language in our nation, while welcoming the ethnic diversity in the United States and the territories, including language. Immigrants should be encouraged to learn English. English is the accepted language of business, commerce, and legal proceedings, and it is essential as a unifying cultural force. It is also important, as part of cultural integration, that our schools provide better education in U.S. history and civics for all children, thereby fostering a commitment to our national motto, *E Pluribus Unum.*

We are grateful to the thousands of new immigrants, many of them not yet citizens, who are serving in the Armed Forces. Their patriotism is inspiring; it should remind the institutions of civil society of the need to embrace newcomers, assist their journey to full citizenship, and help their communities avoid patterns of isolation.

Welcoming Refugees

Our country continues to accept refugees from troubled lands all over the world. In some cases, these are people who stood with America in dangerous times, and they have first call on our hospitality. We oppose, however, the granting of refugee status on the basis of lifestyle or other non-political factors

2012

The Rule of Law: Legal Immigration

The greatest asset of the American economy is the American worker. Just as immigrant labor helped build our country in the past, today's legal immigrants are making vital contributions in every aspect of our national life. Their industry and commitment to American values strengthens our economy, enriches our culture, and enables us to better understand and more effectively compete with the rest of the world. Illegal immigration undermines those benefits and affects U.S. workers. In an age of terrorism, drug cartels, human trafficking, and criminal gangs, the presence of millions of unidentified persons in this country poses grave risks to the safety and the sovereignty of the United States. Our highest priority, therefore, is to secure the rule of law both at our borders and at ports of entry.

We recognize that for most of those seeking entry into this country, the lack of respect for the rule of law in their homelands has meant economic exploitation and political oppression by corrupt elites. In this country, the rule of law guarantees equal treatment to every individual, including more than one million immigrants to whom we grant permanent residence every year. That is why we oppose any form of amnesty for those who, by intentionally violating the law, disadvantage those who have obeyed it. Granting amnesty only rewards and encourages more law breaking. We support the mandatory use of the Systematic Alien Verification for Entitlements (S.A.V.E.) program—an internet-based system that verifies the lawful presence of applicants—prior to the granting of any State or federal government entitlements or IRS refunds. We insist upon enforcement at the workplace through verification systems so that jobs can be available to all legal workers. Use of the E-verify program—an internet-based system that verifies the employment authorization and identity of employees—must be made mandatory nationwide. State enforcement efforts in the workplace must be welcomed, not attacked. When Americans need jobs, it is absolutely essential that we protect them from illegal labor in the workplace. In addition, it is why we demand tough penalties for those who practice identity theft, deal in fraudulent documents, and traffic in human beings. It is why we support Republican legislation to give the Department of Homeland Security long-term detention authority to keep dangerous but undeportable aliens off our streets, expedite expulsion of criminal aliens, and make gang membership a deportable offense.

The current Administration's approach to immigration has undermined the rule of law at every turn. It has lessened work-site enforcement—and even allows the illegal aliens it does uncover to walk down the street to the next employer—and challenged legitimate State efforts to keep communities safe, suing them for trying to enforce the law when the federal government refuses to do so. It has created a backdoor amnesty program unrecognized in law, granting worker authorization to illegal aliens, and shown little regard for the life-and-death situations facing the men and women of the border patrol.

Perhaps worst of all, the current Administration has failed to enforce the legal means for workers or employers who want to operate within the law. In contrast, a Republican Administration and Congress will partner with local governments through cooperative enforcement agreements in Section 287g of the Immigration and Nationality Act to make communities safer for all and will consider, in light of both current needs and historic practice, the utility of a legal and reliable source of foreign labor where needed through a new guest worker program. We will create humane procedures to encourage illegal aliens to return home voluntarily, while enforcing the law against those who overstay their visas.

State efforts to reduce illegal immigration must be encouraged, not attacked. The pending Department of Justice lawsuits against Arizona, Alabama, South Carolina, and Utah must be dismissed immediately. The double-layered fencing on the border that was enacted by Congress in 2006, but never completed, must finally be built. In order to restore the rule of law, federal funding should be denied to sanctuary cities that violate federal law and endanger their own citizens, and federal funding should be denied to universities that provide in-state tuition rates to illegal aliens, in open defiance of federal law.

We are grateful to the thousands of new immigrants, many of them not yet citizens, who are serving in the Armed Forces. Their patriotism should encourage us all to embrace the newcomers legally among us, assist their journey to full citizenship, and help their communities avoid isolation from the mainstream of society. To that end, while we encourage the retention and transmission of heritage tongues, we support English as the nation's official language, a unifying force essential for the educational and economic advancement of—not only immigrant communities—but also our nation as a whole.

Source: Republican Party.

Glossary

A

acculturation. The process by which immigrants take on aspects of American culture and blend them with their native culture.

affidavit of support. A legal document required of someone who wants to sponsor an immigrant, stating that this person will take financial responsibility for the immigrant once she or he enters the country.

Alien Contract Labor Law. An 1885 law (also known as the Foran Act) that restricted the importation of contract laborers.

Alien Enemies Act. A 1798 law that gave the president the right to deport aliens engaging in treasonous activity; allowed to lapse in 1801.

Alien Land Law. A 1913 California law that prohibited landownership by "aliens ineligible for citizenship"; it primarily targeted Japanese immigrants.

alien migrant interdiction operations (AMIOs). U.S. Coast Guard operations intended to control seagoing illegal immigration to the United States.

Alien Registration Act. A 1940 law that required all aliens over the age of fourteen to register annually with the government.

aliens. Nationals of another country living in the United States.

American Colonization Society. An organization established in 1816 to resettle freed slaves and free blacks from the United States in the African colony and, after 1847, country of Liberia.

American Defense Society. An anti-German and anti-immigration organization formed during World War I.

American GI Forum. A political organization created in 1948 by Mexican American veterans of the U.S. armed forces.

American Party. *See* Know-Nothings.

American Protective League. An anti-German organization of the World War I era.

Americanization. The effort to force or teach immigrants to adopt American ways of life.

AMIOs. *See* alien migrant interdiction operations.

Amish. A group of Germans who immigrated to Pennsylvania in the 1700s to practice their dissenting Christian faith.

amnesty. Permission granted by the government for an illegal immigrant to stay in the United States legally.

Anglo-Saxon. Technically the term for people of English descent, it is commonly applied to all white, native-born Protestant Americans.

antimiscegenation laws. Laws that once banned marriage between people of different races; ruled unconstitutional by the U.S. Supreme Court in 1967.

Armenians. A primarily Christian minority of the Middle East.

Ashkenazim. The Hebrew word for Jews from Eastern Europe.

assimilation. The process by which immigrants exchange aspects of their native culture for those of an American way of life.

Assyrians. A Christian minority of Iraq.

asylum. The status of a refugee who is permitted to stay in a host country.

Austria-Hungary. A pre–World War I empire in central and Eastern Europe that sent millions of immigrants to the United States in the late nineteenth and early twentieth centuries.

Aztlán. A Mexican American term for the Southwestern region of the United States that belonged to Mexico before the Mexican-American War of 1846–1848; also used to refer to the historic homeland of the indigenous Nahua people of Mexico.

B

Back to the Soil. A Jewish immigrant movement of the late nineteenth and early twentieth centuries that sought to establish agricultural colonies in the United States.

Bala-vihar. An organization that offers religious instruction to young Hindu immigrants.

barrio. A predominantly Latino neighborhood.

Basques. A minority ethnic group from northern Spain and southern France.

Bilingual Education Act. Title VII of the Elementary and Secondary Education Act, this 1968 act provides funds for planning and implementation of language-education programs for minority-language speakers.

birth rule. Under the Immigration and Nationality Act of 1965, this rule defined an individual's origin as the place where the person was born, not where he or she last lived.

Black Hand. Late nineteenth-century criminal gangs among Italian immigrants.

black-market babies. Foreign-born babies who are acquired illegally and adopted by American parents.

BMNA. *See* Buddhist Mission of North America.

boat people. Southeast Asian refugees who fled the region's communist-led countries in the late 1970s and 1980s, largely on unseaworthy craft.

Bolsheviks. A popular term for leftist radicals who supported the Russian Revolution of 1917; often applied to immigrants.

Border Patrol. The division of the U.S. Department of Homeland Security charged with guarding the nation's land borders and some coastal waters.

Bracero Program. From 1942 to 1964, a program that granted temporary residence in the United States to farm laborers from Mexico; also known as the Labor Importation Program of 1942–1964.

braceros. Farm laborers from Mexico who were allowed to work in the United States temporarily between 1942 and 1964 as part of the Bracero Program.

brain drain. A popular term for a phenomenon whereby highly educated or skilled people from the developing world move to the industrialized countries of the West.

Buddhist Churches of America. *See* Buddhist Mission of North America.

Buddhist Mission of North America (BMNA). Originally the Young Men's Buddhist Association, an organization founded in San Francisco in 1899 that provided services to Japanese and other Buddhist immigrants to the United States; later called the Buddhist Churches of America.

Buford. The name of the ship on which hundreds of supposed communist aliens were deported to the Soviet Union in 1919.

Bureau of Immigration. Established in 1891, the first federal agency charged with regulating immigration to the United States; merged with the Bureau of Naturalization in 1933 to form the U.S. Immigration and Naturalization Service.

Burlingame Treaty. An 1868 treaty (also known as the Burlingame-Seward Treaty) between China and the United States that allowed free immigration between the two countries.

C

Cajuns. Slang for Acadians, a French-speaking people from eastern Canada who immigrated to Louisiana in the eighteenth century after the French and Indian War led to the British takeover of Canada.

Camorra. An organized crime syndicate among emigrants from Naples, Italy.

Canada-Quebec Accord. A 1991 agreement that allowed the province of Quebec to manage its own immigration affairs.

CANF. *See* Cuban American National Foundation.

casita. Spanish for "little house," a small structure built to remind Puerto Ricans and other Latino immigrants of their homeland.

CBP. *See* Customs and Border Protection.

Celestials. A pejorative nineteenth-century term for immigrants from China, the so-called Celestial Kingdom.

chain migration. A scholarly term for the process by which one member of a family or a community immigrates first, followed by other members of the same family or community.

Chicana. A Mexican American woman.

Chicano. A Mexican American man.

Chinese Exclusion Act. An 1882 act that banned virtually all Chinese immigration to the United States for ten years; the law was renewed in 1892 and 1902, made permanent in 1904, and repealed in 1943.

Chinese Six Companies. Benevolent associations that provided guidance, lodging, and care for Chinese immigrants in the United States.

CIC. *See* Citizenship and Immigration Canada.

Citizenship and Immigration Canada (CIC). The main government agency in Canada charged with immigration and naturalization affairs.

closet ethnics. People who try to hide their ethnicity so as to blend into the majority culture.

colonias. Literally "colonies," a Spanish term for makeshift communities of migrant workers; often used in Mexican and U.S. border regions.

Colyer et al. v. Skeffington. A 1920 ruling by the U.S. District Court in Massachusetts that declared that membership in the Communist Party was not, in and of itself, a legal cause for deportation. (On other grounds, the U.S. Court of Appeals for the First Circuit reversed this ruling in 1922 in *Skeffington v. Katz eff.*)

Committee of Vigilance. An anti-immigrant organization formed in the 1850s in San Francisco.

Comprehensive Plan of Action (CPA). A 1989 program implemented jointly by the United Nations and the Vietnamese government to allow for the orderly emigration of Vietnamese nationals.

conditional entrants. A bureaucratic term for refugees.

conquistadores. Literally "conquerors," a Spanish term for the Spaniards who conquered and settled the Americas in the sixteenth, seventeenth, and eighteenth centuries, especially Mexico, Peru, and the Southern and Southwestern parts of the present-day United States.

contiguous zone. A region 12 to 24 miles (20 to 40 kilometers) off the U.S. coast, just outside American territorial waters; under international law, countries may interdict illegal immigrants within this zone.

contract labor. A term for immigrants whose journey to the United States is paid for by prospective employers or their agents; usually brought in groups and forced to work off the cost of the journey.

Contras. A U.S.-financed guerrilla army that attacked the leftist Sandinista government of Nicaragua in the 1980s.

contratista. A Mexican Spanish term for a person who brings contract laborers into the United States.

coolies. A derogatory term applied to Chinese workers in the nineteenth century.

core nations. A term referring to the developed or industrialized countries of Western Europe, North America, Japan, Australasia, and elsewhere.

Cosa Nostra, La. *See* Mafia.

cottage industry. Manufacturing that goes on in the home.

Court Interpreters Act. A 1978 federal law that requires foreign-language interpreters in civil cases initiated by the U.S. government in which the plaintiff or defendant cannot adequately speak English.

coyote. A slang term for someone who smuggles immigrants over the Mexican border into the United States for a fee.

CPA. *See* Comprehensive Plan of Action.

CPS. *See* Current Population Survey.

Creole. A term for people from the Caribbean and Latin America who are of mixed European, African, and Native American heritage; also a hybrid European, African, and Native American language spoken among many people in the Caribbean and Latin America.

Cuban American National Foundation (CANF). The main organization representing the interests of exiled Cubans in the United States; active in anti–Fidel Castro politics.

Current Population Survey (CPS). Annual analysis of the U.S. population conducted by the U.S. Bureau of Labor Statistics and the U.S. Census Bureau; includes data on immigrants and ethnic groups.

Customs and Border Protection. Since 2003, the agency within the U.S. Department of Homeland Security responsible for protecting America's borders and ports of entry against illegal aliens, smuggled goods, and contraband; successor agency to the U.S. Customs Service and the Border Patrol division of the U.S. Immigration and Naturalization Service.

D

diaspora. The voluntary or involuntary exile of a community or ethnic group to other countries or regions of the globe.

displaced persons (DPs). The official term for World War II–era European refugees.

Displaced Persons Act. A 1948 law that permitted 200,000 refugees displaced by World War II, most of them Europeans, to immigrate to the United States.

DPs. *See* displaced persons.

DREAM Act. An acronym for the Development, Relief, and Education for Alien Minors Act, a proposed law first introduced in the U.S. Congress in 2001—but not passed—that would grant amnesty to teenage and young adult immigrants who were brought into the United States illegally as minors; the term also is used to refer to a 2012 executive order issued by President Barack Obama granting a two-year waiver from deportation for the same group of illegal immigrants. Also used to refer to some state acts, enacted in lieu of federal legislation.

Dutch. A variation of *Deutsch,* meaning "German," that refers to Americans of German descent in the eighteenth and nineteenth centuries.

E

Edict of Nantes. A 1598 edict that allowed for tolerance of Protestant Huguenots in France; its revocation in 1685 sent thousands of Huguenots to America.

el Norte. Spanish for "the north," a popular Latino immigrant term for the United States.

émigré. A person who emigrates from his or her native country; also used for someone who emigrates because of political or ethnic persecution.

employer sanctions. Fines assessed against employers who hire undocumented workers.

employment-based preference. A legal category that allows immigrants with special skills or talents to live and work in the United States.

enclave. A geographically contained community of immigrants from a particular country or region, such as a Chinatown or a Latino barrio.

enganchista (or *enganchador*). A Mexican Spanish term for a person who brings contract laborers into the United States.

English-only. The name of a movement to make English the official language of the United States.

Enhanced Border Security and Visa Entry Reform Act. A 2002 law aimed at enhancing security against illegal border crossings and people who try to enter the United States under false pretenses or stay beyond the limit set by legal visas.

ESL. English as a second language.

Espionage Act. A 1917 law intended to prosecute aliens, mostly Germans, who obstructed the military draft during World War I.

ethnic cleansing. A process by which members of a specific ethnic or religious group are forced to leave a country or region, typically under the threat of or as the result of violence.

Executive Order 9066. A 1942 order issued by President Franklin D. Roosevelt that called for the internment of Japanese nationals and Japanese Americans living in the Western United States.

exile. A person who is unable to return to his or her homeland for political or legal reasons; sometimes a voluntary situation in which the person chooses not to go back.

expansionist. A term for someone who wants to maintain or expand the number of visas granted to legal permanent residents in the United States.

F

FAIR. *See* Federation for American Immigration Reform.

Federation for American Immigration Reform (FAIR). An organization that advocates strict limits on legal immigration and tougher controls on illegal immigration.

Federation of Hindu Associations (FHA). An umbrella group for advocacy and service organizations that aid immigrants of the Hindu faith.

female genital mutilation (FGM). A custom prevalent in Africa and the Middle East whereby a woman's genitalia are mutilated in order to prevent sexual arousal.

FGM. *See* female genital mutilation.

FHA. *See* Federation of Hindu Associations.

fifth column. A popular term for traitors, often used against immigrants, especially in wartime.

first world. A term referring to the industrialized or developed parts of the globe.

G

Galicia. A region in present-day Poland that sent many immigrants to the United States in the late nineteenth and early twentieth centuries.

Gam Saan. Literally "Gold Mountain," a Chinese term referring to California and the United States in the nineteenth century.

genocide. The total or near-total destruction of an ethnic or religious group.

Gentlemen's Agreement. An accord reached between President Theodore Roosevelt and the imperial government of Japan in 1907 that restricted Japanese immigration to the United States.

glasnost. A Russian term meaning "openness" that refers to the lifting of restrictions on political expression in the Soviet Union following the rise to power of Mikhail Gorbachev in 1985.

global theory. A political science theory postulating that the developed world dominates the developing world in a pattern similar to the way in which the ruling class within a country dominates all other classes.

globalization. The process by which the world's economy becomes increasingly integrated.

Gold Mountain. *See Gam Saan.*

Great Migration. The large flow of Puritans from England to New England from 1629 to 1640; also refers to the vast movement of African Americans from the rural South to the urban North and West in the twentieth century.

green card. A popular term for a permit to live and work in the United States on a permanent basis; so called for the former color of the document.

Guadalupe Hidalgo, Treaty of. An 1848 treaty that ended the Mexican-American War; among other provisions, it granted full U.S. citizenship to Mexican nationals living in territory ceded to the United States.

Guantánamo Bay. An American military base in Cuba that is often used to hold illegal immigrants from Haiti trying to make their way into the United States; also used as a detention center for "enemy combatants" captured in the War on Terror following the September 11, 2001, terrorist attacks.

Gullah. People of African descent who live on the offshore islands of Georgia and South Carolina; also refers to the distinct Afro-English language that they speak.

H

H-1B visa. A special visa that allows foreigners with certain desirable skills to work in the United States.

H-2A Temporary Agricultural Program. Under the Immigration Reform and Control Act (IRCA) of 1986, this program allows for the employment of immigrant workers in agriculture if no American citizens are available for such work.

Haitian Refugee Immigration Fairness Act. A 1998 law designed to allow more Haitian refugees to enter the United States legally.

Hart-Celler Bill. Congressional bill upon which the Immigration and Nationality Act of 1965 was based.

hate crime. A violent attack motivated by hatred for a person's race, religion, ethnicity, sexual preference, or other group identity.

head tax. A tax imposed during the nineteenth and early twentieth centuries on shipping companies or ship captains for every immigrant brought into the United States.

hegemony. A political science term referring to the process by which one class within a nation or one nation within a region dominates those around it.

Hispanic. A term used for people who come from Spanish- and Portuguese-speaking countries in Latin America and Europe; sometimes used interchangeably with the term "Latino."

Hmong. A mountain people from Laos who aided the United States during the Vietnam War and immigrated in large numbers to the United States after the communist takeover of Laos in 1975.

Huguenots. French Protestants, many of whom were forced to immigrate to America in the seventeenth and eighteenth centuries because of official religious persecution.

hui. See kye.

I

ICE. *See* Immigrations and Customs Enforcement.

IIRIRA. *See* Illegal Immigration Reform and Immigrant Responsibility Act.

ILGWU. *See* International Ladies' Garment Workers' Union.

Illegal Immigration Reform and Immigrant Responsibility Act (IIRIRA). A 1996 law intended to stop the flow of illegal immigrants into the United States through stepped-up border controls and increased fines and penalties.

Immigration Act of 1990. Legislation that modified the Immigration Reform Act of 1986; the law changed the immigration preference system by making family reunification easier and opening up more immigration to people with specialized skills and occupations.

Immigration and Customs Enforcement (ICE). The successor agency to the criminal investigative, detention, and deportation components of the U.S. Immigration and Naturalization Service, as well as the U.S. Customs Service; began operation in 2003 as part of the U.S. Department of Homeland Security.

Immigration and Nationality Act. A 1952 law (also known as the McCarran-Walter Act) that removed some restrictions on immigration but added others; also the popular name for a landmark 1965 law that ended national-origins quotas for immigration, which technically were amendments to the 1952 act.

Immigration and Naturalization Service (INS). Prior to 2003, the agency within the U.S. Department of Justice that executed U.S. immigration and naturalization law; since then, the responsibilities of the INS have been divided among several agencies, including U.S. Immigration and Customs Enforcement and U.S. Citizenship and Immigration Services, under the aegis of the U.S. Department of Homeland Security.

Immigration Reform Act. *See* Illegal Immigration Reform and Immigrant Responsibility Act.

Immigration Reform and Control Act (IRCA). A 1986 law (also known as the Simpson-Mazzoli Act) designed to reduce illegal immigration by penalizing employers who hire undocumented workers and stepping up border patrols; also granted amnesty to many illegal immigrants residing in the United States since 1982.

incorporation. The process by which immigrants fit themselves into the culture and society of their adopted land.

indentured servants. From the colonial and early national period of American history, immigrants whose passage across the Atlantic Ocean was paid in exchange for a term of labor, usually four to seven years.

Indochina Migration and Refugee Assistance Act. A 1975 law designed to ease entry and settlement of Southeast Asian refugees after the Vietnam War.

Indochinese Refugee Assistance Program (IRAP). A U.S. program of the late 1970s created to deal with the large influx of refugees from Southeast Asia; supplanted by the more comprehensive Refugee Act of 1980.

INS. *See* Immigration and Naturalization Service.

Integrated Surveillance Intelligence System (ISIS). A system for monitoring illegal immigration activity along the U.S.–Mexican border during the 1990s.

Internal Security Act. A restrictive 1950 immigration law.

International Ladies' Garment Workers' Union (ILGWU). The main union of immigrant garment workers in the early twentieth century; in 1995, it became part of UNITE, the Union of Needletrades, Industrial and Textile Employees.

internment, Japanese. An effort during World War II to relocate and incarcerate more than 120,000 West Coast Japanese nationals and Japanese Americans in internment camps scattered throughout the United States.

IRAP. *See* Indochinese Refugee Assistance Program.

IRCA. *See* Immigration Reform and Control Act.

Irish Immigration Reform Movement. A movement organized by Irish American politicians to ease the entry of Irish immigrants into the United States.

Iron Curtain. A Cold War–era term for the border between communist Eastern Europe and capitalist Western Europe.

ISIS. *See* Integrated Surveillance Intelligence System.

issei. A Japanese term for first-generation immigrants in America.

J

JACL. *See* Japanese American Citizens League.

Japanese American Citizens League (JACL). A self-help organization for Japanese Americans founded in 1930.

K

Khmer Rouge. The murderous communist government of Cambodia in the late 1970s that caused millions of deaths and sent hundreds of thousands of refugees abroad.

KKK. *See* Ku Klux Klan.

Know-Nothings. Officially the American Party, an anti-immigrant political party of the mid-nineteenth century; the name refers to the organization's secrecy—members were told to answer "I know nothing" if asked about the party.

ko. See kye.

Ku Klux Klan (KKK). An antiblack terrorist organization founded in the South during Reconstruction and resurrected in the early 1900s as an antiblack, anti-immigrant, anti-Jewish, and anti-Catholic organization.

Kurds. A non-Arab Muslim minority in Iran, Iraq, Turkey, and Syria.

kye. A Korean term for a rotating credit association in which members invest funds and receive combined assets on a rotating basis; also known as a *ko* in Japanese and a *hui* in Chinese.

L

La Raza. A Spanish phrase meaning "the race," used to denote people of Latino background.

Latina. A woman who comes from Mexico, Central America, South America, or the Spanish-speaking islands of the Caribbean.

Latino. A man who comes from Mexico, Central America, South America, or the Spanish-speaking islands of the Caribbean; sometimes used interchangeably with the term "Hispanic."

Lau v. Nichols. A precedent-setting U.S. Supreme Court ruling in 1974 that ordered the San Francisco school district to take affirmative steps to ensure a proper education for minority-language students.

Law of Return. A 1950 Israeli law allowing for the free immigration of all Jewish people to Israel.

League of United Latin American Citizens (LULAC). An important Latino self-help organization that fights for immigrant rights.

Lesbian and Gay Immigration Rights Task Force. The primary U.S. advocacy organization for gay and lesbian immigrants.

Literacy Act. A 1917 law (also known as the Literacy Test Act or the Immigration Act of 1917) that required all immigrants to be literate in their own language or in English.

Lo Wa Kiu. A contemporary term for Chinese who immigrated to the United States several generations ago.

lottery. A system by which immigration visas are granted based on the random drawing of applicant names.

LULAC. *See* League of United Latin American Citizens.

M

Mafia. A term that originally referred to an organized crime syndicate among immigrants from Sicily, also known as La Cosa Nostra; now applied to all organized crime syndicates regardless of ethnic background.

mail-order brides. Women imported to the United States to become brides of American men; many come from the Philippines and Eastern Europe.

Marielitos. Cuban immigrants who came to the United States in large numbers as part of the so-called Mariel boatlift in 1980; named for Puerto Mariel, the Cuban port from which they departed.

McCarran-Walter Act. *See* Immigration and Nationality Act.

MEChA. *See* Movimiento Estudantil Chicano de Aztlán.

melting pot. A somewhat dated expression for the process by which immigrants from various countries merge to form a common American culture.

Mennonites. Religious dissenters who emigrated from Germany to the Middle Colonies of North America in the eighteenth century.

MexAmerica. A popular term for the region along the U.S.–Mexican border.

Mezzogiorno. Italian for "midday," refers to the impoverished region of southern Italy, which was a major sender of immigrants to America in the late nineteenth and early twentieth centuries.

microenterprises. Business enterprises that require very little capitalization to initiate.

Middle Immigration Series. A U.S. Census Bureau population projection that assumes current levels of immigration into the United States.

Minuteman Project. Founded in 2005, a private effort to stop illegal immigrants from entering the United States across the U.S.–Mexican border.

miscegenation. A term for marriage or sexual mixing among people of different races; once considered derogatory.

model minority. A term used to describe high-achieving Asian immigrants; although it is meant positively, it is viewed by the Asian American community as a stereotype.

Molly Maguires. A radical and violent labor movement among Irish immigrants, largely in the mining areas of Pennsylvania, in the late nineteenth century.

Mona Passage. The straits between the Dominican Republic and Puerto Rico through which many illegal immigrants from the Dominican Republic and Haiti seek entrance into the United States.

mosaic. A recent term used to replace "melting pot" to refer to the process by which immigrants fit into American society; emphasizes how immigrant groups retain their native culture as they adjust, rather than blending into a homogeneous American identity.

Movimiento Estudantil Chicano de Aztlán (MEChA). The Chicano Student Movement of Aztlán, a Mexican American student organization created in 1970 by the merger of the United Mexican American Students and the Mexican American Youth Organization.

mutual assistance associations. Self-help organizations established by Vietnamese refugees in the 1970s under federal government supervision.

mutualista. Spanish for "mutual aid society," or self-help organizations among Mexican Americans.

N

NAFTA. *See* North American Free Trade Agreement.

National Council of La Raza. A major Latino pro-immigration organization.

National Security League. An anti-German, anti-immigrant organization that was formed during World War I.

nativism. An anti-immigrant political ideology.

naturalization. The process by which a person gives up one nationality for another and becomes a citizen.

Naturalization Act of 1790. The first American law setting residency and racial requirements for citizenship.

new immigration. A term used to describe the most recent wave of immigrants; in the early and mid-twentieth century, it referred to immigrants from Southern and Eastern Europe who arrived between 1885 and World War I; in the late twentieth and early twenty-first centuries, it referred to immigrants who arrived after 1965, when national-origins quotas were ended.

New Irish. Irish immigrants since the 1980s.

newly industrialized countries (NICs). Mainly in East Asia, those countries that achieved rapid economic development in the late twentieth century.

NICs. *See* newly industrialized countries.

nikkeijin. A Japanese term for foreign nationals of Japanese descent.

nisei. A Japanese term for second-generation immigrants in America.

North American Free Trade Agreement (NAFTA). A 1994 treaty that established a free trade zone encompassing Canada, Mexico, and the United States.

O

ODP. *See* Orderly Departure Program.

Office of Refugee Resettlement. A temporary federal agency established in 1975 to oversee the integration of Vietnamese refugees into American life; turned into a permanent agency by federal legislation in 1980, it is now part of the Department of Health and Human Services.

olim. A Hebrew term for immigrants to Israel.

Operation Blockade. A program implemented during the 1990s, also known as Operation Hold the Line, to control illegal immigration over the U.S.–Mexican border in El Paso, Texas.

Operation Boulder. A 1970s program designed to combat terrorism; criticized for being anti–Arab American.

Operation Eagle Pull. A 1975 operation that pulled those who had worked for the United States out of Cambodia following that country's takeover by the communist Khmer Rouge regime.

Operation Gatekeeper. A 1990s program designed to strengthen the U.S.–Mexican border at San Diego, California, against illegal immigrant entries.

Operation Hold the Line. *See* Operation Blockade.

Operation Safeguard. A 1990s program designed to strengthen the U.S.–Mexican border in Arizona against illegal immigrant entries.

Operation Wetback. A program implemented in the 1950s to locate and deport Mexican immigrants living illegally in the United States.

Orderly Departure Program (ODP). A joint effort by the United Nations and the Vietnamese government to allow people who wanted to leave Vietnam to do so in a safe and orderly manner; it was begun in 1979 and suspended in 1986.

P

Pale of Settlement, the. An area within pre-1917 Russia outside of which Jews could not legally reside; corresponds largely to present-day eastern Poland, Belarus, and Ukraine.

Palmer raids. Raids conducted in 1919 and 1920 by U.S. Attorney General A. Mitchell Palmer largely against immigrant radicals.

paper sons/paper daughters. Chinese immigrants who came to the United States prior to the 1965 immigration reforms by falsely claiming to be members of families who were already living legally in the United States.

parachute kids. A popular expression for the children of wealthy Asian parents who attend and live at private schools in the United States.

parochial school. A school that is run by a religious denomination.

pensionado. A Filipino student whose education in the United States was paid for by the U.S. government; the Pensionado Program lasted from 1903 to 1943.

perestroika. A Russian term for "restructuring" that refers to the dismantling of restrictions on private enterprise in the Soviet Union following the rise to power of Mikhail Gorbachev in 1985.

peripheral nations. A term referring to developing or third-world countries.

permanent legal resident status. The status under which an immigrant legally can live and work in the United States indefinitely without becoming a citizen.

Personal Responsibility and Work Opportunity Reconciliation Act. A 1996 law (also known as the Welfare Reform Act) that ended existing welfare programs, thereby cutting off many benefits to both legal and illegal immigrants.

picture brides. Japanese women who were married to Japanese men in America after their photos were sent to the latter in the late nineteenth and early twentieth centuries.

piecework. Work that is paid for by the piece rather than by the hour; once a mainstay of the garment industry.

pogrom. Systematic attacks and massacres by Cossack (a warrior ethnic group) militia groups on Jews in pre-1917 Russia; often instigated by the czarist government.

post-traumatic stress disorder. A psychological condition of acute fear and stress that is frequent among refugees from war and political persecution.

potato famine. The failure of the Irish potato crop in the 1840s that produced widespread starvation and spurred mass immigration to the United States and Canada; also known as the Irish potato famine or the Great Famine.

Proposition 187. A referendum passed by California voters in 1994 that aimed to cut off most public services for illegal immigrants; ruled largely unconstitutional by federal courts.

Proposition 227. A referendum passed by California voters in 1998 that virtually ended bilingual education in the state's public schools.

PTKs. Professional, technical, and kindred workers; a term used by the U.S. Citizenship and Immigration Services.

public charge. A term for someone—including immigrants—who cannot support himself or herself financially and must receive government aid.

Punjabis. A largely Sikh people from the Punjabi provinces of India and Pakistan; because of their predominance among South Asian immigrants, "Punjabi" has become a catchall term used to describe all Indian and Pakistani immigrants.

Puritans. English religious dissenters who emigrated to New England in the seventeenth century.

Q

Quakers. *See* Society of Friends.

Quota Act of 1921. Legislation (also known as the first Quota Act or the Emergency Quota Act) that limited immigration of various nationalities to 3 percent of their total in the United States as of 1910.

Quota Act of 1924. Legislation (also known as the second Quota Act or the Immigration Act of 1924) that limited immigration of various nationalities to 2 percent of their total in the United States as of 1890.

quotas. A set limit of immigrants allowed into the United States, usually from a specific country or region of the world.

R

Rastafarians. Jamaican immigrants who practice a syncretic faith that combines Christianity and African nationalism.

Real ID Act. A 2005 law that created an enhanced and coordinated national identification system to monitor, among other things, the legal status of U.S. residents and citizens.

Red Scare. The popular name for an anticommunist, antiradical hysteria that swept the United States after World War I, resulting in the arrest and deportation of thousands of left-wing immigrants.

refoulement. A French word meaning "to be driven back" and an international term for sending refugees back to probable persecution in their native land; prohibited under United Nations protocols.

refugee. A person who flees his or her native land because of war, persecution, or natural disaster; generally used to refer to those not leaving for specifically economic reasons.

Refugee Act. A 1980 law that disconnected refugee and immigration policies and adopted the United Nations definition of refugees.

Refugee Relief Act. A 1953 law that granted entry to escapees from communist countries.

remittance. Money sent back to the home country by an immigrant living in another country.

restrictionist. A term for someone who wants to restrict the number of visas granted to legal permanent residents in the United States.

retablo. Spanish for "votive painting," created to express a Catholic devotee's gratitude, for example, for safe passage to the United States.

return immigrants. People who return to their home country after living in another country.

rotating credit association. *See kye.*

S

San Yi Man. A Chinese term for new immigrants.

sanctuary. A place where illegal immigrants are hidden from government authorities.

sanctuary movement. A movement during the 1980s of churches and other concerned groups that protected Central American immigrants who feared persecution in their native countries.

Santeria. A faith popular among Caribbean immigrants that combines indigenous Native American and African religious practices with Catholicism.

satsang. A religious organization for Hindu immigrants.

SAVE. *See* Systematic Alien Verification for Entitlements.

SAW. *See* Special Agricultural Worker exemption.

SB 1070. Formally known as the Support Our Law Enforcement and Safe Neighborhoods Act, SB 1070 (Senate Bill 1070) was a 2010 Arizona law that required, among other things, all immigrants to maintain residency documentation on their person at all times and required local and state law enforcement to inquire into the immigration status of anyone whom officers suspected of being in the country illegally; all of SB 1070 except the last element was declared unconstitutional by the U.S. Supreme Court in 2012.

Scotch-Irish. *See* Scots-Irish.

Scots-Irish. Immigrants originally from Scotland who were resettled by English authorities in what is now Northern Ireland beginning in the sixteenth century.

seasoning. Refers to the initial period of arrival during which settlers physically adjusted to the climate of North America in the seventeenth and eighteenth centuries.

Secure Fence Act. A 2006 law that authorized the construction of a security system, including electronic surveillance and barriers of various kinds, to keep out drugs, terrorists, and illegal aliens along the U.S.–Mexican border.

segmented assimilation. The process by which immigrants absorb some elements of their adopted culture and retain elements of their native culture.

Sephardim. A Hebrew term for Jews from the Middle East, North Africa, and parts of Southern Europe.

Sharia. Islamic law based on the Koran and the life teachings of the Prophet Muhammad.

Sikhs. People from India and Pakistan who practice a syncretic religion that combines elements of Hinduism and Islam.

Simpson-Mazzoli Act. *See* Immigration Reform and Control Act.

Slavs. The largest ethnic group in Eastern Europe and Russia.

SLIAG. *See* State Legalization Impact Assistance Grant.

snakehead. A slang term for a person who smuggles Asian immigrants into the United States for a fee.

social capital. Networks of people who can provide human and other resources for economic development.

social Darwinism. A philosophy of the late nineteenth century that maintained that certain ethnic groups—generally Western Europeans—were superior to others and more fit to rule.

social mobility. The capacity to move from one economic level or class to another.

Society of Friends. Popularly known as Quakers, a group of religious dissenters who migrated from England in the seventeenth century and established the colony of Pennsylvania.

Southern Cone. The countries of southern South America: Argentina, Chile, Paraguay, and Uruguay.

Special Agricultural Worker (SAW) exemption. A clause in the 1986 Immigration Reform and Control Act that allowed employers of agricultural workers time to adjust their recruiting and hiring practices to fit the new law; also referred to as the SAW Program.

sponsorship. A system whereby a U.S. citizen may take fiscal or legal responsibility for someone who wants to immigrate.

State Legalization Impact Assistance Grant (SLIAG). Federal government reimbursement to states for the social service costs of immigrants; authorized under the Immigration Reform and Control Act of 1986.

sweatshop. A popular term for a small factory that employs low-wage, low-skilled workers, usually in urban areas and often in the garment industry.

Systematic Alien Verification for Entitlements (SAVE). A computer system used in the 1980s to assist states in determining the immigration status of applicants for social services.

T

temporary protected status. A legal category for refugees who are allowed to stay in the United States until political conditions improve in their home country.

tenement. Often crowded, substandard apartment housing for immigrants in urban areas.

third world. A term referring to the less economically developed parts of the globe.

TNC. *See* transnational corporation.

TOEFL. Test of English as a Foreign Language; a test of an individual's ability to use and understand the English language.

transnational corporation (TNC). A corporation headquartered in one country but operating in many.

transnationalism. The process by which immigrants retain political, economic, and social connections with their home country.

U

UFW. *See* United Farm Workers.

Ulsterites. An eighteenth- and nineteenth-century term for Scots-Irish immigrants from Ulster, or Northern Ireland.

undocumented. Residing in the United States without legal documentation.

UNHCR. *See* United Nations High Commissioner for Refugees.

United Farm Workers (UFW). The main union for migrant agricultural laborers from Mexico, the Philippines, and other countries.

United Nations High Commissioner for Refugees (UNHCR). Established in 1950, the main United Nations agency responsible for refugees.

United Nations Protocol Relating to the Status of Refugees. Key United Nations rules concerning the rights of refugees; first adopted in 1951 and amended in 1967.

United States Citizenship and Immigration Services (USCIS). Created as part of the U.S. Department of Homeland Security, the USCIS began operation in 2003, taking on the administrative functions of the U.S. Immigration and Naturalization Service, including adjudicating claims to residency and asylum status as well as granting naturalization and citizenship services to legal immigrants.

U.S. English. An organization that advocates making English the official language of the United States.

U.S. ex rel. Negron v. New York. A 1970 court case that established the constitutional right to foreign-language interpreters in criminal trials in which a defendant cannot adequately speak English.

USA PATRIOT Act. An acronym for the Uniting and Strengthening America by Providing Appropriate Tools Required to Intercept and Obstruct Terrorism Act, an omnibus national security act passed in the aftermath of the September 11, 2001, terrorist attacks that called for tightened border security and more scrupulous reviews of visa applications.

USCIS. *See* United States Citizenship and Immigration Services.

V

Virginia Company. The royally chartered company that founded the colony of Virginia in 1607.

visa. A legal document allowing a person to visit or reside in another country.

Voter ID laws. State laws that require people to provide identification before voting.

W

war brides. Foreign women who marry U.S. servicemen.

War Brides Act. A 1945 law that allowed the immigration of women and men who had married Americans serving in the U.S. Armed Forces during World War II.

War Refugee Board (WRB). A cabinet-level agency created by President Franklin D. Roosevelt on January 24, 1944, to aid Jewish refugees escaping from Nazi-occupied Europe.

War Relocation Authority. A World War II–era U.S. government agency in charge of Japanese internment.

WASPs. White Anglo-Saxon Protestants.

Welfare Reform Act. *See* Personal Responsibility and Work Opportunity Reconciliation Act.

wet feet, dry feet. An unofficial term for the U.S. policy whereby illegal immigrants apprehended at sea have no right to refugee screenings, whereas those who make it to American territory do.

Workingmen's Party of California. A radical nineteenth-century political party that advocated banning Chinese immigration.

WRB. *See* War Refugee Board.

X

Xenophobia. A fear or hatred of foreigners.

Y

Young Lords. A radical political organization of the 1960s and 1970s among young Puerto Ricans in the United States.

Young Men's Buddhist Association. *See* Buddhist Mission of North America.

Z

Zero Immigration Series. A U.S. Census Bureau population projection that assumes no further immigration into the country.

Zero Population Growth (ZPG). An anti–population growth organization that advocates limits on immigration.

Zionism. A Jewish nationalist movement.

ZPG. *See* Zero Population Growth.

Bibliography

Books

Abdul Rauf, Feisal. *Moving the Mountain: Beyond Ground Zero to a New Vision of Islam in America.* New York: Free Press, 2012.

Abraham, Nabeel, Sally Howell, and Andrew Shryock, eds. *Arab Detroit 9/11: Life in the Terror Decade.* Detroit, MI: Wayne State University Press, 2011.

Abusharaf, Rogaia Mustafa. *Wanderings: Sudanese Migrants and Exiles in North America.* Ithaca, NY: Cornell University Press, 2002.

Ackerman, Kenneth D. *Young J. Edgar: Hoover, the Red Scare, and the Assault on Civil Liberties.* New York: Carroll & Graf, 2007.

Acosta, Yesenia D., and G. Patricia de la Cruz. *The Foreign-Born from Latin America and the Caribbean: 2010.* American Community Survey Briefs No. 10-15. Washington, DC: U.S. Census Bureau, 2011.

Acuña, Rodolfo. *Occupied America: A History of Chicanos.* 5th ed. New York: Pearson Longman, 2004.

Adam, Thomas, and Ruth Gross, eds. *Traveling Between Worlds: German-American Encounters.* College Station: Texas A&M University Press, 2006.

Adams, Gregory P., ed. *Immigration and Nationality Law Handbook 2005–2006.* Washington, DC: American Immigration Lawyers Association, 2005.

Adepoju, Aderanti. *Migration in Sub-Saharan Africa.* Uppsala, Sweden: Nordic Africa Institute, 2008.

Agius Vallejo, Jody. *Barrios to Burbs: The Making of the Mexican American Middle Class.* Stanford, CA: Stanford University Press, 2012.

Aguilar-Gaxiola, Sergio A., and Thomas P. Gulotta, eds. *Depression in Latinos: Assessment, Treatment, and Prevention.* New York: Springer, 2008.

Ahlstrom, Sydney A. *A Religious History of the American People.* New Haven, CT: Yale University Press, 2004.

Alba, Richard. *Blurring the Color Line: The New Chance for a More Integrated America.* Cambridge, MA: Harvard University Press, 2009.

Alba, Richard, and Victor Nee. *Remaking the American Mainstream: Assimilation and Contemporary Immigration.* Cambridge, MA: Harvard University Press, 2003.

Alba, Richard, Albert J. Raboteau, and Josh DeWind, eds. *Immigration and Religion in America: Comparative and Historical Perspectives.* New York: New York University Press, 2009.

Alden, Edward. *The Closing of the American Border: Terrorism, Immigration, and Security Since 9/11.* New York: Harper, 2008.

Aleandri, Emelise. *The Italian-American Immigrant Theatre of New York City.* New York: Arcadia, 1999.

Alexander, June Granatir. *Daily Life in Immigrant America, 1870–1920: How the Second Great Wave of Immigrants Made Their Way in America.* Rev. ed. Chicago: Ivan R. Dee, 2009.

Alperen, Martin J. *Foundations of Homeland Security: Law and Policy.* Hoboken, NJ: Wiley, 2011.

Alsultany, Evelyn. *Arabs and Muslims in the Media: Race and Representation After 9/11.* New York: New York University Press, 2012.

Alsultany, Evelyn, and Ella Shohat, eds. *Between the Middle East and the Americas: The Cultural Politics of Diaspora.* Ann Arbor: University of Michigan Press, 2012.

Anagnostou, Yiorgos. *Contours of White Ethnicity: Popular Ethnography and the Making of Usable Pasts in Greek America.* Athens: Ohio University Press, 2009.

Anbinder, Tyler G. *Nativism and Slavery: The Northern Know Nothings and the Politics of the 1850s.* New York: Oxford University Press, 1994.

Anderson, Gary Clayton. *The Indian Southwest, 1580–1830: Ethnogenesis and Reinvention.* Norman: University of Oklahoma Press, 2009.

Anderson, Margo J., Constance F. Citro, and Joseph J. Salvo, eds. *Encyclopedia of the U.S. Census.* 2nd ed. Washington, DC: CQ, 2013.

Anderson, Margo J., and Stephen E. Fienberg. *Who Counts? The Politics of Census-Taking in Contemporary America.* New York: Russell Sage Foundation, 1999.

Anderson, Philip J., and Dag Blanck, eds. *Norwegians and Swedes in the United States: Friends and Neighbors.* St. Paul: Minnesota Historical Society, 2012.

Andreas, Peter, and Timothy Snyder, eds. *The Wall Around the West: State Borders and Immigration Controls in North America and Europe.* Lanham, MD: Rowman & Littlefield, 2000.

Angel, Jacqueline L., Fernando Torres-Gil, and Kyriakos Markides, eds. *Aging, Health, and Longevity in the Mexican-Origin Population.* New York: Springer, 2012.

Anrig, Greg, Jr., and Tova Andrea Wang, eds. *Immigration's New Frontiers: Experiences from the Emerging Gateway States.* New York: Century Foundation Press, 2006.

Ansari, Abdolmaboud. *Iranian Immigrants in the United States.* New York: Associated Faculty, 1988.

Antin, Mary. *The Promised Land.* 1912. New York: Arno, 1980.

Aranda, Elizabeth M. *Emotional Bridges to Puerto Rico: Migration, Return Migration, and the Struggles of Incorporation.* Lanham, MD: Rowman & Littlefield, 2006.

Archdeacon, Thomas J. *Becoming American: An Ethnic History.* New York: Free Press, 1983.

Ari, Lilach Lev. *The American Dream—for Men Only? Gender, Immigration, and the Assimilation of Israelis in the United States.* New York: LFB Scholarly, 2008.

Arthur, John A. *African Women Immigrants: Crossing Transnational Borders.* New York: Palgrave Macmillan, 2009.

Arthur, John A., Joseph Takougang, and Thomas Owusu, eds. *Africans in Global Migration: Searching for Promised Lands.* Lanham, MD: Lexington, 2012.

Artico, Ceres I. *Latino Families Broken by Immigrations: The Adolescents' Perceptions.* El Paso, TX: LFB Scholarly, 2003.

Asbury, Herbert. *The Gangs of New York.* New York: Alfred A. Knopf, 1928.

Askeland, Lori, ed. *Children and Youth in Adoption, Orphanages, and Foster Care: A Historical Handbook and Guide.* Westport, CT: Greenwood, 2006.

Baily, Samuel L. *Immigrants in the Lands of Promise: Italians in Buenos Aires and New York City, 1870–1914.* Ithaca, NY: Cornell University Press, 2003.

Bailyn, Bernard. *From Protestant Peasants to Jewish Intellectuals: The Germans in the Peopling of America.* New York: Berg, 1988.

Bailyn, Bernard, and Philip D. Morgan, eds. *Strangers Within the Realm: Cultural Margins of the First British Empire.* Chapel Hill: University of North Carolina Press, 1991.

Bakalian, Anny. *Armenian Americans: From Being to Feeling Armenian.* New Brunswick, NJ: Transaction, 1993.

Bakalian, Anny, and Medhi Bozorgmehr. *Backlash 9/11: Middle Eastern and Muslim Americans Respond.* Berkeley: University of California Press, 2009.

Baldoz, Rick. *The Third Asiatic Invasion: Empire and Migration in Filipino America, 1898–1946.* New York: New York University Press, 2011.

Ball, Howard. *U.S. Homeland Security: A Reference Handbook.* Santa Barbara, CA: ABC-CLIO, 2005.

Balmer, Randall. *Blessed Assurance: A History of Evangelicalism in America.* Boston: Beacon, 1999.

Barber, Pauline Gardiner, and Winnie Lem, eds. *Migration in the 21st Century: Political Economy and Ethnography.* New York: Routledge, 2012.

Barde, Robert Eric. *Immigration at the Golden Gate: Passenger Ships, Exclusion, and Angel Island.* Westport, CT: Praeger, 2008.

Barkan, Elliott Robert. *And Still They Come: Immigrants and American Society, 1920 to the 1990s.* Wheeling, IL: Harlan Davidson, 1996.

———. *From All Points: America's Immigrant West, 1870s–1952.* Bloomington: Indiana University Press, 2007.

———, ed. *A Nation of Peoples: A Sourcebook on America's Multicultural Heritage.* Westport, CT: Greenwood, 1999.

Barrett, James R. *The Irish Way: Becoming American in the Multi-Ethnic City.* New York: Penguin, 2012.

———. *Work and Community in the Jungle: Chicago's Packinghouse Workers, 1894–1922.* Urbana: University of Illinois Press, 2002.

Barrett, Paul M. *American Islam: The Struggle for the Soul of a Religion.* New York: Farrar, Straus and Giroux, 2007.

Bartlett, Lesley, and Ofelia Garcia. *Additive Schooling in Subtractive Times: Bilingual Education and Dominican Immigrant Youth in the Heights.* Nashville, TN: Vanderbilt University Press, 2011.

Basaran, Tugba. *Security, Law, and Borders: At the Limits of Liberties.* New York: Routledge, 2010.

Batalova, Jeanne. *Skilled Immigrant and Native Workers in the United States: The Economic Competition Debate and Beyond.* New York: LFB Scholarly, 2006.

Bayor, Ronald H. *Race and Ethnicity in America: A Concise History.* New York: Columbia University Press, 2003.

Bean, Frank D., and Gillian Stevens. *America's Newcomers and the Dynamics of Diversity.* New York: Russell Sage Foundation, 2003.

Bean, Frank D., et al., eds. *At the Crossroads: Mexican Migration and U.S. Policy.* New York: Rowman & Littlefield, 1997.

Behdad, Ali. *A Forgetful Nation: On Immigration and Cultural Identity in the United States.* Durham, NC: Duke University Press, 2005.

Beltrán, Cristina. *The Trouble with Unity: Latino Politics and the Creation of Identity.* Oxford, UK: Oxford University Press, 2010.

Bender, Daniel E., and Richard A. Greenwald, eds. *Sweatshop USA: The American Sweatshop in Historical and Global Perspective.* New York: Routledge, 2003.

Bender, Steven W. *Run for the Border: Vice and Virtue in U.S.–Mexico Border Crossings.* New York: New York University Press, 2012.

Bennett, David H. *The Party of Fear: From Nativist Movements to the New Right in American History.* 2nd ed. New York: Vintage Books, 1995.

Bergquist, James M. *Daily Life in Immigrant America, 1820–1870: How the First Great Wave of Immigrants Made Their Way in America.* Chicago: Ivan R. Dee, 2009.

Berlin, Ira. *The Making of African America: The Four Great Migrations.* New York: Viking, 2010.

———. *Many Thousands Gone: The First Two Centuries of Slavery in North America.* Cambridge, MA: Belknap Press, 1998.

Bernstein, Iver. *The New York City Draft Riots: Their Significance for American Society and Politics in the Age of the Civil War.* Lincoln: University of Nebraska Press, 2010.

Beserra, Bernadette. *Brazilian Immigrants in the United States: Cultural Imperialism and Social Class.* New York: LFB Scholarly, 2003.

Betts, Alexander, and Gil Loescher, eds. *Refugees in International Relations.* Oxford, UK: Oxford University Press, 2011.

Bhatia, Sunil. *American Karma: Race, Culture, and Identity in the Indian Diaspora.* New York: New York University Press, 2007.

Bhugra, Dinesh, and Susham Gupta, eds. *Migration and Mental Health.* New York: Cambridge University Press, 2011.

Bilici, Mucahit. *Finding Mecca in America: How Islam Is Becoming an American Religion.* Chicago: University of Chicago Press, 2012.

Binder, Frederick M., and David M. Reimers. *All the Nations Under Heaven: An Ethnic and Racial History of New York City.* New York: Columbia University Press, 1995.

Bloemraad, Irene. *Becoming a Citizen: Incorporating Immigrants and Refugees in the United States and Canada.* Berkeley: University of California Press, 2006.

Bloom, Stephen G. *Postville: A Clash of Cultures in Heartland America.* New York: Mariner, 2001.

Bodnar, John. *The Transplanted: A History of Immigrants in Urban America.* Bloomington: Indiana University Press, 1985.

Boehm, Lisa Krissoff. *Making a Way out of No Way: African American Women and the Second Great Migration.* Jackson: University Press of Mississippi, 2009.

Boeri, Tito, Herbert Brücker, Frédéric Docquier, and Hillel Rapoport, eds. *Brain Drain and Brain Gain: The Global Competition to Attract High-Skilled Migrants.* Oxford, UK: Oxford University Press, 2012.

Bohme, Frederick G. *200 Years of Census Taking: Population and Housing Questions, 1790–1990.* Washington, DC: U.S. Census Bureau, 1989.

Bon Tempo, Carl J. *Americans at the Gate: The United States and Refugees During the Cold War.* Princeton, NJ: Princeton University Press, 2008.

Bonacich, Edna, and Richard P. Appelbaum. *Behind the Label: Inequality in the Los Angeles Apparel Industry.* Berkeley: University of California Press, 2000.

Borjas, George J. *Heaven's Door: Immigration Policy and the American Economy.* Princeton, NJ: Princeton University Press, 2001.

Breen, T.H. *Tobacco Culture: The Mentality of the Great Tidewater Planters on the Eve of the Revolution.* 2nd ed. Princeton, NJ: Princeton University Press, 2001.

Brick, Kate, A.E. Challinor, and Marc R. Rosenblum. *Mexican and Central American Immigrants in the United States.* Washington, DC: Migration Policy Institute, 2010.

Bridenbaugh, Carl. *Vexed and Troubled Englishmen, 1590–1642.* New York: Oxford University Press, 1968.

Briggs, Vernon M., Jr. *Mass Immigration and the National Interest: Policy Directors for the New Century.* Armonk, NY: M.E. Sharpe, 2003.

Brimelow, Peter. *Alien Nation: Common Sense About America's Immigration Disaster.* New York: Random House, 1996.

Brinkerhoff, Jennifer M. *Digital Diasporas: Identity and Transnational Engagement.* New York: Cambridge University Press, 2009.

Brittain, Carmina. *Transnational Messages: Experiences of Chinese and Mexican Immigrants in American Schools.* New York: LFB Scholarly, 2002.

Brook, Vincent. *Land of Smoke and Mirrors: A Cultural History of Los Angeles.* New Brunswick, NJ: Rutgers University Press, 2012.

Brown, E. Richard, Victoria Ojeda, Roberta Wynn, and Rebecka Levan. *Racial and Ethnic Disparities in Access to Health Insurance and Health Care.* Los Angeles: University of California, Los Angeles, Center for Health Policy Research, 2000.

Brown, Judith M. *Global South Asians: Introducing the Modern Diaspora.* New York: Cambridge University Press, 2006.

Brown, Linda Joyce. *The Literature of Immigration and Racial Formation: Becoming White, Becoming Other, Becoming American in the Late Progressive Era.* New York: Routledge, 2004.

Buff, Rachel Ida, ed. *Immigrant Rights in the Shadows of Citizenship.* New York: New York University Press, 2008.

Buhle, Paule, and Dan Georgakas, eds. *The Immigrant Left in the United States.* Albany: State University of New York Press, 1996.

Bukowczyk, John J. *A History of the Polish Americans.* New Brunswick, NJ: Transaction, 2008.

Bukowczyk, John J., et al. *Permeable Border: The Great Lakes Basin as Transnational Region, 1650–1990.* Pittsburgh, PA: University of Pittsburgh Press, 2005.

Burton, William L. *Melting Pot Soldiers: The Union's Ethnic Regiments.* New York: Fordham University Press, 1998.

Caldwell, Gillian. *Bought and Sold.* DVD. Washington, DC: Global Survival Network, 1997.

Camarota, Steven A. *Welfare Use by Immigrant Households with Children: A Look at Cash, Medicaid, Housing, and Food Programs.* Washington, DC: Center for Immigration Studies, 2011.

Cambridge, Vibert C. *Immigration, Diversity, and Broadcasting in the United States, 1990–2001.* Athens: Ohio University Press, 2005.

Campanella, Richard. *Geographies of New Orleans: Urban Fabrics Before the Storm.* Lafayette: Center for Louisiana Studies, 2006.

Cannato, Vincent J. *American Passage: The History of Ellis Island.* New York: Harper, 2009.

Canniff, Julie G. *Cambodian Refugees' Pathways to Success: Developing a Bi-Cultural Identity.* New York: LFB Scholarly, 2001.

Capps, Randy, Marc R. Rosenblum, Cristina Rodríguez, and Muzaffar Chishti. *Delegation and Divergence: A Study of 287(g) State and Local Immigration Enforcement.* Washington, DC: Migration Policy Institute, 2011.

Carmack, Sharon DeBartolo. *A Genealogist's Guide to Discovering Your Immigrant and Ethnic Ancestors: How to Find and Record Your Unique Heritage.* Cincinnati, OH: Betterway, 2000.

Carnevale, Nancy C. *A New Language, a New World: Italian Immigrants in the United States, 1890–1945.* Urbana: University of Illinois Press, 2009.

Cary, Francine Curro, ed. *Washington Odyssey: A Multicultural History of the Nation's Capital.* Washington, DC: Smithsonian Institution Press, 2003.

Castles, Stephen, and Mark J. Miller. *The Age of Migration: International Population Movements in the Modern World.* 4th ed. New York: Guilford, 2009.

Center for Applied Linguistics. *Education for Adult English Language Learners in the United States: Trends, Research, and Promising Practices.* Washington, DC: Center for Applied Linguistics, 2010.

Chacón, Justin Akers, and Mike Davis. *No One Is Illegal: Fighting Racism and State Violence on the U.S.–Mexico Border.* Chicago: Haymarket, 2006.

———. *Survivors: Cambodian Refugees in the United States.* Urbana: University of Illinois Press, 2004.

———. *This Bittersweet Soil: The Chinese in California Agriculture, 1860–1910.* Berkeley: University of California Press, 1986.

———, ed. *The Vietnamese American 1.5 Generation: Stories of War, Revolution, Flight, and New Beginnings.* Philadelphia: Temple University Press, 2006.

Chan, Sucheng, and Madeline Y. Hsu, eds. *Chinese Americans and the Politics of Race and Culture.* Philadelphia: Temple University Press, 2008.

Chan, Yuk Wah, ed. *The Chinese/Vietnamese Diaspora: Revisiting the Boat People.* New York: Routledge, 2011.

Chang, Iris. *The Chinese in America: A Narrative History.* New York: Viking, 2003.

Chang-Muy, Fernando, and Elaine P. Congress, eds. *Social Work with Immigrants and Refugees: Legal Issues, Clinical Skills, and Advocacy.* New York: Springer, 2009.

Chavez, Leo R. *The Latino Threat: Constructing Immigrants, Citizens, and the Nation.* Stanford, CA: Stanford University Press, 2008.

Cheah, Joseph. *Race and Religion in American Buddhism: White Supremacy and Immigrant Adaptation.* New York: Oxford University Press, 2011.

Chee, Maria W.L. *Taiwanese American Transnational Families: Women and Kin Work.* New York: Routledge, 2005.

Chen, Carolyn. *Getting Saved in America: Taiwanese Immigration and Religious Experience.* Princeton, NJ: Princeton University Press, 2008.

Chen, Yong. *Chinese San Francisco, 1850–1943: A Trans-Pacific Community.* Stanford, CA: Stanford University Press, 2000.

Chi, Sang, and Emily Moberg Robinson, eds. *Voices of the Asian American and Pacific Islander Experience.* Santa Barbara, CA: Greenwood, 2012.

Chin, Ko-lin. *Smuggled Chinese: Clandestine Immigration to the United States.* Philadelphia: Temple University Press, 1999.

Chishti, Muzaffer A., et al. *America's Challenge: Domestic Security, Civil Liberties, and National Unity After September 11.* Washington, DC: Migration Policy Institute, 2003.

Chiswick, Barry R., and Paul W. Miller, eds. *Recent Developments in the Economics of International Migration.* Cheltenham, UK: Edward Elgar, 2012.

Chomsky, Aviva. *"They Take Our Jobs!": And 20 Other Myths About Immigration.* Boston: Beacon, 2007.

Choy, Catherine Ceniza. *Empire of Care: Nursing and Migration in Filipino American History.* Durham, NC: Duke University Press, 2003.

Christgau, John. *Enemies: World War II Alien Internment.* Lincoln: University of Nebraska Press, 2009.

Chuang, Susan S., and Robert P. Moreno, eds. *Immigrant Children: Change, Adaptation, and Cultural Transformation.* Lanham, MD: Lexington, 2011.

Cinel, Dino. *The National Integration of Italian Return Migration, 1870–1929.* New York: Cambridge University Press, 2002.

Coan, Peter Morton. *Ellis Island Interviews: In Their Own Words.* New York: Facts on File, 1977.

———. *Toward a Better Life: America's New Immigrants in Their Own Words: From Ellis Island to the Present.* Amherst, NY: Prometheus, 2011.

Cohen, Deborah. *Braceros: Migrant Citizens and Transnational Subjects in Postwar United States and Mexico.* Chapel Hill: University of North Carolina Press, 2011.

Cohen, Gerard Daniel. *In War's Wake: Europe's Displaced Persons in the Postwar Order.* Oxford, UK: Oxford University Press, 2012.

Cohn, Raymond L. *Mass Migration Under Sail: European Immigration to the Antebellum United States.* New York: Cambridge University Press, 2009.

Coll, Cynthia Garcia, and Amy Kerivan Marks. *Immigrant Stories: Ethnicity and Academics in Middle Childhood.* New York: Oxford University Press, 2009.

Collet, Christian, and Pei-te Lien, eds. *The Transnational Politics of Asian Americans.* Philadelphia: Temple University Press, 2009.

Collins, Randall. *The Credential Society: An Historical Sociology of Education and Stratification.* New York: Academic Press, 1979.

Conklin, Nancy Faires, and Margaret Lourie. *A Host of Tongues: Language Communities in the United States.* New York: Free Press, 1983.

Connell, John. *Migration and the Globalisation of Health Care: The Health Worker Exodus?* Cheltenham, UK: Edward Elgar, 2010.

Constable, Nicole. *Romance on a Global Stage: Pen Pals, Virtual Ethnography, and "Mail-Order" Marriages.* Berkeley: University of California Press, 2003.

Conway, Dennis, and Robert B. Potter, eds. *Return Migration of the Next Generations: 21st Century Transnational Mobility.* Burlington, VT: Ashgate, 2009.

Cornelius, Wayne A., Philip L. Martin, and James F. Hollifield, eds. *Controlling Immigration: A Global Perspective.* Stanford, CA: Stanford University Press, 2004.

Cottle, Simon, ed. *Ethnic Minorities and the Media: Changing Cultural Boundaries.* Philadelphia: Open University Press, 2000.

Coughlin, Reed, and Judith Owens-Manley. *Bosnian Refugees in America: New Communities, New Cultures.* New York: Springer, 2006.

Cowart, David. *Trailing Clouds: Immigrant Fiction in Contemporary America.* Ithaca, NY: Cornell University Press, 2006.

Crèvecoeur, J. Hector St. John de. *Letters from an American Farmer.* Ed. Susan Manning. New York: Oxford University Press, 2009.

Cruz, Wilfredo. *City of Dreams: Latino Immigration to Chicago.* Lanham, MD: University Press of America, 2007.

Cruz-Malavé, Arnaldo, and Martin F. Manalansan IV. *Queer Globalizations: Citizenship and the Afterlife of Colonization.* New York: New York University Press, 2002.

Cummins, Jim. *Language, Power, and Pedagogy: Bilingual Children in the Crossfire.* Tonawanda, NY: Multilingual Matters, 2000.

Curiel, Jonathan. *Al'America: Travels Through America's Arab and Islamic Roots.* New York: New Press, 2008.

Curtin, Philip D. *The Atlantic Slave Trade: A Census.* Madison: University of Wisconsin Press, 1969.

Dalla, Rochelle L., John Defrain, Julie Johnson, and Douglas A. Abbott. *Strengths and Challenges of New Immigrant Families: Implications for Research, Education, Policy, and Service.* Lanham, MD: Lexington, 2009.

Dana, Léo-Paul, ed. *Handbook of Research on Ethnic Minority Entrepreneurship: A Co-Evolutionary View on Resource Management.* Northampton, MA: Edward Elgar, 2007.

Daniels, Roger. *Coming to America: A History of Immigration and Ethnicity in American Life.* 2nd ed. New York: Harper Perennial, 2002.

———. *Guarding the Golden Door: American Immigration Policy and Immigrants Since 1882.* New York: Hill and Wang, 2004.

Das, Mitra. *Between Two Cultures: The Case of Cambodian Women in America.* New York: Peter Lang, 2007.

Das Gupta, Monisha. *Unruly Immigrants: Rights, Activism, and Transnational South Asian Politics in the United States.* Durham, NC: Duke University Press, 2006.

Dashefsky, Arnold, Jan De Amicis, Bernard Lazerwitz, and Ephraim Tabory. *Americans Abroad: A Comparative Study of Emigrants from the United States.* New York: Plenum, 1992.

Dauvergne, Catherine. *Making People Illegal: What Globalization Means for Migration and Law.* New York: Cambridge University Press, 2008.

Deaux, Kay. *To Be an Immigrant.* New York: Russell Sage Foundation, 2006.

DeBiaggi, Sylvia Duarte Dantas. *Changing Gender Roles: Brazilian Immigrant Families in the U.S.* New York: LFB Scholarly, 2010.

Debouzy, Marianne. *In the Shadow of the Statue of Liberty: Immigrants, Workers, and Citizens in the American Republic, 1880–1920.* Urbana: University of Illinois Press, 1992.

DeForest, Robert W., and Lawrence Veiller, eds. *The Tenement House Problem.* 2 vols. New York: Macmillan, 1903. Reprint, Charleston, SC: Nabu, 2011.

Delgado, Richard. *Justice at War: Civil Liberties and Civil Rights During Times of Crisis.* New York: New York University Press, 2003.

Dempsey, Corrine G. *The Goddess Lives in Upstate New York: Breaking Convention and Making Home at a North American Hindu Temple.* New York: Oxford University Press, 2006.

Der-Martirosian, Claudia. *Iranian Immigrants in Los Angeles: The Role of Networks and Economic Integration.* New York: LFB Scholarly, 2008.

Dessens, Nathalie. *From Saint-Domingue to New Orleans: Migration and Influences.* Gainesville: University Press of Florida, 2007.

Dhingra, Pawan. *Life Behind the Lobby: Indian Motel Owners and the American Dream.* Stanford, CA: Stanford University Press, 2012.

DiCarlo, Lisa. *Migrating to America: Transnational Social Networks and Regional Identity Among Turkish Migrants.* New York: Tauris Academic, 2008.

DiMaggio, Paul, and Patricia Fernández-Kelly, eds. *Arts in the Lives of Immigrant Communities.* New Brunswick, NJ: Rutgers University Press, 2010.

Diner, Hasia R. *Erin's Daughters in America: Irish Immigrant Women in the Nineteenth Century.* Baltimore: Johns Hopkins University Press, 1983.

———. *Hungering for America: Italian, Irish, and Jewish Foodways in the Age of Migration.* Cambridge, MA: Harvard University Press, 2001.

———. *The Jews of the United States.* Berkeley: University of California Press, 2004.

Dinnerstein, Leonard. *America and the Survivors of the Holocaust.* New York: Columbia University Press, 1982.

Diouf, Sylviane A. *Dreams of Africa in Alabama: The Slave Ship* Clotilda *and the Story of the Last Africans Brought to America.* New York: Oxford University Press, 2007.

DiSipio, Louis, and Rodolfo O. de la Garza. *Making Americans, Remaking America: Immigration and Immigrant Policy.* Boulder, CO: Westview, 1998.

DiStasi, Lawrence, ed. *Una Storia Segreta: The Secret History of Italian American Evacuation and Internment During World War II.* Berkeley, CA: Heyday, 2001.

Dobbs, Michael. *Saboteurs: The Nazi Raid on America.* New York: Alfred A. Knopf, 2004.

Dodson, Howard, and Sylviane A. Diouf, eds. *In Motion: The African-American Migration Experience.* Washington, DC: National Geographic, 2004.

Dolan, Jay P. *The Irish Americans: A History.* New York: Bloomsbury, 2008.

Domínguez, Silvia. *Getting Ahead: Social Mobility, Public Housing, and Immigrant Networks.* New York: New York University Press, 2011.

Douglass, William A., and Jon Bilbao. *Amerikanuak: Basques in the New World.* Reno: University of Nevada Press, 2005.

Dreby, Joanna. *Divided by Borders: Mexican Migrants and Their Children.* Berkeley: University of California Press, 2010.

Duany, Jorge. *Blurred Borders: Transnational Migration Between the Hispanic Caribbean and the United States.* Chapel Hill: University of North Carolina Press, 2011.

———. *The Puerto Rican Nation on the Move: Identities on the Island and in the United States.* Chapel Hill: University of North Carolina Press, 2001.

Dunn, Timothy J. *The Militarization of the U.S.–Mexico Border, 1978–1992: Low-Intensity Conflict Doctrine Comes Home.* Austin: University of Texas, Center for Mexican American Studies, 1996.

Ebaugh, Helen Rose, and Janet Saltzman Chafetz, eds. *Religion and the New Immigrants: Continuities and Adaptations in Immigrant Congregations.* Walnut Creek, CA: AltaMira, 2000.

Eckstein, Susan Eva. *The Immigrant Divide: How Cuban Americans Changed the U.S. and Their Homeland.* New York: Routledge, 2009.

Eich-Krohm, Astrid. *German Professionals in the United States: A Gendered Analysis of the Migration Decision of Highly Skilled Families.* New York: LFB Scholarly, 2012.

Eisen, George, and David K. Wiggins, eds. *Ethnicity and Sport in North American History and Culture.* Westport, CT: Greenwood, 1994.

Ennis, Sharon R., Merarys Ríos-Vargas, and Nora G. Albert. *The Hispanic Population: 2010.* 2010 Census Brief No. C2010BR-04. Washington, DC: U.S. Census Bureau, 2011.

Erickson, John H. *Orthodox Christians in America.* New York: Oxford University Press, 1999.

Ervin, Clark Kent. *Open Target: Where America Is Vulnerable to Attack.* New York: Palgrave Macmillan, 2006.

Espenshade, Thomas J., ed. *Keys to Successful Immigration: Implications of the New Jersey Experience.* Washington, DC: Urban Institute Press, 1997.

Espiritu, Yen Le. *Home Bound: Filipino American Lives Across Cultures, Communities, and Countries.* Berkeley: University of California Press, 2003.

Ettinger, Patrick. *Imaginary Lines: Border Enforcement and the Origins of Undocumented Immigration, 1882–1930.* Austin: University of Texas Press, 2009.

Evans, Timothy, Margaret Whitehead, Finn Diderichsen, Abbas Bhuiya, and Meg Wirth, eds. *Challenging Inequities in Health: From Ethics to Action.* New York: Oxford University Press, 2001.

Ewing, Katherine Pratt, ed. *Being and Belonging: Muslims in the United States Since 9/11.* New York: Russell Sage Foundation, 2008.

Faulkner, Caroline L. *Economic Mobility and Cultural Assimilation Among Children of Immigrants.* El Paso, TX: LFB Scholarly, 2011.

Feingold, Henry L., ed. *The Jewish People in America.* 5 vols. Baltimore: Johns Hopkins University Press, 1992.

———. *Zion in America: The Jewish Experience from Colonial Times to the Present.* Mineola, NY: Dover, 2002.

Fentress, James. *Eminent Gangsters: Immigrants and the Birth of Organized Crime in America.* Lanham, MD: University Press of America, 2010.

Fernández-Kelly, Patricia, and Alejandro Portes. *Health Care and Immigration: Understanding the Connections.* New York: Routledge, 2013.

Ferriss, Susan, and Ricardo Sandoval. *The Fight in the Fields: Cesar Chavez and the Farmworkers Movement.* Ed. Diana Hambree. New York: Harcourt Brace Jovanovich, 1997.

Finan, Christopher M. *From the Palmer Raids to the Patriot Act: A History of the Fight for Free Speech in America.* Boston: Beacon, 2007.

Finke, Roger, and Rodney Stark. *The Churching of America, 1776–1990: Winners and Losers in Our Religious Economy.* Rev. ed. New Brunswick, NJ: Rutgers University Press, 2005.

Fisher, James T. *Communion of Immigrants: A History of Catholics in America.* New York: Oxford University Press, 2008.

Fishman, Joshua, Robert L. Cooper, and Roxana Ma. *Bilingualism in the Barrio.* Bloomington: Indiana University Press, 1971.

Fitzgerald, David. *A Nation of Emigrants: How Mexico Manages Its Migration.* Berkeley: University of California Press, 2009.

Fix, Michael E., ed. *Immigrants and Welfare: The Impact of Welfare Reform on America's Newcomers.* New York: Russell Sage Foundation, 2011.

Florida, Richard. *The Flight of the Creative Class: The New Global Competition for Talent.* New York: HarperBusiness, 2005.

Foley, Neil. *The White Scourge: Mexicans, Blacks, and Poor Whites in Texas Cotton Culture.* Berkeley: University of California Press, 1999.

Foner, Nancy, ed. *Across Generations: Immigrant Families in America.* New York: New York University Press, 2009.

———. *From Ellis Island to JFK: New York's Two Great Waves of Immigration.* New Haven, CT: Yale University Press, 2000.

———, ed. *New Immigrants in New York.* New York: Columbia University Press, 2001.

———, ed. *One Out of Three: Immigrant New York in the Twenty-First Century.* New York: Columbia University Press, 2013.

Foner, Nancy, Rubén G. Rumbaut, and Steven J. Gold, eds. *Immigration Research for a New Century: Multidisciplinary Perspectives.* New York: Russell Sage Foundation, 2000.

Fortunati, Leopoldina, Raul Pertierra, and Jane Vincent, eds. *Migration, Diaspora and Information Technology in Global Societies.* New York: Routledge, 2011.

Frazier, John W., and Eugene L. Tettey-Fio. *Race, Ethnicity, and Place in a Changing America.* Albany: State University of New York Press, 2006.

Friedman, Lester D., ed. *Unspeakable Images: Ethnicity and the American Cinema.* Urbana: University of Illinois Press, 1991.

Friedman-Kasaba, Kathie. *Memories of Migration: Gender, Ethnicity, and Work in the Lives of Jewish and Italian Women in New York, 1870–1924.* New York: State University of New York Press, 2012.

Fritz, Catarina. *Brazilian Immigration and the Quest for Identity.* El Paso, TX: LFB Scholarly, 2010.

Fujiwara, Lynn. *Mothers Without Citizenship: Asian Immigrant Families and the Consequences of Welfare Reform.* Minneapolis: University of Minnesota Press, 2008.

Gabaccia, Donna R. *Foreign Relations: American Immigration in Global Perspective.* Princeton, NJ: Princeton University Press, 2012.

———. *We Are What We Eat: Ethnic Food and the Making of Americans.* Cambridge, MA: Harvard University Press, 2000.

Galarza, Ernesto. *Merchants of Labor: The Mexican Bracero Story.* Santa Barbara, CA: McNally and Loftin, 1964.

Gambino, Christine, and Thomas Gryn. *The Foreign-Born with Science and Engineering Degrees: 2010.* American Community Survey Briefs No. 10-06. Washington, DC: U.S. Census Bureau, 2011.

Gaquin, Deirdre A., and Gwenavere White Dunn. *The Who, What, and Where of America: Understanding the American Community Survey.* 3rd ed. Lanham, MD: Bernan, 2012.

García, John A. *Latino Politics in America: Community, Culture, and Interests.* 2nd ed. Lanham, MD: Rowman & Littlefield, 2012.

García, Juan Ramon. *Operation Wetback: The Mass Deportation of Mexican Undocumented Workers in 1954.* Westport, CT: Greenwood, 1980.

García, María Cristina. *Havana USA: Cuban Exiles and Cuban Americans in South Florida, 1959–1994.* Berkeley: University of California Press, 1996.

Gems, Gerald R. *The Athletic Crusade: Sport and American Cultural Imperialism.* Lincoln: University of Nebraska Press, 2006.

Gems, Gerald R., Linda J. Borish, and Gertrud Pfister. *Sports in American History: From Colonization to Globalization.* Champaign, IL: Human Kinetics, 2008.

Generazio, Marc R. *Immigration Law: A Guide to Laws and Regulations.* Chicago: American Bar Association, 2011.

Gerber, David A. *American Immigration: A Very Short Introduction.* New York: Oxford University Press, 2011.

Gerber, David A., and Alan M. Kraut. *American Immigration and Ethnicity: A Reader.* New York: Palgrave MacMillan, 2005.

Gerstle, Gary, and John Mollenkopf, eds. *E Pluribus Unum? Contemporary and Historical Perspectives on Immigrant Political Incorporation.* New York: Social Science Research Council, 2000.

Getahun, Solomon Addis. *The History of Ethiopian Immigrants and Refugees in America, 1900–2000: Patterns of Migration, Survival, and Adjustment.* New York: LFB Scholarly, 2007.

GhaneaBassiri, Kambiz. *A History of Islam in America: From the New World to the New World Order.* New York: Cambridge University Press, 2010.

Ghosh, Bimal. *Gains from Global Linkages: Trade in Services and the Movement of People.* New York: St. Martin's, 1997.

Gibson, Annie McNeill. *Post-Katrina Brazucas: Brazilian Immigrants in New Orleans.* New Orleans: University of New Orleans Press, 2012.

Gilbert, Felix. *To the Farewell Address: Ideas of Early American Foreign Policy.* Princeton, NJ: Princeton University Press, 1961.

Gilkes, Alwyn D. *The West Indian Diaspora: Experiences in the United States and Canada.* New York: LFB Scholarly, 2007.

Gimpel, James G., and James R. Edwards, Jr. *The Congressional Politics of Immigration Reform.* Boston: Allyn and Bacon, 1999.

Gjerde, Jon. *The Minds of the West: Ethnocultural Evolution in the Rural Middle West, 1830–1917.* Chapel Hill: University of North Carolina Press, 1999.

Gleeson, David T., ed. *The Irish in the Atlantic World.* Columbia: University of South Carolina Press, 2010.

Glodava, Mila, and Richard Onizuka. *Mail-Order Brides: Women for Sale.* Fort Collins, CO: Alaken, 1994.

Gmelch, George. *Double Passage: The Lives of Caribbean Migrants Abroad and Back Home.* Ann Arbor: University of Michigan Press, 1992.

Golash-Boza, Tanya Maria. *Immigration Nation: Raids, Detentions, and Deportations in Post-9/11 America.* Boulder, CO: Paradigm, 2011.

Goldin, Ian, Geoffrey Cameron, and Meera Balarajan. *Exceptional People: How Migration Shaped Our World and Will Define Our Future.* Princeton, NJ: Princeton University Press, 2011.

González, Juan. *Harvest of Empire: A History of Latinos in America.* Rev. ed. New York: Penguin, 2011.

Gonzalez-Pando, Miguel. *The Cuban Americans.* Westport, CT: Greenwood, 1998.

Goodfriend, Joyce D., Benjamin Schmidt, and Annette Stott, eds. *Going Dutch: The Dutch Presence in America, 1609–2009.* Boston: Brill, 2008.

Gordon, Jennifer. *Suburban Sweatshops: The Fight for Immigrant Rights.* Cambridge, MA: Belknap Press, 2007.

Gornick, Vivian. *Emma Goldman: Revolution as a Way of Life.* New Haven, CT: Yale University Press, 2011.

Greene, Victor R. *A Passion for Polka: Old-Time Ethnic Music in America.* Berkeley: University of California Press, 1992.

———. *A Singing Ambivalence: American Immigrants Between Old World and New, 1830–1930.* Kent, OH: Kent State University Press, 2004.

Greenhill, Kelly M. *Weapons of Mass Migration: Forced Displacement, Coercion, and Foreign Policy.* Ithaca, NY: Cornell University Press, 2010.

Gregory, James N. *American Exodus: The Dust Bowl Migration and Okie Culture in California.* New York: Oxford University Press, 1989.

Grenier, Guillermo J., and Lisandro Pérez. *The Legacy of Exile: Cubans in the United States.* Boston: Allyn and Bacon, 2003.

Greschke, Heike Mónika. *Is There a Home in Cyberspace? The Internet in Migrants' Everyday Life and the Emergence of Global Communities.* New York: Routledge, 2012.

Grey, Mark A., Michele Devlin, and Aaron Goldsmith. *Postville U.S.A.: Surviving Diversity in Small-Town America.* Boston: Gemma, 2009.

Grieco, Elizabeth M. *The Remittance Behavior of Immigrant Households: Micronesians in Hawaii and Guam.* New York: LFB Scholarly, 2003.

Griffin, Patrick. *The People with No Name: Ireland's Ulster Scots, America's Scots Irish, and the Creation of a British Atlantic World, 1689–1764.* Princeton, NJ: Princeton University Press, 2001.

Groody, Daniel G., and Gioacchino Campese, eds. *A Promised Land, a Perilous Journey: Theological Perspectives on Migration.* Notre Dame, IN: University of Notre Dame Press, 2008.

Grunberger, Michael W., ed. *From Haven to Home: 350 Years of Jewish Life in America.* New York: George Braziller in association with the Library of Congress, 2004.

Gryn, Thomas, and Christine Gambino. *The Foreign-Born from Asia: 2011.* American Community Survey Briefs No. 11-06. Washington, DC: U.S. Census Bureau, 2012.

Gu, Chien-Juh. *Mental Health Among Taiwanese Americans: Gender, Immigration, and Transnational Struggles.* New York: LFB Scholarly, 2006.

Gupta, Suman, and Tope Omoniyi, eds. *The Cultures of Economic Migration: International Perspectives.* Burlington, VT: Ashgate, 2007.

Gustafson, Sandra M. *Imagining Deliberative Democracy in the Early American Republic.* Chicago: University of Chicago Press, 2011.

Gyory, Andrew. *Closing the Gate: Race, Politics, and the Chinese Exclusion Act.* Chapel Hill: University of North Carolina Press, 1998.

Haddad, Yvonne Yazbeck. *Not Quite American? The Shaping of Arab and Muslim Identity in the United States.* Waco, TX: Baylor University Press, 2004.

Haenni, Sabine. *The Immigrant Scene: Ethnic Amusements in New York, 1880–1920.* Minneapolis: University of Minnesota Press, 2008.

Hagan, Jacqueline Maria. *Migration Miracle: Faith, Hope, and Meaning on the Undocumented Journey.* Cambridge, MA: Harvard University Press, 2008.

Haines, David W. *Safe Haven? A History of Refugees in America.* Sterling, VA: Kumarian, 2010.

Haley, Brian D. *Reimagining the Immigrant: The Accommodation of Mexican Immigrants in Rural America.* New York: Palgrave Macmillan, 2009.

Hamamoto, Darrell Y. *Monitored Peril: Asian Americans and the Politics of TV Representation.* Minneapolis: University of Minnesota Press, 1994.

Hamamoto, Darrell Y., and Rodolfo D. Torres, eds. *New American Destinies: A Reader in Contemporary Asian and Latino Immigration.* New York: Routledge, 1997.

Hamermesh, Daniel S., and Frank D. Bean, eds. *Help or Hindrance? The Economic Implications of Immigration for African Americans.* New York: Russell Sage Foundation, 1998.

Hamerow, Theodore S. *Why We Watched: Europe, America, and the Holocaust.* New York: W.W. Norton, 2008.

Hao, Lingxin. *Color Lines, Country Lines: Race, Immigration, and Wealth Stratification in America.* New York: Russell Sage Foundation, 2007.

Hapke, Laura. *Sweatshop: The History of an American Idea.* New Brunswick, NJ: Rutgers University Press, 2004.

Harzig, Christiane, ed. *Peasant Maids, City Women: From the European Countryside to Urban America.* Ithaca, NY: Cornell University Press, 1997.

Hatamiya, Leslie T. *Righting a Wrong: Japanese Americans and the Passage of the Civil Liberties Act of 1988.* Stanford, CA: Stanford University Press, 1993.

Hatton, Timothy J., and Jeffrey G. Williamson. *Global Migration and the World Economy: Two Centuries of Policy and Performance.* Cambridge, MA: MIT Press, 2005.

Haycox, Stephen. *Alaska: An American Colony.* Seattle: University of Washington Press, 2002.

Hayduk, Ron. *Democracy for All: Restoring Immigrant Voting Rights in the United States.* New York: Routledge, 2006.

Hayes, Helene. *U.S. Immigration Policy and the Undocumented: Ambivalent Laws, Furtive Lives.* Westport, CT: Praeger, 2001.

Haynes, John Earl, and Harvey Klehr. *In Denial: Historians, Communism and Espionage.* San Francisco: Encounter, 2005.

Heer, David M. *Immigration in America's Future: Social Science Findings and the Policy Debate.* Boulder, CO: Westview, 1996.

Hellman, Judith Adler. *The World of Mexican Migrants: The Rock and the Hard Place.* New York: New Press, 2008.

Helweg, Arthur W. *Strangers in a Not-So-Strange Land: Indian American Immigrants in the Global Age.* Belmont, CA: Wadsworth, 2004.

Henderson, Timothy J. *Beyond Borders: A Concise History of Mexican Migration to the United States.* Malden, MA: Wiley-Blackwell, 2011.

Herman, Richard T., and Robert L. Smith. *Immigrant, Inc.: Why Immigrant Entrepreneurs Are Driving the New Economy (and How They Will Save the American Worker).* Hoboken, NJ: Wiley, 2010.

Hertzberg, Arthur. *The Jews in America: Four Centuries of Uneasy Encounter: A History.* New York: Columbia University Press, 1997.

Higham, John. *Strangers in the Land: Patterns of American Nativism, 1860–1925.* New Brunswick, NJ: Rutgers University Press, 2002.

Higman, B.W. *A Concise History of the Caribbean.* New York: Cambridge University Press, 2011.

Hillstrom, Kevin. *The Dream of America: Immigration, 1870–1920.* Detroit, MI: Omnigraphics, 2009.

Hing, Bill Ong. *Defining America Through Immigration Policy*. Philadelphia: Temple University Press, 2004.

———. *Deporting Our Souls: Values, Morality, and Immigration Policy*. New York: Cambridge University Press, 2006.

Hirobe, Izumi. *Japanese Pride, American Prejudice: Modifying the Exclusion Clause of the 1924 Immigration Act*. Stanford, CA: Stanford University Press, 2001.

Hofmann, Annette R. *The American Turner Movement: A History from Its Beginning to 2000*. Indianapolis, IN: Max Kade, 2010.

Holli, Melvin G., and Peter d'A. Jones, eds. *The Ethnic Frontier: Essays in the History of Group Survival in Chicago and the Midwest*. Grand Rapids, MI: Eerdmans, 1977.

Holmes, Kenneth L., ed. *Covered Wagon Women: Diaries and Letters from the Western Trails, 1840–1849*. Lincoln, NE: Bison, 1995.

Holsiner, Jennifer Leila. *Residential Patterns of Arab Americans: Race, Ethnicity and Spatial Assimilation*. El Paso, TX: LFB Scholarly, 2009.

Holsti, Ole R. *To See Ourselves as Others See Us: How Publics Abroad View the United States After 9/11*. Ann Arbor: University of Michigan Press, 2008.

Holtzman, Jon D. *Nuer Journeys, Nuer Lives: Sudanese Refugees in Minnesota*. 2nd ed. Boston: Allyn and Bacon, 2007.

Hom, Marlon K., ed. and trans. *Songs of Gold Mountain: Cantonese Rhymes from San Francisco Chinatown*. Berkeley: University of California Press, 1987.

Hondagneu-Sotelo, Pierrette. *Doméstica: Immigrant Workers Cleaning and Caring in the Shadows of Affluence*. Berkeley: University of California Press, 2001.

———, ed. *Religion and Social Justice for Immigrants*. New Brunswick, NJ: Rutgers University Press, 2007.

Honeck, Mischa. *We Are the Revolutionists: German-Speaking Immigrants and American Abolitionists After 1848*. Athens: University of Georgia Press, 2011.

Howe, Daniel Walker. *What Hath God Wrought: The Transformation of America, 1815–1848*. New York: Oxford University Press, 2009.

Howe, Irving. *The World of Our Fathers: The Journey of the Eastern European Jews to America and the Life They Found and Made*. New York: New York University Press, 2005.

Hudson, Charles. *Knights of Spain, Warriors of the Sun: Hernando de Soto and the South's Ancient Chiefdoms*. Athens: University of Georgia Press, 1997.

Hudson, John C. *Across This Land: A Regional Geography of the United States and Canada*. Baltimore: Johns Hopkins University Press, 2002.

Hunt, Michael H. *Ideology and U.S. Foreign Policy*. 2nd ed. New Haven, CT: Yale University Press, 2009.

Hunter, Robert. *Tenement Conditions in Chicago*. Chicago: City Homes Association, 1901. Reprint, RareBooksClub.com, 2012.

Hurh, Won Moo. *The Korean Americans*. Westport, CT: Greenwood, 1998.

Ianni, Francis A.J. *Black Mafia: Ethnic Succession in Organized Crime*. New York: Simon & Schuster, 1974.

Iglehart, Alfreda P., and Rosina M. Becerra. *Social Services and the Ethnic Community: History and Analysis*. Long Grove, IL: Waveland, 2011.

Ignatiev, Noel. *How the Irish Became White*. New York: Routledge, 1996.

Inada, Lawson Fusao, ed. *Only What We Could Carry: The Japanese-American Internment Experience*. Berkeley, CA: Heyday, 2000.

Jacobs, Jaap. *The Colony of New Netherland: A Dutch Settlement in Seventeenth-Century America*. Ithaca, NY: Cornell University Press, 2009.

Jacobsen, Robin Dale. *The New Nativism: Proposition 187 and the Debate over Immigration*. Minneapolis: University of Minnesota Press, 2008.

Jacobson, David, ed. *The Immigration Reader: America in a Multidisciplinary Perspective*. Malden, MA: Blackwell, 1998.

———. *Place and Belonging in America*. Baltimore: Johns Hopkins University Press, 2002.

———. *Rights Across Borders: Immigration and the Decline of Citizenship*. Baltimore: Johns Hopkins University Press, 1997.

Jacobson, Matthew Frye. *Whiteness of a Different Color: European Immigrants and the Alchemy of Race*. Cambridge, MA: Harvard University Press, 1998.

Jamero, Peter. *Vanishing Filipino Americans: The Bridge Generation*. Lanham, MD: University Press of America, 2011.

Jaroszyńska-Kirchmann, Anna D. *The Exile Mission: The Polish Political Diaspora and Polish Americans, 1939–1956*. Athens: Ohio University Press, 2004.

Jayaraman, Sarumathi, and Immanuel Ness. *The New Urban Immigrant Workforce: Innovative Models for Labor Organizing*. Armonk, NY: M.E. Sharpe, 2005.

Jefferson, Thomas. *Notes on the State of Virginia*. ForgottenBooks.com, 2012.

Jenks, Rosemary. *The Enhanced Border Security and Visa Entry Reform Act of 2002: A Summary of H.R. 3525*. Washington, DC: Center for Immigration Studies, 2002.

———. *The USA PATRIOT Act of 2001: A Summary of the Anti-Terrorism Law's Immigration-Related Provisions*. Washington, DC: Center for Immigration Studies, 2001.

Johnson, Ericka. *Dreaming of a Mail-Order Husband: Russian-American Internet Romance*. Durham, NC: Duke University Press, 2007.

Johnson, Kevin R. *The "Huddled Masses" Myth: Immigration and Civil Rights.* Philadelphia: Temple University Press, 2004.

Jonas, Suzanne, and Suzie Dod Thomas, eds. *Immigration: A Civil Rights Issue for the Americas.* Wilmington, DE: Scholarly Resources, 1999.

Jones, Katharine W. *Accent on Privilege: English Identities and Anglophilia in the U.S.* Philadelphia: Temple University Press, 2001.

Jones-Correa, Michael. *Between Two Nations: The Political Predicament of Latinos in New York City.* Ithaca, NY: Cornell University Press, 1998.

Joppke, Christian, ed. *Challenge to the Nation-State: Immigration in Western Europe and the United States.* New York: Oxford University Press, 1998.

———. *Immigration and the Nation State: The United States, Germany, and Great Britain.* New York: Oxford University Press, 1999.

Jordan, Don, and Michael Walsh. *White Cargo: The Forgotten History of Britain's White Slaves in America.* New York: New York University Press, 2008.

Joselit, Jenna Weissman. *Parade of Faiths: Immigration and American Religion.* New York: Oxford University Press, 2008.

Junn, Jane, and Kerry L. Haynie, eds. *New Race Politics in America: Understanding Minority and Immigrant Politics.* New York: Cambridge University Press, 2008.

Jurik, Nancy C. *Bootstrap Dreams: U.S. Microenterprise Development in an Era of Welfare Reform.* Ithaca, NY: ILR, 2005.

Kamphoefner, Walter D., and Wolfgang Helbich, eds. *Germans in the Civil War: The Letters They Wrote Home.* Trans. Susan Carter Vogel. Chapel Hill: University of North Carolina Press, 2006.

Kan, Sergei. *Memory Eternal: Tlingit Culture and Russian Orthodox Christianity Through Two Centuries.* Seattle: University of Washington Press, 1999.

Kane, Abdoulaye, and Todd H. Leedy, eds. *African Migrations: Patterns and Perspectives.* Bloomington: Indiana University Press, 2012.

Kanellos, Nicolás. *Hispanic Immigrant Literature: El Sueño del Retorno.* Austin: University of Texas Press, 2011.

Kanellos, Nicolás, with Helvetia Martell. *Hispanic Periodicals in the United States, Origins to 1960: A Brief History and Comprehensive Bibliography.* Houston, TX: Arte Público, 2000.

Kanstroom, Daniel. *Deportation Nation: Outsiders in American History.* Cambridge, MA: Harvard University Press, 2007.

Karim, Jamillah. *American Muslim Women: Negotiating Race, Class, and Gender Within the Ummah.* New York: New York University Press, 2009.

Kasinitz, Philip. *Caribbean New York: Black Immigrants and the Politics of Race.* Ithaca, NY: Cornell University Press, 1992.

Kasintz, Philip, John H. Mollenkopf, Mary C. Waters, and Jennifer Holloway. *Inheriting the City: The Children of Immigrants Come of Age.* New York: Russell Sage Foundation, 2010.

Kaye, Jeffrey. *Moving Millions: How Coyote Capitalism Fuels Global Immigration.* Hoboken, NJ: Wiley, 2010.

Kehoe, Alice B. *North American Indians: A Comprehensive Account.* 3rd ed. Englewood Cliffs, NJ: Prentice Hall, 2005.

Kelly, John. *The Graves Are Walking: The Great Famine and the Saga of the Irish People.* New York: Henry Holt, 2012.

Keogan, Kevin. *Immigrants and the Cultural Politics of Place: A Comparative Study of New York and Los Angeles.* El Paso, TX: LFB Scholarly, 2010.

Kessell, John L. *Pueblos, Spaniards, and the Kingdom of New Mexico.* Norman: University of Oklahoma Press, 2010.

Kettner, James H. *The Development of American Citizenship, 1608–1870.* Chapel Hill: University of North Carolina Press, 2005.

Khory, Kavita R., ed. *Global Migration: Challenges in the Twenty-First Century.* New York: Palgrave Macmillan, 2012.

Kibria, Nazli. *Becoming Asian American: Second-Generation Chinese and Korean American Identities.* Baltimore: Johns Hopkins University Press, 2002.

Kilgour, David, and David T. Jones. *Uneasy Neighbo(u)rs: Canada, the USA and the Dynamics of State, Industry and Culture.* Toronto: Wiley Canada, 2007.

Kim, Kwang Chung, ed. *Koreans in the Hood: Conflict with African Americans.* Baltimore: Johns Hopkins University Press, 1999.

Kim, Nadia Y. *Imperial Citizens: Koreans and Race from Seoul to LA.* Stanford, CA: Stanford University Press, 2008.

Kirsch, George B., Othello Harris, and Claire E. Nolte, eds. *Encyclopedia of Ethnicity and Sports in the United States.* Westport, CT: Greenwood, 2000.

Kiser, George C., and Martha Woody Kiser. *Mexican Workers in the United States: Historical and Political Perspectives.* Albuquerque: University of New Mexico Press, 1979.

Kishinevsky, Vera. *Russian Immigrants in the United States: Adapting to American Culture.* New York: LFB Scholarly, 2004.

Kivisto, Peter, ed. *Incorporating Diversity: Rethinking Assimilation in a Multicultural Age.* Boulder, CO: Paradigm, 2005.

Klapper, Melissa R. *Small Strangers: The Experiences of Immigrant Children in America, 1880–1925.* Chicago: Ivan R. Dee, 2007.

Klein, Herbert S. *The Atlantic Slave Trade.* 2nd ed. New York: Cambridge University Press, 2010.

———. *A Population History of the United States.* 2nd ed. New York: Cambridge University Press, 2012.

Kleinknecht, William. *The New Ethnic Mobs: The Changing Face of Organized Crime in America.* New York: Free Press, 1996.

Knippling, Alpana Sharma, ed. *New Immigrant Literatures in the United States: A Sourcebook to Our Multicultural Literary Heritage.* Westport, CT: Greenwood, 1996.

Kochhar, Rakesh, and Ana Gonzalez-Barrera, with Daniel Dockterman. *Through Boom and Bust: Minorities, Immigrants, and Homeownership.* Washington, DC: Pew Hispanic Center, 2009.

Koehn, Peter H., and James N. Rosenau. *Transnational Competence: Empowering Professional Curricula for Horizon-Rising Challenges.* Boulder, CO: Paradigm, 2010.

Kosak, Hadassa. *Cultures of Opposition: Jewish Immigrant Workers, New York City, 1881–1905.* Albany: State University of New York Press, 2000.

Koshy, Susan, and R. Radhakrishnan. *Transnational South Asians: The Making of a Neo-Diaspora.* New Delhi, India: Oxford University Press, 2008.

Kosoko-Lasaki, Sade, Cynthia T. Cook, and Richard L. O'Brien, eds. *Cultural Proficiency in Addressing Health Disparities.* Sudbury, MA: Jones and Bartlett, 2009.

Kraut, Alan. *The Huddled Masses: The Immigrant in American Society, 1880–1921.* Arlington Heights, IL: Harlan Davidson, 2001.

Kretsedemas, Philip. *The Immigration Crucible: Transforming Race, Nation, and the Limits of the Law.* New York: Columbia University Press, 2012.

Kretsedemas, Philip, and Ana Aparicio, eds. *Immigrants, Welfare Reform, and the Poverty of Policy.* Westport, CT: Praeger, 2004.

Kubrin, Charis E., Marjorie S. Zatz, and Ramiro Martinez, Jr. *Punishing Immigrants: Policy, Politics, and Injustice.* New York: New York University Press, 2012.

Kwong, Peter. *Forbidden Workers: Illegal Chinese Immigrants and American Labor.* New York: New Press, 1998.

Kwong, Peter, and Dušanka Miščević. *Chinese America: The Untold Story of America's Oldest New Community.* New York: New Press, 2005.

Kyle, David. *Transnational Peasants: Migrations, Networks, and Ethnicity in Andean Ecuador.* Baltimore: Johns Hopkins University Press, 2000.

Kyle, David, and Rey Koslowski, eds. *Global Human Smuggling: Comparative Perspectives.* Baltimore: Johns Hopkins University Press, 2001.

La Sorte, Michael. *La Merica: Images of Italian Greenhorn Experience.* Philadelphia: Temple University Press, 2003.

Laglaron, Laureen, Cristina Rodríguez, Alexa Silver, and Sirithon Thanasombat. *Regulating Immigration at the State Level: Highlights from the Database of 2007 State Immigration Legislation and Methodology.* Washington, DC: National Center for Immigration Integration Policy, Migration Policy Institute, 2008.

Laham, Nicholas. *Ronald Reagan and the Politics of Immigration Reform.* Westport, CT: Praeger, 2000.

Lai, Eric, and Dennis Arguelles. *The New Asian Pacific America: Numbers, Diversity and Change in the 21st Century.* San Francisco: Asian Week, 2003.

Lai, Him Mark, Genny Yim, and Judy Yung, eds. *Island: Poetry and History of Chinese Immigrants on Angel Island, 1910–1940.* Seattle: University of Washington Press, 1991.

Laliotou, Ioanna. *Transnational Subjects: Acts of Migration and Cultures of Transnationalism Between Greece and America.* Chicago: University of Chicago Press, 2004.

Lamphere, Louise, Alex Stepick, and Guillermo J. Grenier, eds. *Newcomers in the Workplace: Immigrants and the Restructuring of the U.S. Economy.* Philadelphia: Temple University Press, 1994.

Lau, Estelle T. *Paper Families: Identity, Immigration Administration, and Chinese Exclusion.* Durham, NC: Duke University Press, 2006.

Law, Anna O. *The Immigration Battle in American Courts.* New York: Cambridge University Press, 2010.

Laxer, James. *The Border: Canada, the U.S. and Dispatches from the 49th Parallel.* Toronto: Doubleday Canada, 2003.

Lay, J. Celeste. *A Midwestern Mosaic: Immigration and Political Socialization in Rural America.* Philadelphia: Temple University Press, 2012.

Leach, Kristine. *In Search of a Common Ground: Nineteenth and Twentieth Century Immigrant Women in America.* San Francisco: Austin & Winfield, 1995.

Lederhendler, Eli. *Jewish Immigrants and American Capitalism, 1880–1920: From Caste to Class.* New York: Cambridge University Press, 2009.

Lee, Erika. *At America's Gates: Chinese Immigration During the Exclusion Era, 1882–1943.* Chapel Hill: University of North Carolina Press, 2007.

Lee, Erika, and Judy Yung. *Angel Island: Immigrant Gateway to America.* New York: Oxford University Press, 2010.

Lee, J.J., and Marion R. Casey, eds. *Making the Irish American: History and Heritage of the Irish in the United States.* New York: New York University Press, 2006.

Lee, Jennifer 8. *The Fortune Cookie Chronicles: Adventures in the World of Chinese Food.* New York: Twelve, 2008.

Lee, Josephine, Imogene L. Lim, and Yuko Matsukawa, eds. *Re/collecting Early Asian America: Essays in Cultural History.* Philadelphia: Temple University Press, 2002.

Lee, Maggy, ed. *Human Trafficking.* Portland, OR: Willan, 2007.

Lehmann, Hartmut, Hermann Wellenreuther, and Renate Wilson, eds. *In Search of Peace and Prosperity: New German Settlements in Eighteenth-Century Europe and America.* University Park: Pennsylvania State University Press, 2000.

Leighley, Jan E. *Strength in Numbers? The Political Mobilization of Racial and Ethnic Minorities.* Princeton, NJ: Princeton University Press, 2001.

Lemann, Nicholas A. *The Promised Land: The Great Black Migration and How It Changed America.* New York: Vintage, 1991.

LeMay, Michael C. *Illegal Immigration: A Reference Handbook.* Santa Barbara, CA: ABC-CLIO, 2007.

———. *Transforming America: Perspectives on U.S. Immigration.* New York: Praeger, 2012.

Lemekh, Halyna. *Ukrainian Immigrants in New York: Collision of Two Worlds.* New York: LFB Scholarly, 2010.

Leonard, Karen Isaksen. *Making Ethnic Choices: California's Punjabi Mexican Americans.* Philadelphia: Temple University Press, 1992.

Lester, Paul M., ed. *Images That Injure: Pictorial Stereotypes in the Media.* Westport, CT: Praeger, 1996.

Levine, Bruce C. *The Spirit of 1848: German Immigrants, Labor Conflict, and the Coming of the Civil War.* Urbana: University of Illinois Press, 1992.

Levine, Robert M., and Moisés Asís. *Cuban Miami.* New Brunswick, NJ: Rutgers University Press, 2000.

Levitt, Peggy. *God Needs No Passport: Immigrants and the Changing American Religious Landscape.* New York: New Press, 2007.

Levitt, Peggy, and Mary C. Waters, eds. *The Changing Face of Home: The Transnational Lives of the Second Generation.* New York: Russell Sage Foundation, 2006.

Levy, Amnon, and João Ricardo Faria, eds. *Economic Growth, Inequality and Migration.* Northampton, MA: Edward Elgar, 2002.

Lewis, Ronald L. *Welsh Americans: A History of Assimilation in the Coalfields.* Chapel Hill: University of North Carolina Press, 2008.

Ley, David. *Millionaire Migrants: Trans-Pacific Life Lines.* Malden, MA: Wiley-Blackwell, 2010.

Li, Wei. *Ethnoburb: The New Ethnic Community in Urban America.* Honolulu: University of Hawaii Press, 2009.

Lien, Pei-te, M. Margaret Conway, and Janelle Wong. *The Politics of Asian Americans: Diversity and Community.* New York: Routledge, 2004.

Light, Ivan H. *Deflecting Immigration: Networks, Markets, and Regulation in Los Angeles.* New York: Russell Sage Foundation, 2006.

Light, Ivan H., and Edna Bonacich. *Immigrant Entrepreneurs: Koreans in Los Angeles, 1965–1982.* Berkeley: University of California Press, 1988.

Light, Ivan H., and Steven Gold. *Ethnic Economies.* San Diego, CA: Academic Press, 2000.

Lin, Jan. *Reconstructing Chinatown: Ethnic Enclave, Global Change.* Minneapolis: University of Minnesota Press, 1998.

Lindenfeld, Jacqueline. *The French in the United States: An Ethnographic Study.* Westport, CT: Praeger, 2000.

Ling, Amy, ed. *Yellow Light: The Flowering of Asian American Arts.* Philadelphia: Temple University Press, 1999.

Ling, Huping, ed. *Emerging Voices: Experiences of Underrepresented Asian Americans.* New Brunswick, NJ: Rutgers University Press, 2008.

Lipset, Seymour Martin, and Earl Raab. *The Politics of Unreason: Right-Wing Extremism in America, 1790–1977.* 2nd ed. Chicago: University of Chicago Press, 1978.

Lipsitz, George. *The Possessive Investment in Whiteness: How White People Profit from Identity Politics.* Philadelphia: Temple University Press, 2006.

Longley, Clifford. *Chosen People: The Big Idea That Shaped England and America.* London: Hodder & Stoughton, 2002.

Lonn, Ella. *Foreigners in the Confederacy.* Chapel Hill: University of North Carolina Press, 2001.

López-Garza, Marta, and David R. Diaz, eds. *Asian and Latino Immigrants in a Restructuring Economy: The Metamorphosis of Los Angeles.* Stanford, CA: Stanford University Press, 2001.

Lott, Juanita Tamayo. *Common Destiny: Filipino American Generations.* Lanham, MD: Rowman & Littlefield, 2006.

Louie, Vivian S. *Compelled to Excel: Immigration, Education, and Opportunity Among Chinese Americans.* Stanford, CA: Stanford University Press, 2004.

———. *Keeping the Immigrant Bargain: The Costs and Rewards of Success in America.* New York: Russell Sage Foundation, 2012.

Luebke, Frederick C., ed. *European Immigrants in the American West: Community Histories.* Albuquerque: University of New Mexico Press, 1998.

———. *Germans in the New World: Essays in the History of Immigration.* Urbana: University of Illinois Press, 1990.

Lynch-Brennan, Margaret. *The Irish Budget: Irish Immigrant Women in Domestic Service in America, 1840–1930.* Syracuse, NY: Syracuse University Press, 2009.

Lyons, Terrence, and Peter Mandaville, eds. *Politics from Afar: Transnational Diasporas and Networks.* New York: Columbia University Press, 2012.

Maciel, David R., and María Herrera-Sobek, eds. *Culture Across Borders: Mexican Immigration and Popular Culture.* Tucson: University of Arizona Press, 1998.

Magaña, Lisa. *Straddling the Border: Immigration Policy and the INS.* Austin: University of Texas Press, 2003.

Mahler, Sarah J. *American Dreaming: Immigrant Life on the Margins.* Princeton, NJ: Princeton University Press, 1995.

Mahoney, Annette S. *The Health and Well-Being of Caribbean Immigrants in the United States.* New York: Routledge, 2005.

Maira, Sunaina Marr. *Missing: Youth, Citizenship and Empire After 9/11.* Durham, NC: Duke University Press, 2009.

Malik, Iftikhar H. *Islam and Modernity: Muslims in Europe and the United States.* Sterling, VA: Pluto, 2004.

Mann, Gurinder Singh, Paul David Numrich, and Raymond B. Williams. *Buddhists, Hindus, and Sikhs in America: A Short History.* New York: Oxford University Press, 2008.

Marcelli, Enrico, Colin C. Williams, and Pascale Joassart, eds. *Informal Work in Developed Nations.* New York: Routledge, 2010.

Margolis, Maxine L. *An Invisible Minority: Brazilians in New York City.* Gainesville: University Press of Florida, 2009.

Maril, Robert Lee. *The Fence: National Security, Public Safety, and Illegal Immigration Along the U.S.–Mexico Border.* Lubbock: Texas Tech University Press, 2011.

Marquardt, Marie Friedmann, Timothy J. Steigenga, Phillip J. Williams, and Manuel A. Vasquez. *Living "Illegal": The Human Face of Unauthorized Immigration.* New York: New Press, 2011.

Marre, Diana, and Laura Briggs, eds. *International Adoption: Global Inequalities and the Circulation of Children.* New York: New York University Press, 2009.

Marrus, Michael R. *The Unwanted: European Refugees from the First World War to the Cold War.* Philadelphia: Temple University Press, 2002.

Martin, Philip. *Importing Poverty? Immigration and the Changing Face of Rural America.* New Haven, CT: Yale University Press, 2009.

Martin, Philip, Michael Fix, and J. Edward Taylor. *The New Rural Poverty: Agriculture and Immigration in California.* Washington, DC: Urban Institute Press, 2006.

Martinez, Ramiro, Jr., and Abel Valenzuela, Jr. *Immigrants and Crime: Ethnicity, Race, and Violence.* New York: New York University Press, 2006.

Mason, Ronald J. *Inconstant Companions: Archaeology and North American Indian Oral Traditions.* Tuscaloosa: University of Alabama Press, 2006.

Massey, Douglas S., Jorge Durand, and Nolan J. Malone. *Beyond Smoke and Mirrors: Mexican Immigration in an Era of Economic Integration.* New York: Russell Sage Foundation, 2002.

———. *New Faces in New Places: The Changing Geography of American Immigration.* New York: Russell Sage Foundation, 2008.

Matsaganis, Matthew D., Vikki S. Katz, and Sandra J. Ball-Rokeach. *Understanding Ethnic Media: Producers, Consumers, and Societies.* Thousand Oaks, CA: Sage, 2011.

McCarthy, Angela, and Catharine Coleborne, eds. *Migration, Ethnicity, and Mental Health: International Perspectives, 1840–2010.* New York: Routledge, 2012.

McKinney, Louise. *New Orleans: A Cultural History.* New York: Oxford University Press, 2006.

McWilliams, Carey. *Factories in the Field: The Story of Migratory Labor in California.* 1939. Berkeley: University of California Press, 2000.

Meissner, Doris, and Donald Kerwin. *DHS and Immigration: Taking Stock and Correcting Course.* Washington, DC: Migration Policy Institute, 2009.

Melendez, Edwin. *Los que se van y los que regresan: Puerto Rican Migration to and from the United States, 1982–1988.* New York: Center for Puerto Rican Studies, 1993.

Menchaca, Martha. *Naturalizing Mexican Immigrants: A Texas History.* Austin: University of Texas Press, 2011.

Mendoza, Louis, and S. Shankar, eds. *Crossing into America: The New Literature of Immigration.* New York: New Press, 2003.

Menjívar, Cecilia. *Fragmented Ties: Salvadoran Immigrant Networks in America.* Berkeley: University of California Press, 2000.

Merrill, Ellen C. *Germans of Louisiana.* Gretna, LA: Pelican, 2005.

Merskin, Debra L. *Media, Minorities, and Meaning: A Critical Introduction.* New York: Peter Lang, 2011.

Messamore, Barbara J., ed. *Canadian Migration Patterns: From Britain to North America.* Ottawa, Canada: University of Ottawa Press, 2002.

Messina, Anthony M., and Gallya Lahav, eds. *The Migration Reader: Exploring Politics and Policy.* Boulder, CO: Lynne Rienner, 2005.

Miers, Suzanne. *Slavery in the Twentieth Century: The Evolution of a Global Problem.* Walnut Creek, CA: AltaMira, 2003.

Migration Policy Institute. *Coming to America Two Years After September 11, 2001.* Washington, DC: Migration Policy Institute, 2003.

Milkman, Ruth, ed. *Organizing Immigrants: The Challenge for Unions in Contemporary California.* Ithaca, NY: ILR, 2000.

Milkman, Ruth, and Kent Wong. *Voices from the Front Lines: Organizing Immigrant Workers in Los Angeles.* Los Angeles: University of California, Los Angeles, Center for Labor Research and Education, 2000.

Miller, Aaron R., ed. *U.S. Visa Policies, Programs and Considerations.* Hauppauge, NY: Nova Science, 2011.

Miller, Donald L. *City of the Century: The Epic of Chicago and the Making of America.* New York: Simon & Schuster, 1996.

Milner, Clyde A., Carol A. O'Connor, and Martha A. Sandweiss, eds. *The Oxford History of the American West.* New York: Oxford University Press, 1994.

Min, Pyong Gap. *Caught in the Middle: Korean Communities in New York and Los Angeles.* Berkeley: University of California Press, 1996.

———. *Preserving Ethnicity Through Religion in America: Korean Protestants and Indian Hindus Across Generations.* New York: New York University Press, 2010.

Mirak, Robert. *Torn Between Two Lands: Armenians in America, 1890 to World War I.* Cambridge, MA: Harvard University Press, 1983.

Mize, Ronald L., and Alicia C.S. Swords. *Consuming Mexican Labor: From the Bracero Program to NAFTA.* Toronto: University of Toronto Press, 2011.

Mobasher, Mohsen M. *Iranian Immigrants in Texas: Migration, Politics, and Ethnic Identity.* Austin: University of Texas Press, 2012.

Model, Suzanne. *West Indian Immigrants: A Black Success Story?* New York: Russell Sage Foundation, 2008.

Moloney, Mick. *Far from the Shamrock Shore: The Story of Irish-American Immigration Through Song.* Cork, Ireland: Collins, 2002.

Mooney, Peter J. *The Impact of Immigration on the Growth and Development of the U.S. Economy, 1890–1920.* New York: Garland, 1990.

Moran, Rachel F. *Interracial Intimacy: The Regulation of Race and Romance.* Chicago: University of Chicago Press, 2001.

Morgan, Charlie V. *Intermarriage Across Race and Ethnicity Among Immigrants: E Pluribus Unions.* El Paso, TX: LFB Scholarly, 2009.

Morgan, Edmund S. *American Slavery, American Freedom: The Ordeal of Colonial Virginia.* New York: W.W. Norton, 2003.

Mosk, Carl. *Trade and Migration in the Modern World.* New York: Routledge, 2005.

Moskos, Charles, Jr. *Greek Americans: Struggle and Success.* Englewood Cliffs, NJ: Prentice Hall, 1980.

Moslund, Sten Pultz. *Migration Literature and Hybridity: The Different Speeds of Transcultural Change.* New York: Palgrave Macmillan, 2010.

Mott, Tamar. *African Refugee Resettlement in the United States.* El Paso: LFB Scholarly, 2009.

Moyn, Samuel. *The Last Utopia: Human Rights in History.* Cambridge, MA: Belknap Press, 2010.

Mufwene, Salikoko, John R. Rickford, Guy Bailey, and John Baugh, eds. *African-American English: Structure, History, and Use.* New York: Routledge, 1998.

Muller, Gilbert H. *New Strangers in Paradise: The Immigrant Experience and Contemporary American Fiction.* Lexington: University Press of Kentucky, 1999.

Muller, Thomas. *Immigrants and the American City.* New York: New York University Press, 1993.

Mulrooney, Margaret M., ed. *Fleeing the Famine: North America and Irish Refugees, 1845–1851.* Westport, CT: Praeger, 2003.

Murphy, Andrew R. *Conscience and Community: Revisiting Toleration and Religious Dissent in Early Modern England and America.* University Park: Pennsylvania State University Press, 2001.

Musalo, Karen, Jennifer Moore, and Richard A. Boswell. *Refugee Law and Policy: A Comparative and International Approach.* 4th ed. Durham, NC: Carolina Academic Press, 1997.

Naber, Nadine. *Arab America: Gender, Cultural Politics, and Activism.* New York: New York University Press, 2012.

Naficy, Hamid, ed. *Home, Exile, Homeland: Film, Media, and the Politics of Place.* New York: Routledge, 1999.

Ness, Immanuel, ed. *The Encyclopedia of Global Human Migration.* Hoboken, NJ: Wiley-Blackwell, 2013.

Newton, Lina. *Illegal, Alien, or Immigrant: The Politics of Immigration Reform.* New York: New York University Press, 2008.

Ng, Franklin. *The Taiwanese Americans.* Westport, CT: Greenwood, 1998.

Ngai, Mae M. *Impossible Subjects: Illegal Aliens and the Making of Modern America.* Princeton, NJ: Princeton University Press, 2005.

Nicolas, Guerda, Angela DeSilva, and Stephanie Donnelly. *Social Network and the Mental Health of Haitian Immigrants.* Coconut Creek, FL: Caribbean Studies Press, 2011.

Obidinski, Eugene E., and Helen Stankiewicz Zand. *Polish Folkways in America.* Lanham, MD: University Press of America, 1987.

Oboler, Suzanne, ed. *Latinos and Citizenship: The Dilemma of Belonging.* New York: Palgrave Macmillan, 2006.

Ochoa, Enrique C., and Gilda L. Ochoa, eds. *Latino Los Angeles: Transformations, Communities, and Activism.* Tucson: University of Arizona Press, 2005.

Ofalea, Gregory. *The Arab Americans.* Northampton, MA: Olive Branch, 2006.

O'Hare, William P., and Judy C. Felt. *Asian Americans: America's Fastest Growing Minority Group.* Washington, DC: Population Reference Bureau, 1991.

Okamura, Jonathan Y. *Imagining the Filipino American Diaspora: Transnational Relations, Identities, and Communities.* New York: Garland, 1998.

Okpewho, Isidore, and Nkiru Nzegwu, eds. *The African Diaspora.* Bloomington: Indiana University Press, 2009.

Olson, Laura Katz, ed. *Age Through Ethnic Lenses: Caring for the Elderly in a Multicultural Society.* Lanham, MD: Rowman & Littlefield, 2001.

Olsson, Eva-Karin, and Lan Xue, eds. *SARS from East to West.* Lanham, MD: Lexington, 2012.

Olupona, Jacob K., and Regina Gemignani, eds. *African Immigrant Religions in America.* New York: New York University Press, 2007.

O'Neil, Kevin. *Hazleton and Beyond: Why Communities Try to Restrict Immigration.* Washington, DC: Migration Policy Institute, 2010.

Ono, Hiroshi, and Madeline Zavodny. "Race, Internet Usage, and E-Commerce." Working Paper No. 2002-01, Federal Reserve Bank of Atlanta, January 2002.

Orellana, Marjorie Faulstich. *Translating Childhoods: Immigrant Youth, Language, and Culture.* New Brunswick, NJ: Rutgers University Press, 2009.

Orsi, Robert A. *The Madonna of 115th Street: Faith and Community in Italian Harlem, 1880–1950.* 2nd ed. New Haven, CT: Yale University Press, 2002.

Overmyer-Velázquez, Mark, ed. *Beyond la Frontera: The History of Mexico–U.S. Migration.* New York: Oxford University Press, 2011.

Özden, Çağlar, and Maurice Schiff, eds. *International Migration, Remittances, and the Brain Drain.* Washington, DC: World Bank, 2006.

Pacyga, Dominic A. *Polish Immigrants and Industrial Chicago: Workers on the South Side, 1880–1922.* Chicago: University of Chicago Press, 2003.

Paerregaard, Karsten. *Peruvians Dispersed: A Global Ethnography of Migration.* Lanham, MD: Lexington, 2008.

Palfrey, John, and Urs Gasser. *Born Digital: Understanding the First Generation of Digital Natives.* New York: Basic Books, 2008.

Pallares, Amalia, and Nilda Flores-González, eds. *¡Marcha!: Latino Chicago and the Immigrant Rights Movement.* Urbana: University of Illinois Press, 2010.

Parascandola, Louis J., ed. *"Look for Me All Around You": Anglophone Caribbean Immigrants in the Harlem Renaissance.* Detroit, MI: Wayne State University Press, 2005.

Park, Keumjae. *Korean Immigrant Women and the Renegotiation of Identity: Class, Gender, and the Politics of Identity.* El Paso, TX: LFB Scholarly, 2009.

Park, Kyeyoung. *The Korean American Dream: Immigrants and Small Business in New York City.* Ithaca, NY: Cornell University Press, 1997.

Park, Lisa Sun-Hee. *Consuming Citizenship: Children of Asian Immigrant Entrepreneurs.* Stanford, CA: Stanford University Press, 2005.

———. *Entitled to Nothing: The Struggle for Immigrant Health Care in the Age of Welfare Reform.* New York: New York University Press, 2011.

Park, Robert E. *The Immigrant Press and Its Control.* New York: Harper & Brothers, 1922.

Parks, Virginia. *The Geography of Immigrant Labor Markets: Space, Networks, and Gender.* New York: LFB Scholarly, 2005.

Parrillo, Vincent N. *Strangers to These Shores: Census Update.* 10th ed. New York: Prentice Hall, 2011.

Passel, Jeffrey S. *The Size and Characteristics of the Unauthorized Migrant Population in the U.S.* Washington, DC: Pew Hispanic Center, 2006.

Pawel, Miriam. *The Union of Their Dreams: Power, Hope, and Struggle in Cesar Chavez's Farm Worker Movement.* New York: Bloomsbury, 2009.

Payant, Katherine B., and Toby Rose, eds. *The Immigrant Experience in North American Literature: Carving Out a Niche.* Westport, CT: Greenwood, 1999.

Pearce, Susan C., Elizabeth J. Clifford, and Reena Tandon. *Immigration and Women: Understanding the American Experience.* New York: New York University Press, 2011.

Peck, Gunther. *Reinventing Free Labor: Padrones and Immigrant Workers in the North American West, 1880–1930.* Cambridge, UK: Cambridge University Press, 2000.

Pedraza, Silvia. *Political Disaffection in Cuba's Revolution and Exodus.* New York: Cambridge University Press, 2007.

Pedraza, Silvia, and Rubén G. Rumbaut, eds. *Origins and Destinies: Immigration, Race, and Ethnicity in America.* Belmont, CA: Wadsworth, 1996.

Penn, William. *Narratives of Early Pennsylvania, West New Jersey and Delaware, 1630–1707,* ed. Albert Cook Myers. New York: Charles Scribner's Sons, 1912. Reprint, Charleston, SC: Nabu, 2010.

Perea, Juan F., ed. *Immigrants Out! The New Nativism and the Anti-Immigrant Impulse in the United States.* New York: New York University Press, 1997.

Pfeifer, Mark Edward, Monica Chiu, and Kou Yang, eds. *Diversity in Diaspora: Hmong Americans in the Twenty-First Century.* Honolulu: University of Hawaii Press, 2013.

Phillips, Nicola, ed. *Migration in the Global Political Economy.* Boulder, CO: Lynne Rienner, 2011.

Piatt, Bill. *Only English? Law and Language Policy in the United States.* Albuquerque: University of New Mexico Press, 1990.

Plascencia, Luis F.B. *Disenchanting Citizenship: Mexican Migrants and the Boundaries of Belonging.* New Brunswick, NJ: Rutgers University Press, 2012.

Plender, Richard. *Basic Documents on International Migration Law.* 3rd ed. Boston: Martinus Nijhoff, 2007.

Portes, Alejandro, ed. *The Economic Sociology of Immigration: Essays on Networks, Ethnicity, and Entrepreneurship.* New York: Russell Sage Foundation, 1995.

———, ed. *The New Second Generation.* New York: Russell Sage Foundation, 1996.

Portes, Alejandro, and Robert L. Bach. *Latin Journey: Cuban and Mexican Immigrants in the United States.* Berkeley: University of California Press, 1985.

Portes, Alejandro, and Rubén G. Rumbaut. *Immigrant America: A Portrait.* 3rd ed. Berkeley: University of California Press, 2006.

———. *Legacies: The Story of the Immigrant Second Generation.* Berkeley: University of California Press, 2001.

Potocky-Tripodi, Miriam. *Best Practices for Social Work with Refugees and Immigrants.* New York: Columbia University Press, 2002.

Potowski, Kim, ed. *Language Diversity in the USA.* New York: Cambridge University Press, 2010.

Preston, William, Jr. *Aliens and Dissenters: Federal Suppression of Radicals.* 2nd ed. Urbana: University of Illinois Press, 1994.

Pula, James S., ed. *The Polish American Encyclopedia.* Lafayette, NC: McFarland, 2011.

Pumar, Enrique S., ed. *Hispanic Migration and Urban Development: Studies from Washington, DC.* Bingley, UK: Emerald Group, 2012.

Ramirez, Bruno. *Crossing the 49th Parallel: Migration from Canada to the United States, 1900–1930.* Ithaca, NY: Cornell University Press, 2001.

Ramos, Henry A.J. *The American GI Forum: In Pursuit of the Dream, 1948–1983.* Houston, TX: Arte Publico, 1998.

Raphael, Marc Lee, ed. *The Columbia History of Jews and Judaism in America.* New York: Columbia University Press, 2008.

———. *The Synagogue in America: A Short History.* New York: New York University Press, 2011.

Reid, Ira de Augustine. *The Negro Immigrant: His Background, Characteristics and Social Adjustment, 1899–1937.* New York: Columbia University Press, 1939.

Reimers, David M. *Other Immigrants: The Global Origins of the American People.* New York: New York University Press, 2005.

———. *Still the Golden Door: The Third World Comes to America.* 2nd ed. New York: Columbia University Press, 1992.

———. *Unwelcome Strangers: American Identity and the Turn Against Immigration.* New York: Columbia University Press, 1998.

Reitz, Jeffery G. *Warmth of the Welcome: The Social Causes of Economic Success for Immigrants in Different Nations and Cities.* Boulder, CO: Westview, 1998.

Repak, Terry A. *Waiting on Washington: Central American Workers in the Nation's Capital.* Philadelphia: Temple University Press, 1995.

Reyes, Angela. *Language, Identity, and Stereotype Among Southeast Asian American Youth: The Other Asian.* Mahwah, NJ: Lawrence Erlbaum, 2007.

Richardson, Chad, and Michael J. Pisani. *The Informal and Underground Economy of the South Texas Border.* Austin: University of Texas Press, 2012.

Richardson, Steven O. *The Political Economy of Bureaucracy.* New York: Routledge, 2011.

Ricourt, Milagros. *Dominicans in New York City: Power from the Margins.* New York: Routledge, 2002.

Rieff, David. *Going to Miami: Exiles, Tourists, and Refugees in the New America.* Gainesville: University Press of Florida, 1999.

———. *Los Angeles: Capital of the Third World.* New York: Simon & Schuster, 1991.

Riis, Jacob A. *How the Other Half Lives: Studies Among the Tenements of New York.* New York: Charles Scribner's Sons, 1890. Reprint, ReadaClassic.com, 2010.

Rivera-Batiz, Francisco, and Carlos Santiago. *Puerto Ricans in the United States: A Changing Reality.* Washington, DC: National Puerto Rican Coalition, 1994.

Robila, Mihaela. *Eastern European Immigrant Families.* New York: Routledge, 2012.

Robinson, Greg. *After Camp: Portraits in Midcentury Japanese American Life and Politics.* Berkeley: University of California Press, 2012.

———. *A Tragedy of Democracy: Japanese Confinement in North America.* New York: Columbia University Press, 2009.

Robinson, W. Courtland. *Terms of Refuge: The Indochinese Exodus and the International Response.* New York: Zed, 1998.

Rodríguez, Havidán, Rogelio Sáenz, and Cecilia Menjívar, eds. *Latinas/os in the United States: Changing the Face of América.* New York: Springer, 2008.

Rogin, Michael. *Blackface, White Noise: Jewish Immigrants in the Hollywood Melting Pot.* Berkeley: University of California Press, 1996.

Romero, Fernando. *Hyperborder: The Contemporary U.S.–Mexican Border and Its Future.* Princeton, NJ: Princeton Architectural Press, 2008.

Rosenbaum, Emily, and Samantha Friedman. *The Housing Divide: How Generations of Immigrants Fare in New York's Housing Market.* New York: New York University Press, 2007.

Rosenblum, Marc R. *The Transnational Politics of U.S. Immigration Policy.* La Jolla: University of California, San Diego, Center for Comparative Immigration Studies, 2004.

Rosenwaike, Ira. *Population History of New York City.* Syracuse, NY: Syracuse University Press, 1972.

Ross, Robert. *Slaves to Fashion: Poverty and Abuse in the New Sweatshops.* Ann Arbor: University of Michigan Press, 2007.

Roth, Wendy D. *Race Migrations: Latinos and the Cultural Transformation of Race.* Stanford, CA: Stanford University Press, 2012.

Rothenberg, Daniel. *With These Hands: The Hidden World of Migrant Farmworkers Today.* New York: Harcourt Brace, 1998.

Rozek, Barbara J. *Come to Texas: Attracting Immigrants, 1865–1915.* College Station: Texas A&M University Press, 2003.

Rubin, Rachel, and Jeffrey Melnick. *Immigration and American Popular Culture: An Introduction.* New York: New York University Press, 2007.

Rubio-Goldsmith, Raquel, Celestino Fernández, and Maribel Álvarez, eds. *No Vale Nada La Vida: Migrant Deaths in the Arizona Desert.* Tucson: University of Arizona Press, 2014.

Ruble, Blair A. *Creating Diversity Capital: Transnational Migrants in Montreal, Washington, and Kyiv.* Baltimore: Johns Hopkins University Press, 2005.

Rumbaut, Rubén G., and Alejandro Portes, eds. *Ethnicities: Children of Immigrants in America.* Berkeley: University of California Press, 2001.

Russo, Jean B., and J. Elliot Russo. *Planting an Empire: The Early Chesapeake in British North America.* Baltimore: Johns Hopkins University Press, 2012.

Sahay, Anjali. *Indian Diaspora in the United States: Brain Drain or Gain?* Lanham, MD: Lexington, 2009.

Salomone, Rosemary C. *True American: Language, Identity and the Education of Immigrant Children.* Cambridge, MA: Harvard University Press, 2010.

Sánchez, Augustin, ed. *Iraqi Refugees: A Humanitarian Crisis?* New York: Nova Science, 2010.

Sandrow, Nahma. *Vagabond Stars: A World History of Yiddish Theater.* Syracuse, NY: Syracuse University Press, 1996.

Sarna, Jonathan D. *American Judaism: A History.* New Haven, CT: Yale University Press, 2005.

Sassen, Saskia. *The Global City: New York, London, Tokyo.* 2nd ed. Princeton, NJ: Princeton University Press, 2001.

Sawhney, Deepak Narang, ed. *Unmasking L.A.: Third Worlds and the City.* New York: Palgrave Macmillan, 2002.

Saxton, Alexander. *The Indispensable Enemy: Labor and the Anti-Chinese Movement in California.* Berkeley: University of California Press, 1995.

———. *The Rise and Fall of the White Republic: Class Politics and Mass Culture in Nineteenth-Century America.* New York: Verso, 1990.

Scarpaci, Vincenza. *The Journey of the Italians in America.* Gretna, LA: Pelican, 2008.

Schaie, K. Warner, and Peter Uhlenberg, eds. *Social Structures: Demographic Changes and the Well-Being of Older Persons.* New York: Springer, 2007.

Schain, Martin A. *The Politics of Immigration in France, Britain, and the United States: A Comparative Study.* New York: Palgrave Macmillan, 2008.

Schattle, Hans. *Globalization and Citizenship.* Lanham, MD: Rowman & Littlefield, 2012.

Schmidt Camacho, Alicia. *Migrant Imaginaries: Latino Cultural Politics in the U.S.–Mexico Borderlands.* New York: New York University Press, 2008.

Schoenberger, Karl. *Levi's Children: Coming to Terms with Human Rights in the Global Marketplace.* New York: Atlantic Monthly, 2000.

Schotel, Bas. *On the Right of Exclusion: Law, Ethics and Immigration Policy.* New York: Routledge, 2011.

Schrag, Peter. *Not Fit for Our Society: Immigration and Nativism in America.* Berkeley: University of California Press, 2010.

Schuck, Peter H. *Citizens, Strangers, and In-Betweens: Essays on Immigration and Citizenship.* Boulder, CO: Westview, 1998.

Seager, Richard Hughes. *Buddhism in America.* Rev. ed. New York: Columbia University Press, 2012.

Segura, Denise A., and Patricia Zavella, eds. *Women and Migration in the U.S.–Mexico Borderlands: A Reader.* Durham, NC: Duke University Press, 2007.

Segura, Rosamaría. *Central Americans in Los Angeles.* Charleston, SC: Arcadia, 2010.

Selznick, Barbara J. *Global Television: Co-Producing Culture.* Philadelphia: Temple University Press, 2008.

Sen, Rinku, with Fekkak Mamdouh. *The Accidental American: Immigration and Citizenship in the Age of Globalization.* San Francisco: Berrett-Koehler, 2008.

Shaub, Marvin H. *Transitions: Adjustment Strategies of American Immigrants.* Lanham, MD: University Press of America, 2009.

Shavarini, Mitra K. *Educating Immigrants: Experiences of Second-Generation Iranians.* New York: LFB Scholarly, 2004.

Shaw-Taylor, Yoku, and Steven A. Tuch, eds. *The Other African Americans: Contemporary African and Caribbean Immigrants in the United States.* New York: Rowman & Littlefield, 2007.

Sheffer, Gabriel. *Diaspora Politics: At Home Abroad.* New York: Cambridge University Press, 2003.

Shelley, Louise. *Human Trafficking: A Global Perspective.* New York: Cambridge University Press, 2010.

Shell-Weiss, Melanie. *Coming to Miami: A Social History.* Gainesville: University Press of Florida, 2009.

Sher, Leo and Alexander Vilens, eds. *Immigration and Mental Health: Stress, Psychiatric Disorders, and Suicidal Behavior Among Immigrants and Refugees.* Hauppauge, NY: Nova Science, 2010.

Shukla, Sandhva, and Heidi Tinsman, eds. *Imagining Our Americas: Toward a Transnational Frame.* Durham, NC: Duke University Press, 2007.

Simon, Rita J., and Susan H. Alexander. *The Ambivalent Welcome: Print Media, Public Opinion, and Immigration.* Westport, CT: Praeger, 1993.

Simone, Roberta. *The Immigrant Experience in American Fiction: An Annotated Bibliography.* Lanham, MD: Scarecrow, 1995.

Sinclair, Upton. *The Jungle.* 1906. Blacksburg, VA: Wilder, 2010.

Singer, Audrey, Susan W. Hardwick, and Carolina B. Brettell, eds. *Twenty-First Century Gateways: Immigrant Incorporation in Suburban America.* Washington, DC: Brookings Institution Press, 2008.

Sirkeci, Ibrahim, Jeffrey D. Cohen, and Dilip Ratha, eds. *Migration and Remittances during the Global Financial Crisis and Beyond.* Washington, DC: World Bank, 2012.

Slobin, Mark. *Tenement Songs: The Popular Music of the Jewish Immigrants.* Urbana: University of Illinois Press, 1982.

Small, Cathy A. *Voyages: From Tongan Villages to American Suburbs.* 2nd ed. Ithaca, NY: Cornell University Press, 2011.

Smedley, Brian D., Adrienne Y. Stith, and Alan R. Nelson, eds. *Unequal Treatment: Confronting Racial and Ethnic Disparities in Health Care.* Washington, DC: National Academy Press, 2003.

Smith, James P., and Barry Edmonston, eds. *The New Americans: Economic, Demographic, and Fiscal Effects of Immigration.* Washington, DC: National Academy Press, 1997.

Smith, Jane L. *Islam in America.* 2nd ed. New York: Columbia University Press, 2010.

Smith, Michael Peter, and Matt Bakker. *Citizenship Across Borders: The Political Transnationalism of El Migrante.* Ithaca, NY: Cornell University Press, 2008.

Smith, Michael Peter, and Luis Eduardo Guarnizo. *Transnationalism from Below.* New Brunswick, NJ: Transaction, 1998.

Smith, Peter H. *Talons of the Eagle: Latin America, the United States, and the World.* 4th ed. New York: Oxford University Press, 2012.

Smith-Hefner, Nancy J. *Khmer American: Identity and Moral Education in a Diasporic Community.* Berkeley: University of California Press, 1999.

Sobczak, Michael. *American Attitudes Toward Immigrants and Immigration Policy.* El Paso, TX: LFB Scholarly, 2010.

Sokolovsky, Jay, ed. *The Cultural Context of Aging: Worldwide Perspectives.* 3rd ed. Westport, CT: Praeger, 2009.

Sonnert, Gerhard, and Gerald Holton, eds. *Helping Young Refugees and Immigrants Succeed: Public Policy, Aid, and Education.* New York: Palgrave Macmillan, 2010.

Southern Poverty Law Center. *Alabama's Shame: HB 56 and the War on Immigrants.* Montgomery, AL: Southern Poverty Law Center, 2012.

Spickard, Paul. *Japanese Americans: The Formation and Transformations of an Ethnic Group.* Rev. ed. New Brunswick, NJ: Rutgers University Press, 2009.

Spinney, Robert G. *City of Big Shoulders: A History of Chicago.* DeKalb: Northern Illinois University Press, 2000.

Staudt, Kathleen, Tony Payan, and Z. Anthony Kruszewski, eds. *Human Rights Along the U.S.–Mexico Border: Gendered Violence and Insecurity.* Tucson: University of Arizona Press, 2009.

Stavans, Ilan, ed. *Becoming Americans: Four Centuries of Immigrant Writing.* New York: Library of America, 2009.

Stephenson, George. *A History of American Immigration, 1829–1924.* Boston: Ginn, 1926.

Stepick, Alex, Guillermo Grenier, Max Castro, and Marvin Dunn. *This Land Is Our Land: Immigrants and Power in Miami.* Berkeley: University of California Press, 2003.

Stockwell, Foster. *A Sourcebook for Genealogical Research: Resources Alphabetically by Type and Location.* Jefferson, NC: McFarland, 2004.

Stoecker, Sally, and Louise Shelley, eds. *Human Traffic and Transnational Crime: Eurasian and American Perspectives.* Lanham, MD: Rowman & Littlefield, 2005.

Stolarik, M. Mark, ed. *Forgotten Doors: The Other Ports of Entry to the United States.* Philadelphia: Balch Institute Press, 1988.

———. *Where Is My Home? Slovak Immigration to North America (1870–2010).* New York: Peter Lang, 2012.

Strobel, Christoph. *Daily Life of the New Americans: Immigration Since 1965.* Santa Barbara, CA: Greenwood, 2010.

Struna, Nancy L. *People of Prowess: Sport, Leisure, and Labor in Early Anglo-America.* Urbana: University of Illinois Press, 1996.

Suárez-Orozco, Carola, and Marcelo M. Suárez-Orozco. *Children of Immigration.* Cambridge, MA: Harvard University Press, 2001.

Suárez-Orozco, Carola, Marcelo M. Suárez-Orozco, and Irina Todorova. *Learning a New Land: Immigrant Students in American Society.* Cambridge, MA: Belknap Press, 2008.

Suárez-Orozco, Marcelo M., ed. *Crossings: Mexican Immigration in Interdisciplinary Perspectives.* Cambridge, MA: Harvard University Press, 1998.

Sung, Kyu-taik. *Respect and Care for the Elderly: The East Asian Way.* Lanham, MD: University Press of America, 2007.

Sussman, Nan M. *Return Migration and Identity: A Global Phenomenon, A Hong Kong Case.* Hong Kong: Hong Kong University Press, 2011.

Takaki, Ronald. *A Different Mirror: A History of Multicultural America.* Rev. ed. New York: Little, Brown, 2008.

———. *Strangers from a Different Shore: A History of Asian Americans.* Rev. ed. Boston: Little, Brown, 1998.

Tate, E. Mowbray. *Transpacific Steam: The Story of Steam Navigation from the Pacific Coast of North America to the Far East and the Antipodes, 1867–1941.* New York: Cornwall, 1986.

Taylor, Alan. *American Colonies: The Settling of North America.* New York: Penguin, 2002.

Taylor, Eric Robert. *If We Must Die: Shipboard Insurrections in the Era of the Atlantic Slave Trade.* Baton Rouge: Louisiana State University Press, 2006.

Tehranian, John. *Whitewashed: America's Invisible Middle Eastern Minority.* New York: New York University Press, 2009.

Terrell, John Upton. *American Indian Almanac.* New York: Barnes and Noble, 1991.

Thai, Hung Cam. *For Better or For Worse: Vietnamese International Marriages in the New Global Economy.* New Brunswick, NJ: Rutgers University Press, 2008.

Thomas, Hugh. *The Slave Trade: The Story of the Atlantic Slave Trade, 1440–1870.* New York: Simon & Schuster, 1997.

Tichenor, Daniel J. *Dividing Lines: The Politics of Immigration Control in America.* Princeton, NJ: Princeton University Press, 2002.

Tilly, Charles. *Identities, Boundaries, and Social Ties.* Boulder, CO: Paradigm, 2005.

Tocqueville, Alexis de. *Democracy in America.* Trans. George Lawrence, ed. J.P. Mayer. 1848. New York: Harper & Row, 1969.

Tolzmann, Don Heinrich. *German-American Achievements: 400 Years of Contributions to America.* Bowie, MD: Heritage, 2001.

Tong, Benson. *The Chinese Americans.* Westport, CT: Greenwood, 2000.

Toohey, David E. *Borderlands Media: Cinema and Literature as Opposition to the Oppression of Immigrants.* Lanham, MD: Lexington, 2012.

Torres-Saillant, Silvio, and Ramona Hernández. *The Dominican Americans.* Westport, CT: Greenwood, 1998.

Trager, Lillian, ed. *Migration and Economy: Global and Local Dynamics.* Lanham, MD: AltaMira, 2005.

Trommler, Frank, and Elliott Shore, eds. *The German-American Encounter: Conflict and Cooperation Between Two Cultures, 1800–2000.* New York: Berghahn, 2001.

Trulock, Notra. *Code Name Kindred Spirit: Inside the Chinese Nuclear Espionage Scandal.* New York: Encounter, 2003.

Tsuda, Takeyuki. *Diasporic Homecoming: Ethnic Return Migration in Comparative Perspective.* Stanford, CA: Stanford University Press, 2009.

Tsui, Bonnie. *American Chinatown: A People's History of Five Neighborhoods.* New York: Free Press, 2009.

Turner, Lowell, and Daniel B. Cornfield, eds. *Labor in the New Urban Battlegrounds: Local Solidarity in a Global Economy.* Ithaca, NY: ILR, 2007.

Ugalde, Antonio, and Gilberto Cárdenas, eds. *Health and Social Services Among International Labor Migrants: A Comparative Perspective.* Austin: University of Texas Press, 1998.

Ulam, Adam B. *The Bolsheviks: The Intellectual and Political History of the Triumph of Communism in Russia.* Cambridge, MA: Harvard University Press, 1998.

United Nations High Commissioner for Refugees. *Climate Change, Natural Disasters and Human Displacement: A UNHCR Perspective.* Geneva, Switzerland: United Nations, 2008.

Ural, Susannah J., ed. *Civil War Citizens: Race, Ethnicity, and Identity in America's Bloodiest Conflict.* New York: New York University Press, 2010.

U.S. Census Bureau. *Historical Statistics of the United States: Colonial Times to 1970.* Washington, DC: U.S. Government Printing Office, 1975.

———. *Statistical Abstract of the United States: 2010.* 129th ed. Washington, DC: U.S. Government Printing Office, 2009.

U.S. Department of Agriculture, Food and Nutrition Service. *Supplemental Nutrition Assistance Program Participation.* Washington, DC: U.S. Government Printing Office, 1995–2010.

U.S. Department of Health and Human Services. *TANF: Total Number of Families, Fiscal and Calendar Overview.* Washington, DC: U.S. Government Printing Office, 1995–2009.

U.S. Department of Homeland Security, Office of Immigration Statistics. *2010 Yearbook of Immigration Statistics.* Washington, DC: U.S. Government Printing Office, 2011.

———. *2011 Yearbook of Immigration Statistics.* Washington, DC: U.S. Government Printing Office, 2012.

U.S. Immigration and Naturalization Service. *An Immigrant Nation: United States Regulation of Immigration, 1798–1991.* Washington, DC: U.S. Government Printing Office, 1991.

Vallejo, Jody Agius. *Barrios to Burbs: The Making of the Mexican American Middle Class.* Stanford, CA: Stanford University Press, 2012.

Vang, Chia Youvee. *Hmong America: Reconstructing Community in Diaspora.* Urbana: University of Illinois Press, 2010.

Vargas, Lucila. *Latina Teens, Migration, and Popular Culture.* New York: Peter Lang, 2009.

Varsanyi, Monica W., ed. *Taking Local Control: Immigration Policy Activism in U.S. Cities and States.* Stanford, CA: Stanford University Press, 2010.

Vasquez, Jessica M. *Mexican Americans Across Generations: Immigrant Families, Racial Realities.* New York: New York University Press, 2011.

Vernez, Georges. *Immigrant Women in the U.S. Workforce: Who Struggles? Who Succeeds?* Lanham, MD: Lexington, 1999.

Vertovec, Steven. *Transnationalism.* New York: Routledge, 2009.

Vigdor, Jacob L. *From Immigrants to Americans: The Rise and Fall of Fitting In.* Lanham, MD: Rowman & Littlefield, 2009.

Virden, Jenel. *Good-bye Piccadilly: British War Brides in America.* Urbana: University of Illinois Press, 1996.

Von der Mehden, Fred R., ed. *The Ethnic Groups of Houston.* Houston, TX: Rice University Studies, 1984.

Voss, Kim, and Irene Bloemraad, eds. *Rallying for Immigrant Rights: The Fight for Inclusion in 21st Century America.* Berkeley: University of California Press, 2011.

Waldinger, Roger. *Still the Promised City? African Americans and New Immigrants in Postindustrial New York.* Cambridge, MA: Harvard University Press, 1996.

———, ed. *Strangers at the Gates: New Immigrants in Urban America.* Berkeley: University of California Press, 2001.

Waldinger, Roger, Howard Aldrich, Robin Ward, et al. *Ethnic Entrepreneurs: Immigrant Business in Industrial Societies.* Newbury Park, CA: Sage, 2006.

Waldinger, Roger, and Michael I. Lichter. *How the Other Half Works: Immigration and the Social Organization of Labor.* Berkeley: University of California Press, 2003.

Walsh, James P. *The San Francisco Irish, 1850–1976.* San Francisco: Irish Literary and Historical Society, 1978.

Walters, Nathan P., and Edward N. Trevelyan. *The Newly Arrived Foreign-Born Population of the United States: 2010.* American Community Survey Briefs No. 10-16. Washington, DC: U.S. Census Bureau, 2011.

Walz, Eric. *Nikkei in the Interior West: Japanese Immigration and Community Building, 1882–1945.* Tucson: University of Arizona Press, 2012.

Warner, R. Stephen, and Judith G. Wittner, eds. *Gatherings in Diaspora: Religious Communities and the New Immigration.* Philadelphia: Temple University Press, 1998.

Warren, Robert. *Estimates of the Undocumented Immigrant Population Residing in the United States: October 1996.* Washington, DC: Office of Policy and Planning, Immigration and Naturalization Service, U.S. Department of Justice, 1997.

Waters, Mary C., and Reed Ueda. *The New Americans: A Guide to Immigration Since 1965.* Cambridge, MA: Harvard University Press, 2007.

Waters, Tony. *Crime and Immigrant Youth.* Thousand Oaks, CA: Sage, 1999.

Weber, David J. *The Spanish Frontier in North America.* New Haven, CT: Yale University Press, 2009.

Wenger, Beth S. *History Lessons: The Creation of American Jewish Heritage.* Princeton, NJ: Princeton University Press, 2010.

Wennersten, John R. *Leaving America: The New Expatriate Generation.* Westport, CT: Praeger, 2008.

West, Darrell M. *Brain Gain: Rethinking U.S. Immigration Policy.* Washington, DC: Brookings Institution Press, 2010.

West, Thomas G. *Vindicating the Founders: Race, Sex, Class, and Justice in the Origins of America.* Lanham, MD: Rowman & Littlefield, 1997.

Whalen, Carmen Teresa, and Victor Vázquez-Hernández, eds. *The Puerto Rican Diaspora: Historical Perspectives.* Philadelphia: Temple University Press, 2005.

White, Roger, and Bedassa Tadesse. *International Migration and Economic Integration: Understanding the Immigrant–Trade Link.* Northampton, MA: Edward Elgar, 2011.

Wierzbicki, Susan. *Beyond the Immigrant Enclave: Network Change and Assimilation.* El Paso, TX: LFB Scholarly, 2004.

Wilkerson, Isabel. *The Warmth of Other Suns: The Epic Story of America's Great Migration.* New York: Random House, 2010.

Williams, Peter W. *America's Religions: From Their Origins to the Twenty-First Century.* Urbana: University of Illinois Press, 2002.

Wills, Chuck. *Destination America: The People and Cultures That Created a Nation.* New York: DK, 2005.

Wong, Carolyn. *Lobbying for Inclusion: Rights Politics and the Making of Immigration Policy.* Stanford, CA: Stanford University Press, 2006.

Wong, Janelle S. *Democracy's Promise: Immigrants and American Civic Institutions.* Ann Arbor: University of Michigan Press, 2006.

Wong, Kent, and Julie Monroe, eds. *Sweatshop Slaves: Asian Americans in the Garment Industry.* Los Angeles: University of California, Los Angeles, Center for Labor Research, 2006.

World Bank. *Migration and Remittances Factbook 2011.* Washington, DC: World Bank, 2011.

World Health Organization. *WHO Global Code of Practice on the International Recruitment of Health Personnel.* Geneva, Switzerland: World Health Organization, 2010.

Worth, Richard. *Jewish Immigrants.* New York: Facts on File, 2005.

Wright, Ronald. *Stolen Continents: 500 Years of Conquest and Resistance in the Americas.* New York: First Mariner, 2005.

Wroe, Andrew. *The Republican Party and Immigration Politics: From Proposition 187 to George W. Bush.* New York: Palgrave Macmillan, 2008.

Wyman, Mark. *Round Trip to America: The Immigrants Return to Europe, 1880–1930.* Ithaca, NY: Cornell University Press, 1996.

Wynar, Lubomyr R., and Anna T. Wynar. *Encyclopedic Directory of Ethnic Newspapers and Periodicals in the United States.* 2nd ed. Littleton, CO: Libraries Unlimited, 1976.

Yee, Shirley. *An Immigrant Neighborhood: Interethnic and Interracial Encounters in New York Before 1930.* Philadelphia: Temple University Press, 2012.

Yoshikawa, Hirokazu. *Immigrants Raising Citizens: Undocumented Parents and Their Young Children.* New York: Russell Sage Foundation, 2012.

Yu, Bin. *Chain Migration Explained: The Power of the Immigration Multiplier.* New York: LFB Scholarly, 2008.

Yuh, Ji-Yeon. *Beyond the Shadow of Camptown: Korean Military Brides in America.* New York: New York University Press, 2002.

Yung, Judy, Gordon H. Chang, and Him Mark Lai, eds. *Chinese American Voices: From the Gold Rush to the Present.* Berkeley: University of California Press, 2006.

Zahniser, Steven S. *Mexican Migration to the United States: The Role of Migration Networks and Human Capital Accumulation.* New York: Garland, 1999.

Zentella, Ana Celia. *Growing Up Bilingual: Puerto Rican Children in New York.* Malden, MA: Blackwell, 1997.

Zéphir, Flore. *The Haitian Americans.* Westport, CT: Greenwood, 2004.

Zhang, Donghui. *Between Two Generations: Language Maintenance and Acculturation Among Chinese Immigrant Families.* El Paso, TX: LFB Scholarly, 2008.

Zhang, Sheldon X. *Smuggling and Trafficking in Human Beings: All Roads Lead to America.* Westport, CT: Praeger, 2007.

Zhao, Xiaojian. *The New Chinese America: Class, Economy, and Social Hierarchy.* New Brunswick, NJ: Rutgers University Press, 2010.

Zhou, Min. *Contemporary Chinese America: Immigration, Ethnicity, and Community Transformation.* Philadelphia: Temple University Press, 2009.

Ziegler-McPherson, Christina A. *Americanization in the States: Immigrant Social Welfare Policy, Citizenship, and National Identity in the United States, 1908–1929.* Gainesville: University Press of Florida, 2009.

Zinzius, Birgit. *Chinese America: Stereotype and Reality: History, Present, and Future of the Chinese Americans.* New York: Peter Lang, 2004.

Zlolniski, Christian. *Janitors, Street Vendors, and Activists: The Lives of Mexican Immigrants in Silicon Valley.* Berkeley: University of California Press, 2006.

Zolberg, Aristide R. *A Nation by Design: Immigration Policy in the Fashioning of America.* New York: Russell Sage Foundation, 2006.

Zúñiga, Víctor, and Rubén Hernández-León, eds. *New Destinations: Mexican Immigration in the United States.* New York: Russell Sage Foundation, 2005.

Zunz, Olivier. *The Changing Face of Inequality: Urbanization, Industrial Development, and Immigrants in Detroit, 1880–1920.* Chicago: University of Chicago Press, 2000.

Web Sites

American Civil Liberties Union, Immigrant Rights Page. www.aclu.org/immigrants-rights

American Immigration Lawyers Association. www.aila.org

Aspiration, Acculturation, and Impact. Immigration to the United States, 1789. http://ocp.hul.harvard.edu/immigration/

Center for Immigration Studies. www.cis.org

Center for Migration and Development, Princeton University. www.princeton.edu/cmd/

Center for Migration Studies. www.cmsny.org

Department of Homeland Security. www.dhs.gov

Digital History, Ethnic America. www.digitalhistory.uh.edu/historyonline/ethnic_am.cfm

Immigration Policy Center. www.immigrationpolicy.
   org
International Labour Organization. www.ilo.org
International Organization for Migration. www.iom.
   int
Migration Information Source. www.
   migrationinformation.org
National Archives Immigration Records. www.
   archives.gov/research/immigration
National Genealogical Association. www.
   ngsgenealogy.org
National Network for Immigrant and Refugee Rights.
   www.nnirr.org
New America Media National Ethnic Media Directory.
   http://news.newamericamedia.org/directory
Pew Research Center. www.pewresearch.org
The Statue of Liberty—Ellis Island Foundation. www.
   ellisisland.org

United Nations, International Migration. http://
   unstats.un.org/unsd/demographic/sconcerns/
   migration/
United Nations High Commissioner for Human
   Rights. www.ohchr.org
U.S. Census Bureau. www.census.gov
U.S. Citizenship and Immigration Services. www.uscis.
   gov
U.S. Department of Health and Human Services, Child
   Welfare Information Gateway. www.childwelfare.
   gov
U.S. Department of Health and Human Services,
   Office of Refugee Resettlement. www.acf.hhs.gov/
   programs/orr
U.S. Department of State, Bureau of Consular Affairs,
   Intercountry Adoption. www.adoption.state.gov
U.S. Department of State, Bureau of Population,
   Refugees, and Migration. www.state.gov/j/prm

Index

Page numbers in *italics* indicate illustrations, figures, or tables; page numbers followed by *f* and *t* are figures and tables.

A

Abalone industry, **1**:153
Abbott, Grace, **3**:737; **4**:926–932
ABC (television network), **2**:404
ABE. *See* Adult basic education
Abe-Kim, Jennifer, **2**:493
Abercrombie, John W., **1**:202
Abie's Irish Rose (Broadway comedy), **2**:*385,* 386
Abie's Irish Rose (film), **2**:386
Abie's Irish Rose (radio series), **2**:386
Abolitionism, **2**:627; **3**:728, 729
  See also Slave trade
Abu Ghraib, **1**:9
Abusive marriages, **1**:65; **2**:338
Abwehr (German intelligence), **1**:206
Acadia (Nova Scotia), **3**:676, 723
Acadians, **3**:676
Acculturation. *See* Assimilation and acculturation
ACLU. *See* American Civil Liberties Union
"Across the Borderline" (song, Cooder), **2**:391
"Across the Wire" (song, Calexico), **2**:391
Act Banning Naturalization of Anarchists (1903), **4**:922
Act of Union (Britain, 1800), **1**:138
Act to Establish an Uniform Rule of Naturalization, An. *See* Naturalization Act (1790)
Activism. *See* Labor activism and labor unions; Politics, immigrant
Actos (dramatic sketches), **2**:356
Adamic, Louis, **1**:168
Adams, John, **1**:6, 134, 147; **2**:543; **4**:893
Adams, John Quincy, **1**:147
Adams Morgan, Washington, D.C., **3**:853, 855

Adaptation. *See* Assimilation and acculturation
ADC. *See* Aid to Families with Dependent Children
Addams, Jane, **1**:57; **2**:511
Addy, Samuel, **1**:307
Adepoju, Aderanti, **3**:635
Adler, Jacob, **1**:187
Admission laws, **2**:521–532
  international law and immigration, **3**:868–869
  pre-restriction era (1800s–1910s), **2**:521–527
    antebellum federal immigration legislation, **2**:521–523
    turn of the twentieth century, **2**:525–527, *526*
    wartime, Reconstruction, and westward expansion, **2**:523–525
  prevention of "undesirables," **2**:522–523
  restriction era (1920s–present), **2**:527–532, *528*
    end of national-origins quotas and start of mass immigration, **2**:530–532
    years of limited immigration, **2**:528–530
  See also specific legislative acts
Adolescents. *See* Children and adolescents
Adoption, **1**:47–51, *50*
  adoption process, **1**:49–50
  agencies, **1**:49–50
  child's country of origin, **1**:49, 51
  of Chinese children, **1**:*50*
  controversies, **1**:51
  domestic adoption, **1**:47
  eligible children, **1**:47–48
  eligible parents, **1**:48–49
  expenses, **1**:49
  home study, **1**:50
  international adoption, **1**:47, 49, 51
  of Korean children, **1**:252
  legislation, **2**:530

Adoption *(continued)*
  of Russian children, **1**:50
  statistics, **1**:*50,* 51
  timing of, **1**:49
  USCIS documentation, **1**:50–51
  war orphans, **3**:760
Adult basic education (ABE), **1**:58, 61
Advertising, **1**:73; **3**:719
Afghan immigrants
  National Security Entry-Exit Registration System, **1**:288
  refugees and asylees, **1**:44–45, 260; **3**:665
  statistics
    as percentage of South Asian–origin in the United States (2010), **3**:665
    permanent legal resident status (2001–2011), **3**:*665t*
    population (2010), **3**:663
    refugees and asylees, **3**:665
  war brides, **3**:668
Afghanistan
  border protection, **1**:294
  migration corridor with Iran, **3**:863
  refugees in Pakistan, **1**:31
  Soviet invasion, **3**:665
AFL (American Federation of Labor), **1**:184; **2**:538
AFL–CIO (American Federation of Labor–Congress of Industrial Organizations), **2**:421, 472, 480–481, 556
Africa
  brain drain, **3**:865
  Cold War, **3**:644
  colonization, **3**:642
  impact of slave trade on, **1**:122
  mass migration, **3**:635
  refugees, **1**:42; **3**:635
  See also specific countries and regions
African American English, **2**:376, 378, 379
African Americans, **3**:649–653
  Caribbeanization, **3**:829
  children and adolescents, **2**:331, 349

H

T